The New World of Work

The
New World
of Work

Challenges and Opportunities

Edited by

Cary L. Cooper

Manchester School of Management, University of
Manchester Institute of Science and Technology, UK

and

Ronald J. Burke

York University, Canada

BLACKWELL
Business

Copyright © Blackwell Publishers Ltd 2002
Editorial matter and arrangement copyright © Cary L. Cooper and Ronald J. Burke 2002

The moral right of Cary L. Cooper and Ronald J. Burke to be identified as authors of the editorial material has been asserted in accordance with the Copyright, Designs and Patents Act 1988.

First published 2002

2 4 6 8 10 9 7 5 3 1

Blackwell Publishers Ltd
108 Cowley Road
Oxford OX4 1JF
UK

Blackwell Publishers Inc.
350 Main Street
Malden, MA 02148
USA

British Library Cataloguing in Publication Data

A CIP catalogue record for this book is available from the British Library.

Library of Congress Cataloging-in-Publication Data

The new world of work : challenges and opportunities / edited by Cary L. Cooper and Ronald J. Burke.
        p.   cm. — (Manchester business and management)
    Includes bibliographical references and index.
    ISBN 0–631–22278–2 (hbk : alk. paper) — ISBN 0–631–22279–0 (pbk : alk. paper)
    1. Organizational change.   2. Personnel management.   3. Work environment.
    4. Employment forecasting.   5. Telecommuting.   6. Work and family.
    7. Contracting out.   I. Cooper, Cary L.   II. Burke, Ronald J.   III. Series.

    HD58.8 .N493 2002
    658.3—dc21

                                                                2001037563

Typeset in 10 on 12 pt Sabon by Ace Filmsetting Ltd, Frome, Somerset
Printed in Great Britain by TJ International, Padstow, Cornwall

This book is printed on acid-free paper.

Contents

Contributors

Ronald J. Burke, York University
Rita Campos e Cunha, Universidade Nova de Lisboa
Wayne F. Cascio, University of Colorado
B. G. Dale, Manchester School of Management, UMIST
Linda Duxbury, Carleton University, Ottawa
Jackie Dyer, UMIST
Daniel C. Feldman, University of South Carolina
Daniel G. Gallagher, James Madison University
Jeffrey H. Greenhaus, Drexel University
Douglas T. Hall, Boston University School of Management
Christopher Higgins, University of Western Ontario
Pierre-Guy Hourquet, Department of Management, ESC Tours
William A. Kahn, Boston University School of Management
Edward E. Lawler III, University of Southern California
Mary Dean Lee, McGill University
Suzan Lewis, Manchester Metropolitan University
Shelley M. MacDermid, Purdue University
Mary C. Mattis, Catalyst, New York
Saroj Parasuraman, Drexel University
Terri A. Scandura, University of Miami
Romila Singh, Drexel University
Ethlyn A. Williams, University of South Florida

About the Editors

Cary L. Cooper

Cary L. Cooper is currently BUPA Professor of Organizational Psychology and Health in the Manchester School of Management, and Deputy Vice-Chancellor (External Activities) of the University of Manchester Institute of Science and Technology (UMIST). He is the author of over 80 books (on occupational stress, women at work and industrial and organizational psychology), has written over 300 scholarly articles for academic journals, and is a frequent contributor to national newspapers, TV and radio. He is currently Founding Editor of the *Journal of Organizational Behavior*, Co-Editor of the medical journal *Stress Medicine*, and Co-Editor of the *International Journal of Management Review*. He is a Fellow of the British Psychological Society, the Royal Society of Arts, the Royal Society of Medicine, and the Royal Society of Health. Professor Cooper is the President of the British Academy of Management, is a Companion of the (British) Institute of Management, and one of the first UK-based Fellows of the (American) Academy of Management (having also won the 1998 Distinguished Service Award for his contribution to management science from the Academy of Management). Professor Cooper is the Editor (jointly with Professor Chris Argyris of Harvard Business School) of the international scholarly Blackwell Encyclopedia of Management (12-volume set). He has been an advisor to the World Health Organisation, ILO, and recently published a major report for the EU's European Foundation for the Improvement of Living and Work Conditions on "Stress Prevention in the Workplace". In 2001 Professor Cooper was awarded the Commander of the Order of the British Empire (CBE) by the Queen for his contribution to health and safety.

Ronald J. Burke

Ronald J. Burke (Ph.D., University of Michigan) is currently Professor of Organizational Behavior, School of Business, York University Toronto, Canada. He was the founding editor of the *Canadian Journal of Administrative Sciences* and serves on the editorial boards of a dozen other journals. His research interests include work stress and health, career development in organizations, and gender issues in management. He has consulted with organizational clients on management development, advancing managerial women, and restructuring and downsizing.

Acknowledgments

I thank Cary Cooper for 20 years of friendship. Our first book together emerged around a pool in San Diego, this one at a restaurant at Chicago's O'Hare airport. I acknowledge our international contributors and friends at Blackwell.

Interestingly, most of my support and research collaborations since graduate school have come from women. I am grateful to all of them: Anne Burke, Patricia Burke, Marilyn Davidson, Esther Greenglass, Carol McKeen, Debra Nelson, Susan Pothecary, and Tamara Weir.

Ronald J. Burke
Toronto, Canada

Introduction:
The New World of Work[1]

RONALD J. BURKE AND CARY L. COOPER

This collection is a sequel to our earlier volume *The Organization in Crisis: Downsizing, Restructuring, and Privatization* (Burke and Cooper, 2000). In that book, we chronicled the many changes that employees and organizations have faced during the past 20 years, why these changes occurred and are occurring with increasing frequency, and the impact of these changes on individuals, organizations, and the broader society.

More organizations are downsizing, restructuring, and outsourcing, which means more workers in the future will be selling their services to organizations on short-term contract or freelance bases. What are the implications for the health of the individual, his/her family, and future organizations? Can individuals commit to organizations that do not commit to them? Can families survive the conflicts surrounding the changing role of men and women? Will women become the main breadwinners, given their flexible approach to work? Will these developments create "virtual organizations" with more teleworkers? These are some of the issues addressed in this volume.

The last half-century has seen an enormous change in the nature of society and the workplace. The 1960s epitomized the limitless possibilities of change, as society confronted the horrors of the Vietnam War and the traditional and established lifestyles of the post-war period. It was an era that embraced new technology, some suggesting a leisure age of 20-hour weeks. This was followed by the 1970s, a period of industrial strife, conflict, and retrenchment. The workplace became the battleground between employers and workers, between the middle classes and the working classes, between liberal and conservative thinking.

Out of the turmoil of the 1970s came the "enterprise culture" of the 1980s, a decade of privatizations, statutory constraints on industrial relations, mergers and acquisitions, strategic alliances, joint ventures, process re-engineering and the like, transforming workplaces into free market, hot-house cultures. Although this entrepreneurial period improved the economic competitiveness of some countries domestically and in international markets, there were also the first signs of strain, as "stress" and "burnout" became concepts in the everyday vocabulary of working people.

By the end of the 1980s and into the early 1990s, the sustained recession, together with the privatizing mentality with regard to the public sector, laid the groundwork for potentially the most profound changes in the workplace since the Industrial Revolution. The early years of the 1990s were dominated by the effects of recession and efforts to get out of it, as organizations "downsized," "delayered," "flattened" or "right-sized." Whatever euphemism you care to use, the hard reality experienced by many was job loss and constant change. There were fewer people, doing more work, and feeling more insecure. The rapid expansion of information technology also meant the added burden of information overload and the accelerating pace of work, with people demanding more information, quicker and quicker. The mid-1980s through the 1990s also saw the massive expansion of women in the workplace, with a noticeable pushing (not shattering) of the glass ceiling further upwards. The changing role of men and women at work and at home added another dimension to the enormity of change taking place in the offices, factory floors, and techno-cultures of industry.

Three types of organizational transitions have received increasing attention during the past few years: mergers and acquisitions, restructurings and downsizings, and privatizations (Burke and Nelson, 1998). These three newly emerging sources of organizational change share some common features. First, they are interrelated since all represent the effects of the economic recession and attempts by organizations to survive and to increase productivity (Marks, 1994). Second, being fairly recent areas of research, relatively little empirical work has been completed (Kozlowski, Chao, Smith, and Hedlund, 1993). Third, these changes have vast implications for both practice and intervention at both individual and organizational levels (Cascio, 1995; Cameron, Freeman, and Mishra, 1991).

Some of the dramatic changes affecting work and organizations include increased global competition, the impact of information technology, the re-engineering of business processes, smaller companies that employ fewer people, the shift from making a product to providing a service, and the increasing disappearance of the job as a fixed collection of tasks (Cascio, 1995; Martin and Freeman, 1998). These forces have produced wrenching changes in all industrialized economies. These changes have impacted most profoundly in terms of job losses.

In addition, companies were not downsizing simply because they were losing money. Fully 81 percent of companies that downsized in a given year were profitable in that year. Major reasons reported in the American Management Association's 1994 survey on downsizing were strategic or structural (to improve productivity, plant obsolescence, mergers and acquisitions, transfer of location, new technology).

The economic downturns of the 1980s highlighted the stress of not having a job. In the US, 10.8 million people lost their jobs between 1981 and 1988 (Fraze, 1988). Even in the growth periods from 1985 to 1989, 4.3 million American workers lost their jobs (Herz, 1991). From June 1990 through July 1991, 1.6 million lost their jobs (Greenwald, 1991). In the European countries of France, Germany, Italy, the Netherlands, and the UK, 2.1 million lost their jobs in 1989. In this same year, 320,000 Japanese and 522,000 Canadians lost jobs (Sorrentino, 1993). And in Central and Eastern Europe, 3.7 million lost jobs (OECD, 1992). Global job loss is predicted to continue as organizational retrenchment and restructuring continue (Haugen and Meisenheimer, 1991).

Other studies have shown that anticipation or concern about job loss may be as damaging as job loss itself (Latack and Dozier, 1986). Job insecurity has been found to be associated with increased medical consultations for psychological distress (Catalano, Rook, and Dooley, 1986) and with increased disability claims for back pain (Volinn, Lai, McKinney, and Loeser, 1988). Job insecurity of parents can also affect their children's work beliefs and attitudes (Barling, Dupre, and Hepburn, 1998).

Furthermore, laid-off workers who return to the job market often take pay cuts. Downward mobility is common (*Business Week*, 1994). Of approximately 2,000 workers terminated by RJR Nabisco, 72 percent eventually found jobs but at wages averaging about half their previous pay (Baumohl, 1993). And jobs that were lost were being lost permanently as a result of new technology, improved machinery, and new ways of structuring work. They were not being lost temporarily because of a recession.

Organizations are becoming leaner and meaner. More and more are focussing on their core competencies and outsourcing everything else. Continental Bank Corporation, for example, has contracted its legal, audit, cafeteria, and mailroom operations to outside companies. American Airlines is contracting out customer service jobs at thirty airports. There are no longer any guarantees to managers and workers. Flattened hierarchies also mean that there will be fewer managers in smaller remaining organizations.

The increasing globalization of business has exposed many organizations to more competition than they've ever experienced before. Differential wage rates between developed and developing countries have added to these pressures. One implication of these forces is that companies are increasingly concerned about managing their costs. Levels of management have been removed; cost cutting has taken place.

Now concepts of management, organization, and work have been introduced (e.g. Lawler, 1996; Bridges, 1990). Management has become more informational based on knowledge workers, knowledge, management, and learning organization concepts. Organizational structures have also changed dramatically from hierarchical, command and control structures to flatter, and in some cases network, structures. Organizations are increasingly becoming flexible, more people-centered, and fluid.

The pattern of employees' daily working lives has also changed dramatically. Career structures have been most heavily impacted. More employees are insecure; motivation and commitment have been reduced and loyalty may be dead (Worrall, Cooper, and Campbell, 2000). There is also a sense that many employing organizations have handled these transitions badly.

Worrall and Cooper (1997, 1998) have embarked on a five-year longitudinal study of 5,000 UK managers examining the impact of organizational changes on their work lives to provide a "more socially complete" picture of changes in organizational structures and working patterns in Britain.

They found that 59 percent of respondents (N = 1,362) experienced some form of organizational change in 1997. This figure increased slightly in 1998 to 62 percent (N = 1,313). There was considerable organizational change in both years and respondents indicating change in 1997 were also likely to indicate an organizational change in 1998. The most common organizational changes were cost reduction (57 percent), culture change (49 percent), redundancies (45 percent), delayering (32 percent), use of temporary staff (31 percent), use of contract staff (28 percent), closure of sites (29 percent), and use of outsourcing (18 percent).

Those managers having experienced an organizational change in 1998 saw the results as mixed (Worrall, Cooper, and Campbell, 2000). Participation and flexibility were seen to have been increased, speed of decision-making was about the same, but loss of valued skills was observed. Increased accountability, profitability, and productivity were seen as rising as well.

Respondents at higher organizational levels indicated more benefits resulting from two organizational changes than did respondents at lower organizational levels.

Organizational changes were seen as having a negative effect on employee loyalty, morale, motivation, and job security. These conclusions are consistent with human and social costs typically found to be associated with such changes (Burke and Nelson, 1998; Marks, 1994; Noer, 2000). Once again, lower-level mangers reported lower levels on all these indicators.

• The Changing Workplace •

The downsizing and the rapidity of change took its toll in the 1990s. An Institute for Social Research (ISR) survey published in 1995, of 400 companies in 17 countries including 8 million workers throughout Europe, found that over the last ten years the UK's employee satisfaction level dropped from 64 percent in 1985 to 53 percent by 1995, the biggest drop of any European country. In addition, the sickness absence rates rose during much of this period, recently hitting an all-time high of £12 billion cost to industry in one year. This had its effects on the family, as more and more two-earner families/couples emerged in a climate which was anything but "family friendly." The BT Forum's report *The Cost of Communication Breakdown* found that by 1991 the UK had the highest divorce rate in Europe with over 171,000 divorces, while the proportion of people living in one-parent families increased fourfold between 1961 and 1991, with the prediction that over 3 million children and young people would grow up in step-families by the year 2000.

This is in no small measure partly a result of a "long working hours" culture in most public and private sector organizations in the UK. DEMOS's report *Time Squeeze* in 1995 found that 25 percent of British male employees worked more than 48 hours a week; one-fifth of all manual workers worked more than 50 hours; one in eight managers worked more than 60-hour weeks and seven out of ten British workers want to work a 40-hour week but only three out of ten do.

This scenario is cause for concern but the trend toward outsourcing is also leading toward a more insidious work environment, the short-term contract or freelance culture. This privatizing of the private sector no doubt stems from our insatiable appetite for privatizing the public sector in the 1980s. This has led to what employers refer to euphemistically as "the flexible work force," although it is anything but flexible. The psychological contract between employer and employee in terms of "reasonably permanent employment for work well done" is being undermined, as more employees no longer regard their employment as secure and many more are engaged in part-time working. From 1984 to 1994 the number of men working part-time doubled, with the number of people employed by firms of more than 500 employees having slumped to just over a third of the employed population and with over one in eight British workers now self-employed.

There may be nothing inherently wrong with this trend but a recent *Quality of Working Life* survey by the Institute of Management and UMIST – which has and will continue to survey 5,000 managers each year over the next five years – found disturbing results among Britain's managers (Worrall and Cooper, 1997). Organizations at the end of the 1990s were found to be in a state of constant change, with 61 percent of this national sample of managers having undergone a major restructuring over the last 12 months. The consequences of this change, even among a group supposedly in control of events, were increased job insecurity, lowered morale, and the erosion of motivation and loyalty.

Most changes involved downsizing, cost reduction, delayering, and outsourcing. Yet, although they led to an increase in profitability and productivity, decision-making was slower and, more importantly, the organization was deemed to have lost the right mix of human resource skills and experience in the process. In addition, the impact on working patterns, contract hours, and evening and weekend working was penal. It was found that 82 percent of managers in the UK regularly work more than 40 hours a week, 38 percent report working over 50-hour weeks, and 41 percent always or often work at weekends.

Poor communications and concern about future employability were some of the reasons for managers' insecurity: 60 percent feel they are in the dark about their organization's future strategies, while 48 percent say their biggest worry is financial security and employability in the wide job market. Due to outsourcing and intrinsic job insecurity, 89 percent of managers say they will need to develop new skills (e.g. IT, information management) over the next five years, presumably as they foresee the selling of their services to organizations on a freelance or short-term contract basis (Sparrow and Cooper, 1998).

This snapshot of corporate life from Britain's managers highlights the workplace of the future. Most organizations will have only a small core of full-time, permanent employees, working from a conventional office. They will buy most of the skills they need on a contract basis, either from individuals working at home and linked to the company by computers and modems (teleworking), or by hiring people on short-term contracts to do specific jobs or projects. In this way companies will maintain the flexibility they need to cope with a rapidly changing world. This change is already happening: BT claim that more than 2.5 million people are already working wholly or partly from home and predicted this would rise to 4 million by the millennium. There is also a significant rise in the provision of interim management agencies to supply senior management on a project management basis to industry. All the trends are in the direction of what has been termed the "contingent workforce," an army of blue-collar, white-collar and managerial temps (Rousseau, 1996).

● Is there a Healthy Side to Transition and Change? ●

Marks (1994) contends that people are saturated with change and transition, and efforts must be made to help them deal with the pain of the past before they can move on to accept future changes. Most organizations in the 1980s and 1990s went through mergers, acquisitions, downsizing, restructuring, re-engineering, culture change, and leadership succession. Many have had several of these and often overlapping. These events have not only changed organizational systems; they have had a major effect on workers in them – mostly negative. Victims, survivors, destroyed careers and career paths; cynicism is up, trust in organizational leadership is down. Survivors work harder with fewer rewards. Multiple downsizings are seen over a few years (Armstrong-Stassen, 1997). Those who lost their jobs may in fact be better off – they can now get on with new things. And employees see no end to the changes – and feel powerless to influence them.

Yet organizations must continue to change to remain competitive (Nolan and Croson, 1995). New technology and increased competition will hasten the rate of change (Marks, 1994). Senior managers are excited about opportunities; middle managers are angry, depressed, and tired. The negative psychological, behavioral, and business consequences of these changes weigh heavily upon them.

● Consequences of Change ●

As more people work from home, whether part-time or on a short-term contract, we will be increasingly creating "virtual organizations." How will this virtual organization of the future manage a dispersed workforce? Communications difficulties are already apparent in existing organizational structures, as found by the IM–UMIST survey.

With two out of three families/couples pursuing dual careers, how will working from home affect the delicate balance between home and work or indeed the roles between men and women? As employers increasingly look for and recruit "flexible workers," will women be preferred to men, given their history of flexibility? For example, there are currently five times as many women working part-time than men, and although twice as many men are now working part-time than a decade ago, women are historically more experienced at discontinuous career patterns, flowing in and out of the labour market, working part-time and on short-term contracts.

Since the Industrial Revolution, few white-collar, managerial, and professional workers have experienced high levels of job insecurity; even blue-collar workers who were laid off in heavy manufacturing industries of the past were frequently re-employed when times got better. The question society has to ask is, "Can human beings cope with permanent job insecurity, without the safety and security of organizational structures, which in the past provided training, development, and careers?" The European survey by ISR on employment security provides some cause for concern in this regard, showing the UK with the worst decline in employee satisfaction in terms of employment security of any of its competitors, from 70 percent satisfaction levels in 1985 to 48 percent by 1995, at a time when the UK has been moving faster toward a contingent workforce than all of its European counterparts.

Will this trend toward stable insecurity, freelance working, and virtual organizations continue? More importantly, can organizations, virtual or otherwise, continue to demand commitment from employees they don't commit to? In comparative terms the UK economy is doing remarkably well but the levels of job insecurity and dissatisfaction are high. Developing and maintaining a "feel good" factor at work and in our economy generally is not just about bottom-line factors, such as higher salaries, a penny off income tax or increased profitability; in a civilized society it should be about quality of life issues as well, like hours of work, family time, manageable workloads, control over one's career, and some sense of job security.

As Sparrow (2000) has observed, the same forces that have impacted on management, organizations, and jobs, have also impacted the employee–employer relationship, bringing about a new employment contract. And implementing this new employment relationship will not be easy.

Feldman (2000) has noted the increased pursuit of self-employment, small business proprietorships, and entrepreneurship as alternative career paths following from organizational downsizing. This increase has been particularly evident among women and minorities.

McCarthy and Hall (2000) suggest the individuals have been forced to adopt a "protean" career in response to the widespread redefinition and restructuring of the psychological contract. A protean career is characterized by constant adaptation and individual responsibility for career direction. Individuals must "add value." Employers must provide an environment for growth and learning. What emerges is a type of contingent loyalty. That is, both employees and employing organizations hope things will work out well. The employment relationship has both relational and transitional elements.

McCarthy and Hall (2000) identify some problems and issues with the new employment contract. These include a growing gap between those having the resources (e.g. education, self-confidence, ability to learn, resources that support learning and development) and those that don't; a "me first," "winner take all" mentality, whether the competencies necessary for survival in the new world of work can be developed, unclear responsibilities of firms for employee development, and increasingly complicated work and life balance issues.

The new world of work is also characterized by increasing diversity among employees. Dimensions among which employees may differ include gender, age, marital status, parental status, race, ethnicity, education, sexual orientation, job tenure and experience, and physical disability. There is a sense that diversity has both potential benefits as well as disadvantages. The benefits include a more inclusive and representative workforce, a workforce that mirrors prospective customers and clients resulting in better products and services, and more innovation as a consequence of the existence of multiple perspectives. Disadvantages are thought to include heightened tensions between various sub-groups, a need for greater managerial sensitivity to the needs and interests of various sub-groups, and more flexibility in meeting these needs.

Organizations are also facing greater challenges in motivating and managing a workforce whose members include several generations of employees, each having unique attitudes and values, many of which are significantly different across these generations (Zemke, Raines, and Filipczak, 2000).

Zemke, Raines, and Filipczak (2000) consider issues surrounding different generations at work. Four generations might be present in some workplaces.

- The Veterans, 1922–1943 (52 million people). Those born prior to World War II and those whose earliest memories and influences are associated with that world-engulfing event.
- The Baby Boomers, 1943–1960 (73.2 million people). Those born during or after World War II and raised in the era of extreme optimism, opportunity, and progress.
- Generation Xers, 1960–1980 (70.1 million people). Those born after the blush of the Baby Boom who came of age deep in the shadow of the Boomers and the rise of the Asian tiger.
- Generation Nexters, 1980–2000 (69.7 million people to date). Those born of the Baby Boomers and early Xers and into our current high-tech, neo-optimistic time.

Zemke and his colleagues suggest that considerable confusion, misunderstanding, and conflict exist between these groups when members of the various generations have to work side by side. Generational diversity, while holding out opportunity, is becoming increasingly problematic. These generations differ in "values, ambitions, issues, mind sets and demographics" (Zemke et al., 2000: 9). Each of these four cohort groups faced different sociological, political, and economic circumstances as well as differing in size.

These four generations have unique work ethics, different views on work, unique and preferred ways of managing and being managed, varied styles, and different perspectives on organizational issues such as quality service, attendance, and punctuality. Managing these four generations can be daunting.

Zemke and his colleagues suggest that mixed generations can work well together if: (1) aggressive communication of issues across the generational groups is encouraged and supported, along with the much needed listening. Talking and communication helps; (2) there is a use of employees with different backgrounds, viewpoints, and skills to strategically strengthen work units and departments: Generational differences are valued and seen as strengths. Efforts to create a homogeneous culture are unlikely to be successful.

The workforce is becoming increasingly diverse as more women and numbers of other "minority" groups enter the world of work. Organizations seem to be doing a reasonable job at attracting and hiring these non-traditional employees into entry-level jobs; few have reached levels of executive leadership. This will be an increasingly important challenge in the new world of work as organizations strive to obtain high levels of talent.

Family structures have also changed. Historically as organizations emerged and grew in the early 1900s the typical employee was a married man with a partner who was employed as a homemaker and who shouldered almost all of the family responsibilities. Today this pattern represents about 15 percent of family structures. This raises huge needs for flexibility on the part of organizations and adaptability or resilience on the part of individuals and families.

There is also a belief that teamwork and the use of teams will be a major factor in the way work is carried out. Project teams and project management will be more common. This focus places a much higher emphasis on the "softer" shells, interpersonal competencies such as listening, communication, conflict management, negotiation, and coaching without reducing the technical and competitive requirements necessary to perform successfully in newly evolving jobs.

The leadership role is also evolving away from the "autocratic manager as expert" position to one requiring visionary and empowering skills, with the leader serving as a coach, cheerleader, and motivator. Managers will increasingly be required to inspire staff to put forth high levels of commitment with meaningful projects.

The new world of work is also still taking shape. We can identify some themes that are now developing with some continuity (transition and change, greater use of teams), but other aspects of the new world of work, and their effects, are "in process." It is not clear, for example, how the move to e-commerce (the dot.com) will affect organization, careers, managing, and work–personal life issues.

It is also not clear how these forces and events will impact levels of satisfaction and psychological well-being of individuals and their families. There is some agreement that levels of demands and stress are likely higher now than two decades ago. Levels of income have increased during this time (at least for many), but these increases have not been present in personal happiness. How will employees and their families (and communities) respond to these demands? Whose responsibility is this? The individual's? The organization's? Society's?

NOTE

1   Preparation of this chapter was supported in part by the School of Business, York University and the Manchester School of Management, UMIST.

REFERENCES

Armstrong-Stassen, M. (1997). The effect of repeated management downsizing and surplus designation on remaining managers: An exploratory study. *Anxiety, Stress, and Coping*, 10, 377–84.

Barling, J., Dupre, K.E., and Hepburn, C.G. (1998). Effects of parents' job insecurity on children's work beliefs and attitudes. *Journal of Applied Psychology*, 83, 112–18.

Baumohl, B. (1993, March 15). When downsizing becomes dumbsizing. *Time*, 55.

Bridges, W. (1990). *Job Shift*. Reading, MA: Addison-Wesley.

Burke, R.J., and Cooper, C.L. (2000). *The Organization in Crisis: Downsizing, Restructuring, and Privatization*. Oxford: Blackwell Publishers.

Burke, R.J., and Nelson, D.L. (1998). Mergers and acquisitions, downsizing, and privatization: A North American perspective. In M.K. Gowing, J.D. Kraft, and J.C. Quick (eds). *The New Organizational Reality: Downsizing, Restructuring and Revitalization*. Washington D.C.: American Psychological Association, 21–54.

Cameron, K., Freeman, S.J., and Mishra, A.K. (1991). Best practices in white-collar downsizing: Managing contradictions. *Academy of Management Executive*, 5, 57–73.

Cascio, W.F. (1995). Whither industrial and organizational psychology in a changing world of work? *American Psychologist*, 50, 928–39.

Catalano, R., Rook, K., and Dooley, D. (1986). Labor markets and help seeking: A test of the employment security hypothesis. *Journal of Health and Social Behavior*, 27, 227–37.

Cooper, C.L. (1998a). The psychological implications of the changing patterns of work. *Royal Society of Arts Journal*, 1, 4, 74–81.

Cooper, C.L. (1998b). The future of work: A strategy for managing the pressures. *Journal of Applied Management Studies* (forthcoming).

Cooper, C.L., and Lewis, S. (1994). *Managing the New Work Force: The Challenge of Dual Income Families*. San Diego: Pfeiffer.

Feldman, D.C. (2000). Down but not out: Career trajectories of middle-aged and older workers after downsizing. In R.J. Burke and C.L. Cooper (eds). *The Organization in Crisis: Downsizing, Restructuring, and Privatization*. Oxford: Blackwell Publishers, pp. 188–201.

Fraze, J. (1988). Displaced workers: Oakies of the 80s. *Personnel Administration*, 33, 42–51.

Greenwald, J. (1991, September 9). Permanent pink slips. *Time*, pp. 54–6.

Haugen, S. E., and Meisenheimer, J.R. (1991). U.S. labor market weakened in 1990. *Monthly Labor Review*, 114, 3–16.

Herz, D.E. (1991). Worker displacement still common in the late 1980s. *Monthly Labor Review*, 114, 3–9.

ISR (1995). *Employee Satisfaction: Tracking European Trends*. London: Institute for Social Research.

Kozlowski, S.W.J., Chao, G.T., Smith, E.M., and Hedlund, J. (1993). Organizational downsizing: Strategies, interventions, and research implications. In C.L. Cooper and I.T. Robertson (eds). *International Review of Industrial and Organizational Psychology*. New York: Wiley, pp. 263–332.

Latack, J.C., and Dozier, J.B. (1986). After the axe falls: Job loss as a career transition. *Academy of Management Review*, 11, 375–92.

Lawler, E.E. (1996). *From the Ground Up: Set Principles for Building the New Logic Corporation*. San Francisco: Jossey-Bass.

Marks, M.L. (1994). *From Turmoil to Triumph*. New York: Lexington Books.

Martin, R.E., and Freeman, S.J. (1998). The economic content of the new organizational reality. In M.K. Gowing, J.D. Kraft, and J.C. Quick (eds). *The New Organizational Reality*. Washington, D.C.: American Psychological Association, pp. 5–20.

McCarthy, J.F., and Hall, D.T. (2000). Organizational crisis and change: The new career contract at work. In R.J. Burke and C.L. Cooper (eds). *The Organization in Crisis: Downsizing, Restructuring, and Privatization*. Oxford: Blackwell Publishers, pp. 202–19.

Noer, D. (1993). *Healing the Wounds: Overcoming the Trauma of Layoffs and Revitalizing Downsized Organizations*. San Francisco: Jossey Bass.

Noer, D. (2000). Leading organizations through survivor sickness: A framework for the new millennium. In R.J. Burke and C.L. Cooper (eds). *The Organization in Crisis: Downsizing, Restructuring, and Privatization*. London: Blackwell, pp. 235–50.

Nolan, R.L., and Croson, D.C. (1995). *Creative Destruction: A Six-Stage Process of Transforming the Organization*. Boston: Harvard Business School Press.

OECD (Organization for Economic Cooperation and Development) (1992). *Economic Outlook*. Paris: OECD Perspectives of Employment.

Rousseau, D.M. (1996). Changing the deal while keeping the people. *Academy of Management Executive*, 10, 50–61.

Sorrentino, C. (1993). International comparisons of unemployment indicators. *Monthly Labor Review*, 116, 3–9.

Sparrow, P. (2000). The new employment contract: Psychological implications of future work.

In R.J. Burke and C.L. Cooper (eds). *The Organization in Crisis: Downsizing, Restructuring, and Privatization*. Oxford: Blackwell Publishers, pp. 167–87.

Sparrow, P., and Cooper, C.L. (1998). New organizational forms: The strategic relevance of future psychological contract scenarios. *Canadian Journal of Administrative Sciences*, 15, 336–71.

Volinn, E., Lai, D., McKinney, S., and Loeser, J.D. (1988). When back pain becomes disabling: A regional analysis. *Pain*, 33, 33–9.

Worrall, L., and Cooper, C.L. (1997). IM-UMIST, *The Quality of Working Life: The 1997 Survey of Managers' Experiences*. London: Institute of Management.

Worrall, L., and Cooper, C.L. (1998a). *The Quality of Working Life: The 1998 Survey of Managers' Experiences*. London: Institute of Management.

Worrall, L., Cooper, C.L., and Campbell, F. (2000). The impact of organizational change on UK managers' perceptions of their working lives. In R.J. Burke and C.L. Cooper (eds). *The Organization in Crisis: Downsizing, Restructuring, and Privatization*. Oxford: Blackwell Publishers.

Zemke, R.M., Raines, C., and Filipczak, B. (2000). *Generations at Work*. New York: AMACOM.

I

The Changing Work Environment

Organizational Transitions[1]

RONALD J. BURKE

Hardly a day goes by without stories about organizational restructuring, downsizing, merging or closing appearing in the popular press. These events are taking place throughout the industrialized world. Consider the following newspaper headlines:

"Laidlaw's U.S. ambulance unit hit with job cuts" (*Financial Post*, April 19, 1999)

"Mitsubishi to cut 14,500 jobs in massive restructuring" (*Financial Post*, April 11, 1999)

"AOL to trim staff after Netscape deal" (*Financial Post*, March 25, 1999)

"Siemens to buy Redstone, cut jobs" (*Financial Post*, March 19, 1999)

"Olivetti proposes large job cuts in takeover bid" (*Financial Post*, March 18, 1999)

"Telecom Italia plans 40,000 job cuts" (*Financial Post*, March 15, 1999)

The early 1990s were characterized by economic slowdown, plant closings and layoffs, and budget cutbacks (Gowing, Kraft, and Quick, 1998). This mood of austerity has affected private and public sector organizations alike, and is expected to continue through the early 2000s and beyond.

Organizations are becoming leaner and meaner (Burke and Nelson, 1998). More and more are focussing on their core competencies and outsourcing everything else. Continental Bank Corporation, for example, has contracted its legal, audit, cafeteria, and mailroom operations to outside companies. American Airlines is contracting out customer service jobs at thirty airports. There are no longer any guarantees to managers and workers. Flattened hierarchies also mean that there will be fewer managers in smaller remaining organizations.

● Why Downsize or Restructure? ●

Downsizing refers to the voluntary actions of an organization to reduce expenses. This is usually, but not exclusively, accomplished by shrinking the size of the workforce. But the term covers a whole range of activities from personnel layoffs and hiring freezes to consolidation and mergers of units. Downsizing refers to an array of initiatives implemented by an organization in response to a decision to reduce headcount.

Wrenching changes have forced organizations to look for ways to compete. The globalization of the marketplace, sweeping technological advances, and changes to a service-based economy are but a few of these forces (Martin and Freeman, 1998). Global benchmarking, in particular, has led companies to compare their overhead costs with those of global competitors, and to cut their payrolls in response. It must also be acknowledged that downsizing is sometimes the price paid for mismanagement and strategic errors at the top of the organization (Kets de Vries and Balazs, 1997).

The outcomes that organizations seek from restructuring may include increased productivity, improved quality, enhanced competitive advantage, and potential regeneration of success (Hoskisson and Hitt, 1994). In addition, organizations hope to achieve lower overhead, less bureaucracy, more effective decision-making, improved communication, and greater innovativeness.

However, companies were not downsizing simply because they were losing money. Fully 81 percent of companies that downsized in a given year were profitable in that year. Major reasons reported in the American Management Association's 1994 survey on downsizing were strategic or structural (to improve productivity, plant obsolescence, mergers and acquisitions, transfer of location, new technology).

Although we might like to think that the reasons for downsizing are well thought out, many of the reasons are purely social ones (McKinley, Mone, and Barker, 1998; McKinley, Zhao, and Garrett Rust, 2000). McKinley, Sanches, and Schick (1995) proposed that three social forces that precipitate downsizing efforts are constraining forces, cloning forces, and learning forces. Constraining forces place pressures on executives to do the "right thing" in terms of legitimate managerial actions. Managers are expected to reduce their workforces, and those who make drastic cuts are often cast in the media as heroes. Cloning forces are the result of imitation or benchmarking. Reacting to uncertainty, managers want to display that they are doing something to address the decline. They look to other organizations within their industries to demonstrate some initiative, and then they follow suit. Learning, the third social force that brings about downsizing efforts, takes place through educational institutions and professional associations. Cost accounting methods encourage downsizing as a legitimate business activity. Organizations thus choose to downsize for a variety of reasons, some of them economic and some of them social. The rationale for downsizing is an integral part of the issue of whether downsizing efforts are effective, or whether they fail.

Various levels of government throughout the industrialized world have also focussed their attention in recent years on balancing their budgets and reducing the size of their financial deficits (Armstrong-Stassen, 1998). In the US, between 1979 and

1993, 454,000 public service jobs were lost (Uchitelle and Kleinfield, 1996). They have also cut costs by reducing levels of financial support provided to the health care system. These efforts have been associated with hospital restructuring, mergers, and closures as the health care system has had to provide the same levels of service with fewer resources. In the US, 828 hospitals closed between 1980 and 1992 (Godfrey, 1994).

Since 1992, health care institutions in Canada have had to manage with a reduction of government allocation. As a result of severe cutbacks in federal funding to the provinces, the equivalent of $2.5 billion was expected to be cut from health care in 1996–7 (Canadian College of Health Services Executives, 1995). The government of Ontario was planning to close ten hospitals in Toronto, downgrading two others to outpatient clinics, merging programs and downloading a whole host of services onto municipalities, a strategy expected to save $430 million annually in health care costs. As hospitals have closed, merged or restructured, hospital workers, and in particular nurses, are at risk of losing their jobs (Doyle-Driedger, 1997).

Three types of organizational transitions have received increasing attention during the past few years: mergers and acquisitions, restructurings and downsizings, and privatization (Burke and Nelson, 1998). These three newly emerging sources of organizational change share some common features. First, they are interrelated since all represent the effects of the economic recession and attempts by organizations to survive and to increase productivity (Marks, 1994). Second, being fairly recent areas of research, relatively little empirical work has been completed (Kozlowski, Chao, Smith, and Hedlund, 1993). Third, these changes have vast implications for both practice and intervention at both individual and organizational levels (Cascio, 1995; Cameron, Freeman, and Mishra, 1991; Gowing, Kraft, and Quick, 1998).

● Extent of Restructuring and Downsizing ●

Worrall, Cooper, and Campbell (2000) present data on the extent of organizational change in organizations in the UK. They report that 59 percent of managerial respondents had experienced some form of organizational change in the past year (1998); the figure was 62 percent in 1998. The same respondents participated in both surveys, indicating the persistence and increasing pace of change. Mangers in large organizations reported more change. They also found that organizational restructuring was highest in the public sector and the former public sector (utilities, education, health care). Most common forms of restructuring were cost reduction (57 percent of managers indicating a restructuring in the past year), culture change (45 percent), layoffs (45 percent), delayering (32 percent), using a contract staff (28 percent), plant or site closures (27 percent), use of temporary staff (31 percent), and outsourcing (18 percent). Restructuring was seen to have mixed levels of benefits; benefits of increasing accountability, profitability, and productivity were noted. Top management were significantly more likely to see benefits than were the rank and file. Significant deterioration in levels of loyalty, morale, motivation, and perceived job security were evident. This data raised concerns about both the need for such large and rapid change and the way changes have been implemented and managed. The use of job loss in restructuring was found to have particularly negative effects. The loss of key skills and knowledge, heightened job insecurity, and employee motivation and morale were most strongly impacted by redundancies (Sennett, 1998).

● Effects of Restructuring and Downsizing ●

Research has indicated some common patterns of change in the work environment of organizations during downsizing. Organizational communication seems to deteriorate (Cascio, 1993; Dougherty and Bowman, 1995; Noer, 1993) during downsizing, though it is likely to be particularly important at these times (Rosenblatt, Rogers, and Nord 1993). Organizational trust also has been observed to fall (Buch and Aldridge, 1991; Cascio, 1993) coupled with an increase in fear (Buch and Aldridge, 1991). Downsizing organizations have been found to exhibit heightened resistance to change and increased rigidity (Cameron, Sutton, and Whetton, 1987). The work environments of downsizing organizations are characterized by heightened uncertainty and turbulence (Tombaugh and White, 1990).

Staw, Sandelands, and Dutton (1992) propose that under conditions of threat, an external event or situation which individuals, groups or organizations perceive as having negative or harmful consequences (e.g., downsizing), organizations undergo a "mechanistic shift" (p. 516). Organizations centralize information, restrict communication, and rely on familiar habitual responses, responses that are likely to be dysfunctional.

Studies that examine survivors' attitudes in the aftermath of corporate layoffs consistently indicate that survivors' job attitudes such as job satisfaction, job involvement, organizational commitment, and intention to remain with the organization become more negative (Brockner, Grover, Reed, and Dewitt, 1992; Brockner, Konovsky, Cooper-Schneider, Folger, Martin, and Bies, 1994; Hallier and Lyon, 1996). These negative reactions, combined with the fact that survivors must do more with less, make the aftermath of layoffs difficult to deal with.

Common symptoms among survivors are particularly strong in organizations that have historically taken great care of their employees. Employees often deny survivor symptoms. Noer (1993) uses the term "psychic numbing" to describe the denial, which is stronger the higher the organizational level and among those who plan and implement downsizing (HR specialists). Survivor Sickness has elements of psychic numbing. Some symptoms include denial, job insecurity, feelings of unfairness, depression, stress and fatigue, reduced risk-taking and motivation, distrust and betrayal, lack of reciprocal commitment, wanting it to be over, dissatisfaction with planning and communication, anger at the layoff process, lack of strategic direction, lack of management credibility, short-term profit focus, and a sense of permanent change (O'Neill and Lenn, 1995). There were also some unexpected findings with regard to survivors, including little survivor guilt, some optimism, lots of blaming others, and a thirst for information.

Interestingly, both survivors and victims shared common symptoms. Noer, in fact, believes the terms (survivors and victims) become reversed; that those who leave become survivors, and those who stay become victims (Wright and Barling, 1998). The organization typically provides resources to those who leave; however, they do not compensate survivors for the end to job security provided by organizations. The only way to have job security is to have up-to-date work experiences and skills. Rational decisions about non-human resources can be contrasted with the random decisions about human resources. Unlike discarding machines, discarding people has an effect on those who remain (Gottlieb and Conkling, 1995).

● Do Downsizing Efforts Work? ●

Evidence for the effectiveness of downsizing is not impressive. Many efforts produce results that are dismal, and unintended consequences that are devastating. Two-thirds of firms that downsized during the 1980s were behind industry averages for the 1990s. Despite lower unit labor costs, less than half the firms that downsized in the US in the 1990s improved profits or productivity. Seventy-four percent of managers in downsized companies said that morale, trust, and productivity dropped following downsizing, and half of the 1,468 firms in still another survey reported that productivity suffered after downsizing (Henkoff, 1994). A majority of organizations that downsized in another survey failed to realize desired results, only 9 percent indicating an improvement in quality. Evidence suggests that quality, productivity, and customer service often decline over time, and financial performance, while often improving in the short run following downsizing due to promised savings and lower costs, diminish over the long run (Cascio, Young, and Morris, 1997; Morris, Cascio, and Young, 1999).

A four-year study of downsizing that attempted to identify best practices demonstrated a significant negative relationship between organizational effectiveness and downsizing accomplished through layoffs (Freeman and Cameron, 1993). Another study of 1,005 firms showed that less than half of these firms had reduced expenses, on a third increased profits, and one-fifth increased productivity. Two-thirds of the firms reported that morale was seriously affected by the downsizing (Bennett, 1991).

Cascio (1998) provided recent evidence that underscores these findings in a study of 311 companies that downsized employees by more than 3 percent in any year between 1980 and 1990. He concluded that the level of employee downsizing did not lead to improved company financial or stock performance. A pure downsizing strategy, then, is unlikely to be effective.

In a study of 281 acute care hospitals, morbidity and mortality rates were 200 percent to 400 percent higher in hospitals that downsized in the traditional head-count reduction, across-the-board way (Murphy, 1994). That is, patient deaths were significantly higher when downsizing occurred in an imprecise fashion. Moreover, the cost savings associated with downsizing dissipated in twelve to eighteen months, and costs rose to pre-downsizing levels in a relatively short time.

Some organizations, however, have seen benefits from downsizing. There can be a healthy side to restructuring and downsizing. In a Canadian study of 1,034 organizations by Axmith (1995), 85 percent cut costs, 63 percent improved earnings,

58 percent improved productivity, and 36 percent reported improved customer service. Cameron (1998) found, contrary to expectations, that downsizing of one military command was associated with favorable results. First, there was considerable cost savings ($90 million in three years). Second, on-time delivery and order-processing time decreased. Third, quality of products delivered also improved. Fourth, employee grievances dropped. Fifth, customer complaints dropped while their satisfaction improved. In sum, substantial improvement took place on a variety of objective performance indicators over this three-year period. When questionnaire measures of the process dimensions of downsizing, the general approach to downsizing, and the effects of downsizing were compared at the start and at the end of the three-year period, the responses were significantly more favorable at the end of this period. The command was seen as more effective and downsizing was seen as a contributor to this improvement. The majority of evidence suggests, however, that most downsizing efforts fall short of meeting objectives. Despite its dismal track record, downsizing remains a strategy of choice of organizations faced with excess capacity, bloated employee ranks, sky-high costs, and declining efficiency. In order to learn from the experience of downsizing, the many failures and few successes must be examined.

● Why Do Restructuring and Downsizing Fail? ●

A recent survey of 1,142 firms conducted by the American Management Association (Greenberg, 1990) reported that more than half of them were unprepared for the downsizing, with no policies or programs in place to reduce the effects of the cutbacks (Rosenblatt and Mannheim, 1996). Surviving managers find themselves working in new and less friendly environments, stretched thin managing more people and jobs, working longer. In addition, these companies sometimes replace staff functions with expensive consultants. Some severed employees will be hired back permanently while others will return to work part-time as consultants.

What about productivity? More than half of 1,468 firms surveyed by the Society for Human Resources Management reported that productivity either stayed the same or deteriorated following downsizing. Similarly a study of 30 firms in the automobile industry indicated that in most productivity deteriorated relative to pre-downsizing levels.

Studies consistently show that after a downsizing, survivors become narrow-minded, self-absorbed, and risk-averse. Morale drops, productivity lessens. Survivors distrust management (Brockner, 1998). The long-term implications of survivor syndrome – lowered morale and commitment – are likely to be damaging for organizations. How likely are such employees to strive towards goals of high-quality services and products?

Cascio (1993) reviewed the literature on the economic and organizational consequences of downsizing. He concluded that in many firms, expected economic benefits were not realized (e.g., higher profits, lower expense ratios, higher stock prices, greater return on investment). Similarly, many expected organizational benefits were not achieved (e.g., better communication, greater productivity, lower overhead, greater entrepreneurship). Cascio attributed this failure to continued use of traditional structures and management practices. Instead, he advocated that downsizing be viewed as a process of continuous improvement that included restructuring, along with other initiatives to reduce waste, inefficiencies, and redundancy.

Cameron, Whetten, and Kim (1987) identified twelve dysfunctional organizational consequences of any organization decline. These include: centralization, the absence of long-range planning, the curtailment of innovation, scapegoating, resistance to change, turnover, decreased morale, loss of slack, the emergence of special interest groups (politics), loss of credibility of top management, conflict and in-fighting, and across-the-board rather than prioritized cuts.

Four of ten companies that downsized had unintended business consequences (Marks, 1994). These included need for retraining, more use of temporary workers, more overtime, increased retiree health costs, contracting out, loss of the wrong people, loss of too many people, and severance costs greater than anticipated (Bedeian and Armenakis, 1998).

● Mergers and Acquisitions ●

Mergers appear to be taking place with ever-increasing regularity today. And these mergers are occurring in all industrial countries, often involve organizations in two or more countries, and are larger in scale, now topping $100 billion. But many of these combinations fail. Marks and Mirvis (1998) state that more than three-quarters of corporate combinations fail to achieve anticipated business results. Most produce higher than expected costs and lower than expected profits. These failures are the results of several factors: price, a lack of strategy for the combination, corporate politics and clashing cultures, and poor planning. There are potential benefits from combining, but the costs (e.g., heightened levels of stress, increased workloads, job losses, corporate culture clashes, systems and structures that do not mesh) reduce the benefits.

A productive combination results when the combining organizations are now better able to reach strategic and financial objectives. These productive combinations achieve capacity or asset not present before. There are many legitimate reasons for combining. These include: expanding product or service offerings, vertical integration, globalization, spreading risk, gaining access to new technology and resources, obtaining economies of scale, cost-cutting and efficiency, greater flexibility in the use of company assets, and the creation of new and innovative products and services.

Marks and Mirvis (1998) highlight important differences in the typical and successful combinations of firms at the three phases. In the pre-combination phase, the typical emphasis was financial; on the successful combination it was strategic. In the combination phase, the typical emphasis was political while in the successful combination it was combination planning. Finally, in the post-combination phase, the typical emphasis was damage control while in the successful combination it was combination management.

Common problems in the pre-combination phase (Marks and Mirvis, 1998) include: unclear business strategy, weak core business, poor combination strategy, pressure to do a deal, hurried diligence, and over-valued objectives and over-estimated benefits. Common problems in the combination phase include: integration seen as a distraction from the real work, not understanding synergies and critical business success factors, psychological effects denied or ignored, and culture clash denied or ignored. Common problems in the post-combination phase include: renewed merger syndrome, a rushed implementation, not enough resources used, unanticipated imple-mentation obstacles, coordination snags, ignoring team-building, not paying enough attention to desired cultural norms, overlooking the human side of im-plementation, and not capitalizing on opportunities to reinforce the new combination's culture.

Marks and Mirvis (1998) identify symptoms of "merger syndrome" as a major cause of the failure of many mergers. Merger syndrome results from stress reactions and crisis management. Personal reactions to merger stress include personal preoccu-pation, the creation of worst-case scenarios, spreading rumours, reactions from job performance, and psychosomatic reactions.

Organizational reactions to merger stress include crisis management, centraliza-tion of decision-making, less communication, a war-room mentality at the top, inter-personal and inter-group tensions, and more conformity and group think. Cultural reactions to merger stress include clashes between the two cultures, a "we" versus "them" mentality, superior versus inferior thinking, criticize and defend, win-lose positions, and flawed decision-making characterized by force, horse trading or de-fault (Mirvis and Marks, 1994).

Marks and Mirvis (1998) offer their insights on how to improve the odds that a merger, acquisition or alliance will be successful. They divide their model into three phases: precombination, combination, and post-combination. The pre-combination phase describes planning and cultural analyses of the combining organizations as well as the emotional and psychological issues that emerge as individuals anticipate the combination. The combination phase places emphasis on top management's lead-ership, the role of transition teams, building enthusiasm throughout the workforce, the reduction of stress and the importance of being sensitive to symptoms of culture clash. The post-combination phase involves the integration of structures, policies and practices, and the development and reinforcement of the desired culture. This phase also helps employees adapt to the new organizational realities and works on the development of effective work teams.

● Privatization ●

A large number of formerly government-managed organizations have been priva-tized throughout the industrialized world. The impetus for this is the belief that the private sector can manage these organizations in more efficient and effective ways. The widespread use of privatization by governments began under Margaret Thatcher in the UK and spread to other countries. New Zealand, for example, intro-duced privatization to many formerly government-managed programs. Although privatization is a major social and organizational experiment, it has not received much research attention. Most attention has been paid to possible economic benefits; less attention has been paid to potential human and organizational gains.

Cunha (2000) evaluated the impact of privatization on the organizational culture, human resource management practices, and employee well-being (perceived occupational stress, job satisfaction, mental and physical ill-health). She studied four industrial companies, three of which had been privatized and one about to be privatized. The study was longitudinal with two and three waves of data being collected in various companies. She found that efforts to privatizate increased both people and performance orientations. Staff reductions also took place in all cases. Perceptions of occupational stress increased. Self-reports of physical and emotional health symptoms also increased during the privatization process. Job satisfaction was found to increase over time during the privatization process.

Nelson, Cooper, and Jackson (1995) conducted a workforce study during the process of two major organizational transitions. The organization was a regional water authority about to move from public to private ownership as part of government policy to privatize the UK water industry. Two significant events took place during the period covered by the research (October 1989 – July 1991): (1) privatization, at the end of November 1989, and (2) structural reorganization in March 1991. These changes occurred in the context of previous changes, including staff reductions. Between 1983 and 1989 the workforce had been reduced 25 percent from 6,000 to 4,500, a reduction in levels of management and employees, with some changing jobs. The privatization plans called for a major restructuring and rationalization of the existing system of autonomous geographic regions, each with its own service functions. These service functions (e.g., personnel, finance) were to be centralized at the head office. These changes would have significant effects on large numbers of employees (new reporting relationships, changes in jobs and responsibilities, relocation to other sites). The research examined the effects of these changes on employee morale and well-being. From a total workforce of 6,500, every third employee from each of the nine divisions of the organization was selected (N = 1,500). Data were collected from 332 employees (84 percent male) at three time periods: pre-privatization, November 1989; post-privatization, June 1990; post-reorganization, July 1991. Three dependent variables were included: job satisfaction, mental health symptoms, and physical health symptoms. Job satisfaction dropped following privatization and increased following reorganization. Mental health symptoms increased following privatization. There was also a significant increase in physical health symptoms following privatization.

Ferrie and her colleagues (1995, 1998) have considered this question in an important longitudinal study of a group of middle-aged men and women white-collar civil servants working in a department facing privatization. Self-reported health status of individuals anticipating privatization deteriorated when compared to the health status of individuals not experiencing privatization. Health behaviors of individuals facing privatization were found to be more positive both before and during privatization when compared to control civil servants. The before and during privatization measures were obtained using questionnaires four years apart.

This department was ultimately sold to the private sector. Ferrie et al. (1998) compared self-reported and clinical measures of health as the department was transferring in ownership with control civil servants. They report that self-reported morbidity and physiological risk factors tended to increase among respondents in the privatized department compared with those in other departments.

• Job Insecurity •

Each of these organization transitions has resulted in actual job loss and increased potential of job loss. Studies have shown that anticipation or concern about job loss may be as damaging as job loss itself (Latack and Dozier, 1986). Job insecurity has been found to be associated with increased medical consultations for psychological distress (Catalano, Rook, and Dooley, 1986) and with increased disability claims for back pain (Volinn, Lai, McKinney, and Loeser, 1988). Job insecurity of parents can also affect their children's work beliefs and attitudes (Barling, Dupre, and Hepburn, 1998).

Dekker and Schaufeli (1995) conducted a repeated measures study of the effects of job insecurity in a large Australian public transport organization undergoing significant change and downsizing. At the time of the study (1990–1), the organization employed about 20,000 people and provided train, streetcar, and bus service to passengers in urban and rural areas. Four departments were identified as having an objective threat of having surplus workers or closure. Data were collected via questionnaires distributed twice – two months apart. Job insecurity was associated with a deterioration of psychological health (psychological health and burnout) as well as job and organizational withdrawal. Interestingly Dekker and Schaufeli (1995) found that being certain about the worst (those transport workers who knew they would lose their jobs) seemed to reduce symptoms of psychological stress and burnout, while prolonged job insecurity was associated with continued high levels of psychological stress and burnout.

Roskies and Louis-Guerin (1990) examined reactions to job insecurity as a chronic ambiguous threat in a sample of 1,291 Canadian managers. Two high-risk and one low-risk company participated in the study. Significantly more managers in the high-risk companies saw themselves as insecure than in the low-risk company. Various facets of insecurity showed different effects. Thus, less than 5 percent of all respondents reported high likelihood of termination or demotion in the short term; 15 percent reported high likelihood of deteriorating work conditions, and over 40 percent reported a high likelihood of job loss in the long term. They also found significant relationships between the measures of insecurity and health problems: the higher the levels of perceived insecurity, the greater the number of health symptoms. A similar pattern was found on relationships between levels of job insecurity and work-related outcomes: the higher the level of perceived insecurity, the lower the job commitment and more negative the appraisal of one's career. Interestingly, subjective perceptions of job insecurity had significantly stronger relationships with the physical health measures than did the objective index.

● Coping with Change and Transition ●

Callan and Terry (1994) deliberately set out to study how individuals cope with organizational change. Data were obtained from 100 Australian lawyers. Respondents indicated both the magnitude and stressfulness of organizational change experienced by their firms. Lawyers perceiving higher levels of organizational change also reported greater anxiety and depression; lawyers indicating higher levels of appraised stress also reported greater depression. Both personal (self-esteem and internal loss of control) and social resources (professional support) were also related to levels of anxiety and depression.

Terry, Callan, and Sartori (1996) empirically tested a stress-coping model of employee adjustment to an organizational merger. Event characteristics, how the event was appraised, coping strategies used in response to the change, and individuals' coping resources (neuroticism and social support) were examined. They found that appraisal of the merger and coping responses mediated the effects of merger characteristics on psychological well-being. They found considerable support for their model. Thus the processes by which the merger was introduced (consultation, communication, visible leadership) were associated with lower stress appraisals, and lower appraisals of the stress of the merger were associated with greater job satisfaction and psychological well-being. Use of escapist coping was associated with levels of psychological well-being and job satisfaction. Supervisor support, but not co-worker support, was also important. Supervisor support was associated with more favorable merger processes, less appraised merger stress, and greater job satisfaction and psychological well-being.

Terry and Callan (2000) tested a model of adjustment to organizational change, a merger between two airlines using a large sample of pilots and flight engineers. Participants who had perceived the merger's implementation in a positive manner reported higher levels of job satisfaction and less psychological distress. They also perceived the merger as less threatening. In addition, participants having more positive views on the implementation of the merger were more likely to use problem-focussed coping responses. Level of threat seemed to be a key variable. Adjustment to the change was better if employees were kept informed of the change process, if they were consulted about the change and its implementation, and if effective leadership was present.

A second study examined predictors of employees' adjustment to the integration of two public sector organizations and the large internal reorganization that resulted. Participants were middle managers and supervisors. Perceptions of uncertainty and stress predicted psychological distress. Amount of change also emerged as a significant predictor of distress.

● Is There a Healthy Side to Transition and Change? ●

Marks (1994) contends that people are saturated with change and transition, and efforts must be made to help them deal with the pain of the past before they can move on to accept future changes. Most organizations in the 1980s and 1990s went through mergers, acquisitions, downsizing, restructuring, re-engineering, culture change, and leadership succession. Many had several of these and often overlapping. These events have not only changed organizational systems; they have had a major effect on workers in them – mostly negative (Ferrie, Shipley, Marmot, Stansfeld, and Smith, 1998; Kivimaki, Vahtera, Thomson, Griffiths, Cox, and Penti, 1997). Victims, survivors, destroyed career paths; cynicism is up, trust in organizational leadership is down. Survivors work harder with fewer rewards. Multiple downsizings are seen over a few years (Armstrong-Stassen, 1997). Those who lost their jobs may in fact be better off – they can now get on with new things. And employees see no end to the changes – and feel powerless to influence them.

Yet organizations must continue to change to remain competitive (Nolan and Croson, 1995). New technology and increased competition will hasten the rate of change (Marks, 1994). Senior managers are excited about opportunities; middle managers are angry, depressed, and tired. The negative psychological, behavioral, and business consequences of these changes weigh heavily upon them.

There is a healthy side to transition and change. Some organizations were bloated: they needed to rightsize by eliminating unnecessary work (and people) and responding to the forces mentioned above. The point of Marks' book is the theme of using transitions such as mergers and acquisitions, restructuring, and downsizing to spur organizational renewal. This is easier said than done. Most organizations simply do not do this very well (Baumohl, 1993). If organizations did not change they would stagnate and decline. Some restructurings, mergers, and downsizings are wise business decisions. The merger of Molson's Breweries and Carling O'Keefe is one Canadian example of such a decision. Many companies in the red may be wise to reduce their workforces. Companies can be revitalized and individuals can be renewed . . . if the emphasis is rightsizing rather than downsizing (Bruton, Keels, and Shook, 1996).

● Individual Responses to Transition ●

Mishra and Spreitzer (1998) identified four types of survivor responses to downsizing: cynical, fearful, obliging, and hopeful. Two dimensions underlay these responses: constructive/destructive and active/passive. Constructive survivors do not view a significant threat or harm from the downsizing and willingly cooperate with management in its implementation. Destructive survivors feel threatened or perceive potential harm from the downsizing and are less willing to cooperate in its implementation. Active survivors believe they can cope with the downsizing and they behave assertively. Passive survivors believe they are unable (less able) to cope with the downsizing and they make no efforts in this regard. Hopeful responders are active advocates and excited about the future. Obliging responders are faithful followers who cooperate in the downsizing by following orders. Cynical responders are vocal critics of the change. Fearful responders are the walking wounded, frightened, worried, and helpless in the face of the change.

Mishra and Spreitzer propose that high levels of both trust in management and perception of justice in the way the downsizing is implemented and managed will increase the constructiveness of survivor responses. In addition, feelings of empowerment and downsizing efforts that enrich the content of some jobs serve to increase active responses by survivors.

Speitzer and Mishra (2000) empirically examined this framework of survivor responses to downsizing in a sample of 350 aerospace workers at a plant that had recently announced a downsizing. They found support for many of their predicitions. Thus perceptions of procedural and distributive justice were related to more constructive survivor responses. There was modest evidence that perceptions of empowerment would be related to active survivor responses. Neither task variety nor trust were related to more active survivor responses as hypothesized. Interestingly, the independent variables were better predictors of the hopeful survivor responses and the cynical survivor responses. Both justice perceptions and empowerment were important predictors of the hopeful response. Hopeful survivors were also more likely to be the primary breadwinner in their family and were younger. Cynical responders perceived less justice and less task variety.

On the practical side, efforts to develop perceptions of fairness in survivors would appear to be useful. Empowering survivors, while difficult, had desirable consequences. In addition, keeping workload levels within manageable limits had further value in influencing survivor responses.

Noer (1993) identifies four individual responses to change and transitions. Individuals vary in their capacity for changing (the ability to learn from their experience) and their comfort with change (the readiness to learn):

- *The Entrenched* (30–60 percent of employees) possess low comfort with change and a high capacity for change. Their primary behavior in response to transition involves tenaciously clinging to narrow learnings that worked in the past but have limited value in the new reality.
- *The Overwhelmed* (30–40 percent) exhibit low comfort with change and low capacity for change. Their common response to transition is to withdraw, thus avoiding the change where possible and forgoing the necessary learning.
- *The BSers* (10–15 percent) display high comfort with change but low capacity for change. BSers delude themselves and others. They "talk a good game" but fail to deliver.
- *The Learners* (15–20 percent) possess high comfort with change and a high capacity for change. Learners actively and positively engage the change and acquire the new and relevant skills for succeeding in the new reality.

• Successful Organizational Transformation •

What characterizes an organization that can successfully adapt and change itself? Day (1999) suggests that the most common feature of failed or flawed change programs is a lack of commitment to the deep-seated changes needed. Why do we need to change? What is the path to the desired end-state? What does the end-state look like? Day examined four different change programs (Fidelity Investments, Sears Roebuck, Eurotunnel, Owens Corning) and others that failed, distilling six conditions that ensure change program success. Focussing specifically on changes that make an organization more market-driven, Day believes that organizations must tailor the design of a change program to the particular challenges of understanding, attracting, and keeping valuable customers.

Day writes that successful change programs have six overlapping stages:

1. Demonstrating leadership commitment. A leader owns and champions the change, invests time and resources, and creates a sense of urgency.
2. Understanding the need for change. Key implementers understand the challenges facing the organization, know the changes needed, and see the benefits of the change initiative.
3. Shaping the vision. All employees know what they are trying to accomplish, understand how to create superior value, and see what to do differently.
4. Mobilizing commitment at all levels. Those responsible have experience and credibility and know how to form a coalition of supporters to overcome resistance.
5. Aligning structures, systems, and incentives. Key implementers have the resources they need to create a credible plan for alignment.
6. Reinforcing the change. Those responsible know how to start the program, keep attention focussed on the change and benchmark measures, and ensure an early win.

Waterman (1997) also studied organizations that seemed to be effectively managing change. He identified eight themes in organizations capable of renewing themselves:

1. Informed opportunism. Renewing organizations set direction for their companies, using information and flexibility to capitalize on opportunities.
2. Direction and empowerment. Renewing companies treat everyone as a source of creative input in the pursuit of results.
3. Friendly facts, congenial controls. Renewing companies use information and financial controls as benchmarks of progress and challenge.
4. A different mirror. Renewing companies have the motivation and discipline to break old habits.
5. Teamwork, trust, politics, and power. Renewing companies fostered trust, collaboration, the skillful use of politics and power.
6. Stability in motion. Renewing companies operated in fluid, flexible ways.
7. Attitudes and attention. Management in renewing organizations spoke and behaved in ways that focussed attention on key issues.
8. Causes and commitment. Renewing organizations were able to generate commitment to their cultural purpose and mission.

Pascale, Millemann, and Gioja (1997) similarly observe that many efforts at transformational change fail to achieve expected results. The problem is not the improvement programs but the fact that the responsibilities for and the burden of changes are borne by so few individuals. Companies can only be successful here if all employees eagerly respond to the challenges of transformation and revitalization. Pascale and his colleagues distilled three sources of revitalization by tracking the change efforts at three of the world's largest organizations (Sears Roebuck, Royal Dutch Shell, the US army). These were: all employees are involved in grappling with the key business challenges facing the company; leadership that maintains employee involvement; and changes in the job behaviors of all employees.

● Managing Organizational Transitions ●

Marks (1994) makes a distinction between change and transition. A change refers to a path to a known state; a transition is a path to an unknown state. Transitions can be of two types: event-driven and large-scale organizational transformations. Event-driven transitions include mergers or acquisitions, restructuring or delayering, downsizing, the adoption of new technology, the addition of a large number of new employees or the appearance of a new CEO. The second type of transition involves a planed large-scale culture change or the adoption of TQM philosophy. It is necessary to help organizations and their employees recover from transition. This is due to the human pain involved and the resulting organizational inefficiencies that accompany transitions.

Bridges (1991) also makes a distinction between change and transition. Change is situational: the new job, the new manager, the new policies. Transition is the psychological process people go through to come to terms with the new situation. Change is external; transition is internal.

Transition starts with an ending (Bridges, 1980, 1991). One must let go of the old. The failure to identify and prepare for the losses and endings that change produces is the largest problem that organizations in transition face. The next stage is the neutral zone, a confusing place between the old and the new. The neutral zone is characterized by confusion, fear, and flight. Bridges believes that the neutral zone is the individual's and the organization's best opportunity for renewal and development. The neutral zone then is the most important stage of the transition process.

Bridges (1991) offers practical suggestions for navigating each stage in the transition process. Some suggestions for the first stage include: identify who's losing what, accept the reality and importance of loss, expect over-reaction, acknowledge losses openly, encourage grieving, compensate for the losses, provide information fully and frequently, define what is over and what isn't, mark endings, treat the past with respect, take some of the past into the future, and highlight ways in which endings will guarantee the continuing of the organization.

Some suggestions for managing the neutral zone include: normalize people's feelings and reactions, reframe the neutral zone in more positive terms, provide structure and support, build teamwork, gather data on how the transition is unfolding, and strive to develop new and better ways of working.

• What Organizations Can Do •

Considerable guidance is now available to senior organizational managers on how best to implement organizational restructuring and downsizing (Burke and Nelson, 1997; Nelson and Burke, 1998). Handled properly, we propose that revitalization can re-energize tired workers and heighten their aspirations, shift the organization's focus to future opportunities, strengthen the pay-for-performance link, increase investment in training and development, encourage innovation, improve communication, and produce a clearer mission. Downsizing may, in fact, be part of the revitalization process, but only a part.

Successfully managing transitions such as mergers and acquisitions, downsizing, and other restructurings requires considerable commitment from organizations. The research literature provides guidance for managers who are leading such transitions (Moser Illes, 1996).

Schweiger and DeNisi (1991) considered the impact of a realistic merger preview, a program of realistic information on employees of an organization that had just announced a merger. Employers from one plant received the merger preview while those in another plant received only limited information. Data were collected at four points in time: before the merger was announced, following the announcement but before the realistic merger preview program was introduced, and twice following the realistic merger program. The study extended for a five-month period overall. Both objective and self-report data were obtained.

The following conclusions were drawn. First, the announcement of the merger was associated with significant increases in global stress, perceived uncertainty and absenteeism, and decreases in job satisfaction, commitment, and perceptions of the company's trustworthiness, honesty, and caring, and no change in self-reported performance. There were no differences between the two plants following the announcement of the merger. The experimental plant was significantly lower on perceived uncertainty and significantly higher on job satisfaction, commitment, and perceptions of the company's trustworthiness, honesty, and caring following the realistic merger preview program. These same differences were also present three months later.

Parker, Chmiel, and Wall (1997) report findings from a four-year longitudinal study of strategic downsizing showing that the use of deliberate work organization and change-management strategies minimized the negative effects of staff reductions. The company intended to downsize, and the downsizing was accompanied by an empowerment philosophy. This longitudinal study involved repeated measures over a four-year period. Four work characteristics were assessed: demands, control, clarity, and participation in change. During the four years, the workforce was reduced to about 60 percent of its original size. Most of the downsizing was voluntary through early retirement. Employees losing their jobs received counseling and outplacement help and generous severance. The empowerment initiative involved multiskilling, delayering, and restructuring into business and support teams. Managers were given training to support the empowerment strategy. During the study there was a significant increase in performance. Demand, control, and participation increased over time.

There was no change in strain over time. Both clarity and participation were important predictors of well-being. In summary, this study showed that there was no decrease of employee well-being during the downsizing despite an increase in demands. Potential negative effects of high demands seemed to be counterbalanced by improvements in other work characteristics (particularly clarity and participation). The negative consequences of downsizing can be partially addressed by establishing clear roles and responsibilities, developing a vision for the future and thoughts on how this will be achieved, along with more staff involvement. In addition, the existence of a positive work environment before downsizing had significant relationships with well-being four years later. Paying attention to the design of work and the broader work environment is more likely to result in effective and successful downsizing.

Noer (1993) offers a four-level process for handling layoffs and their effects. The first level of intervention addresses the layoff process itself. Organizations that more effectively manage the layoff process will reduce (but not eliminate) layoff survivor sickness. The second level of intervention addresses the grieving process by providing an opportunity for catharsis in releasing repressed feelings and emotions. The third level of intervention helps survivors regain their sense of control, confidence, self-esteem, and efficacy. The fourth level of intervention develops organizational policies, procedures, and structures that will prevent future layoff survivor sickness. This includes the use of job enrichment and employee participation, employee autonomy, non-traditional career paths, short-term job planning, and the encouragement of employee independence and empowerment (Mishra and Spreitzer, 1998).

Government policies have been helpful, particularly advance notification provisions, extended unemployment benefits, and worker retraining programs. Advance notification gives workers more time to find new employment, decreasing the length of unemployment and emotional distress. Extended unemployment benefits lessen the economic distress. Retraining programs help the unemployed find new jobs. Company programs such as outplacement initiatives have also been of some help.

Cascio (1993) also offers some guidelines for managing downsizing effectively. First, to downsize effectively, be prepared to manage apparent contradictions – for example, between the use of top-down authority and bottom-up empowerment, between short-term strategies (headcount reduction) and long-term strategies (organization redesign and systemic changes in culture). To bring about sustained improvements in productivity, quality, and effectiveness, integrate reductions in head count with planned changes in the way that work is designed. Downsizing was not a one-time, quick-fix solution to enhance competitiveness. Rather, it should be viewed as part of a process of continuous improvement.

• There is No Quick Fix •

One of the reasons for the failure of many downsizing efforts was an overly simplistic approach. Senior management equated downsizing with cutting costs through staff reduction. This approach has often been short-sighted, focussing on perceived internal efficiencies rather than examining the way the organization conducts its business. Simply cost-cutting is unlikely to improve the competitive position of most organizations over the long haul in the global marketplace. Kets de Vries and Balazs (1997) suggest that companies that implemented downsizing seem to be more concerned with their past than their future; long-term investments are postponed to realize short-term gains. They propose instead that downsizing be reframed "as a continuous process of corporate transformation and change, a way to plan for the continuity of the organization" (p. 11). In its broadest sense, downsizing can mean changing the firm's fundamental business practices, and even its corporate culture. Responsible restructuring focusses on how to use the current people more effectively and as part of continuous improvement efforts, and constitutes a more effective approach. A wider definition serves to place downsizing under the umbrella of continuous corporate renewal.

● A Three-Stage Approach to Revitalization ●

We propose that organizations approach revitalization efforts within the framework of comprehensive organizational change (Burke and Nelson, 1997; Nelson and Burke, 1998). Large-scale changes can be recast within the three-stage framework of initiation, implementation, and institutionalization. A careful examination of the literature on downsizing and restructuring yields guidance for managers in each of the three stages.

● Initiation: Planning Revitalization Efforts ●

Planning is an essential element in any change process. Graddick and Cairo (1998) note the importance of up-front planning. This includes the establishment of timeframes, goals, and objectives for the restructuring, the establishment of deadlines to monitor progress, and the establishment of principles to ensure consistency and integrity of the process. Reframing the restructuring in a broader way offers a more constructive way of viewing the process. This new mindset opens up possibilities for learning and novel solutions to performance, productivity, and cost concerns (Caplan and Teese, 1997).

Attempts to revitalize organizations should begin with a goal, and should be a part of a long-term strategy rather than a quick fix. It is possible to downsize without layoffs. If the reasons for reducing the workforce are cost-related, managers should consider cutting costs elsewhere. Process improvements may be more effective than reducing headcount. In addition, a thorough organizational diagnosis should be conducted, and specific areas of inefficiency should be targeted. Employees should be given information about the financial state of the business, and when they are informed they can draw their own conclusions about actions that need to be taken. The individuals affected can provide input on cutting costs if they are made aware of the need to do so. When employees understand that the organization's performance affects them personally, they respond by helping to improve that performance (Burke and Nelson, 1997).

If downsizing is deemed a necessity, there are several short-term alternatives to be considered, each with advantages and disadvantages. Such options include attrition, hiring freezes, wage containment, limits in work hours, and alternative forms of termination (Knowdell, Branstead, and Moravec, 1994). Interestingly, Cameron (1998) found that type of downsizing tactics used (e.g., use of layoffs, early retirement, severance packages, transfers, demotions) was unrelated to command effectiveness or performance improvements following downsizing. In addition, other factors such as salary or hiring freezes, number of management levels reduced or amount of outsourcing undertaken had no effect on these closures.

Whatever option is taken, managers must clearly explain the criteria for workforce reductions. The decision of what method to use requires in-depth analysis and careful forethought. This explanation must be characterized by open communication, candor, and repetition. Multiple methods of communication should be used, but face-to-face communication may be most effective. In addition, managers should be trained on how to effectively communicate the downsizing (Mishra, Spreitzer, and Mishra, 1998). Managers must be prepared to give bad news with empathy and be prepared to deal with the emotional reactions of employees.

● Implementation: The Change is Underway ●

The way in which the transition plan is executed has a dramatic effect on the long-term success of the effort, and particularly affects the victims' and survivors' reactions to the process. Adkins (1998) advocated the use of broadly based change management teams in describing the military base closure. Graddick and Cairo (1998) concur with this point, and propose that transition teams formed in the planning stage be heavily involved in implementing the change process. Participation in the implementation of change gives employees a sense of control over their destinies and a means of influencing events that threaten their livelihoods and well-being.

Communication during the implementation stage is essential. Managers must tell the truth, and overcommunicate (Mishra, Spreitzer, and Mishra, 1998). Managers should carefully and thoroughly explain the criteria for layoffs, and clarify the role of performance valuations in the layoff process (Leana and Feldman, 1992). Using a procedure that is perceived as fair can build employee trust, especially when the outcome is negative, as in a layoff (Brockner, Wiesenfeld, and Martin, 1995). The communication process must be two-way; employees must be engaged in communication to determine their reactions to the process and their level of understanding.

Providing support to all affected employees is critical. All employees must be treated with respect and dignity. Providing laid-off employees with honest information and social support can help them face the future with more confidence. Also, employees should be given the bad news in person by someone they know rather than via mail or by someone they do not know. Laid-off workers and survivors should be allowed to grieve, and to say goodbye to each other. Generosity to those departing will benefit both victims and survivors. Providing clear explanations and treating people with respect while implementing a layoff are actions that are not costly in economic terms, but add to the perceptions of procedural fairness. Managers should provide laid-off workers with fair recommendations to future employers. Providing outplacement assistance for employees is a critical part of managing the transition process. These services can be provided by company career centers, or can be outsourced. One outplacement intervention that has been demonstrated to be helpful to displaced employees is stress management training. Participants in a stress management training program were able to maintain effective coping resources and minimize increases in distress and strain, while members of the control group either increased their distress levels or decreased their use of coping skills (Maysent and Spera, 1995). The program was also evaluated by participants, who indicated that one of the informal benefits of the training was the forum it provided for sharing their own frustrations and concerns about the job search process.

Continuous monitoring of progress during the implementation stage will help the organization assess its efforts and spot trouble early. Monitoring processes can help the transition teams adjust the plan along the way. The emotions and well-being of employees should be monitored as well, and managers should be especially vigilant for signals of distress and burnout (Graddick and Cairo, 1988). In conjunction with the monitoring process, managers should not expect immediate payoffs. Cameron (1998), in describing the downsizing of the military command, indicated that one factor that differentiated this case from typical downsizing efforts was an expectation of temporary downturns during the process, and subsequent moderate-term recovery.

• Institutionalization: Revitalization and Renewal •

If downsizing is required, then revitalization of the organization is a key third step in the transformation process. In their study of the trivestiture of AT&T, Graddick and Cairo (1998) distilled seven lessons learned about revitalization:

1. Avoid ignoring past accomplishments and qualities, but emphasize why changes are required for future success.
2. Ensure that employees understand the new business direction, opportunities for growth, and how they can contribute to these. Clarify requirements for change, including new skills and competencies, culture changes, and leadership behaviors.
3. Celebrate and recognize important accomplishments.
4. Drive process improvements so that the smaller, downsized workforce does not end up doing the same amount of work as the pre-downsizing workforce had done.
5. Communicate the new employment contract between employees and the company (i.e., clarify mutual expectations).
6. Align goals throughout the organization and clarify roles and responsibilities.
7. Realign human resources processes and programs (e.g., compensation, workforce planning, education and training, performance management, leadership development) with the new business direction.

These suggestions are in accordance with the view of downsizing as part of organizational redesign and systemic changes in organizational cultures.

Helping survivors cope with the trauma of the transition should be a major part of revitalization efforts. Layoff survivors' symptoms do not go away, and some even intensify over time. These symptoms include an increase in resignation, fear, and depression, deepening sense of loss of control, and heightened, more focused anger (Noer, 1993). Survivors' social support systems have been disrupted or destroyed, they are confused about role expectations, and fear the overload of work that will be passed along to them. They may suffer feelings of guilt from wondering "Why not me?" Managers must allow for a period of grieving and disruptions in productivity, and treat survivors gently following the transition (Leana and Feldman, 1992). Support groups can help employees feel safe in expressing their feelings.

Investment in the retraining and development of survivors is important because some organizations want to demonstrate some immediate improvements in bottom line from the downsizing efforts (Gutknecht and Keys, 1993). The new organizational reality, however, dictates that new strategies and even new organizational cultures be passed along through training and development efforts. It cannot be assumed that survivors will understand how to carry out their new jobs after downsizing. They will need new skills to tackle the work left behind by former colleagues. Adkins (1998) suggested that education and training efforts should include job training, transition skills, personal change, and stress management. Training can help the survivors to feel more competent and empowered in the throes of uncertainty (Mishra, Spreitzer, and Mishra, 1998).

Downsizing may necessitate a movement from the old employment contract, focussed on long-term tenure and co-dependency, to the new employment contract, which views employees as self-employed entrepreneurs (Noer, 1993). Rather than emphasizing lifetime employment, the new psychological contract emphasizes employability. Workers are trained in transferable skills. Whereas long-term career planning was a part of the old psychological contract, the new environment requires career management programs for survivors that focus on opportunities for growth and development rather than advancement (Feldman, 1996). Providing survivors with growth opportunities that allow them to develop portfolios of transferable skills is an important support mechanism. It signals that the company believes in investing in human resources.

● Conclusion: Leadership is Vital ●

A major theme that can be gleaned from the studies of successful revitalization efforts is that effective leadership is a critical element in the transformation process. The competence, knowledge, dynamism, and accessibility of senior managers and their ability to articulate a vision that provides motivation for the future increases the likelihood of positive outcomes. Consistent, strong, effective leaders must develop and communicate a new vision and motivate employees to embrace this vision. Changes in leadership are likely to affect the process adversely, particularly if trust – a key ingredient – is jeopardized.

The behavior of senior management, particularly their treatment of survivors, is an important determinant of the success or failure of the downsizing process. The way senior managers handle layoffs has a major impact on survivors' attitudes and work behaviors. Many senior managers underestimate the importance of little details in the downsizing and restructuring process implementation on the productivity of those remaining. It is also a mistake to tell those that remain they should consider themselves fortunate and work hard since they still have jobs.

NOTE

1   Preparation of this chapter was supported in part by the School of Business, York University. I thank my colleague and friend Debra Nelson for her insights on managing organizational transitions. Tijen Harcar assisted in collecting material for the chapter and Sandra Osti prepared the typescript.

REFERENCES

Adkins, J.A. (1998). Base closure: A case study in occupational stress and organisational decline. In M.K.L. Gowing, J.D. Kraft, and J.C. Quick (eds). *The New Organizational Reality: Downsizing, Restructuring and Revitalization.* Washington, D.C.: American Psychological Association, pp. 111–42.

Armstrong-Stassen, M. (1997). The effect of repeated management downsizing and surplus designation on remaining managers: An exploratory study. *Anxiety, Stress, and Coping*, 10, 377–84.

Armstrong-Stassen, M. (1998). Downsizing the Federal Government: A longitudinal study of managers' reactions. *Canadian Journal of Administrative Sciences*, 15, 310–21.

Axmith, M. (1995). 1995 Canadian Dismissal Practices Survey. Toronto, Ontario: Author.

Barling, J., Dupre, K.E., and Hepburn, C.G. (1998). Effects of parents' job insecurity on children's work beliefs and attitudes. *Journal of Applied Psychology*, 83, 112–18.

Baumohl, B. (1993, March 15). When downsizing becomes dumbsizing. *Time*, 55.

Bedeian, A.G., and Armenakis, A.A. (1998). The cesspool syndrome: How dreck floats to the top of declining organizations. *Academy of Management Executive*, 12, 58–67.

Bennett, A. (1991). Downscoping doesn't necessarily bring an upswing in corporate profitability. *The Wall Street Journal*, June 4, B-1, B-4.

Bridges, W. (1980). *Transitions*. Reading, MA: Addison-Wesley.

Bridges, W. (1991). *Managing Transitions: Making the Most of Change*. Reading, MA: Addison-Wesley.

Brockner, J. (1998). The effects of work layoffs on survivors: Research, theory and practice. In B.M. Staw and L.L. Cummings (eds). *Research in Organizational Behavior* (vol. 10). Greenwich, CT: JAI Press.

Brockner, J., Grover, S., Reed, T., and Dewitt, R. (1992). Layoffs, job insecurity, and survivors' work effort: Evidence of an inverted-U relationship. *Academy of Management Journal*, 35, 413–25.

Brockner, J., Konovsky, M., Cooper-Schneider, R., Folger, R., Martin, C., and Bies, R. (1994). Interactive effects of procedural justice and outcome negativity on victims and survivors of job loss. *Academy of Management Journal*, 37, 397–409.

Brockner, J., Wiesenfeld, B.M., and Martin, C.L. (1995). Decision frame, procedural justice, and survivors' reactions to job layoffs. *Organizational Behavior and Human Decision Processes*, 63, 59–68.

Bruton, G.D., Keels, J.K., and Shook, C.L. (1996). Downsizing the firm: Answering the strategic questions. *Academy of Management Executive*, 10, 38–45.

Buch, K., and Aldridge, J. (1991). O.D. under conditions of organizational decline. *Organization Development Journal*, 9, 1–5.

Burke, R.J., and Nelson, D.L. (1997). Downsizing and restructuring: Lessons from the firing line for revitalizing organizations. *Leadership and Organization Development Journal*, 18, 325–34.

Burke, R.J., and Nelson, D. L. (1998). Mergers and acquisitions, downsizing, and privatization: A North American perspective. In M.K. Gowing, J.D. Kraft, and J.C. Quick (eds). *The New Organizational Reality: Downsizing, Restructuring and Revitalization*. Washington, D.C.: American Psychological Association, pp. 21–54.

Callan V.J., and Terry, D.J. (1994). Coping resources, coping strategies and adjustment to organizational change: Director buffering effects? *Work & Stress*, 8, 372–83.

Cameron, K. (1998). Strategic organizational downsizing: An extreme case. In C.L. Cooper and D. Rouseau (eds). *Trends in Organizational Behavior*. New York: John Wiley, pp. 72–95.

Cameron K., Freeman, S.J., and Mishra, A.K. (1991). Best practices in white-collar downsizing: Managing contradictions. *Academy of Management Executive*, 5, 57–73.

Cameron, K.S., Suttor, R.I., and Whetton, D.A. (1987). *Readings in Organizational Decline: Frameworks, Research and Prescriptions*. Cambridge, MA: Ballinger.

Cameron, K.S., Whetten, D.A., and Kim, M.U. (1987). Organizational dysfunctions of decline. *Academy of Management Journal*, 30, 126–37.

Canadian College of Health Services Executives (1995). *Special Report – External Environmental Analysis and Health Reform Update*. Summer. Ottawa.

Caplan, G., and Teese, M. (1997). *Survivors: How to Keep your Best People on Board after Downsizing*. Palo Alto, CA: Davies-Black.

Cascio, W.F. (1993). Downsizing: What do we know? What have we learned? *Academy of Management Executive*, 7, 95–104.

Cascio, W.F. (1995). Whither industrial and organizational psychology in a changing world of work? *American Psychologist*, 50, 928–39.

Cascio, W.F. (1998). Learning from outcomes: Financial experiences of 311 firms that have downsized. In M.K. Gowing, J.D. Kraft, and J.C. Quick (eds). *The New Organizational Reality: Downsizing, Restructuring and Revitalization*. Washington, D.C.: American Psychological Association, pp. 55–70.

Cascio, W.F., Young, C.E., and Morris, J.R. (1997). Financial consequences of employment change decisions in major US corporations. *Academy of Management Journal*, 40, 1175–89.

Catalano, R., Rook, K., and Dooley, D. (1986). Labor markets and help seeking: A test of the employment security hypothesis. *Journal of Health and Social Behavior*, 27, 227–37.

Cunha, R.C. (2000). Impact of privatization in Portugal. In R.J. Burke and C.L. Cooper (eds). *The Organization in Crisis*. London: Blackwell, in press.

Day, G. (1999) Creating a market-driven organization. *Sloan Management Review*, 41, 11–22.

Dekker, S.W.A. and Schaufeli, W.B. (1995). The effects of job insecurity on psychological health and withdrawal: A longitudinal study. *Australian Psychologist*, 30, 57–63.

Dougherty, D., and Bowman, E. (1995). The effects of organizational downsizing on product innovation. *California Management Review*, 37, 28–44.

Doyle-Driedger, S. (1997, April 28). The Nurses. *MacLean's*, 106, 24–27.

Feldman, D.C. (1996). Managing careers in downsizing firms. *Human Resource Management*, 35, 145–61.

Ferrie, J.E., Shipley, M.J., Marmot, M.G., Stansfield, S.A., and Smith, G.D. (1995). Health effects of anticipation of job change and non-employment: Longitudinal data from the Whitehall II study. *British Medical Journal*, 311, 1264–9.

Ferrie, J.E., Shipley, M.J., Marmot, M.G., Stansfeld, S., and Smith G.D. (1998). The health effects of major organizational change and job insecurity. *Social Science and Medicine*, 46, 243–54.

Freeman, S.J., and Cameron, K.S. (1993). Organizational downsizing: A convergence and reorientation framework. *Organization Science*, 4, 10–29.

Godfrey, C. (1994). Downsizing: Coping with personal pain. *Nursing Management*, 25, 90–3.

Gottlieb, M.R. and Conkling, L. (1995). *Managing the Workplace Survivors: Organizational Downsizing and the Commitment Gap*. New York: Quorum Books.

Gowing, M.K., Kraft, J.D., and Quick, J.C. (1998). Helping people and organizations deal with the impact of competitive change: An AT&T case study. In M.K. Gowing, J.D. Kraft, and J.C. Quick (eds). *The New Organizational Reality: Downsizing, Restructuring and Revitalization*. Washing, D.C.: American Psychological Association pp. 77–98.

Graddick, M. M., and Cairo, P.C. (1998). Helping people and organizations deal with the impact of competitive change: An AT&T case study. In M.K. Gowing, J.D. Kraft, and J.C. Quick (eds). *The New Organizational Reality: Downsizing, Restructuring and Revitalization*. Washington, D.C.: American Psychological Association, pp. 77–98.

Greenberg, E.R. (1990). The latest AMA survey on downsizing. *Compensation and Benefits Review*, 22, 66–71.

Gutknecht, J.E., and Keys, J.B. (1993). Mergers, acquisitions and takeovers: Maintaining morale of survivors and protecting employees. *Academy of Management Executive*, 7, 26–36.

Hallier, J., and Lyon, P. (1996). Job insecurity and employees' commitment: Managers' reactions to the threat and outcomes of redundancy selection. *British Journal of Management*, 7, 107–23.

Henkoff, R. (1994, January 10). Getting beyond downsizing. *Fortune*, 58–64.

Hoskisson, R.E., and Hitt, M.A. (1994). *Downscoping: Hot to Tame the Diversified Firm*. New York: Oxford University Press.

Kets de Vries, M.F.R., and Balazs, K. (1997). The downside of downsizing. *Human Relations*, 50, 11–50.

Kivimaki, M., Vahtera, J., Thomson, L., Griffiths, A., Cox, T., and Penti, J. (1997). Psychosocial factors predicting employee sickness absence during economic decline. *Journal of Applied Psychology*, 82, 858–72.

Knowdell, R.L., Branstead, E., and Moravec, M. (1994). *From Downsizing to Recovery: Strategic Transition Options for Organizations and Individuals*. Palo Alto, C.A: Cpp Books.

Kozlowski, S.W.J., Chao, G.T., Smith, E.M., and Hedlund, J. (1993). Organizational downsizing: Strategies, interventions, and research implications. In C.L. Cooper and I.T. Robertson (eds). *International Review of Industrial and Organizational Psychology*. New York: Wiley, pp. 263–332.

Latack, J.C., and Dozier, J.B. (1986). After the axe falls: Job loss as a career transition. *Academy of Management Review*, 11, 375–92.

Leana, C.R., and Feldman, D.C. (1992). *Coping with Job Loss: How Individuals, Organizations and Communities Respond to Layoffs*. New York: Macmillan/Lexington Books.

Marks, M.L. (1994). *From Turmoil to Triumph*. New York: Lexington Books.

Marks, M.L., and Mirvis, P.H. (1998). *Joining Forces*. San Francisco: Jossey-Bass.

Martin, R.E., and Freeman, S.J. (1998). The economic context of the new organizational reality. In M.K. Gowing, J.D. Kraft, and J.C. Quick (eds). *The New Organizational Reality: Downsizing, Restructuring and Revitalization*. Washington, D.C.: American Psychological Association, pp. 5–20.

Maysent, M., and Spera, S. (1995). Coping with job loss and career stress: Effectiveness of stress management training with outplaced employees. In L.R. Murphy, J.J. Hurrell, Jr., S.L. Sauter, and G.P. Keita (eds). *Job Stress Interventions*. Washington, D.C.: American Psychological Association, pp. 159–70.

McKinley, W., Mone, M.A., and Barker, V.L (1998). Some ideological foundations for organizational downsizing. *Journal of Management Inquiry*, 7, 198–212.

McKinley, W., Sanchez, C.M., and Schick, A.G. (1995). Organizational downsizing: Constraining, cloning, learning. *Academy of Management Executive*, 9, 32–42.

McKinley, W., Zhao, J., and Garrett Rust, K. (2000). A sociocognitive interpretation of organizational downsizing. *Academy of Management Executive*, 25, 227–43.

Mirvis, P.H., and Marks, M.L. (1994). *Managing the Merger: Making it Work*. Upper Saddle River, N.J.: Prentice Hall.

Mishra, A.K., and Spreitzer, G.M. (1998). Explaining how survivors respond to downsizing: The role of trust, empowerment, justice and work redesign. *Academy of Management Review*, 23, 567–88.

Mishra, K.E., Spreitzer, G.M., and Mishra, A.K. (1998). Preserving employee morale during downsizing. *Sloan Management Review*, 39, 83–95.

Morris, J.R., Cascio, W.F., and Young, C.E. (1999). Downsizing after all these years: Questions and answers about who did it, how many did it, and who benefitted from it. *Organizational Dynamics*, 27, 78–87.

Moser Illes, L. (1996). *Sizing Down*. Ithaca, NY: Cornell University Press.

Murphy, E.C. (1994). *Strategies for Health Care Excellence*. Washington, D.C.: American Society for Work Redesign.

Nelson, A., Cooper, C.L., and Jackson, P.R. (1995). Uncertainty amidst change: The impact of privatization on employee job satisfaction and well-being. *Journal of Occupational and Organizational Psychology*, 68, 57–71.

Nelson, D.L., and Burke, R.J. (1998). Lessons learned. *Canadian Journal of Administrative Sciences*, 15, 372–81.

Noer, D. (1993). *Healing the Wounds: Overcoming the Trauma of Layoffs and Revitalizing Downsized Organizations*. San Francisco: Jossey-Bass.

Nolan, R.L., and Croson, D.C. (1995). *Creative Destruction: A Six-Stage Process of Transforming the Organizations*. Boston: Harvard Business School Press.

O'Neill, H.M., and Lenn, J. (1995). Voices of survivors: Words that downsizing CEOs should hear. *Academy of Management Executive*, 9, 23–34.

Parker, S.K., Chmiel, N., and Wall, T.D. (1997). Work characteristics and employee well-being within a context of strategic downsizing. *Journal of Occupational Health Psychology*, 2, 289–303.

Pascale, R., Millemann, M., and Gioja, L. (1997). Changing the way we change. *Harvard Business Review*, 75, 126–39.

Reynolds Fisher, S., and White, M.A. (2000). Downsizing in a learning organization: Are there hidden costs? *Academy of Management Review*, 25, 244–51.

Rosenblatt, Z., and Mannheim, B. (1996). Workforce cutback decisions of Israeli managers: A test of a strategic model. *International Journal of Human Resources Management*, 7, 437–54.

Rosenblatt, Z., Rogers, K.S., and Nord, W.R. (1992). Toward a political framework for flexible management of decline. *Organization Science*, 4, 76–91.

Roskies, E., and Louis-Guerin, C. (1990). Job insecurity in managers: Antecedents and consequences. *Journal of Organizational Behavior*, 11, 345–59.

Schweiger, D.M., and DeNisi, A.A. (1991). Communication with employees following a merger: A longitudinal field experiment. *Academy of Management Journal*, 34, 110–35.

Sennett, R. (1998). *The Corrosion of Character: The Personal Consequences of Work in the New Capitalism*. New York: Norton.

Spreitzer, G.M., and Mishra, A.K. (2000). An empirical examination of a stress-based framework of survivor responses to downsizing. In R.J. Burke and C.L. Cooper (eds). *The

Organization in Crisis: Downsizing, Restructuring, and Privatization. London: Blackwell, in press.

Staw, B.M., Sandelands, L.E., and Dutton, J.E. (1992). Threat-rigidity effects in organizational behavior: A multi-level analysis. *Administrative Science quarterly*, 26, 501–24.

Terry, D. J., and Callan, V.J. (2000). Employee adjustment to an organizational change: A stress and coping perspective. In P. Dewe, M. Leiter, and T. Cox (eds). *Coping, Health and Organizations*. London: Taylor & Francis, pp. 259–76.

Terry D.J., and Callan, V.J., and Sartori, G. (1996). Employee adjustment to an organizational merger: Stress, coping and intergroup differences. *Stress Medicine*, 12, 105–22.

Tombaugh, J.R., and White, L.P. (1990). Downsizing: An empirical assessment of survivors' perceptions in a post layoff environment. *Organization Development Journal*, 8, 32–43.

Uchitelle, L., and Kleinfeld, N.R. (1996). The price of jobs lost. In the New York Times Special Report (eds). *The Downsizing of America*. New York: The New York Times Company Inc., pp. 37–76.

Volinn, E., Lai, D., McKinney, S., and Loeser, J.D. (1988). When back pain becomes disabling: A regional analysis. *Pain*, 33, 33–9.

Waterman, R.H. J. (1987). *The Renewal Factor*. New York: Bantam Books.

Worrall, L., Cooper, C.L., and Campbell, F. (2000). The impact of organizational change on UK managers' perceptions of their working lives. In R.J. Burke and C.L. Cooper (eds). *The Organization in Crisis: Downsizing, Restructuring, and Privatization*. London; Blackwell, in press.

Wright, B., and Barling, J. (1998). "The executioner's song": Listening to downsizers reflect on their experiences. *Canadian Journal of Administrative Sciences*, 15, 339–55.

2

Privatization and Outsourcing

RITA CAMPOS E CUNHA

● Introduction ●

This book is about the New World of Work. Since the last decade, the world of work has been deeply affected by two worldwide phenomena, from developed to emerging economies: privatization and outsourcing.

Over US$700 billion in assets have been privatized around the world, according to the World Bank (1998). The basic rationale behind this economic policy is to improve economic development and performance by increasing the role of competitive market forces. Privatization helps reduce the public sector deficit and alleviate constraints on financing under which companies operate due to the restraining of government expenditures. Furthermore, state monopolies are broken and competition introduced, leading to increased efficiency. Citizens may expect higher transparency in the costing of public services and in the regulation of natural monopolies. For the privatized companies, status change leads to profound internal changes, from organizational goals to managerial incentives and corporate governance.

Outsourcing, on the other hand, is also on the rise. According to the December 1997 Outsourcing Index, released by Dun & Bradstreet Corporation and the Outsourcing Institute (1997), US companies with over $80 million in revenue increased expenditures for services outsourced to approximately $146 billion. In Europe, a survey of 5,822 companies in 14 countries revealed that while about 29 percent did not use outsourcing, 37 percent increased and 30 percent maintained outsourcing contracts. Only about 5 percent of the companies reported to have decreased their subcontracting activities (Cranet, 1996). The reasons behind this dramatic increase in outsourcing vary from cost-cutting to having access to resources not available internally or to concentrate on core competencies. In a way, we may even look at privatization as a particular case of outsourcing, which is usually the way privatization is looked at in the literature about the privatization of government functions.

Common objectives may therefore be reported to account for privatization and outsourcing efforts: improvement of efficiency and effectiveness. Some common secondary effects may also be expected to derive from these two activities, particularly in what concerns human resources. Both policies go far to increase numerical flexibility, for their association with downsizing. In that sense, they both contribute to new organizational arrangements and work contracts, which according to Cooper (1999) are euphemistically called the "flexible workforce."

The purpose of this chapter is to consider some of the likely effects of privatization and outsourcing for human resource systems. We will start by briefly describing these two strategies and their objectives and will then consider some of their expected results in terms of employees' attitudes towards work and their companies, as well as firms' competitive advantage.

● Privatization ●

Privatization involves the transfer of assets and activities from the public to the private sector and it generally means the sale of at least 50 percent of the shares of a state-owned enterprise (SOE) to private shareholders, although other privatization forms have been used, such as franchising and concessions, whereby management is private and ownership remains public. It aims at increasing efficiency through competition, deregulation, and improvement of customer service, at strengthening the capital markets, at stimulating employee productivity and at reducing the state's liabilities in order to carry on micro- and macroeconomic restructuring. Governments in emerging, developing or developed economies pursue these purposes, although there are significant differences in the institutional backgrounds of these economies, as Newman (2000) points out.

Zahra, Ireland, Gutierrez, and Hitt (2000) presented a multidimensional model of privatization describing the antecedents of privatization (both macro and micro), their influence on the modes and processes of privatization strategies, the organizational transformation expected to follow privatization, and the entrepreneurial outcomes, in terms of innovation and venturing. This model suggests that the macro and micro antecedents of privatization, such as political factors or industrial sectors, will determine the chosen form of privatization, which may vary from asset sale to franchising, as well as the implementation process. It also states that important outcomes may result from privatization, creating wealth for both nations and companies. The authors distinguish first-order and second-order effects associated with the organizational transformation that is inevitably generated by change in company status. The first-order effects referred to are managerial incentives and organizational structure and culture. Second-order effects include improved organizational learning, increased technological opportunities, and gaining access to networks. Privatization and the change process it unleashes will also produce two entrepreneurial outcomes: innovation and new ventures. Product and process innovation, whether radical or incremental, may be expected to result from organizational change, new ownership, new strategies and mindsets, different managerial incentives, increased market demands, new company-specific capabilities and competencies. New domestic or international ventures are made possible by the changed economic environment and institutional contexts. In this model of privatization there are, thus, implicit benefits, both for companies and economies.

Although the model *per se* has not been empirically tested, there are several studies that support some of the advanced propositions. Megginson, Nash, and Randenborgh (1992) reported substantial increases in profitability and operational efficiency in fully or partially privatized companies, partly due to increases in capital expenditure, better use of human resources, decreased financial leverage, and significant output growth. Boubakri and Cosset (1998) examined financial and operating performance of 79 privatized firms in 21 developing countries and found significant increases in profitability, operating efficiency, capital investment spending, output, employment levels, and dividends. These benefits were also found to be greater for companies headquartered in countries with higher income per capita. Cragg and Dyck (1999) analyzed managerial incentives in the UK and concluded that top management in state-owned enterprises received about half the compensation of their counterparts in private companies, with no pay-for-performance, whereas after privatization compensation levels increased as well as the intensity of pay-for-performance.

Other studies, on the other hand, present less positive results, such as the ones by Parker and Hartley (1991) and Parker (1992) who found that privatization does not appear to guarantee improved performance. The authors suggest that other factors, that accompany the status change, jointly contribute to performance improvements: introduction of competition, new management, and incentive-type employment contracts.

The research studies reported and the privatization model presented by Zahra et al. (2000) are lacking in terms of the effects of privatization for the human resources. This issue will be developed in the next section of this chapter.

● Impact of Privatization on the Human Factor ●

This section will summarize the results of a longitudinal research study on the impact of privatization on corporate culture, human resource management policies, and the employees, which was conducted in Portugal, a country where a large-scale privatization program was launched in the early 1990s (Cunha, 2000). Three industrial companies participated in the study. Company One (C1) is a holding in the paper pulp sector, divided into several companies, only one of them having been partially privatized. Data were collected in two periods: before privatization and after partial privatization. Companies Two and Three (C2 and C3), in the cement sector, have been partially and fully privatized respectively, and had two data collections after privatization. It was felt that a longitudinal design was needed since some of the effects were expected to be experienced immediately while others were expected to take a longer period of time to manifest themselves.

Several measurement instruments were used in this study:

1.   A questionnaire about organizational culture, which was developed for this study, with four cultural dimensions: *organizational integration*, dealing with openness of internal communication and cooperation between individuals and units, *performance*

orientation, concerning individual accountability for objectives and results, and pay-for-performance; *people orientation*, or the concern the organization shows for its members and their development, as well as team spirit, and *market orientation*, re-flecting responsiveness to market opportunities and benchmarking.

2.   The Occupational Stress Indicator (Cooper, Sloan, and Williams, 1988), to assess perceived occupational stress, locus of control, job satisfaction, and mental and physical ill-health.

3.   Intensive semi-structured interviews with human resource managers, to assess the changes in human resource management practices.

   Several problems were encountered in the course of the study: privatization is a very sensitive political issue, since corporate governance is changed and major restructur-ing usually follows (and sometimes even antecedes). Most companies are therefore reluctant to give permission to researchers collecting data on issues related to human resources, and it is quite difficult to get access to privatizing corporations. A second type of problem is missing data. Although a longitudinal design is the most adequate to study the impact of privatization, the vast majority of employees did not respond to all the surveys, creating a sample size too small for a repeated measures analysis.

   For this reason, cross-sectional analyses were performed for the three companies, based on the first data-collection period, with three levels of privatization: public, partially privatized, and fully privatized. With C1, the paper pulp holding, a quasi-longitudinal design was used based on four independent samples of subjects: two composed of employees from the units that were not privatized, before and after the partial privatization, and two others composed of employees from the plc that was partially privatized, before and after partial privatization. The results from this analysis were used to validate the results obtained in the cross-sectional analyses.

   The hypotheses being tested concerned changes in corporate culture and human resource management practices as well as the impact on individual employees fol-lowing privatization. Findings from this study will be presented next.

Corporate culture

Corporate culture has been defined as the "internalization of a set of values, feelings, attitudes and expectations, which provide meaning, order and stability to organiza-tional members' lives and influence their behavior" (Cartwright and Cooper, 1992: 56). As such, it is only natural that leadership will play a crucial role not only in the initial stages of culture formation, but also in the processes of deep change to guaran-tee that new and better solutions are developed and to provide security to help the group cope with the insecurity of giving up old behaviors while new ones are being learned and tested (Schein, 1984). This proposition is even more pertinent in privati-zation processes that include not only new ownership (and leadership), but also new rules and goals in a different competitive environment.

   According to agency theory, managers of state-owned companies are the agents hired to pursue the principal's objectives. The public, the citizens, are the principal (Andrews and Dowling, 1998), but they have little organized power to influence the way the company is managed. Managers, on the other hand, are hired by government officers who represent the public. There is, therefore, an enormous potential for agency conflicts, managerial objectives are quite ambiguous, leadership turnover is high, responsibility for corporate results is low and, over time, a "no-owner company" culture is installed, where bureaucracy is usually the dominant value.

Privatization, involving a transfer of ownership from the public to the private sector, unleashes a deep change in corporate goals towards value maximization. Additionally, privatization is associated with market liberalization and increased competition, namely international competition, which leads to change in the values and beliefs under which companies operate. Corporate culture should, therefore, move to a different paradigm.

In the cross-sectional analysis of this study, significant differences were found in three of the four cultural dimensions: *performance orientation* and *people orientation* are significantly higher as we move from the public to the partially privatized and from this to the fully privatized levels. For *organizational integration* there is a significant increase from the public to the partially privatized levels, but not from this to the fully privatized one. No significant changes were found for *market orientation*.

Results obtained from the quasi-longitudinal analysis in C1 were consistent with the cross-sectional ones. As may be observed in figure 2.1, in the first data collection (time 1), perceptions concerning *organizational integration*, *performance orientation*, and *people orientation* were significantly higher for employees belonging to the business units that were not privatized than for employees of the unit that would be partially privatized. However, in the second data collection (time 2), almost two years later, perceptions of *organizational integration* and *people orientation* increased significantly for the employees of the unit that was partially privatized and decreased for the others. Perceptions of *performance orientation* significantly increased for the two samples and no change was found for *market orientation*.

In this study, results suggest that organizational culture evolves towards a greater emphasis on the definition of individual objectives, on the development of human resources, and on the creation of meritocracies, as well as the opening of communication channels between different organizational units. The fact that *market orientation* did not significantly change may be related to the period of preparation for privatization, in which financial performance was a main concern for the shareholder, in order to improve selling prospects.

Similar results have been found by Nwankwo, Aiyeku, and Ogbuehi (1998), who did a case study of PowerGen, a company that successfully emerged from the privatization of the electricity industry in the UK. These authors reported that new values were introduced in this company, through a value-focussed approach that emphasized "the need to work together through shared responsibility, teamwork, open and honest communication, valuing colleagues' contributions, and fairness and respect" (Nwankwo, Aiyeku, and Ogbuehi, 1998: 27). A study carried out by United Research (1990) also pointed to the change of a culture "that was non-commercial or even anti-commercial" (p. 6) toward an appreciation of efficiency, quality, and innovation, whereby people must learn new ways of doing things.

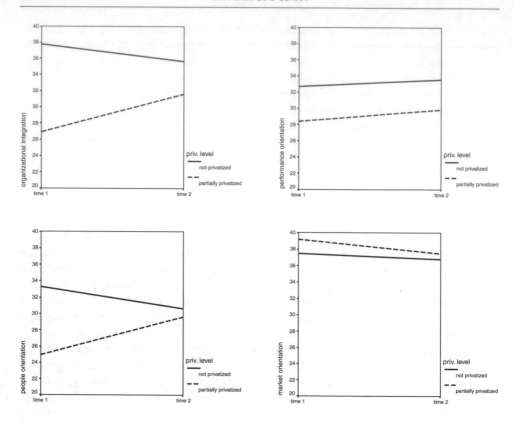

Figure 2.1 Quasi-longitudinal analysis for the cultural dimensions in C1

Human resource management practices

The interviews with the human resource managers of the companies that participated in this study demonstrated some common trends covering the following issues:

1. *Role of personnel function*: human resource managers increased their involvement in the process of strategic definition and, as a consequence, were more prone to
develop coherent human resource strategies.

2. *Reduction of headcount, recruitment, and selection*: downsizing was considered
to be one of the greatest challenges human resource managers had to face. In these
companies, reductions were mainly done by early retirement and negotiated termina-
tions. Recruitment was basically done for some technical areas, such as information
technology and marketing, and the use of some flexible working arrangements increased, such as outsourcing, flexitime, and part-time and fixed-term contracts.

3. *Training and development*: large investments in training and development were reported, namely in such areas as functional flexibility, service to client, change management, and quality.

4. *Performance appraisal*: greater emphasis was given to performance appraisal systems, which received stronger commitment from top management and were used for the introduction of performance pay practices, as well as for individual development purposes.

5. *Compensation policy*: pay-for-performance systems were refined and the proportion of variable pay increased. Criteria used for these incentive programs included company and unit results, like production and profit margins, as well as individual results and absenteeism.

6. *Labor relations*: a decrease in the influence of trade unions was reported, although these were still recognized for collective bargaining purposes. Additionally, direct individual communication with employees was increased, as well as upwards communication.

These changes are consistent with the role that the human resource management function has to play in the process of strategic and cultural change that is expected to accompany privatization processes. Some of these changes were also reported by other researchers, such as labor reductions and a decrease in the role of trade unions (Haskel and Szymanski, 1994), changes in compensation practices (Bishop and Thompson, 1994) or the emphasis in training and development programs (United Research, 1990).

Impact on individual employees

Since privatization is associated with the restructuring of companies, in order to become more effective and efficient individual employees have to cope with the increased uncertainty stemming from this process.

The impact on the individual employees, in terms of perceptions of occupational stress and its negative consequences, and in terms of job satisfaction and physical and psychological ill-health, was also studied.

The results from the cross-sectional analyses showed that perceptions of occupational stress were higher in the company preparing for privatization, whereas they were lower for the companies that were already privatized, which may point to the proposition that privatization represents a critical event in a company's life. As expected, job satisfaction increased as companies moved towards the already privatized status. However, reports of symptoms of both physical and mental ill-health tended to increase in the already privatized companies.

Locus of control was found to have a significantly negative correlation with occupational stress, i.e., individuals with internal locus of control reported lower levels of perceived pressure, which implies that increasing the sense of control individual employees have over decision-making may have a strong impact in the management of these change processes.

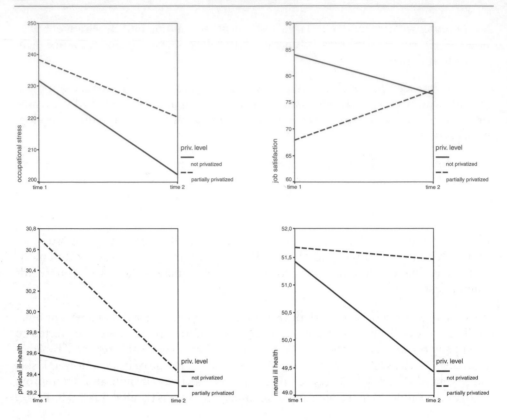

Figure 2.2 Quasi-longitudinal analysis of occupational stress, job satisfaction, physical and mental ill-health in C1

These results were also obtained in the quasi-longitudinal analysis at C1, with the exception of physical ill-health symptoms. As figure 2.2 shows, in time 1, when the holding company was being prepared for privatization, perceptions of stress were higher, particularly for the unit that would be partially privatized, than at time 2, when partial privatization had already occurred. Job satisfaction followed the expected pattern, but it can be seen that, in time 2, there was a significant increase in the unit that was privatized, while the other units presented a decrease in reported job satisfaction. Mental ill-health followed the results obtained in the cross-sectional analysis, but the physical ill-health ones did not replicate the cross-sectional ones.

The fact that mental health (and maybe physical health) is poorer in the already privatized companies, while job satisfaction is higher and occupational stress lower, may be explained if we consider that these consequences are deferred and take longer to disappear.

Using a longitudinal design in a regional water authority in the UK, Nelson, Cooper, and Jackson (1995) measured job satisfaction, physical health, and mental health symptoms over three stages of the organization's transition from the public to the private sector. During this two-year period, the company was privatized and structurally reorganized. The authors found that during the periods of greater uncertainty, levels of job satisfaction and mental and physical health declined significantly, particularly for those positions of less control, such as manual workers. After the post-privatization reorganization, when the organizational structure was more clearly defined, job satisfaction and physical and mental health improved, although in a less marked fashion for the health variables (Nelson, Cooper, and Jackson, 1995).

In summary, research results seem to indicate that privatization does have important effects on the human side of the enterprise. When properly managed, privatization is associated with major internal reorganization, namely in human resource management policies, leading over time to a change in corporate culture. As this reorganization is anxiety-provoking, employees will suffer from higher levels of occupational stress and a decline in job satisfaction, physical health, and mental health may be expected to occur. These symptoms will tend to improve, as the new rules of the game are settled and the organizational structure is more clearly defined.

The next sections of this chapter will focus on outsourcing, where we will consider some of its potential effects for the world of work, based on published research.

● Outsourcing ●

Outsourcing generally means purchasing from external vendors goods and services that could be produced inside the firm. Just as privatization may take different forms, outsourced services can vary in size, level of sophistication, and amount of control by the outsourcing firm, from the mere performance of a support function by an external vendor, to "blending," in which services of in-house and external suppliers are mixed, to the creation of outsourcers through spin-offs or even to contracting temporary employment agencies to manage the temporary workforce in a given location (Medcoff and Needham, 1998).

According to the Outsourcing Index (Dun & Bradstreet and the Outsourcing Institute, 1997) durable and non-durable manufacturers are the heavier users of outsourcing, accounting for nearly two-thirds of all outsourcing activity, followed by telecommunications and technology companies (13 percent of all activity). Information technology represents about 30 percent of all outsourcing expenditures, while human resources account for about 16 percent. No wonder most research in outsourcing is explicitly dealing with these two major areas of outsourcing.

Outsourcing may be viewed as the search for labor flexibility (Benson and Ieronimo, 1996), since firms can cover new work tasks or production methods, link payments to productivity and adjust labor to the production requirements. Additionally, outsourcing clients always have the option of putting an end to the contract with the vendors, which is another source of flexibility. In fact, certain outsourcing contracts may eventually be strategically considered as real options (Amram and Kulatilaka, 1999), since firms are acquiring the opportunity to make a decision of producing the good or service later on, after seeing how events unfold.

As Deavers (1997) explains, changes in the competitive environment, such as rapid technological change, increased risk and the search for flexibility, greater emphasis on core corporate competencies and globalization, are responsible for the increased level of outsourcing and not just the quest for lower labor costs. Wages are primarily determined by productivity, not by outsourcing. However, as some large firms in protected markets, with highly unionized workforces, start outsourcing, it is likely that wages will be under pressure, as these firms try to escape high labor costs through outsourcing. By and large, however, this is not the main reason for outsourcing.

Whatever the reasons for the increasing levels of outsourcing, from cost-cutting to strategic reorganization, this phenomenon will have an impact on human resources, and this impact is probably quite similar to the one of privatization, namely in terms of the perceived occupational stress and its negative consequences, because of the uncertainty regarding career prospects and work. As companies become increasingly "virtual" by externalizing business functions, corporate culture is equally likely to change. The human resource management policies themselves will surely change to accommodate the different needs of the "flexible" workforce.

In the next section, we will outline some propositions about the effects that outsourcing is likely to produce at the human resources level.

● Effects of Outsourcing for Organizational Behavior ●

The above review of outsourcing has shown that, like privatization, it is also intended to improve efficiency and effectiveness, through reduction of fixed costs, the pursuit of labor flexibility, and the improvement of product/service differentiation and company performance. Given the acceptance these two policies have gained, we may assume that both privatization and outsourcing are here to stay. However virtuous the goals may be, there is no beauty without a beast, i.e., although we may understand and defend the need to improve company performance, in the new economic and technological environment, the "dark side of flexibility", "with its often merciless displacement of both white- and blue-collar workers" (Harrison, 1994: p.45) must be faced, namely by policy-makers, in order to find ways to maintain civilized labor and living standards, and encourage companies to compete on technological improvement and human skills upgrading.

According to the resource-based view of the firm (Barney, 1991; Wright, McMahan, and McWilliams, 1994) strategic resources may be a source of sustained competitive advantage for firms, when they create value, and are rare and difficult for competitors to imitate. Human resources, defined as competencies, knowledge, experience, and motivation, may become the most important source of competitive advantage, because they create value by enhancing the firm's capabilities and by being especially difficult to imitate. This difficulty lies in the causal ambiguity of the factors that are responsible for performance: a complex network of historical and cultural social relationships that are longitudinally developed.

In a resource-based view of the firm, tacit knowledge, which is acquired through company tenure, socialization, and learning by doing, is firm-specific and therefore more immobile. However, it is dependent upon a process of knowledge creation and transference which is slow and complex, involving long-term commitment, trust, and adequate incentive systems. According to Lado and Wilson (1994), human resource functions such as selection, socialization, developmental performance appraisal, on-the-job training, and skill-based pay constitute investments in firm-specific human capital and may be potent sources of sustained competitive advantage.

When companies increasingly rely on outsourcing as a way to achieve numerical and financial flexibility alone, they may be destroying competence and endangering their long-term success by not guaranteeing the necessary conditions for these to develop.

We will now consider some of the likely effects of outsourcing for the human resource system. Not intended to be exhaustive, five issues will be discussed, other than the ones described for privatization: control over operations, change in the psychological contract, impact on organizational citizenship behavior and trust, impact on innovation and entrepreneurship, and impact on organizational knowledge.

Control

Companies extensively resorting to outsourcing may have to deal with compatibility problems between the outsourced systems (for example, HR systems and information technology) as well as encounter disclosure and confidentiality problems (Medcoff and Needham, 1998). It is important for the effective use of both that these systems are compatible, giving easy access to all important information for all interested actors, as well as making sure that contract discontinuance will not disrupt operations.

On the other hand, effective performance will, in many instances, depend on the free communication of some information and protection of other, proprietary, information. When sensitive information is shared with external vendors, who may be involved with other companies, there's a risk competitors will gain access to strategic information and even to confidential data regarding individual employees. Companies in this situation should develop their own strategies for information disclosure and confidentiality.

Kelley (1995) has also pointed out that managers often complain about loss of control over their own process technologies and work standards, since most of the work that used to be performed by their subordinates is now being done by outsiders, over whom control is less close. The potential loss of competencies will be discussed in the section on organizational knowledge below.

Additionally, it is quite likely that some outsourcing contracts will be incomplete and need to be modified during the term of the contract, exposing the company to the risk of opportunistic behavior by the contractor, on whom the company has become dependent. Klaas, McClendon, and Gainey (1999) found that where firm-specific practices are emphasized, such as human capital development and recruitment and selection, outsourcing will expose companies to greater opportunistic behavior by service providers, limiting the advantages offered by economies of scale and therefore suppressing cost advantages.

The psychological contract

Psychological contracts are not written documents, rather they imply mutual expectations and satisfaction of needs arising from the relationships between individual employees and their organizations, involving a process of mutual giving and receiving. These expectations cover a wide range of duties and obligations, rights and privileges, which are not part of a formal agreement, but nevertheless influence individual behavior. Employees, for example, expect a safe working environment, fair company policies, respectful treatment, recognition for good work, employment security, and even involvement in decision-making. Organizations, on the other hand, expect that employees work efficiently towards corporate goals, accept authority and responsibility, and comply with company rules (Stalker, 2000).

As more and more companies are increasing their levels of outsourcing, employees may feel their psychological contracts have been violated, particularly in terms of job security and opportunities for advancement, which will negatively impact on their work attitudes and work behaviors. As Turnley and Feldman (1999) report, exit intentions and behaviors, decreased loyalty, negative voicing, and neglect behaviors were strongly related to perceived violations of psychological contracts and were more severe for managers in organizations that underwent restructuring and downsizing. Moving to structural arrangements around a small group of core employees and a larger group of peripheral workers, who have no security, benefits or strong involvement in organizational life, may lead to psychological contracts with less reciprocal commitment.

Organizational citizenship behavior and trust

"The biggest disadvantage of contingent employment arrangements is the difficulty of obtaining loyalty, dedication, or willingness to expend extra effort of behalf of the organization" (Pfeffer, 1994: 24). According to Pfeffer, the costs of using subcontractors are more likely to show up over time and are more difficult to capture than the immediate benefits of cost-cutting and adaptation to product demand fluctuations. Organizational citizenship behaviors refer to things people do at work, that are beneficial to the company, but which individuals are not mandated to do, such as, helping co-workers, volunteering for extra-job activities, or otherwise contributing to organizational effectiveness by doing things that are not job tasks. Those extra-role behaviors are supposed to represent a currency of reciprocity towards the company for positive and beneficial actions directed at employees (Lambert, 2000). Organ and Ryan (1995) reported that although job satisfaction, perceived equity, and commitment may be weakly related to productivity, which basically depends on work processes and worker abilities, they strongly correlate with extra-role behaviors. On the other hand, trust is also shown to predict organizational citizenship behavior (Konovsky and Pugh 1994), namely trust generated by procedural fairness, which demonstrates the firm's respect for the rights and dignity of individual employees, in the long-run relationship.

When companies decide to increase their level of outsourcing, it is likely that employees will feel there's a breach in the relational contracts, affecting the social exchange behaviors employees are willing to exert.

Trust is likely not to develop with temporary workers, since they are allocated to short-term projects and there is no time to develop a trust relationship. On the other hand, compensation is different for employees and contractors, the latter receiving greater cash compensation, while employees receive greater fringe benefits and job security. The presence of contractors will thus remind employees "that they are in a market, rather than a familial relationship with the organization, and market actors are expected to exploit their opportunities, not take care of one another" (Pearce, 1993: 1086), making them see the organization as less trustworthy. This hypothesis was supported by Pearce's (1993) findings.

Innovation and entrepreneurship

Outsourcing defenders claim that by having external parties providing the non-core services, companies and their staff may concentrate on their core tasks and competencies, and therefore may invest in doing research on new products and services and other higher value-added activities (Venkatesan, 1992; Venkatraman, 1997).

IT outsourcing, for example, may improve productivity of resources and upgrade technology and skills, leading to cost reduction, service improvement, and distinctive technical expertise, improving critical aspects of business performance and implementing business transformation initiatives including time to market, supply-chain management or engineering operations (DiRomualdo and Gurbaxani, 1998) as well as make firms concentrate on core competencies and speed up the development of new applications for the business units (Huber, 1993).

As positive as these results may be, some caution is recommended. Research on strategic human resource management argues that in order to pursue strategies of innovation, companies need to select highly qualified individuals, providing them a long-term focus and minimal controls, appraising performance for long-run impact (Schuler and Jackson, 1987). "Rather than emphasizing managing people so they work *harder* (cost-reduction strategy) or *smarter* (quality strategy) on the same products or services, the innovation strategy requires people to work *differently*" (Schuler and Jackson, 1987: 210).

Pfeffer (1994) also emphasizes the risks of the "externalization" of employment in terms of the likelihood of obtaining competitive advantage through human resources, particularly because external contractors have less firm-specific knowledge and companies are not as motivated to invest in their training and development, which could affect innovation. Additionally, hiring external providers with a short-term objective of cost-cutting and the numerical flexibility to adjust to market fluctuations constrains not only the establishment of cooperative links between individuals, but also the internalization of company vision and mission, which can consequently inhibit or destroy any innovative and entrepreneurial goals the firm may wish to pursue.

Additionally, downsizing may hinder efforts at innovation, by breaking down the networking that is needed by innovators: to assemble resources and expertise, to work out problems in a trial and error fashion, to sell the project to the company, and to get commitment from senior management (Dougherty and Bowman, 1995).

Organizational knowledge

Organizational knowledge is considered to be a strategic asset that helps firms achieve their competitive advantage due to its inherent characteristics (Chesbrough and Teece, 1996; Narasimha, 2000). Narasimha presents five dimensions of organizational knowledge that contribute to competitive advantage: tacitness and codifiability of knowledge, architectural and component knowledge, exploratory and exploitative knowledge, variety-generating capability of knowledge, and depth and breadth of knowledge. Tacit knowledge is implicitly grasped and used, but not fully articulated as codified knowledge (Chesbrough and Teece, 1996). It is deeply embedded in individuals and companies, making it very difficult for rivals to imitate and to internally transfer. Component knowledge comprehends the core design concepts of particular components, while architectural knowledge embraces the way components are integrated into a coherent whole. Exploratory knowledge refers to the development of new products and processes, whereas exploitative knowledge focusses on the refinement of existing product technology (March, 1991). The variety-generating capability of knowledge provides adaptive abilities and the potential for multiple applicability of knowledge. Depth of knowledge is useful for firms to better understand and exploit their knowledge stocks, while breadth is needed to supplement depth. Narasimha argues that long-tenured employees are necessary for firms to reap the benefits of organizational knowledge, since tacit knowledge must be transferred within the firm, knowledge must be integrated across the distinctive components, exploratory learning, involving "muddling through" and failures, has to be accepted.

The returns that organizational knowledge provide may be reduced or even destroyed with increased use of outsourcing, particularly when companies are going virtual, not to mention changing their management structure (with delayering) and downsizing.

In this section, some concerns regarding potential effects of outsourcing have been discussed. Concretely, some research propositions may be raised to investigate the impact of outsourcing on managerial control over operations, on the psychological contracts, on citizenship behaviors and trust, on innovation and entrepreneurship, and on organizational knowledge. We believe that outsourcing may have either positive or negative results for companies (or both) according to the strategic goals that are being pursued. When well-defined strategic goals are established, that take into account the creation of value and the enhancement of organizational competencies, the negotiation of contracts with the external vendors will be much more favorable for outsourcing companies, as well as in the results for organizational performance, in the short and in the long run.

● Summary and Conclusions ●

In this chapter, we have considered some outcomes of privatization and put forward some propositions regarding the potential effects of outsourcing for the new reality of work.

Table 2.1 Potential positive and negative effects of privatization and outsourcing

Positive effects	Negative effects
Increased efficiency and employee productivity	Compatibility between outsourced systems and control over operations and proprietary information
Better use of human resources	Violation of psychological contracts (job security and opportunities for advancement)
Better managerial compensation and incentives	Decreased organizational citizenship behavior and firm-specific knowledge
Increased company flexibility	Decreased job satisfaction, physical health and mental health
Adaptation to technological change and access to new skills	Perceptions of untrustworthiness
Concentration on core competencies	Lower investments in training and development
Faster development of new products and services	Decreased probability of obtaining a return on knowledge
New ventures	Decreased internal networking

It is not our intention to ride against the wave and assume that all efforts made by companies and governments to outsource have exclusively negative effects. Instead, while recognizing the benefits these practices have for organizations and economies, we wish to alert managers to some likely long-term consequences that may limit the positive contributions they may bring (see table 2.1 for a summary of positive and negative effects).

It is undeniable that changes in the competitive environment, such as the techno-logical advances or globalization, and changes in the political scenario, are driving companies into major restructuring, in order to reduce costs, gain access to new capabilities and capital funds, share risks, and improve company focus. In striving to become flexible, lean, and competitive, governments have been privatizing their state-owned companies and public services and private companies have been increasingly externalizing their human resource infrastructure.

However, many firms have seen their costs increase with outsourcing (Medcoff and Needham, 1998) and privatization has not always produced economic gains and financial improvements (Parker, 1992; Bishop, Kay, and Mayer, 1994). Companies should then carefully analyze the impact of their "externalization of the workforce" decisions, namely the extent to which organizational competencies will be developed and competitive advantage achieved, or, on the contrary, the extent to which these competencies will be destroyed or not fully exploited. Basically, our point is that intangible assets should not be forgotten.

In particular, we emphasize the likelihood of violating psychological contracts, by reducing job security and advancement opportunities. This violation may result in negative behavioral consequences. Job satisfaction and mental and physical health have been shown to decrease in periods of major upheaval, such as privatization and organizational restructuring. Trust and organizational citizenship behaviors may also be decreased, since both develop over time and, in the same fashion, innovative and entrepreneurial behaviors may be hindered. As innovative and entrepreneurial behaviors assume the existence of internal and informal networking and risk tolerance, virtual companies that resort extensively to external contractors may be risking this important asset. They may also be losing the long-term returns provided by organizational knowledge, specifically the ones deriving from the most difficult one to imitate, tacit knowledge.

Organizations are, to a higher or lower degree, a combination of mechanistic and organic systems, and both must be effective. Privatization and outsourcing may certainly help companies become more efficient, have access to new skills and resources, and focus on their core business, as long as the benefits accruing from the intangible assets are achieved and contribute to their sustained competitive advantage. The credibility of an organizational change stemming from privatization or outsourcing is key to its success and may be achieved by employee involvement, clear and realistic communication of expected gains and opportunity costs, consistent human resource management practices that enhance knowledge creation and talent retention, and by maintaining the momentum, not stalling or procrastinating important decisions.

REFERENCES

Amram, M., and Kulatilaka, N. (1999). *Real Options: Managing Strategic Investment In An Uncertain World*. Boston, MA: Harvard Business School Press.

Andrews, W., and Dowling, M. (1998). Explaining performance changes in newly privatized firms. *Journal of Management Studies*, 35, 5, 601–17.

Barney, J. (1991). Firm resources and sustained competitive advantage. *Journal of Management*, 17, 1, 99–120.

Benson, J., and Ieronimo, N. (1996). Outsourcing decisions: Evidence from Australia-based enterprises. *International Labour Review*, 135, 1, 59–73.

Bishop, M., and Thompson, D. (1994). Privatization in the UK: Internal organization and productive efficiency. In M. Bishop, J. Kay, and C. Mayer (eds). *Privatization and Economic Performance*. Oxford: Oxford University Press.

Bishop, M., Kay, J., and Mayer, C. (1994). *Privatization and Economic Performance*, Oxford: Oxford University Press.

Boubakri, N., and Cosset, J.C. (1998). The financial and operating performance of newly privatized firms: Evidence from developing countries. *The Journal of Finance*, 53, 3, 1081–110.

Cartwright, S., and Cooper, C.L. (1992). *Mergers and Acquisitions: The Human Factor*. Oxford: Butterworth Heinemann.

Chesbrough, H., and Teece, D. (1996). When is virtual virtuous? Organizing for innovation, *Harvard Business Review*, January–February, 65–73.

Cooper, C.L. (1999). The changing psychological contract at work. *European Business Journal*, 11, 3, 115–18.

Cooper, C.L., Sloan, S.J., and Williams, S. (1988). *Occupational Stress Indicator Management Guide*. Windsor: NFER-NELSON.

Cragg, M., and Dyck, I. (1999). Management control and privatization in the United Kingdom. *Rand Journal of Economics*, 30, 3, 475–9.

Cranet (1996). Cranet-E 1995/96 Survey Results. Centre for European Human Resource

Management, Cranfield School of Management, UK.

Cunha, R. (2000). Impact of privatization in Portugal. In R. Burke and C.L. Cooper (eds). *The Organization in Crisis: Downsizing, Restructuring, and Privatization*. Oxford: Blackwell Publishers, pp. 44–57.

Deavers, K. (1997). Outsourcing: A corporate competitiveness strategy, not a search for low wages. *Journal of Labor Research*, 18, 4, 503–19.

DiRomualdo, A., and Gurbaxani, V. (1998). Strategic intent for IT outsourcing. *Sloan Management Review*, 39, 4, 67–80.

Dougherty, D., and Bowman, E. (1995). The effects of organizational downsizing on product innovation. *California Management Review*, 37, 4, 28–45.

Dun & Bradstreet and the Outsourcing Institute (1997). *The Outsourcing Index*, 2nd edn. The Outsourcing Institute.

Harrison, Bennett (1994). The dark side of flexible production. *Technology Review*, May/June, 38–45.

Haskel, J., and Szymanski, S. (1994). Privatization and labor market: Facts, theory and evidence. In M. Bishop, J. Kay, and C. Mayer (eds). *Privatization and Economic Performance*. Oxford: Oxford University Press.

Huber, R. (1993). How continental bank outsourced its "crown jewels". *Harvard Business Review*, January–February, 121–9.

Kelley, B. (1995). Outsourcing marches on. *Journal of Business Strategy*, July–August, 40–2.

Klaas, B., McClendon, J., and Gainey, T. (1999) HR outsourcing and its impact: The role of transaction costs. *Personnel Psychology*, 52, 113–36.

Konovsky, M., and Pugh, S. (1994). Citizenship behavior and social exchange. *Academy of Management Journal*, 37, 3, 656–69.

Lado, A., and Wilson, M. (1994). Human resource systems and sustained competitive advantage: A competency-based perspective. *Academy of Management Review*, 19, 4, 699–727.

Lambert, S. (2000). Added benefits: The link between work-life benefits and organizational citizenship behavior. *Academy of Management Journal*, 43, 5, 801–15.

March, J. (1991). Exploration and exploitation in organizational learning. *Organization Science*, 2, 71–87.

Medcoff, J., and Needham, B. (1998). The supra-organizational HRM system. *Business Horizons*, January–February, 43–50.

Megginson, W., Nash, R., and Randenborgh, M. (1992). Efficiency gains from privatization: An international empirical analysis. Preliminary draft, Terry College of Business, University of Georgia, USA.

Narasimha, S. (2000). Organizational knowledge, human resource management, and sustained competitive advantage: Toward a framework. *Competitiveness Review*, 10, 1, 123–35.

Newman, K. (2000). Organizational transformation during institutional upheaval. *Academy of Management Review*, 25, 3, 602–19.

Nwankwo, S., Aiyeku, J., and Ogbuehi, A. (1998). Adjusting to market competition in the UK's privatized utility sector. *Advances in Competitiveness Research*, 6, 1, 20–9.

Organ, D., and Ryan, K. (1995). A meta-analytic review of attitudinal and dispositional predictors of organizational citizenship behavior. *Personnel Psychology*, 48, 775–802.

Parker, D. (1992). Agency status, privatization and improved performance: Some evidence from the UK. *International Journal of Public Sector Management*, 5, 1, 30–8.

Parker, D., and Hartley, K. (1991). Do changes in organizational status affect financial performance? *Strategic Management Journal*, 12, 631–41.

Pearce, J. (1993). Toward an organizational behavior of contract laborers: Their psychological involvement and effects on employee co-workers. *Academy of Management Journal*, 36, 5, 1082–96.

Pfeffer, J. (1994). Competitive advantage through people. *California Management Review*, Winter, 9–28.

Schein, E.H. (1984). Coming to a new awareness of organizational culture. *Sloan Management Review*, Winter, 3–16.

Schuler, R., and Jackson, S. (1997). Linking competitive strategies with human resource management practices. *The Academy of Management Executive*, 1, 3, 207–19.

Stalker, K. (2000). The individual, the organization and the psychological contract. *The British Journal of Administrative Management*, July–August, 28/34.

Turnley, W., and Feldman, D. (1999). The impact of psychological contract violations on exit, voice, loyalty and neglect. *Human Relations*, 52, 7, 895–922.

United Research (1990). *Privatization: Implications for Cultural Change*. Morristown, NJ: United Research.

Venkatesan, R. (1992). Strategic sourcing: To make or not to make. *Harvard Business Review*, November–December, 2–11.

Venkatraman, N. (1997). Beyond outsourcing: Managing IT resources as a value center. *Sloan Management Review*, 38, 3, 51–64.

World Bank (1998). World Debt Tables 1997. Washington, D.C.: World Bank.

Wright, P., McMahan, G., and McWilliams, A. (1994). Human resources and sustained competitive advantage. *International Journal of Human Resource Management*, 5, 301–26.

Zahra, S., and Hansen, C. (2000). Privatization, entrepreneurship and global competitiveness in the 21st century. *Competitiveness Review*, 10, 1, 83–103.

Zahra, S., Ireland, R., Gutierrez, I., and Hitt, M. (2000). Privatization and sustained entrepreneurial transformation: Emerging issues and a future research agenda. *Academy of Management Review*, 25, 3, 509–24.

II

Changing Career Landscapes

3

Developmental Relationships at Work: A Learning Perspective

DOUGLAS T. HALL AND WILLIAM A. KAHN

> "I get by with a little help from my friends."
>
> *The Beatles*

> "No one of us is smarter than all of us."
>
> *Jack Welch*

● Work as the New Schoolhouse ●

The most critical skill for any leader in the new economy is knowing how to learn. As Charles Handy, author of *The Age of Unreason* (1989), pointed out, the key competency in the old economy was being able to say, "I know." In the new economy, the most important requirement is the ability to say, "Let's ask."

Careers as learning cycles

What this means is that the nature of the leader's career has changed. Not only is there a new career contract (Hall and Associates, 1996; Arthur and Rousseau, 1996), in which the individual, not the organization, is the agent responsible for career development, but the definition and course of the career have changed as well. We have moved away from an era of the one-life-one-career imperative (Sarason, 1977; Hall and Associates, 1986), where one series of career stages covered the whole of a person's work life. In its place is a new *protean career*, which consists of a *series of learning cycles* (Hall and Mirvis, 1996). Each learning cycle is like a mini-version of the old lifelong model career stages (Hall, 1976), but the time frame is much shorter. In the new model, first the person explores new areas of career work. Then he or she tries it out, and if it is a good fit, works to become established in that area. Then comes a period of mastery or full performance. But after a period of time (one, two,

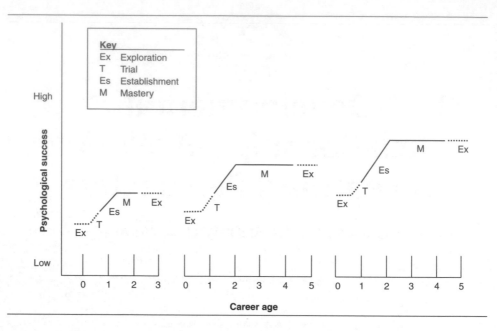

Figure 3.1 A model of careers as *learning cycles*
Source: Adapted from Hall and Mirvis (1996): "The New Protean Career," p. 15.

three years, perhaps) something changes – a new technology, a change in the market, new opportunities, new interests – and the person begins to explore doing something different. And then a new learning cycle would begin. The career thus becomes a series of learning cycles (perhaps on the order of three to five years), with short developmental stages. This new model of career development is shown in figure 3.1.

Organizations that take account of this new employee expectation for learning and growth stand to gain handsomely. A recent Hudson Institute survey found that 56 percent of employees felt that their company did not genuinely care about them, and the same percentage reported that they did not have a strong loyalty to their company (Zipkin, 2000). Zipkin reports that a Gallup Organization survey that found that:

> most workers rate having a caring boss even higher than they value money or fringe benefits. In interviews with two million employees at 700 companies, Gallup found that how long an employee stays at a company and how productive she is there, is determined by her relationship with her immediate supervisor. "People join companies and leave managers," said Marcus Buckingham, a senior managing consultant at Gallup and the primary analyst for the study. (Zipkin, 2000: p. C1)

Zipkin goes on to describe the interest one boss, David Lein, took in her career:

> Mr. Lein . . . summoned her to his office from time to time to discuss her career hopes. After she completed a project for the redesign of a large piece of computer code, he

asked her what she wanted to do next. When she said she wanted to be a software engineer, he recommended classes and gave her the time off to go. Two months ago, Mr. Lein and other managers arranged for Ms. Morse's transfer to a position testing more complex software designs, even though she lacked the experience that was supposedly required for the job. While not technically a promotion, the job required more expertise than her previous one and was a logical step to a higher-paying job.

All the kindness she has received the last two years, Ms. Morse says, is literally worth a million dollars to her [as she turned down a competitive offer worth $1 million in stock options, but the job seemed to be more of a career dead end]. (Zipkin, 2000: p. C10)

If the person does not learn ever-new skills, he or she runs the risk of derailment, and this is exactly what Ms. Morse foresaw, had she accepted the competing (and lucrative) offer. As Morgan McCall (1998) points out, the skills that got a person to their present level are probably not the skills he or she will need to get to the next level. And if he or she persists in applying the current skills, at some point they will be used inappropriately and then become weaknesses. Table 3.1 shows how skills can become weaknesses and how failures to learn new skills can contribute to career derailment.

Learning metacompetencies

As a person like Ms. Morse grows through developmental relationships at work, they develop specific new skills. More important, they often acquire higher-order qualities, or *metacompetencies*, that enhance their abilities to learn. These

Table 3.1   How failures in learning contribute to derailment

Source of derailment	*Dynamics*
Strength becomes weakness	Strengths may be overused. The situation may have changed, so that other strengths are now more important.
Blind spots matter	Flaws that didn't matter or were overlooked before now become central in a new situation.
Success leads to arrogance	Success goes to the person's head, creating overconfidence and ego-centeredness.
Bad luck	May be a run-in with fate that is not an accurate reflection of one's talent. Or, maybe bad luck is aggravated by one of the other dynamics, suggesting that fate does not always work alone.

Source: McCall (1998).

metacompetencies are self-knowledge – a clear sense of *identity* – and *adaptability* (Hall and Associates, 1996; Briscoe and Hall, 1999). If the person has a clear understanding of him- or herself, is skilled at obtaining feedback and learning more about the self, and can take action based on this self-understanding, he or she is likely to be able to recognize when new skills are needed and adapt by finding ways to acquire these skills. Thus, with these two metacompetencies, the person will probably be able to be a continuous learner.

We need to look at identity separately from adaptability. Some people cope with change through serious identity exploration, with lots of personal work, self-assessment, personal questioning, and values clarification, and let that identity work become an end in itself. There can be a lot of "navel-gazing" but not much change (adaptation). Unless the person has developed the ability to adapt his or her behavior based on the learning about the self, he or she may not have really learned better how to learn. On the other hand, if the person becomes expert on adapting to change but does not really look at him- or herself, does not think about how this change is furthering his or her own values, path in life, purpose, etc., then this change could be mere reaction. The person would be reacting blindly to the environment and be controlled by it. The adaptation has to include identity learning in order for it to represent a higher level of personal development.

Metacompetencies represent the primary ways in which organizational members can thrive in the new economy. It is clear that, with no end to downsizing in sight, organizational expenditures for activities such as formal training and development programs will continue to be difficult to justify, and corporate support for external education, such as tuition remission for university programs, will become tighter. And yet, at the same time, in a world of great volatility, uncertainty, change, and ambiguity, the need for continuous learning has never been greater. Yet if learning is not going to happen in company programs or in external programs, where else can it happen? On the job. Organization members must learn how to learn independently, in the context of their work lives. And the way to do that is through acquiring the metacompetencies of identity and adaptability.

We argue here that these two metacompetencies are best and most fully learned in the context of developmental relationships at work. Through good relationships and the feedback and insights of trusted others, the person can obtain new information and perspectives on him- or herself. Through trust and reciprocity, the person can learn to feel more comfortable soliciting feedback about the self and thus develop the skill of enlisting others in his or her development. And through the support, coaching, and confronting of other people with whom one feels comfortable, the person can be helped to act and make fundamental changes in his or her everyday behavior. In this way, relationships that have the right emotional properties can produce truly transformative developmental outcomes.

● What is Relational Learning? ●

Our point here is that today a major source of learning is *relationships*: we do much of our learning through connection with other people. Much of this connection is in face-to-face meetings – in work teams, informal interactions with colleagues, discussions with customers, task forces, and countless daily encounters. And increasingly this connection is also coming in electronic form; with information technology it has never been so easy for one person to have instant access to knowledgeable people on a given topic, anywhere, any time.

Ironically, although many organizational resources are vanishing, the best resources for career development and learning – work challenges and relationships with other people (McCall, 1998; Hall and Associates, 1996) – have never been so plentiful. Indeed, the more turbulent and difficult conditions become in today's work settings, the more naturally occurring work challenges there are, and the more motivated people are to give and receive help, because people realize that banding together is the best bet for survival. Thus, it seems to us that relational learning resources are all around a person in the natural environment of the workplace.

What, then, do we mean by "relational learning"? We define the term as follows: *Relational learning at work is the enlargement of an individual's capacities to approach new situations, integrate and interpret new information, to learn about the self, and act effectively in those situations through relationships with other individuals or groups at work.*

Let us unpack the elements of this definition. First, relational learning happens in the context of a relationship at work. It could be an intentional or a tacit process. It involves the growth of the receiver's capacities, such that the person is more competent after than before. These competencies include the ability to be proactive in recognizing new situations as having learning potential and the ability to receive new information and to integrate it into the person's self-concept or sense of identity. And, finally, relational learning also involves the ability to take action based on what one has learned; that is, it is behavioral as well as cognitive.

The examples of relational learning in the everyday work environment – the "natural resources" for learning through experience – vary in the range and depth of

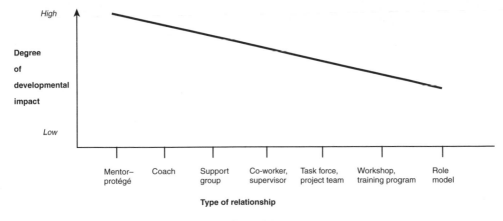

Figure 3.2 A continuum of developmental relationships

Table 3.2 Types of developmental relationships

Type	Definition	Primary functions	Characteristics	Impacts
Mentoring	Intentional relationship focussed on developing self of relatively unseasoned protégé through dialogue and reflection. Implicit focus on development of next generation in context of interpersonal relationships.	Develop protégé's capacities for learning about tasks and self. Transmit information, knowledge, culture and wisdom. Enable mentors and protégés to meet appropriate adult developmental needs.	Relatively intimate cross-generation relationships marked by transmission of stories, lessons, perspectives in response to protégé's needs to learn about self, role, and organization. Focus on whole person of protégé.	Anchors protégés, enabling them to reflect on and learn from their experiences at work. Enhanced functioning based on learning about self-in-role.
Coaching	Intentional relationship focussed on developing specific developmental objectives in regards to relatively junior organization member.	Increase member's capacity to assume increased responsibility for identified role and tasks. Enable coach to delegate, support, and provide resources rather than control.	Interactions marked by coach's increasing movement toward posing questions rather than providing answers, thus building other's capacities for autonomous thinking, acting, and reflecting on specific tasks.	Enhanced capacity of junior member in thought, action, and reflection in regard to specific types of roles and tasks. Coaches move from control to coordination.
Support group/ Network	Formal or informal group of individuals who join around common characteristics, interests, goals, or visions and provide meaningful personal and professional suppport to its members.	Emotional support, in the form of encouragement, reinforcement, and acknowledgment. Instrumental support through network of connections and information.	Focus on maintaining support group through regular meetings, group and subgroup communication efforts, and personal relationships that provide members with sense of shared identity and meaning.	Enables members to feel connected to, supported by and joined with like-minded others at work. Offers sense of identity, meaning, and confidence.

Supervisor/ co-worker	Naturally occurring work relationships centered around given tasks and roles. Development of person is incidental rather than intentional.	Completion of work tasks and goals through various forms of coordination and collaboration. Development of skills and knowledge necessary to perform work.	Relatively frequent, often intense contact determined by task requirements and organizational structures and processes. Can also provide emotional support in context of significant interpersonal relationships at work.	Completion of given tasks, supported by growth in persons's task-related capacities.
Project team/task force	Formally structured work group, focussed on completion of shared goals, requiring intense collaboration.	Completion of work tasks and goals through cross-boundary collaboration. Development of skills and knowledge related to collaboration.	Relatively frequent, often intense contact determined by project requirements and organizational structures and processes.	Completion of given taks, supported by growth in persons's task-related capacities.
Training workshop/ program	Formally structured learning experiences that emphasize transmission of information from experts to learners.	Increase learner's knowledge, skills, and capacities for effective thought and action in specific areas and types of situations.	Academic- or practitioner-based courses and programs that transmit knowledge and information, with varying degree of relatedness to actual work experiences.	Learning of concepts, ideas, techniques, and perspectives that vary in terms of relevance and applicability to work situations.
Role model	Non-reciprocal relationship between person observing and admired other in order to learn desired traits and behaviors.	Provide models of desirable traits and behaviors to emulate – an embodiment of a desired set of skills and knowledge.	Relatively distant relationship marked by observation, study, and comparisons between self and others.	Learning through observation and reflection, to the extent possible without dialogue with other. Offers sense of hope.

relational learning that they can potentially provide. In fact, they can be ordered and placed on a continuum based on their power to provide development to a person. (See figure 3.2 for a model of the relative potency of various types of developmental relationships. Definitions of these types of relationships are shown in table 3.2.)

The most powerful learning is often provided by a traditional mentor–protégé relationship, which provides both task learning and socio-emotional learning that affects the person's adaptability and identity over a long period of time. At the other extreme might be a casual relationship or even a one-sided relationship (that is, a relationship in which the learner is aware of the model, but it is not reciprocal). In this kind of distant relationship modeling can occur based on the meaning that the learner makes of the model's behavior.

To the right of the mentoring relationship might come a coaching or a sponsor relationship, in which the model is aware of the relationship and is intentionally helping the learner with his or her learning agenda. But the learning agenda would be more limited than in a mentoring context, limited to specific developmental objectives, rather than the growth of the whole person. After a coach or sponsor might come a support group. Often in such a group the assistance is primarily emotional (encouraging, reinforcing, and persuasive), rather than instructive, but the impact on the person's motivation and self-confidence can be considerable.

Next most impactful might be naturally occurring work relationships, such as a boss–subordinate or a co-worker relationship. Here the contact is frequent and often intense, and much learning can take place through the person's need to learn in the service of performance. But the help that a boss or co-worker provides is usually incidental, not intentional.

However, there can be a wide variation in the developmental quality of relationships among co-workers, as shown by Kram and Isabella (1985). They show a continuum with three types of co-worker relationships. The relationship with the *information peer* is one with the primary purpose being the exchange of information. Self-disclosure and trust tend to be low. Next most developmental would be the *collegial peer*, with whom more peer mentoring functions are shared: career strategizing, job-related feedback, and friendship. This is a more intimate, trusting, self-disclosing relationship. And at the most developmental end of the continuum of co-worker relationships is the *special peer*. This unusual relationship contains the most mentoring functions: confirmation, emotional support, personal feedback, and friendship. Kram and Isabella (1985: 121) describe the special peer as follows:

> Becoming a special peer often involves revealing central ambivalences and personal dilemmas in work and family realms. Pretense and formal roles are replaced by greater self-disclosure and self-expression. The career histories suggested that the special peer relationship is rare. Individuals in this sample typically mentioned a small number (one to three), or none at all. Special peer relationships generally take several years to develop and tend to endure through periods of change and transition. Thus, they offer not only intimacy and confirmation, but continuity and stability as well.

Similar to working with peers or co-workers in one's own department or work unit, working on a project team or task force requires discovery and new learning in the company of others, but the learning is somewhat limited by the fact that the central purpose of the relationships is instrumental, not developmental. However, the diversity of skills, experiences, and perspectives reflected in such a group (which is usually cross-disciplinary) provides a rich ground for potential learning.

In contrast to a project team or task force, formal courses and training programs have learning as their main objective, but the learning often does not transfer well to the back-home job situation. Thus, such activities may not have strong impact on the person's identity and adaptability.

When all of the relationships along this entire continuum in figure 3.2 are viewed together, the result is part of what Higgins and Kram (2001) describe as the "developmental network," the person's overall constellation of relationships that can contribute to development. Two key dimensions of this relational constellation are the diversity of the network (i.e., the range and density of information that it provides), and the strength of the relationships (i.e., the intensity of the relationships' reciprocity, mutuality, and interdependence; see Fletcher, 1996). We believe that when organization members locate themselves within a meaningful constellation of developmental relationships at work, they are more likely to create conditions that enable them to thrive under the conditions of the increasingly protean organization and career.

● Growth Stages in the Developmental Relationship ●

Locating themselves within such constellations and relationships requires individuals to invest themselves in doing so. Developmental relationships at work must be constructed. They tend to develop through various stages of growth. While what occurs in these stages will vary depending on the type of developmental relationship, the stages themselves offer a template for the growth of developmental relationships more generally. We define growth in terms of development that results in the construction of relationships that serve their developmental purposes exactly. For the more intensive developmental relationships – mentor/protégé, coach, and support groups – growth is defined by the extent to which people are appropriately intimate, disclosing, and present with one another, in ways relevant to the tasks of personal growth (Kahn, 1992; Kram, 1996). In less intensive developmental relationships – supervisor/co-worker, project teams and task forces, training workshops, role models – growth is defined less in terms of the development of conditions enabling safety and vulnerability and more in terms of conditions enabling appropriate communication, feedback loops, and transfer of knowledge. Either way, growth requires the ongoing development of a relationship until its conduct – structure of interactions, level of intimacy and trust, processes of self-correction and sustainability – fits with its purposes and its meaning in the lives of its participants (cf. Gabarro, 1987).

We identify and review below the five stages of development that characterize the growth of developmental relationships at work. The stages – *initiation, formation, construction, maturation,* and *transformation* – are generalized across the various forms of developmental relationships at work (more specifics about the intersection of stage and form are located in table 3.3). Effective developmental relationships at work are those that progress through the stages in the course of meeting people's

Table 3.3 Growth stage sequences in different types of developmental relationships at work

	Initiation	Formation	Construction	Maturation	Transformation
Mentor	Formally assigned mentor; intentional or circumstantial movement toward specific mentor or protégé.	Mentor program with established meeting structures, processes, training; or worked-out initial agreements about meetings and processes.	Develop processes enabling protégés to disclose real issues and receive meaningful support, with increasing sense of trust, safety, and mutual respect.	Safe relationship in which the whole self of the protégé is held in regard and developed. Ongoing mutual investment in relationship; meeting shared needs for cross-generational relationship.	Gradual decrease in frequency and intensity, until relationship diminishes in importance; abrupt endings through job changes; shifts toward equality and friendship; or movements toward partnership.
Coach	Formally assigned coach; intentional or circumstantial movement toward specific coaching relationship, based on organizational role or work project.	Formal coaching process with established parameters, training; or worked-out initial agreements about meetings and processes.	Develop processes enabling coach to guide other's learning of role- or project-related skills. Involves negotiating means to constructively provide and receive help.	Trusting relationship in which coach serves as a secure base for other, who seeks out and receives support and guidance in appropriate situations and develops capacities to learn, think, act, and reflect.	Gradual decrease in frequency and intensity, based on other's developing capacities for autonomy; abrupt endings through job changes; shifts toward collaboration in roles and projects.
Support group/network	Trigger events that coalesce people with shared interests, identities, or goals; social groups whose members begin to offer mutual support and assistance.	Creation of initial means (interactional, technological) by which to share support, information, resources and fellowship. Formation via isolated connections that network or creation of a group as a whole.	Develop communication systems and processes enabling members to experience connection, support, identity, and meaning through personal relationships.	Set of relationships marked by interdependence, mutuality, and reciprocity that allow members to provide and receive emotional and instrumental support from others at work.	Gradual decrease in group frequency and intensity, based on resolution of trigger events; shifts away from group and toward specific relationships; abrupt endings through job changes; inclusion of others to deepen and revitalize group.

Supervisor/co-worker	Assigned hierarchical, departmental or project-related work relationship based on fit between individuals and jobs.	Role and task focussed interactions that initially structure types, processes, and content of interactions based on organizational norms.	Develop work processes – coordination, communication, influence and authority, collaboration – enabling task accomplishment and relevant task learning.	Effective, efficient work relationships marked by meaningful collaboration and full exchange of relevant information and learning across hierarchy and roles.	Abrupt endings through job changes, role shifts, and project completions; expansions into friendship, partnership, coaching, or mentorship.
Project team/task force	Assigned departmental or cross-functional project team or task force based on member skills, knowledge, and experience.	Initial group structure developed by formal leaders to enable goal-oriented interactions among team members.	Develop group processes – coordination, communication, influence and authority, collaboration – that enable teamwork and task-related learning.	Effective teamwork marked by collaboration, feedback, exchange of knowledge, and individual and collective learning related to project work.	Endings through project completion or shifts to standing units; re-formation through member changes; expansions into friendship, partnership, coaching, or mentorship.
Training workshop/program	Individual approaches training opportunities through personal desire and/or organizational requirements.	Training parameters for training content and delivery established by training group and instructors, with varying input by participants.	Develop instructional processes that enable participants to become engaged in learning of desired knowledge and skills.	Training process marked by presentation of engaging opportunities for participants to learn and apply relevant knowledge and skills.	Predictable endings through completion of workshop or program; abrupt endings through job shifts; further trainings; enlistment of coaches to reinforce training.
Role model	Individual selects respected role model(s) for the learning of specific skills.	Individual creates or takes advantage of opportunities to observe role model.	Develop means by which to observe role model in relevant situations and reflect on lessons.	Learning process marked by cycle of ongoing observation, reflection, emulation, and trial and error.	Less dependence on role model because skills are learned and integrated, role model proves flawed, or access reduced; relationship becomes mutual.

developmental needs. Ineffective relationships are those that cannot progress through the stages; they are, at some point, derailed, mired in ineffective patterns, or simply collapse from the lack of energy to motivate and sustain them. At each stage, there is some sort of *developmental task* that must be completed in order for the relationship to continue growing (cf. Levinson, Darrow, Klein, Levinson, and McKee, 1978). If such tasks are not successfully completed, a relationship loses its meaning and momentum. In this section, we describe the five stages and the developmental tasks they present for completion.

Initiation

The first stage of a developmental relationship is marked by people moving toward others for the intentional or incidental purpose of development, and the positive reception of those movements by others. Such movements may be externally driven: mentors or coaches are assigned, supervisors, co-workers, and project teams are given, training programs are required. Or they are internally driven, as individuals seek out others from whom to learn and with whom to network or angle for certain job assignments in order to work with certain others. The movements may be in response to some triggering event in the environment (e.g., job change, organizational restructuring, downsizing). Or the triggering event may be more personal; an individual receives difficult feedback or fails or is uncertain and confused and feels the need to learn and develop. In some fashion, individuals are propelled toward opportunities to develop their selves, toward some type of relationship – intimate or distant, formal or informal, short-term or open-ended – in which to learn what they need to know.

The initiation of developmental relationships at work varies in terms of difficulty, according to the circumstances. It is easier to initiate a developmental relationship, for example, in the context of a formal process to do so, as with assigned mentors and coaches, than in the absence of such a context. It is easier as well when a relationship does not carry with it a history that makes it difficult to allow development-related interactions to occur. Such a history might include, for example, a mentor, coach, supervisor, or co-worker who has negative perceptions of an individual based on real or imagined previous interactions. Or the history may include a particular kind of relationship (e.g., senior executive–junior manager, casual acquaintances) that needs to be redefined into another, more development-oriented relationship (e.g., mentor, support system). It is difficult for people to move toward others who are quite distant from them on key dimensions – such as hierarchy, culture, and experience – that present large gaps that need to be bridged.

None of these factors prevent the initiation of a developmental relationship, of course. They simply make such movements toward others more difficult to make. When they are overwhelmingly difficult, initiation does not occur. That is, people do not make movements toward others – sign up for training or mentoring programs, make connections with others who would be likely support systems, ask for help from supervisors and co-workers, seek out a potential role model. Or they make such movements but their signals are not picked up or acknowledged by others, or their efforts at connection are rebuffed – possible mentors and coaches make themselves unavailable, co-workers provide little connection or help, project teams or task forces are unable to perceive or react to developmental needs. Movements toward are met by movements away. This constitutes a failure to complete the initial developmental task: *identifying likely relational vehicles* that will carry individuals on their journeys toward learning and growth. If that task is successfully met, and movements toward others are met with acceptance, developmental relationships can begin to form.

Formation

The second stage of a developmental relationship is marked by the creation of an initial structure to drive and contain initial efforts to form the relationship necessary to meet the needs of its participants. The formation process is, in reality, a series of choices and decisions that individuals make that, together, create a set of conditions in which developmental relationships can ideally flourish. Such choices include decisions about membership, i.e., who is inside the boundary of the relationship. While this is reasonably clear in terms of mentor, coaching, and working relationships – all assigned or chosen during the initiation stage – it is less clear in terms of support groups, networks, and ad hoc task forces. People must make choices about the time they invest in their relationships with others, in terms of frequency and length of contact. And they must choose forms of communication with which to connect with one another, ranging from the relative intimacy of face-to-face meetings to the relative distance of technology-based interactions. Each of these choices represents decisions about how much of their selves people commit to and invest in various forms of developmental relationships.

Some of these choices are externally driven, of course. Formal mentoring and coaching programs may involve guidelines and training that offer initial structures for development-related interactions. Work relationships with supervisors, co-workers, and project team members are structured according to the demands of the tasks that need to be completed and ongoing role relationships. Training workshops and programs have their own structures, dictated by curriculum. Such externally driven structures offer given settings, removing some of the barriers and choices people face in forming developmental relationships.

What is less externally driven, however, are people's choices about how much of their selves they make present in the course of their interactions with one another (Kahn, 1992). During the formation stage, individuals make an initial set of choices related to process, i.e., to how they go about engaging in developmental relationships within the various forms of structures they choose. Thus, people are making an initial set of choices about how much of their selves to disclose (Jourard, 1971), how open they wish to be to learning about themselves (Argyris, 1990), how much they wish to provide and receive meaningful feedback (Rogers, 1958), and, more generally, how personally engaged and present they wish to be in the course of their interactions with others (Kahn, 1992). These initial choices reflect people's sense of what the type of developmental relationship calls for (i.e., a mentoring relationship is related to more self-disclosure for protégés than, say, a training program or project team). They also reflect people's initial stances toward new situations about which they have little data, and as such, usually reflect a great deal about their own personal dispositions and experiences. The initial choices about how to be in the early parts of a developmental relationship thus reflect people's brief coding of the type of relationship, filtered through their own dispositions and experiences.

The result is some type of commitment to join with another, or others, in the exploration of a potentially developmental relationship at work. It is this *joining* that is the developmental task linked to the formation stage. Failures to meet this developmental task occur when people are unable to join with one another. They may discover early that the gaps in interests, desires, and capabilities are too wide to bridge. Or they may discover that their personal dispositions and experiences prevent them from entering certain types of developmental relationships. Such failures appear as people unable to make or follow through on their commitments to one another. When people engage the task of joining successfully, on the other hand, they create scaffolding that frames their relationship and offers a platform on which to build. They create ways to interact that meet appropriate needs and fit with the specific type of developmental relationship. Patterns of interaction are set in motion and people move toward one another in useful ways. It is in the context of the next stage that the initial stances that individuals strike come into contact with the reality of a situation, and they begin to construct a working developmental relationship.

Construction

The third stage of a developmental relationship is marked by building upon the scaffolding created during the formation stage to construct a relationship that works, i.e., is useful and relevant for its participants. Much of the construction focusses on the processes by which people actually interact to create learning and growth, either intentional (in development-oriented relationships) or incidental (in work-oriented relationships). Mentors and protégés need to develop interaction patterns (e.g., dialogue, give-and-take, accepting silences) that enable the latter to disclose real issues and receive meaningful support. Coaches and their charges need to develop their own interaction patterns (e.g., when and how to connect in relation to work tasks) that enable the former to remain close enough to help and distant enough to create autonomy. Support groups need to develop patterns (e.g., times and places to meet, ways of organizing and interacting) that enable participants to experience meaningful connection with one another in contexts that are defined largely by personal relations and shared interests. Project teams, task forces, and supervisor/co-worker relationships need to develop patterns of interaction (e.g., decision-making, task and resource allocations, consensus-building) that enable people to learn what they need to in order to be more effective at their tasks. And people who enroll in training programs or identify role models need to create patterns of interaction with instructors/models (e.g. critical thinking) that enable them to develop areas they wish to develop.

Such patterns of interaction are influenced by what occurred during the early stages of developmental relationships. How people approached or were approached by others set in motion certain patterns, certain tones, that are usually built upon in the early period of a developmental relationship. A mentor seeks out a protégé because she appreciates the younger woman's direct, no-nonsense demeanor during a difficult meeting; a minority support group/network forms around the dismissal of two minority executives; a project team's first meeting contains a thoughtful, blameless review of earlier failures; two new co-workers discover that they both lack a certain skill and seek out training opportunities together. Each of these acts of initiation created an initial set of premises on which participants of developmental relationships based the choices they made during their formation stages. The mentor assumes that direct, honest feedback will be welcomed by the younger woman; the minority support group members assume that outrage is what joins them and shapes their interactions; project team members assume that problems should be surfaced rather than hidden; the new co-workers assume that they can share their lack of knowledge rather than compete with one another. These premises both dictate and constrain what occurs among people.

During the construction stage, such premises are re-evaluated and either built upon to create ongoing relationships or renegotiated and altered to best fit the needs of people investing in developmental relationships. The re-evaluative process occurs in varying forms, but is driven by trial and error. People try different ways of relating with one another and are presented with certain outcomes, from which they judge the efficacy of continuing or altering their interactions. A mentor shares personal stories with his protégé. Whether those stories are tolerated with boredom or serve as a trigger for a thoughtful conversation will determine subsequent patterns of interaction in that relationship. Or a project team leader requests feedback about her leadership from team members. How respectfully she is provided with, and receives, such feedback will determine subsequent patterns of interaction among team members. In these and many similar examples across the range of developmental relationships at work, people are trying various ways of relating with one another, evaluating their outcomes, and making conscious and unconscious decisions about how to construct useful, satisfying relationships.

Such re-evaluation results in some sort of action. People may continue building upon their initial, still-operative premises and move more deeply into their relationships. Or they may try and renegotiate their initial premises upon realizing that the patterns of interaction they are creating are not serving their developmental needs, leave them feeling badly, or are not useful for others. Such renegotiations may be subtle, slight calibrations in how individuals interact that are not even brought up for discussion – a project leader may introduce ideas differently, a coach may make herself more available after specific milestones, a trainer may solicit more input after each session. Or the renegotiations may be more direct. A project team or support group may "storm," its members engaging in overt, direct conflicts around influence and authority and the extent to which participation and consensus are sought and valued. An individual may raise her need for more direct feedback from her coach. The point of such renegotiations is for participants to construct a relationship with which they are each satisfied, from the vantage points of their differing roles.

The developmental task connected to the construction stage is for people to negotiate patterns of interaction that *integrate their differences* – in style, need, abilities, capacities for intimacy and trust, etc. – and come to some resolution on how they wish to work together in ways that promote the desired development. Failure to complete this task occurs when people are unable to move from the initial stances that they created in the formation stage – stances built upon the brief coding of others, filtered through personal and biased lenses – into more realistic patterns of interaction informed by actual experiences with others. When that is not possible, people remain stuck in ineffective patterns that fail to serve appropriate developmental needs. When people are able to bridge the gaps between their initial assumptions and the reality of their experiences with others, they create useful, working relationships in which development, intentional or incidental, can proceed. They successfully construct a relational setting in which development may occur.

Maturation

The fourth stage of developmental relationships is marked by high performance and integration into the lives of their participants. The construction stage ends when people create relationships that serve appropriate developmental needs without extracting costs too high to bear. In the maturation stage, people settle into increasingly efficient operating relationships that meet their respective needs and continue to provide benefits that outweigh costs (e.g., time, energy, political capital). Moreover, they integrate the developmental relationships with the other parts of their personal and professional lives, locating them both psychologically and temporally in places that rest easily with and complement those other parts. A protégé reflects on the dynamics of a difficult work meeting with the help of his mentor, tries to implement the lessons in the context of another project team meeting, and talks with his wife about what he is learning about himself. Two members of a support group remind one another of their shared interests before joining a cross-functional team meeting in which they represent different functions and perspectives. A member of a training program joins with another to try and apply what they are learning about strategy to a project. In each case, developmental pieces join with and enhance the other parts of members' lives, and vice versa. People weave their developmental relationships into the fabric of their personal and professional lives, giving those relationships proper place and meaning.

The nature of highly performing, mature developmental relationships varies according to their specific forms. In mentor–protégé relationships, maturity reflects the extent to which protégés can make their whole selves (i.e., dispositions, skills, experiences, emotions) available in the context of their discussions with their mentors, who make it safe for protégés by treating them carefully, with regard and appreciation (Kahn, 1993; Kram, 1996). In the coaching relationship, maturity reflects coaches' creating secure bases for others, i.e., places to which others may repair for support and guidance during moments of anxiety and uncertainty related to work tasks (Kahn, 1996). Mature support groups and networks offer members a sense of connection and relatedness through which to receive emotional and instrumental support. In these relatively intensive, intimate relationships, there is the possibility that members will experience what Fletcher (1996) defines as three hallmarks of growth-fostering relational interactions: interdependence (i.e., recognition of opportunities to contribute and/or grow through relationships with others), mutuality (i.e., the use of skills to enable and/or be enabled by others), and reciprocity (i.e., mutual sense of responsibility for enacting developmental relationships).

The maturity of other, less intensive developmental relationships reflects the extent to which they enable people to make themselves personally available to their own learning or that of others in appropriate ways. In relations with supervisors, co-workers, and project teams or task forces, mature developmental relationships are marked by people's abilities to give or receive feedback, disclose relevant information, and reflect together on their processes – all of which enables people to take up teaching and learning roles in the course of their given tasks and roles. In each of these relationships, people serve as anchors for others' learning, in ways limited and appropriate to their formal work interactions. The focus on accomplishing work tasks trumps the focus on individual development. Yet even within that limited scope, the maturing of developmental relationships occurs. People simply make themselves appropriately visible in or available for development-related interactions. In training workshops, they bring forth the parts of themselves that need development – a certain skill, perhaps, or base of knowledge. With role models, they remain observers, doing the relevant developmental work elsewhere. Maturity, in these two types of relationships, is defined by the unhindered opportunity for people to learn what they need to learn as they wish to do so.

The developmental task related to the maturation stage is that of *psychological presence*, appropriate to the form of developmental relationship and an individual's role within it. Failure to complete this task occurs when people are unable to make themselves present – emotionally and intellectually – to the extent that they need to do so to sustain a mature developmental relationship. There are a number of factors influencing such presence (Kahn, 1992). Individuals may simply be unable to integrate their developmental relationships with others in their lives in terms of time and energy, or in terms of the psychological work necessary to bring together the different parts of themselves they expose in different settings. Individuals may run up against the limits of their own dispositions; they may find themselves unable to sustain certain types of intimacy after a point, through a lack of basic trust (Erikson, 1980), emotional intelligence (Goleman, 1998), or experience with secure attachments (Bowlby, 1988). Or people's lives may change in ways that render them less available for developmental relationships. People who, through some set of dispositions and circumstances, are able to remain appropriately psychologically present, however, sustain the course of successful, integrated developmental relationships.

Transformation

The fifth and final stage of developmental relationships is marked by their transformation into other forms that fit people's changing needs, circumstances, and relationships. Such changes are inevitable; people learn and grow, change jobs, restructure their personal lives, discover new possibilities. Developmental relationships need to transform as well, having partially or fully served their purposes.

Such transformations take any of a number of identifiable paths. One path is simply the ending of a developmental relationship that has run its course. A project team completes its work and disbands. A mentor retires. A training program concludes. A protégé or individual performer learns how to think, act, and reflect and no longer requires mentoring or coaching. A support group disbands as members retire or move. These relationships served people's developmental needs at a certain time and place in their personal and professional lives. Once those needs concluded, the relationships terminated. The endings may be abrupt – someone quits a job, a task force is suddenly disbanded – or they may be signaled well in advance and marked with some ceremony or another.

Another transformation is a lessening of intensity and frequency of contact rather than a complete ending. The developmental relationship gradually diminishes in the place and meaning that it takes in the lives of its participants. A protégé seeks the counsel of her mentor every six months rather than every two months. A support group meets infrequently. Project team members devote less and less time to reflection and feedback. Supervisors offer less feedback and support to increasingly experienced subordinates. Individuals refer to role models less often. These developmental relationships do not disappear. Rather, they remain touchstones, held in place by the shared history of their participants and available for use should the need arise.

A third type of transformation is a shifting of the shape of a developmental relationship. A relationship may have served its purposes but, rather than gradually lessening or abruptly ending, it offers a structure upon which to base another type of relationship. On this path, people who come together in one venue meet in another, their new relationship informed by their old. A boss becomes a coach, and later, a mentor; or, conversely, a mentor becomes a boss. A support network creates the momentum for a project team. A role model becomes a colleague. To the extent that these reshaped relationships contain developmental aspects, they must again progress through the stages described here. That is, they will require a renewal of commitments, based on the shifting needs and circumstances of people in the context of the new form of their developmental relationship.

The fourth and final transformation that we identify here is a deepening and broadening of the developmental relationship, such that it transcends its original form and shifts into another. Such transformations mark developmental relationships that mature so extensively that their participants grow increasingly present with and useful to one another. A supervisor increasingly invests in a promising performer that they create a coaching, then mentoring relationship. A project team or training seminar shifts into a support group. A coach develops into a close colleague and partner. In each of these transformations, people invest and display increasing amounts of their selves in the context of development-related interactions. These are, after a fashion, new relationships as well. As such, they too will require people to recycle through the stages of developmental relationships – a process made quicker by their familiarity with one another and with the form of the relationship itself.

The developmental task linked to the transformation stage calls for individuals to *locate the next relational structures* appropriate for meeting their shifting developmental needs. Failure to complete this task occurs when people are unable to identify their needs, lack resources or outlets for possible relationships, or have not learned how to adapt their needs to changing circumstances. People are thus left adrift, unable to create or locate relational vehicles that will move them along the next steps of their developmental journeys.

This is not to say that individuals must always be immersed within developmental relationships. There are periods of adult development that are marked by the implementation of what one has learned (Levinson et al., 1978). In such periods, individuals may rely on what they have internalized from their relations with others; they carry with them the wise counsel of a mentor, the memory of the reflective process they engaged in with a coach, the lessons from supervisors and co-workers. Other periods are marked by transitions, however, subtle or large upheavals that strain people's capacities and require them to develop further. To the extent that they have experienced successful developmental relationships – i.e., have beneficially gone through the five stages we have described here – they are more likely to seek them out, in some form or another, to enable their continued growth and development.

● How to Facilitate Relational Development: Creating Favorable Conditions ●

Developmental relationships at work are shaped by certain creating conditions, a set of variables that shape rather than determine individual choices and behaviors in some sort of predictably causal or contingency model. Our premise is that of the theory of multiple possibilities (Tyler, 1983), which maintains that there are many possible outcomes that can emerge in any situation. We believe that there are certain individual and organizational factors that help create the conditions for developmental relationships to occur, which we describe below. Whether such relationships do actually take root and flourish, however, is a matter of an unpredictable mixture of opportunity, desire, and competence, stirred by the timing of circumstance and fortune.

Individual conditions

Individuals are more likely to engage in successful developmental relationships at work when they have both the desire and the competence to do so. Desire shapes people's movements toward or receptivity to others. It determines their willingness to engage in any particular form of developmental relationship. For some individuals, such willingness is dispositional; they are simply drawn toward certain types of relationships as a way of being or learning, and have been consistently reinforced for doing so. They may do this out of a need for affiliation or because they happen to possess strong emotional competencies (Goleman, 1998). Or they may have a learning style whereby they routinely access others (Dalton, 1999). Thus, some people are routinely enrolled in training programs of one kind or another, involved in support groups, observing role models, coaching or being coached by others, or developing work relationships that allow for developmental feedback. This may represent some combination of individual learning styles, dispositional tendencies to look outward for stimulation, and a history of personal experiences that have proven rewarding.

For other individuals, desire is more situational. Circumstances arise that force people to need to learn – about themselves, technical skills, how to collaborate more effectively – in order to meet some important goal or survive in a quickly turbulent situation. People will bring themselves to change when they are in enough pain, or in enough threat of future pain (Havens, 1989). There are sources enough in organizational life of current or future threat of pain: career setbacks; receiving difficult feedback about oneself; failing on a key task because of a lack of technical skill; a seismic change in one's personal or professional life for which one is unprepared; a project that is rapidly disintegrating because of unmanaged group dynamics; and on and on (McCall, 1998). When individuals who are not naturally drawn toward relationships as a source of learning and support find themselves in such situations, they perform a sort of (mostly unconscious) calculus, weighing the pain attached to those situations against that attached to engaging in some particular form of developmental relationship. The result is stasis, or movement toward developmental relationships at work.

If individuals do move toward various developmental relationships, they are more likely to create successful ones if they possess certain competencies. The abilities required to grow a developmental relationship depend, of course, on the form and meaning of that relationship. Each form depends, however, on a certain kind of give and take, whether it be the relatively intimate, expressive dialogue of a mentor–protégé relationship or the relatively scripted interactions of a training session. Individuals can learn the sorts of competencies enabling such give and take, through training of one sort or another. In doing so, some people may have to confront the frustrating paradox of needing to learn *how* to learn with and through others in order to learn with and through others. In such cases, people must develop enough relational competence in order to approach and remain within developmental relationships, enough to learn relational competence. Here, the possession of appropriate relational competencies is a step-by-step affair, occurring in the course of rather than previous to the engagement of a developmental relationship.

The necessary relational competencies vary according to the form of developmental relationship. Creating an effective mentor–protégé relationship requires the competence to create increasingly trust-worthy settings. For mentors, this means performing the essential gestures of caregiving (Kahn, 1993): remaining accessible to, enquiring about, focussing attention on, validating, empathizing with, supporting, maintaining compassion for, and remaining consistent toward protégés. These dimensions envelop those discussed in other terms such as emotional intelligence (Goleman, 1998), active listening (Rogers, 1958), and empathy (Havens, 1989). Appropriate caregiving allows mentors to create settings in which protégés experience themselves as valued and supported; they create a reasonably safe place in which protégés can increasingly make more of their selves visible in the process of developing those selves. For their part, protégés need to know how to make their selves increasingly visible. They must disclose themselves – what they are thinking, feeling, perceiving – in the course of seeking support and guidance (Jourard, 1971; Kram, 1996). But they must do so appropriately, neither revealing themselves too much before the necessary trust is created nor too little such that such trust cannot be created at all.

The same types of competencies are required in other forms of developmental relationships, but in lesser intensities, given that individuals do not need to make as much of their whole selves visible. To create a secure base to which others may return when uncertain, coaches need to enact a certain amount of caregiving – they need to be accessible and supportive, able to guide without getting too close or remaining too distant and detached (Kahn, 1996). As with support group members, coaches need to be competent at providing emotional support, through encouragement, reinforcement, and acknowledgment. Here too, others – support group members, and individuals receiving coaching – need to be able to ask for and receive help, making themselves receptive and open without crossing the boundaries of appropriate work relationships.

The effectiveness of work relationships in which individual development is incidental rather than intentional depends on people's abilities to learn in the course of their work. Various researchers have identified three particular competencies that enable such experiential learning to occur. First, people need to reflect – to take in data, reflect on their meaning, develop abstract lessons to be applied in other situations, and create action plans for doing so (Kolb, 1983). Second, people need to be able to ask for and receive, non-defensively, feedback from others that they use as material upon which to reflect, without rejecting or accepting it uncritically (Gibb, 1968). Third, people need to hold themselves at some remove, or more colloquially, to not take things too personally. That is, they need to be able to examine a situation and their own reactions to that situation as data to be analyzed, interpreted, and used to form testable hypotheses to guide future actions (Argyris, 1990). Together, these competencies make it more likely that individuals can learn in the contexts of their task-focussed interactions with co-workers, supervisors, and project team members, formal workshops, and informal observations of role models.

As we note above, individuals can learn the competencies we discuss here. For some individuals, the learning will come less easily, however. The competencies that people have for engaging effectively in developmental relationships (and their abilities to learn those competencies in the future) are powerfully affected by their individual histories and dispositions. Individuals vary in terms of their ability to risk making themselves vulnerable. Those who have been cared for well in their lives, particularly as children in relations with parents and other primary caregivers, develop a sense of basic trust enabling them to move toward others when they are anxious, secure in the sense that they will find support (Bowlby, 1980; Erikson, 1968). People who lack such experiences create psychological defenses that prevent them from seeking or being receptive to certain forms of developmental relationships (Kahn and Kram, 1994). Lessening the grip of these defenses requires some sort of intervention – a personal or therapeutic relationship in which people experience themselves as cared for, for example, or a work relationship that gradually deepens into a trusting setting. Without such re-modeling, such individuals are not likely to utilize the full extent of developmental relationships available to them in the course of their work lives.

Organizational conditions

Organizations are marked by conditions that make it more or less likely that their members will seek out or engage in developmental relationships at work. Such conditions – which we describe here under the general categories of *formal systems* and *informal norms* – more or less legitimate the use of developmental relationships (or, more specifically, the use of certain forms at certain times). We suggest that the extent to which an organization legitimizes relational learning is woven into its culture. The formal systems and informal norms that shape whether and how developmental relationships form are cultural artifacts (Schein, 1985) – the observable behaviors, systems, and forms of interaction that members routinely use to go about their collective business. These artifacts reflect underlying, taken-for-granted basic assumptions. Schein (1985) notes that one basic assumption characterizing organizations involves the nature of human relationships: organizations develop ways to answer questions about how "openness and intimacy are to be handled in the context of managing the organization's tasks" (p. 66). How they answer those questions determines their collective abilities to enable developmental relationships. Here, we describe formal systems and informal norms that organizations develop to reflect cultures that support relational learning.

One set of formal systems that make developmental relationships more likely to occur involves establishing structures for people to join such relationships. Formal mentoring and coaching programs that pair mentors with protégés, and coaches with individual performers, provide a structure (and, ideally, a process and training) enabling those relationships to flourish. Similarly, organization members may be slotted into training programs that fit with their career developmental needs. Each of these structures initiates a type of developmental relationship, legitimizing it as an important developmental tool. Organizations push that legitimization further when they develop formal performance appraisal and reward systems that explicitly reward members for engaging in various types of developmental relationships. Such systems keep track of the extent to which organization members set and complete goals related to coaching and mentoring others, developing subordinate skills, completing training workshops and programs, becoming involved in quality improvement teams, and the like. While the quality of these relational activities is notoriously difficult to measure, and hence to tie to rewards in any precise way, organizations that develop and utilize simple measures of involvement are likely to generate the use of developmental relationships.

Another set of formal systems focusses on processes that encourage feedback and reflection as an integral part of members' work experiences. This can occur in a variety of settings and forms. Supervisors may be required as part of their roles to routinely conduct developmental (rather than merely evaluative) assessments with their subordinates. This process can be aided by 360-degree feedback, in which members reflect on feedback provided by supervisors, peers, subordinates, and customers. In project teams and task forces, feedback among group members can be woven into meeting structures, in the form of "process checks" that enable people to step back and examine how they are going about working together. After-action reviews (AARs) similarly offer a system by which team members can reflect together on their work, with the express purpose of learning and developing, individually and collectively.

Whether and how members of any organization use these or other formal systems, or in the absence of any such systems, how they aid one another's growth and learning, depends on the informal norms that guide their interactions. Norms – the patterns of behavior that mark a group, organization, or any other social system – spring up to regulate cultures (Schein, 1985). The organizational norms in which we are particularly interested here are apparent in answers to the following questions. How much is feedback encouraged, welcomed, rewarded, acted upon? How often do members seek out and are welcomed by potential mentors and coaches? How often do supervisors, project team leaders and members, and colleagues pause and make time and space for authentic dialogue and reflection? How much and in what ways is the relational work that members do with and for one another made visible, valued, and rewarded? To what extent do stories about respected leaders refer to their involvement in and support of various forms of developmental relationships? Such questions point to the real meaning of developmental relationships in any organizational culture – to their place as important vehicles for the journeys that organization members take, individually and collectively.

● Conclusion: Intentional Use of Relationships for Career Learning ●

In this era of constrained resources, relationships at work are one of the few untapped natural resources that an organization has available for increased work effectiveness and worker fulfillment. As we have attempted to show, simply by being more intentional about cultivating and managing good relationships, and by consciously utilizing them where they occur naturally in settings like project teams and task forces, human development occurs as a simple byproduct of doing work.

A central mechanism that enables good developmental relationships to facilitate an individual's growth is the impact that such relationships can have on the person's metacompetencies. As a source of meaningful feedback and psychological safety for reflection, these relationships contribute to the growth of the person's self-knowledge and his or her ability to seek and use such feedback in the future. This feedback and its new information about the self can also be an important part of the exploration stage of a new career learning cycle. Thus, the relationships serve the enhancement of personal identity and career exploration. Similarly, by providing a safe place to experiment as well as encouragement to take risky action, developmental relationships also promote adaptability. This can help propel the person into the trial stage of a new career learning cycle. These two metacompetencies, identity and adaptability, tend to be relatively enduring properties of the individual, and changing them requires a developmental leap (Kegan, 1983, 1995; Kegan and Lahey, 2000). With the support of strong developmental relationships, the task becomes more manageable.

When individuals perform better and grow, teams and organizations do better, as well. And the members feel better about and more loyal to the collective, as well, as we saw earlier in the example of career-developing Ms. Morse and her rejected $1 million competing offer. The team or organization is strengthened by the new competencies that are now part of the members individually and part of the collective. And thus, as the song goes, "We get by with a little help from our friends."

Thus, we would leave the reader with the following conclusions about tapping the natural developmental potential of relationships at work. First, organization members need to *recognize and value developmental relationships as key learning resources*, in their own lives and in those of others in the organization. These relationships can potentially provide a source of meaning and stability and growth gone missing under the terms of the new contract. They offer a way for people to continue to learn to build their own capacities – which are increasingly their most valuable resource. Second, and related, we believe that *leadership can be understood partly as the ability to utilize developmental relationships to build the business*. The relationally skilled leader can engage in, encourage, model, make visible, and create the conditions for the effective growth and use of developmental relationships in his or her organization. This fits with the ongoing recasting of the role of the organizational leader from someone who dictates to someone who develops the capacities of others to lead themselves.

Third, it is important to *nurture an array of developmental relationships*, for oneself and others. This involves making a conscious commitment to and effort on behalf of relations at work – to devoting the time, energy, and attention to creating the various conditions that enable developmental relationships specifically, and relational learning more generally, to occur in the course of doing business. Fourth, organization members need to *recognize the natural progression – the stages –* that mark the development of various forms of these relationships. This will help normalize their experiences (e.g., dealing with differences in goals and styles as a developmental step), and enable them to examine the warning signs of relationships that are stuck – that is, in which people are unable to complete the tasks that move them into their next stages.

Finally, our defining of the various forms and stages of developmental relationships offers an *opportunity to reflect on the extent to which people have such relationships*, and which types, and how far they develop, and where and why they fail to. This sort of diagnosis can occur at both individual and organizational levels. Individuals can examine the pattern of developmental relationships in their work lives, and reflect on what it is about them that enables or disables those relationships, and the effects on their lives. Together, people can reflect on the underlying basic assumptions and cultures of their organizations, in terms of their desire to facilitate or undermine developmental relationships of a certain nature. It is through such reflection – itself an integral dimension of relational learning – that organization members are most likely to create the conditions for themselves and others that facilitate the growth of developmental relationships to sustain them at work.

REFERENCES

Argyris, C. (1990). Teaching smart people how to learn. *Harvard Business Review*, May/June, 99–109.
Arthur, M.B., and Rousseau, D.R. (1996). *The Boundaryless Career*. New York: Oxford.
Bowlby, J. (1980). *Attachment and Loss* (Vol. 3). New York: Basic.
Bowlby, J. (1988). *The Secure Base*. New York: Basic Books.
Briscoe, J., and Hall, D.T. (1999). Grooming and picking leaders using competency frameworks: Do they work? *Organizational Dynamics*, 3, 37–51.

Dalton, M. (1999). *The Learning Tactics Inventory*. San Francisco: Jossey-Bass and the Center for Creative Leadership.

Erikson, E. (1968). *Identity: Youth and Crisis*. New York: Norton.

Erikson, E.H. (1980). *Identity and the Life Cycle*. New York: Norton.

Fletcher, J.K. (1996). A relational approach to the protean worker. In Douglas T. Hall and Associates, *The Career is Dead – Long Live the Career: A Relational Approach to Careers*. San Francisco: Jossey-Bass, pp.104–15.

Gabarro, J.J. (1987). The development of working relationships. In J. Lorsch (ed.). *Handbook of Organizational Behavior*. Englewood Cliffs: Prentice-Hall, pp. 172–89.

Gibb, J. (1968). Defensive communication. In W. Bennis, E. Schein, F.I. Steele, and D.E. Berlew (eds). *Interpersonal Dynamics*. New York: Irwin.

Goleman, D. (1998). *Working with Emotional Intelligence*. New York: Bantam Books.

Hall, D.T., and Associates (1986). *Career Development in Organizations*. San Francisco: Jossey-Bass.

Hall, D.T., and Associates (1996). *The Career is Dead – Long Live the Career: A Relational Approach to Careers*. San Francisco: Jossey-Bass.

Hall, D.T., and Mirvis, P.H. (1996). The new protean career. In Douglas T. Hall and Associates, *The Career is Dead – Long Live the Career*. San Francisco: Jossey-Bass.

Handy, C. (1989). *The Age of Unreason*. Boston: Harvard Business School Press.

Havens, L. (1989). *A Safe Place*. Cambridge, MA: Harvard University Press.

Higgins, M., and Kram, K.E., (2001). Mentoring networks. *Academy of Management Review* (in press).

Jourard, S.M. (1971). *Self-Disclosure*. New York: Wiley.

Kahn, W.A. (1992). To be fully there: Psychological presence at work. *Human Relations*, 45, 4, 321–49.

Kahn, W.A. (1993). Caring for the caregivers: Patterns of organizational caregiving. *Administrative Science Quarterly*, 38, 4, 539–63.

Kahn, W.A. (1996). Secure base relationships at work. In D. T. Hall and Associates, *The Career is Dead*, pp. 158–179. San Francisco: Jossey-Bass Publishers.

Kahn, W.A., and Kram, K.E. (1994). Authority at work: Internal models and their organizational consequences. *Academy of Management Review*, 19, 1, 17–50.

Kegan, R. (1983). *The Evolving Self*. Cambridge, MA: Harvard University Press.

Kegan, R. (1995). *In Over Our Heads: The Mental Demands of Modern Life*. Cambridge, MA: Harvard University Press.

Kegan, R., and Lahey, L.L. (2000). *How the Way We Talk Can Change the Way We Work: Seven Languages for Transformation*. San Francisco: Jossey-Bass.

Kolb, D.A. (1983). *Experiential Learning: Experience as the Source of Learning and Development*. Englewood Cliffs, NJ.

Kram, K.E. (1996). A relational approach to career development. In D.T. Hall and Associates, *The Career is Dead – Long Live the Career: A Relational Approach to Careers*. San Francisco: Jossey-Bass, pp. 132–57.

Kram, K.E., and Isabella, L.A. (1985). Mentoring alternatives: The role of peer relationships in career development. *Academy of Management Journal*, 28, 1, 110–32.

Levinson, D.J., Darrow, C.N., Klein, E.B., Levinson, M.H., and McKee, B. (1978). *The Seasons of a Man's Life*. New York: Ballantine Books.

McCall, Morgan W., Jr. (1998). *High Flyers: Developing the Next Generation of Leaders*. Boston: Harvard Business School Press.

Rogers, C.R. (1958). The characteristics of a helping relationship. *Personnel and Guidance Journal*, 37, 6–16.

Sarason, S. (1977). *Work, Aging, and Social Change*. New York: Free Press.

Schein, E.H. (1985). *Organizational Culture and Leadership*. San Francisco: Jossey-Bass.
Tyler, L.E. (1983). *Thinking Creatively: A New Approach to Psychology and Individual Lives*.
    San Francisco: Jossey-Bass.
Zipkin, Amy (2000). The wisdom of thoughtfulness. *The New York Times*, May 31, 2000,
    C1, C10.

4

Second Careers and Multiple Careers

DANIEL C. FELDMAN

While journalistic accounts about the prevalence and growth of second careers have been numerous, the amount of theoretical and empirical work on multiple careers has been surprisingly sparse. The present chapter builds upon previous work on second careers in three ways. First, it proposes a conceptualization of "career change" and illustrates its convergent and discriminant validity with such related constructs as job change, organizational change, turnover, and retirement. Second, it presents a series of propositions about the motivations for career change and examines how the extent of career change and reasons for career change vary across career stages. Third, the chapter presents some additional directions for future theory development and empirical research on this topic, particularly in terms of identifying predictors of performance and perseverance in subsequent career paths.

The interest in second careers (and multiple careers) has been building steadily, both among academics and the public in general, for the past thirty years. Beginning with the increase in dual-career couples in the 1970s, intensifying with the downsizings of the 1980s, and broadening with the rise of e-commerce in the 1990s, both the need to pursue second careers and innovative opportunities for doing so have become salient to a wider spectrum of individuals in the labor market.

For many, the shift to a labor market in which career changing is now both feasible and fashionable has been received with great enthusiasm. The rise of multiple careers has been viewed largely as a liberating force for untapped human potential (e.g., Arthur and Rousseau, 1996). For individuals who have been trapped in dead-end jobs, no longer proficient (or even interested) in sustaining high skill levels in their present occupations, the increased social acceptability of switching careers and increased options for pursuing new careers have been a blessing. Employees no longer automatically have to "stick with something they started" or "put in more years to retirement."

Among scholars of gender issues in employment, the rise of second careers has also been seen as increasing the opportunities for both men and women to alter career paths as their marital status and family status change (Gallos, 1989; Schneer and Reitman, 1993). Because career switching might enable both two-career couples and single parents to better balance work and family demands, the phenomenon of career switching has often been viewed very favorably from this perspective as well.

However, theoretical and empirical research on this topic among social scientists has lagged far behind. Indeed, what the term "career change" means and how it differs from other, related constructs (such as job change, organizational change, turnover, and retirement) have not been fully explicated. In addition, there has been surprisingly little empirical research on the extent of career changing, the specific reasons that individuals pursue (or avoid pursuing) multiple careers, and the factors which determine whether individuals persevere and succeed in their new careers.

The present chapter, then, has three related goals. First, it proposes a conceptualization of "career change" and illustrates its convergent and discriminant validity with such related constructs as job change, organizational change, turnover, and retirement. Second, it presents a series of propositions about the motivations for career change and examines how both the extent of career change and the reasons for career change vary across career stages. Last, the chapter concludes with additional directions for future theory development and empirical research on multiple careers, with particular emphasis on identifying predictors of performance and perseverance in subsequent career paths.

• The Construct of Career Change •

For our purposes, we will define *career change* as entry into a new occupation which requires fundamentally different skills, daily routines, and work environments from the present one. While career change may be conceptually similar to other types of job transitions, it can also be conceptually distinguished from them.

The term "job change," for example, refers to taking a different position within an organization or at another organization. A transition from being a first-line supervisor in one department to a first-line supervisor in another, then, is easily classifiable as a job change; the term job change does not necessarily imply fundamental differences in important skills or daily routines. In contrast, for such a transition to be labeled a career change, it would have to entail major shifts in job duties and daily routines, too. Thus, moving from being a first-line supervisor in a plant to being a self-employed software developer would be considered a career change as well.

Similarly, the terms "organization change" and "turnover" imply exit from one firm and entry into another. By way of contrast, career change refers not only to major shifts in work context but also to major shifts in work content. Leaving Company A as a plant manager to become a plant manager at Company B is turnover; leaving Company A as a plant manager to become a professor at a junior college is a career change, too.

As defined by Feldman (1994), "retirement" refers to withdrawal from a long-held position with the intention of decreased psychological involvement in work there-after. Feldman's definition suggests that retirement does not necessarily mean total withdrawal from the workforce. Indeed, although many workers in the US and abroad have left their long-time positions by age 60, the majority still continue to participate in the workforce in some manner after that time. In fact, Doeringer (1990) refers to this phenomenon as "bridge employment"; in other words, bridge employment is work taken after the end of long-term, full-time employment but before total withdrawal from the workforce.

Depending on the nature of post-retirement employment, then, there may be some overlap between the constructs of bridge retirement and career change for older workers (Kim and Feldman, 2000). If a lawyer "retires" at age 50 to establish an internet commerce company, it could be legitimately said that the lawyer is changing careers. He/she uses fundamentally different skills and works in fundamentally different contexts, but still maintains a high level of psychological involvement and commitment in full-time employment. In contrast, if a 65-year-old executive leaves a long-held, full-time position to become a part-time gardener, we would consider that move a transition into "bridge employment" rather than a career change *per se*. The job as a gardener does require different skills and work environments than the job as executive, but is done only on a part-time basis and only with the intention of gradually phasing out of the workforce altogether.

Probably the most difficult distinction to be made among career transitions is when individuals change their major focus of interest within the same broad occupation (Feldman and Bolino, 1997). For example, Schein's (1978) work on career anchors suggests that individuals in marketing may pursue career paths as technical specialists (e.g., market researchers), general managers (e.g., brand managers), positions with high job security (e.g., marketing professors), paths which are largely entrepreneurial in nature (e.g., internet marketers), or careers with high autonomy (e.g., marketing consultants). While all these different career paths might require a graduate degree in marketing, the skills these careers utilize, the daily routines they entail, and the environments in which they are employed are widely different. To what extent should changes among these career paths, then, be considered career changes?

For our purposes, we will consider transitions within the same broad occupational category as career changes only if there are *fundamental* changes in work skills, daily routines, and work contexts between successive positions. Using this rationale, then, moving from being a brand manager to being a marketing professor would be considered a career change. On almost every dimension (except basic marketing knowledge), brand managers use fundamentally different skills, have fundamentally different daily routines, and work in widely different organizational environments than marketing professors do. On the other hand, moving from being a market researcher working for a consumer products company to being a self-employed market research consultant would not be considered a career change, since the job skills, daily routines, and many of the work contexts are very similar between these two career paths.

• The Motivation to Change Careers •

There is always some uncertainty and risk associated with a major career change (Feldman, 1988; Hall, 1976). Moreover, while the attractions of a different career may be highly visible to outsiders, its negative attributes may not be as readily or easily discernible.

In this section of the chapter, then, we examine those factors which influence individuals to change careers despite the potential risks associated with these changes. Here, we discuss individual-level factors (e.g., educational attainment, health, and financial wealth), family-level factors (e.g., marital status and family size), occupation-level factors (e.g., changes in work content or performance expectations), and labor market and industry-wide changes (e.g., downsizings and changes in labor supply) which are likely to be significantly related to career change.

At least in journalistic and anecdotal accounts of career change, most of the focus has been on mid-career changers and their experiences "starting over" in their forties and fifties (e.g., Dunkin, 1996; Kruger, 1994). However, despite the popular fascination with mid-career changes, empirical evidence suggests that switching occupations is actually more prevalent among young adults in their early careers. Indeed, labor economists note that individuals under age 30 are much more likely to change occupations than individuals over age 50 (Monks and Pizer, 1998; Neal, 1999).

Thus, in presenting the motivations for changing careers, we will focus on the different motivations for switching careers in each career stage. Both the factors which predispose individuals to change careers and the factors which inhibit such changes are likely to vary considerably over the course of a lifetime. A summary of these factors appears in table 4.1; a more detailed discussion follows below.

Early career

In the organizational sciences, career changes in young adulthood have been studied much less frequently than those in mid-career – despite the evidence that career switching is, in fact, inversely related to age. Here, we suggest that the amount and type of education, the degree of underemployment in early career jobs, the level of career search and job search activity, and family status all influence young adults' decisions to switch occupations in early career.

Education.   Changing careers is a potentially very expensive course of action. Getting one's career started often requires considerable formal education to build the skills necessary to enter the labor market. To change careers, then, an individual may have to "give up" his/her original investment in education in the first career and "reinvest" in additional training for a second career. Furthermore, to change careers, individuals may have to leave the workforce on a part-time or full-time basis to return to school (Sagen, Dallam, and Laverty, 1999; Vuori and Vesalainen, 1999). Proposition 1 suggests that the lower the level of formal education an individual receives before initially entering the workforce on a full-time basis, the more likely

Table 4.1 Factors associated with career change

Early Career Stage
- Amount of education
- Vocational orientation of education
- Degree of initial underemployment
- Quality of career search
- Amount of job search activity
- Financial support from parents
- Number of children to support

Mid-Career Stage
- Degree of change in occupation
- Degree of organizational decline
- Divorce
- Decrease in number of dependent children to support

Late Career Stage
- Health of employee
- Physical demands of occupation
- Household wealth
- Involvement in hobbies and leisure pursuits
- Occupational tenure
- Organizational tenure

---

he/she is to switch occupations in early career. There are two reasons for this proposition (Booth et al., 1999). First, the lower the level of formal education, the less likely an individual is to earn a substantial salary. Thus, the financial incentive to switch careers is greater for employees with less education. Second, the loss of earnings associated with leaving an occupation which requires little formal education should be small as well. A high-school graduate working as a bank teller has much more to gain and little to lose by pursuing a bachelor's degree in accounting. In contrast, a medical-school graduate has much more to lose and much less to gain by switching from medicine to law.

P1: The lower the level of education before entering the workforce on a full-time basis, the more likely an individual will be to switch occupations in early career.

For similar reasons, Proposition 2 suggests that the more vocationally oriented an individual's formal education, the less likely he/she will be to switch occupations in early career. Part of the rationale for this proposition is that vocationally oriented education is more likely to be instrumental in providing young adults with specific skills to obtain (and perform well in) jobs upon graduation (Sagen et al., 1999). For example, undergraduate accounting students are better prepared to be entry-level accountants than undergraduate psychology students are prepared to be entry-level professional psychologists.

In addition, the decision to pursue vocationally oriented education may itself signal a firm decision about what career to follow upon graduation (Schwab, Rynes, and Aldag, 1987). For example, the decision to pursue an engineering degree is implicitly a decision to pursue a job as a scientist, engineer, or computer specialist. In contrast, the decision to get a general liberal arts degree may put off the decision about career choice to a much later date. Thus, the decision to get a degree in philosophy does not lead to any obvious career path – and therefore the chances of changing careers in young adulthood are much higher.

> **P2:**   The more vocationally oriented an individual's formal education, the less likely he/she will be to switch occupations in early career.

Underemployment.   Another major factor influencing switching occupations in early career is the quality of the first job obtained upon leaving school. For a variety of reasons, many individuals graduating high school and college end up "underemployed" in their first jobs. That is, it appears that about 25 percent of these graduates end up in jobs for which are they over-educated, over-qualified, or which require substantially fewer skills than they possess (Feldman, 1996).

A major consequence of this underemployment is that young adults start to look for new jobs and new careers even within months of starting their initial employment. Both Feldman and Turnley (1995) and Rousseau (1990) found that business school graduates were significantly more likely to start job-hunting again if they felt underemployed in their initial placements. As Proposition 3 suggests, then, the inability to find appropriate jobs upon graduation impels individuals to consider switching occupations in early career.

> **P3:**   The greater the degree of underemployment in early career jobs, the more likely an individual will be to switch careers.

When underemployed young adults are faced with the prospect of pursuing new careers, they are faced with a fundamental choice: Should they return to school in order to get additional (or different) training or should they pursue career changes through finding new occupations in the labor market? Previous research suggests that young adults who are underemployed upon graduation are somewhat ambivalent about pursuing career changes through more schooling (Feldman and Turnley, 1995; Sagen et al., 1999). Some are skeptical about the instrumentality of education in directly improving their job prospects; others feel they need to get more work experience in the "real world" to discover their true interests or to acquire enough money to afford further education.

As potentially costly as returning to school may be, Proposition 4 suggests that young adults who are underemployed are more likely to return to school to switch careers than individuals at other career stages. The opportunity costs (i.e., the amount of salary lost by leaving the workforce) are lower for young adults, while the potential benefits of getting into more lucrative occupations early in life have greater long-term financial rewards. In addition, middle-aged and older workers may be more reluctant to deal with the social awkwardness of returning to school with young adults not much older than their own children (Vuori and Vesalainen, 1999).

> **P4:** Individuals are more likely to pursue career changes via further education in early career than in other career stages.

Career search and job search activity. While part of the reason young adults become underemployed is attributable to external forces (such as general recessions or poor local labor market conditions), another reason young adults become underemployed initially is their own inadequate search for appropriate careers and jobs. Previous research suggests that inadequate initial research on occupational possibilities and lack of time put into job-hunting both contribute to initial underemployment and to subsequent career changing (Feldman and Turnley, 1995; Freeman and Schopen, 1992; Schwab et al., 1987).

In some cases, young adults simply do not put adequate time into getting realistic previews of what careers will be like or seeking out honest advice from people in careers of interest to them (Wanous, 1980). In other cases, students who are graduating procrastinate looking for jobs or do not aggressively pursue job leads (Feldman, 1988). As a result, they end up in poor jobs in their chosen occupation – and then become more easily disillusioned with those initial career choices altogether.

Therefore, Propositions 5 and 6 suggest that the amount of research into careers and the amount of job search activity will both be inversely related to the likelihood of switching occupations. The greater the effort put into picking careers and jobs initially, the less likely young adults will be to switch occupations in early career.

> **P5:** The less research an individual has conducted on occupational choices while in school, the more likely he/she will be to change careers in early career.
>
> **P6:** Amount of job search activity for the first full-time job will be inversely related to the likelihood of switching careers in early career.

Family status. The third set of factors related to career change among young adults concerns family status. The nature of young adults' family relationships can influence the amount of financial distress a change of careers might entail.

Proposition 7 suggests that the greater parents' wealth, the more likely a young adult will be to switch occupations in early career. Starting over, particularly if that means going back to school, can be very costly financially. If young adults can receive monetary support from parents, their willingness to change careers and their financial ability to do so will be enhanced. On the other hand, if young adults have no financial safety net, they may be less willing to take on the financial risks or debts which might be incurred by leaving their present occupations (Holzer, 1987; Steffy, Shaw, and Noe, 1989).

> **P7:**   The greater parents' wealth, the more likely a young adult will be to switch occupations in early career.

Young adults' responsibilities for their own minor children may also influence their ability and willingness to switch careers. Proposition 8 suggests that individuals will be more likely to switch occupations in early career when they have no children (Sterrett, 1999). Because raising children is expensive, young adults with one or more children to support may be less willing to take the financial risks associated with changing careers. In addition, because child-rearing is also time-consuming, young adults who have already started their families may have less time or opportunity to switch careers by going back to school.

> **P8:**   Individuals without children are more likely to switch careers in early career than individuals with children.

Labor economists (e.g., Waddoups and Assane, 1993) often draw distinctions among "independent primary labor markets" (e.g, high-paying professional jobs), "subordinate primary labor markets" (e.g., jobs such as nursing, which have some desirable characteristics but little room for advancement), and "secondary labor markets" (e.g., seasonal and temporary work with little pay or job security). Powell and Mainiero (1992) suggest that as families grow in size, the secondary wage-earner (that is, the spouse/partner who earns less money) is more likely to switch into occupations which demand fewer skills and are lower in this hierarchy of jobs.

For instance, female MBAs who are the secondary wage-earners may switch out of highly demanding positions in large consulting firms to accept part-time employment in public sector jobs which have "family-friendly" hours. As Proposition 9 proposes, then, increases in family size may be positively associated with secondary wage-earners' shifting to lower-skilled occupations with fewer time and travel demands.

> **P9:**   Increases in number of dependent children will be positively associated with secondary wage-earners' switching into lower-skilled occupations.

Mid-career stage

As discussed above, mid-life career changes have received the most attention from researchers and practitioners alike. Part of the reason for this research focus has been the attention mid-career changes have received from early, influential scholars of career stages (e.g., Gould, 1978; Levinson, 1978; Valliant, 1977). In addition, mid-career changes make "better press" than early-career changes; a retail clerk going back to school to become an accountant is a much less exciting story than that of a CEO quitting to be a stay-at-home parent.

Despite the anecdotal and case study evidence on mid-career changes, the amount of theoretical and empirical research on this topic has been surprisingly limited. Below we consider the factors which are most likely to impel individuals in mid career to overcome the inertia of staying their with present course of action in order to switch careers. In general, the factors hypothesized to be most closely associated with mid-career changes are the degree of change in an individual's organization, occupation, and family circumstances over time (cf. table 4.1).

Degree of change in occupation and organization.   By the time individuals reach their forties, there have often been major changes in the nature of the occupations they have chosen (Hermans and Oles, 1999; Levinson, 1978). For example, many faculty members who entered academia in the 1960s because they enjoyed teaching discovered, much to their chagrin, that the rewards and accolades of professional accomplishment in the 1980s were now going to researchers. Similarly, many physicians who entered medicine in the 1970s because of the desire for high income and high professional autonomy discovered in the 1990s that increased governmental regulation and growth of managed care substantially curtailed those positive aspects of medicine.

Proposition 10, then, suggests that the greater the degree of change in the occupation over time, the more likely that the initial attributes which attracted individuals to that occupation will no longer be present or present to the same extent. For instance, there has been relatively little change in the work content or work context of electricians over the past twenty years, and so there is little reason to expect much career switching on their part in mid-career. In contrast, there have been dramatic changes in the content and environment of public school teaching during this time period; consequently, we might reasonably expect more mid-career switching among this occupational group.

P10:   The greater the degree of change in an individual's occupation over time, the more likely he/she is to change occupations in mid-career.

Similarly, Proposition 11 suggests that the greater the degree of decline in an individual's current organization, the more likely he/she is to change occupations in mid-career. For many individuals in mid-career, the need to change organizations in mid-life may spark a desire to change careers at the same time as well.

For example, many mid-career managers forced out of their jobs by downsizing over the past decade have decided to change careers, too (Feldman, 1995; Leana and Feldman, 1995). For some, switching careers has been approached in a positive or proactive perspective; the downsizing has forced them to get out of a rut and pursue a career which is more desirable to them. For others, though, switching occupations at the time of downsizing has been undertaken as a last resort because no other alternatives existed; many steelworkers laid off in the 1980s and 1990s were forced to change careers because the number of jobs in that industry was declining rapidly. Thus, while voluntary turnover is not necessarily related to switching occupations, involuntary turnover in mid-career is more likely to be related to career change.

P11:   The greater the degree of decline in an individual's current organization, the more likely he/she is to change occupations in mid-career.

While career plateauing may occur at any point in an individual's career, previous research suggests that it is more likely to occur in mid-career (Alderfer and Guzzo, 1979; Ference, Stoner, and Warren, 1977; Veiga, 1983). Some plateauing is, of course, attributable to changes in career paths and organizations described above (Feldman and Weitz, 1988). When the job content of an occupation changes dramatically, when the criteria for promotion (or layoff) are altered, or when the current employer is having business reverses, mid-career employees are clearly more likely to plateau. However, some plateauing is also due to middle-aged employees' own career decisions. For example, when employees consistently refuse to update their training or refuse to take any geographical transfers, the probability increases that they will no longer receive any further positions of increased responsibility.

Proposition 12 suggests that employees who have plateaued will also be the most likely to switch occupations in mid-career. Some of these plateaued performers will see the writing on the wall and change occupations of their own volition; others will only be jolted out of their current career paths by involuntary layoffs. In either event, marginal or plateaued performers are more likely to switch careers in mid-career than high performers. For these employees, the potential for future intrinsic and extrinsic rewards is much lower and the potential for future career-ending personnel actions (e.g., firings or layoffs) is much higher.

P12:   Plateaued performers are more likely to switch occupations in mid-career than high performers are.

Changes in family circumstances.   Changes in family circumstances also influence the degree of career change among mid-career employees. Furthermore, changes in family circumstances will have differential effects on the career-switching behavior of primary and secondary wage-earners in marriages or partnerships (Albrecht et al., 1999; Eby, Allen, and Douthitt, 1999).

Depending on the age at which they married and had children, individuals in mid-life may no longer be responsible for financially supporting children or may have fewer children to support. Indeed, even if middle-aged parents are still financially supporting children, their teenaged children are more independent and better able to take care of themselves after school. Consequently, several constraints on mid-career employees' switching occupations may be relaxed as well.

In couples where there is a disparity in amount of income earned between partners, the secondary wage-earner with young children is often forced into the secondary labor market or part-time work. The costs associated with secondary wage-earners having childcare responsibilities are low relative to the costs for primary wage-earners. For these secondary wage-earners, then, the decrease in child-rearing responsibilities creates opportunities to switch out of less demanding career paths and into more highly skilled occupations. As Proposition 13 suggests, when childcare responsibilities decrease, secondary wage-earners are freer to pursue occupations more consistent with their past experience or their potential. For example, a CPA working part-time doing tax returns from home can now become a full-time financial planner.

In contrast, Proposition 14 suggests that decreases in the number of dependent children allow primary wage-earners to shift into less demanding career paths (Kim and Feldman, 1998). When the financial responsibilities for supporting spouses and children are high, primary wage-earners are often reluctant to take any major financial risks associated with switching occupations – particularly any that would decrease current earning power. However, once financial responsibilities in the household decrease, primary wage-earners are freer to pursue careers which might be of more interest to them even if they do not pay as well. For example, an engineering manager no longer responsible for supporting children could switch into secondary science education without as much fear about lost income.

P13: Decreases in number of dependent children to support will be associated with secondary wage-earners' switching into more demanding career paths.

P14: Decreases in number of dependent children to support will be associated with primary wage-earners' switching into less demanding career paths.

Changes in child-rearing responsibilities are not the only alterations in family circumstances which influence the likelihood of switching careers; divorce and separation also impact those changes. As Propositions 15 and 16 suggest, the types of career changes secondary wage-earners pursue after a divorce will be different than the changes faced by primary wage-earners (Becker, 1981; Gray, 1998).

For secondary wage-earners, divorce or separation will often necessitate switching into careers which are more highly skilled and which pay more money (Proposition 15). Previous research suggests that when couples divorce, the secondary wage-earner experiences a greater loss in standard of living than the primary wage-earner. Moreover, after dependent children turn 18, the secondary wage-earner will no longer automatically collect child support payments; the amount of "rehabilitative alimony" may decline after this point as well. Subsequently, middle-aged, divorced individuals who are secondary wage-earners have greater incentives to switch into careers which afford them a higher standard of living.

In contrast, for most primary wage-earners, divorce means considerable financial responsibility for supporting the ex-spouse and dependent children. At least in the short run, then, the divorced primary wage-earner has to support two households. In contrast to secondary wage-earners, then, primary wage-earners getting divorced should be less likely to switch careers (Proposition 16). The financial demands on them are already heavy and the risks of switching careers may be too great for them to undertake at this juncture.

P15:   Divorce will be positively associated with secondary wage-earners' switching into career paths requiring higher skills.

P16:   Divorce will be negatively associated with primary wage-earners' switching occupations in mid-career.

Late-career stage

In late career, individuals have both greater opportunities and greater constraints on their abilities to change careers. On one hand, older workers may have accrued suffi-cient financial resources to afford to take a cut in pay or absorb transaction costs associated with switching occupations. On the other hand, because of their age, older workers may have less energy for changing careers or see less point in doing so (Feldman, 1994). In this section, the following factors are considered as important influences on the degree of career change among older workers: health, wealth, in-volvement in outside hobbies and leisure pursuits, and tenure in the occupation and organization.

Health.   Health has a major impact on the extent to which older workers remain fully involved in the workforce. As individuals age, they are more likely to suffer from chronic health problems (such as arthritis and high blood pressure) and acute health problems (such as heart disease and cancer) which make continued participa-tion in their present occupations more difficult (Anderson and Burkhauser, 1985). While previous research has focused on health as a major predictor of the decision to retire (e.g., Colsher, Dorfman, and Wallace, 1988), here our focus is on health as a predictor of the decision to change careers instead.

Propositions 17 and 18 highlight two ways in which older workers' health is likely to influence the probability of switching occupations. Proposition 17 suggests that the poorer an individual's health, the more likely he/she is to switch into careers which are less physically demanding. Thus, one construction worker may switch into building supply sales as he develops arthritis which makes heavy lifting more diffi-cult, while another without any major health problems may continue in construction well into his sixties.

In a similar vein, Proposition 18 suggests that the fewer the physical demands of a job, the less likely an individual will be to switch occupations in late career. For instance, there are relatively few physical demands in being a professor, a lawyer, or an author. Consequently, age-related health problems are less likely to force individuals out of these occupations. In contrast, the physical demands of being a professional ball player or dancer make career changes in late career much more likely. The speed, coordination, and strength needed for these careers decline with age, and in time, older individuals are unable to compete with younger colleagues on these dimensions.

> **P17:** The poorer an individual's health, the more likely he/she is to switch careers to a less physically demanding occupation in late career.
>
> **P18:** The fewer the physical demands of work, the less likely an individual will be to switch occupations in late career.

Wealth.   Older workers' financial resources also make career changes more possible. As Proposition 19 suggests, savings, pensions, and inheritances enable late-career individuals to enter occupations they find more attractive without having to worry about financial considerations (Kim and Feldman, 1998, 2000). In many cases, these late-career changes are impelled by burnout and boredom. After years and years in the same occupation, older workers who have accumulated wealth are now freer to walk away from occupations in which they no longer have much interest.

> **P19:** The greater the household wealth, the more likely individuals are to switch occupations in late career.

Involvement in outside interests.   Another set of late-career individuals may switch occupations to pursue some activity they have been nurturing as a hobby or a leisure activity over a period of several years (Gratton and Haug, 1983; Hornstein and Wapner, 1985). For example, Kim and Feldman (2000) cite several instances of older workers turning long-time avocations into income-producing vocations in late career: a passion for horses turned into a horse-training enterprise; a long-standing hobby of growing grapes into a viticulture farm; a long-term interest in playing the stock market channelled into a career as a financial advisor. As Proposition 20 suggests, then, long-standing involvement in hobbies and leisure pursuits is likely to be associated with changes in late career as well.

> **P20:** The greater an individual's long-standing involvement in hobbies and leisure pursuits, the more likely an individual is to switch occupations in late career.

<u>Occupational and organizational tenure.</u>   Finally, Propositions 21 and 22 suggest that both occupational and organizational tenure will be inversely related to the likelihood of switching occupations in late career. Primarily, the longer individuals have been in one occupation or organization, the more disruptive any late-career change is likely to be. For example, Atchley's (1989) "theory of continuity" suggests that the longer an individual has been attached to one occupation, the more disruptive changing careers will be and the less likely it is that he/she will do so.

In addition, there are often substantial financial rewards associated with long-time tenure in one organization in terms of pension benefits, extended health coverage, and so on. Consequently, the costs of switching careers are higher for individuals with long organizational tenure than they are for individuals with short organizational tenure (Gustman and Steinmeier, 1991; Ruhm, 1989). Furthermore, long-time tenure in an occupation or an organization appears to be correlated with excellent performance and/or high professional involvement in the present career path (Kim and Feldman, 1998). In other words, older workers who have been in one occupation or one organization a long time may be particularly good at their jobs and/or particularly like them. For these older workers, then, there is neither a push nor a pull to switch career trajectories late in life.

P21:   The longer an individual's tenure in his/her present occupation, the less likely he/she is to switch occupations in late career.

P22:   The longer an individual's organizational tenure, the less likely he/she is to switch occupations in late career.

● Directions for Future Research ●

In this final section, we briefly consider some overall directions for future research on second careers and multiple careers. Here, we focus on four issues in particular: (1) the conceptual refinement of the construct of career change; (2) the identification of predictors of successful career changes; (3) the integration of additional social science theories into research on career changes; and (4) methodological considerations in future empirical research on multiple careers.

Concept of career change

As noted earlier in the chapter, the concept of "career change" has itself been somewhat ambiguous. While the concept of career change can be reasonably distinguished from job change, organization change, and turnover, its distinctiveness from retirement and reorientation within career need further elaboration.

It is not unusual for older workers to start transitioning out of highly intensive careers into less stressful career paths as they age. However, whether these transitions are the early stages of retirement or the beginnings of truly new careers is not

SECOND CAREERS AND MULTIPLE CAREERS

always clear. The distinction is even more blurry when these transitions occur when individuals are in their fifties; is the "new" career simply a form of bridge employ-ment or an entirely different career path with long-term potential? Career issues among older workers, in general, have received considerably less research than career issues facing the young. However, given the increasing longevity of older workers, career changes among 50- and 60-year-olds warrant much closer attention in the years ahead.

The distinction between career changes and changing paths within a career also needs further clarification. This chapter suggests that Schein's (1978) notion of "career anchors" might be a useful avenue for framing future research on this topic. Another potentially fruitful framework for future research on this topic is Feldman and Bolino's (1997) octagonal model of Schein's career anchors, in which career anchors are arrayed in proximity (and distance) to each other on the basis of similar-ity (or dissimilarity) of work demands.

The degree of career change, then, might be able to be conceptualized in terms of degree of distance between career anchors. Thus, the shift from a career anchor of entrepreneurship to one of security and stability might be considered a major career change, since these two anchors are maximally distant from each other in terms of work content and work context. In contrast, the shift from a security and stability anchor to a lifestyle anchor might not be considered a major career change, since there is considerable similarity in the work demands and work environments of these two anchors (Feldman and Bolino, 1997).

Predictors of successful career changes

Somewhat surprisingly, there has been little research on how successful career changes are, either in terms of performance in the new career path or perseverance and lon-gevity in them. Here we suggest that identifying predictors of successful career changes is a particularly important avenue for future research in this area. The factors which appear to be most likely to predict performance and longevity in new careers are individual differences, the nature of the career change process, and the amount of emotional support career changers receive from family and friends.

For instance, previous research on individual differences suggests that personality traits and personal styles may impact how successfully people make the transition from one career to another. Of the "Big 5" personality traits frequently studied in the organizational sciences (Digman, 1989), the two which may be most critical in this regard are extraversion and openness to new experience.

Making a major change in one's career requires a good deal of initiative, seeking out of new information, and networking. Moreover, making a successful career tran-sition often requires individuals to develop personal connections with new colleagues, supervisors, and clients. In general, then, extraversion would facilitate both the "break-ing in" and "settling in" to new careers. Similarly, a major career change often is accompanied by a great deal of uncertainty, ambiguity, and ambivalence. The greater an individual's openness to new experience, the more likely he/she will be to cope effectively with change, master new environments, and persevere in the face of initial adversity.

In terms of characteristics of the transition itself, the opportunity to make the transition into the new career path incrementally may considerably enhance the like- lihood of the career change being successful (Doeringer, 1990; Kim and Feldman, 2000). Since there is a learning curve in entering any new career path, making the transition gradually may allow career changers to master the basic job duties more fully before entering the new occupation full-time. Also, making the transition gradu- ally allows individuals to establish their earning power in the new occupation before having to give up their income from their prior occupation.

Another critical factor which clearly warrants future research attention in this area is whether career changes are made voluntarily by individuals or whether career changes are forced on individuals by external circumstances. For example, if a 30-year-old steelworker gets laid off and there are no longer many jobs in the indus- try, he/she may have to find new employment quickly simply to generate income. Moreover, this sudden need to find an alternative career path decreases both the amount of time individuals have to research new careers and the likelihood they will find new careers which appropriately use their skills and abilities (Feldman, Leana, and Bolino, 2000).

Finally here, changing careers can be an anxiety-arousing and emotionally exhaust- ing experience. Both the decision to change careers and the emotional energy which these transitions demand often create turmoil for the career changers themselves and for family members and friends in the individual's network (Nicholson, 1984). Thus, in predicting success of career changes, the amount of social and emotional support received from parents, spouses, and friends during these difficult periods may play a critical role.

Theoretical perspectives on career changes

Most of the previous research on career transitions has, implicitly or explicitly, relied heavily on expectancy-valence theory, need theory, and stress theory to examine these phenomena. Expectancy-valence theory (cf. Vroom, 1964) suggests that individuals' work decisions are driven by their calculation of the probability of obtaining higher rewards in alternative situations and the value of those rewards to them. Similarly, need theory (cf. Alderfer and Guzzo, 1979) suggests that individuals are driven to change careers when their current occupations no longer fulfill their most important needs. Research on career transitions using the stress paradigm (e.g., Nicholson, 1984) suggests that individuals' difficulty in making career changes is largely attributable to the degree of uncertainty associated with those transitions and the adverse emotional and physiological reactions associated with that uncertainty. Indeed, many of the propositions above are implicitly justified using these theoretical approaches. While there are several additional theoretical perspectives which might be usefully applied to understanding career changes, there are two paradigms, in particular, which might be of interest in this area.

Analogous to cybernetic control theory, behavioral control theory postulates that receipt of discrepant feedback about role performance can cause individuals to reassess and modify their behaviors (cf. Klein, 1989). Control theory might be particularly helpful in understanding which changes in the work environment or one's personal life cue individuals to change careers. In addition, control theory provides interesting insights on how changes in individuals' personal lives affect their decisions to change careers as well. For example, control theory suggests that the boundaries between work and personal life domains are often asymmetrically permeable; that is, the demands of work tend to intrude on the personal domain more than vice versa (Frone, Russell, and Cooper, 1992).

Another potentially useful theoretical perspective here is "family power theory" (cf. Eby et al., 1999; Stephens and Feldman, 1997). One of the most difficult areas to untangle in the research on career changes is the role that gender, marital status, family status, and family income play in those decisions. Rather than consider these variables in isolation, family power theory suggests that partners in a marriage or a relationship have control over career decisions to the extent they make the majority of the household income and have the fewest responsibilities in the household. Thus, women's constraints on changing careers may be attributable to their *relative*, rather than their absolute, earning power and share of child-rearing responsibilities. Family power theory, then, suggests that the traditional focus on career decisions on the part of *one* individual are bound to fail because they do not simultaneously consider the career decisions of others in the family network.

Empirical research on career change

Finally, it is important to note here that descriptive and prescriptive work on career changes has far outpaced empirical research on the topic. Moreover, the empirical research which has been conducted on this topic has had considerable methodological limitations. In future empirical research on this topic, three key issues, in particular, need to be more thoughtfully addressed.

First, much more diverse sampling is needed, both across career stages and across occupations. As the propositions above highlight, the reasons that individuals change careers vary dramatically over the life cycle. Thus, examining career change among only one group of workers (for example, among mid-career males) misses many of the most important dynamics of these transitions.

Equally important, there are many labor market factors which play important roles in determining the likelihood of career change and success in second careers: difficulties of getting retrained, opportunities for part-time participation in the current career, human capital investment in the present career, and the amount of capital investment needed to start a new career. Again, to capture the richness of the career change phenomenon, much broader sampling across initial occupations is needed.

Second, like much organizational science research, the research on career changes is largely self-report and cross-sectional in nature. Certainly, the simultaneous collection of archival data with self-report data – along with longitudinal designs – would give greater confidence in causal inferences in this research area.

Even if these design changes cannot be fully implemented, it is especially critical to examine social desirability response bias (Muller and Boaz, 1988) in this research stream. As some of the research on early retirement suggests, for example, older individuals may give poor health as a reason for taking bridge employment rather than acknowledging declining performance. The fundamental attribution error (Kelly, 1973) would suggest that there is a basic tendency to externalize the factors in one's failure in the current situation. Consequently, it is particularly critical to observe this rating bias, among others, in conducting future research on second careers and multiple careers.

Last, the research on career change in the economics literature and the research on career change in the organizational sciences literature have been largely separate and distinct. That is, researchers in economics have used large archival databases to explain *post hoc* why individuals did change occupations (Albrecht et al., 1999), while researchers in organizational behavior have used small-scale, self-report surveys to explain why individuals might change occupations in the future (Eby et al., 1999). Economics researchers have relied almost exclusively on demographic and financial data in examining this topic, while organizational behavior researchers have relied almost exclusively on the perceptions and emotional reactions of individuals to their job situations. The integration of economic and behavioral perspectives on career change, then, might not only improve the methodological rigor of research on this topic, but its theoretical sophistication as well.

REFERENCES

Albrecht, J.W., Edin, P.A., Sundstrom, M., and Vroman, S.B. (1999). Career interruptions and subsequent earnings: A reexamination using Swedish data. *Journal of Human Resources*, 34, 294–311.

Alderfer, C.P., and Guzzo, R.A. (1979). Life experiences and adults' enduring strength of desires in organizations. *Administrative Science Quarterly*, 24, 347–61.

Anderson, K.H., and Burkhauser, R.V. (1985). The retirement–health nexus: A new measure for an old puzzle. *Journal of Human Resources*, 20, 315–30.

Arthur, M.B., and Rousseau, D.M. (1996). *The Boundaryless Career: A New Employment Principle for a New Organizational Era*. New York: Oxford University Press.

Atchley, R. (1989). A continuity theory of aging. *Gerontologist*, 29, 183–90.

Becker, G.S. (1981). *A Treatise on the Family*. Cambridge, MA: Harvard University Press.

Booth, A.L., Francesconi, M., and Garcia-Serrano, C. (1999). Job tenure and job mobility in Britain. *Industrial and Labor Relations Review*, 53, 43–70.

Colsher, P.L., Dorfman, L.T., and Wallace, R.B. (1988). Specific health conditions and work–retirement status among the elderly. *Journal of Applied Gerontology*, 7, 485–503.

Digman, J.M. (1989). Five robust trait dimensions: Development, stability, and utility. *Journal of Personality*, 57, 195–214.

Doeringer, P.B. (1990). *Bridges to Retirement*. Ithaca, NY: Cornell University ILR Press.

Dunkin, A. 1996. Franchising: A recipe for your second career? *Business Week*, March 4, 128–9.

Eby, L.T., Allen, T.D., and Douthitt, S.S. (1999). The role of nonperformance factors on job-related relocation opportunities: A field study and laboratory experiment. *Organizational Behavior and Human Decision Processes*, 79, 29–55.

Feldman, D.C. (1988). *Managing Careers in Organizations*. Glenview, ILL: Scott Foresman.

Feldman, D.C. (1994). The decision to retire early: A review and conceptualization. *Academy of Management Review*, 19, 285–311.

Feldman, D.C. (1995). The impact of downsizing on organizational career development activities and employee career development opportunities. *Human Resource Management Review*, 5, 189–221.

Feldman, D.C. (1996). The nature, antecedents, and consequences of underemployment. *Journal of Management*, 22, 385–409.

Feldman, D.C., and Bolino, M.C. (1997). Careers within careers: Reconceptualizing the nature of career anchors and their consequences. *Human Resource Management Review*, 6, 89–112.

Feldman, D.C., Leana, C.R., and Bolino, M.C. (2000). Underemployment among downsized executives: Tests of structural equation models. Under editorial review.

Feldman, D.C., and Turnley, W.H. (1995). Underemployment among recent college graduates. *Journal of Organizational Behavior*, 16, 691–706.

Feldman, D.C., and Weitz, B.A. (1988). Career plateaus reconsidered. *Journal of Management*, 14, 69–80.

Ference, T.P., Stoner, J.A.F, and Warren, E.K. (1977). Managing the career plateau. *Academy of Management Review*, 2, 602–12.

Freeman, B., and Schopen, A. (1992). Does the early bird get the worm? An analysis of academic success, early placement preparation, and hiring. *Journal of Employment Counseling*, 29, 183–90.

Frone, M.R., Russell, M., and Cooper, M.L. (1992). Prevalence of work-family conflict: Are work and family boundaries asymmetrically permeable? *Journal of Organizational Behavior*, 13, 723–9.

Gallos, J.V. (1989). Exploring women's development: Implications for career theory, practices, and research. In M.B. Arthur, D.T. Hall, and B.A. Lawrence (eds). *Handbook of Career Theory*. Cambridge, UK: Cambridge University Press, pp. 110–32.

Gould, R. (1978). *Transformations: Growth and Change in Adult Life*. New York: Simon & Schuster.

Gratton, B., and Haug, M.R. (1983). Decision and adaptation. *Research on Aging*, 5, 59–76.

Gray, J.S. (1998). Divorce-law changes, household bargaining, and married women's labor supply. *American Economic Review*, 88, 628–42.

Gustman, A.L., and Steinmeier, T.L. (1991). The effects of pensions and retirement policies on retirement in higher education. *American Economic Review*, 81, 111–15.

Hall, D.T. (1976). *Careers in Organizations*. Pacific Palisades, CA: Goodyear Publishing.

Hermans, H.J.M., and Oles, P.K. (1999). Midlife crisis in men: Affective organization of personal meanings. *Human Relations*, 52, 1403–26.

Holzer, H.J. (1987). Job search by employed and unemployed youth. *Industrial and Labor Relations Review*, 40, 601–11.

Hornstein, G.A., and Wapner, S. (1985). Modes of experiencing and adapting to retirement. *International Journal of Aging and Human Development*, 21, 291–315.

Kelly, H.H. (1973). The process of causal attribution. *American Psychologist*, 28, 105–20.

Kim, S., and Feldman, D.C. (1998). Healthy, wealthy, or wise: Predicting actual acceptances of early retirement incentives at three points in time. *Personnel Psychology*, 51, 623–42.

Kim, S., and Feldman, D.C. (2000). Working in "retirement": The antecedents of bridge employment and its consequences for quality of life in retirement. *Academy of Management Journal*, forthcoming.

Klein, H.J. (1989). An integrated control theory model of work motivation. *Academy of Management Review*, 14, 150–72.

Kruger, A. (1994). The midlife transition: Crisis or chimera? *Psychological Reports*, 75, 1299–305.

Leana, C.R., and Feldman, D.C. (1995). Finding new jobs after a plant closing: Antecedents and outcomes of the occurrence and quality of reemployment. *Human Relations*, 48, 1381–401.

Levinson, D.J. (1978). *The Seasons of a Man's Life*. New York: Knopf.

Monks, J., and Pizer, S.D. (1998). Trends in voluntary and involuntary job turnover. *Industrial Relations*, 37, 440–59.

Muller, C.F., and Boaz, R.F. (1988). Health as a reason or a rationalization for being retired? *Research on Aging*, 10, 37–55.

Neal, D. (1999). The complexity of job mobility among young men. *Journal of Labor Economics*, 17, (237–61).

Nicholson, N. (1984). A theory of work role transitions. *Administrative Science Quarterly*, 29, 172–91.

Powell, G.N., and Mainiero, L.A. (1992). Cross-currents in the river of time: Conceptualizing the complexities of women's careers. *Journal of Management*, 18, 215–37.

Rousseau, D.M. (1990). New hire perceptions of their own and their employer's obligations: A study of psychological contracts. *Journal of Organizational Behavior*, 11, 389–400.

Ruhm, C.J. (1989). Why older workers stop working. *Gerontologist*, 29, 294–99.

Sagen, H.B., Dallam, J.W., and Laverty, J.R. (1999). Job search techniques as employment channels: Differential effects on the initial employment success of college graduates. *Career Development Quarterly*, 48, 74–85.

Schein, E.H. (1978). *Career Dynamics: Matching Individual and Organizational Needs*. Reading, MA: Addison-Wesley.

Schneer, J.A., and Reitman, F. (1993). Effects of alternative family structures on managerial career paths. *Academy of Management Journal*, 36, 830–43.

Schwab, D.P., Rynes, S.L., and Aldag, R.J. (1987). Theories and research on job search and choice. *Research in Personnel and Human Resources Management*, 5, 129–66.

Steffy, B.D., Shaw, K.N., and Noe, A.W. (1989). Antecedents and consequences of job search behaviors. *Journal of Vocational Behavior*, 35, 254–69.

Stephens, G.K., and Feldman, D.C. (1997). A motivational approach for understanding career versus personal life investments. *Research in Personnel and Human Resources Management*, 15, 333–77.

Sterrett, E.A. (1999). A comparison of women's and men's career transitions. *Journal of Career Development*, 25, 249–59.

Valliant, G. (1977). *Adaptation to Life*. Boston: Little, Brown.

Veiga, J.F. (1983). Mobility influences during managerial career stages. *Academy of Management Journal*, 26, 64–85.

Vroom, V.H. (1964). *Work and Motivation*. New York: Wiley.

Vuori, J., and Vesalainen, J. (1999). Labour market interventions as predictors of re-employment, job seeking activity, and psychological distress among the unemployed. *Journal of Occupational and Organizational Psychology*, 72, 523–38.

Waddoups, J., and Assane, D. (1993). Mobility and gender in a segmented labor market: A closer look. *American Journal of Economics and Sociology*, 52, 398–412.

Wanous, J.P. (1980). *Organizational entry*. Reading, MA: Addison-Wesley.

5

The Impact of Family Life on Career Decisions and Outcomes

ROMILA SINGH, JEFFREY H. GREENHAUS, AND
SAROJ PARASURAMAN

The work–family interface has been studied extensively over the past twenty-five years, primarily because of the growing representation of dual-earner partners and single parents in the workforce. Strongly dominated by a conflict perspective (Greenhaus and Parasuraman, 1999), the work–family literature has historically emphasized the effects of work on family life. However, the recent distinction between work-to-family conflict and family-to-work conflict has demonstrated that the interference between work and family lives can go in both directions (Frone, Yardley, and Markel, 1997). Nevertheless, role interference represents only a partial view of the varied ways in which individuals' family experiences may influence their careers. Despite a growing recognition of the influence of family life on work and career, there is a need to systematically review this growing literature.

It is also important to place the family–work research in a larger theoretical context. Although many mechanisms – such as spillover, accommodation, and compensation – have been proposed to explain the relationship between work and family roles, the usefulness of these processes to explain the impact of family on work life needs further attention. Moreover, the persistent differences between men and women regarding participation in – and involvement with – work and family activities (Friedman and Greenhaus, 2000) requires a careful scrutiny of the role of gender in family–work relationships.

Therefore, the purpose of this chapter is to examine the research on the career-related consequences of family life. First, we review the evidence linking multiple indicators of family life to a variety of career decisions and outcomes. Then, we attempt to relate the findings to theoretical perspectives and mechanisms on work–family relationships. Finally, we suggest areas for future research that can advance our understanding of the impact of family experiences on careers.

We identified the following five dimensions of family life to organize the review of the literature:

- *Marriage and spouse*
- *Dependent care*, which primarily includes responsibility for children but also includes responsibility for elders.
- *Family involvement*, which has two indicators: behavioral (time) involvement in family activities and psychological or emotional involvement in the family role (Friedman and Greenhaus, 2000).
- *Family resources*, the most prominent of which is the social support provided by family members.
- *Family role quality*, including family satisfaction and stress experienced within the family role.

These five dimensions of family life were then related to the following career decisions and outcomes:

- *Career role selection*, including occupational choice and job choice.
- *Career involvement*, including behavioral (time) involvement in work and psychological involvement in work.
- *Career development opportunities* such as training, developmental assignments, and coaching.
- *Career success* defined objectively in terms of income and advancement and subjectively in terms of career satisfaction.
- *Career withdrawal*, including organizational and professional turnover and retirement.

● Marriage and Spouse ●

Career role selection

There is some evidence that marriage constrains the career choices of women. It has been observed that married women are more likely than unmarried women to hold low-status and part-time jobs (Drobnic, Blossfeld, and Rohwer, 1999), and that marriage may inhibit women's attainment of upper management positions (Parasuraman and Greenhaus, 1993). There is little indication that marital status affects men's choice of occupations and jobs.

A spouse's employment may have a greater impact than marital status on the selection of career roles, especially those that involve relocations. Several studies of dual-earner couples have shown that women are more likely than men to be the "trailing spouse" (Bielby and Bielby, 1992; Brett, Stroh, and Reilly, 1999; Gill and Haurin, 1998). Thus, women's choices for part-time employment or low-status jobs may partly be in response to the frequent job interruptions and transitions they go through as a result of their partner's transfers (Bielby and Bielby, 1992; Gill and Haurin, 1998).

Work involvement

There is little research on the effects of marriage on the work involvement of employees. More prominent have been studies on the impact of a spouse's employment status on an individual's work involvement. Several studies have reported that dual-earner men have lower job involvement than single-earner men (Brett et al., 1992; Friedman and Greenhaus, 2000; Parasuraman, Greenhaus, Rabinowitz, Bedeian, and Mossholder, 1989). Parallel analyses among women have generally not been conducted because of the relatively small number of women with stay-at-home partners.

Researchers have suggested other mechanisms by which a spouse can influence an employee's work involvement. For example, it has been observed that women's work hours might be affected by their husbands' approval of their employment (Parasuraman and Greenhaus, 1993) as well as the extent to which the husband identifies with the family (Greenhaus and Parasuraman, in press). Further, husbands' work involvement and career priority have a negative effect on their wives' work involvement and priority, whereas husbands' family involvement contributes positively to the priority of their wives' careers (Hammer, Allen, and Grigsby, 1997).

Career development opportunities

Although several studies have revealed no relationship between marriage and the availability of various career development opportunities (Dreher and Ash, 1990; Parasuraman, Singh, and Greenhaus, 1997; Shenhav, 1992; Whitely, Dougherty, and Dreher, 1991), there is limited evidence that marriage can enhance a man's exposure to career-building experiences. Friedman and Greenhaus (2000) observed that married men – but not married women – experienced a "family bonus" in that married men had more autonomy in their jobs (a key ingredient of career growth) than unmarried men. Consistent with this observation was the finding by Eby, Allen, and Douthitt (1999) that married men received higher recommendation ratings for jobs that required relocation as well as a greater number of relocation offers than equally qualified married women.

Moreover, marriage may have an indirect negative influence on the availability of career development opportunities for women because marriage may affect women's representation in certain occupations, functions, and jobs that have limited opportunity structures (Stroh and Reilly, 1999). Although it is not clear whether women are selected out of certain functional areas by organizational power structures or whether they select themselves out of these jobs, positions that are associated with greater opportunities for development, career achievement, and compensation are less likely to be held by women (Herz and Wootton, 1996; Stroh and Reilly, 1999).

Career success

Income.   With some exceptions (Aryee, Chay, and Tan, 1994; Dreher and Ash, 1990; Whitely et al., 1991), the research generally indicates that married employees have higher incomes than unmarried employees (Bretz and Judge, 1994; Judge, Cable, Boudreau, and Bretz, 1995; Korenman and Neumark, 1991; Landau and Arthur, 1992). Nevertheless, the linkage between marital status and income seems more consistent for men than for women. A number of studies that revealed positive effects of marriage on men's income observed either no effect on women's income (Cooney and Uhlenberg, 1991; Landau and Arthur, 1992; Friedman and Greenhaus, 2000) or a negative effect (Bellas, 1992; Jacobs, 1992; Melamed, 1996; Spitze and Loscocco, 1999; Waite, 1995).

Advancement. Although marriage has been associated with high salaries – especially for men – the evidence linking marriage to hierarchical advancement is less convincing. In fact, most of the research has observed no relationship between marital status and advancement (Aryee et al., 1994; Dreher and Ash, 1990; Judge et al., 1995; Korenman and Neumark, 1991; Melamed, 1996; Shenhav, 1992; Tharenou and Conroy, 1994; Whitely et al., 1991). One study observed a positive effect of marriage on advancement in a primarily male sample (Bretz and Judge, 1994), which is consistent with the finding that marriage enhances the advancement of men but not women (Friedman and Greenhaus, 2000; Schneer and Reitman, 1993).

It is possible that the impact of marriage on women's career advancement occurs in a subtle manner. Spousal attainments may either facilitate or impede the other partner's career achievements and outcomes. For example, Philliber and Vannoy-Hiller (1990) found that husbands' career attainments tended to act as a ceiling on their wives' career achievements especially when husbands and wives subscribed to traditional gender role attitudes.

Satisfaction. There is little research that has examined the effect of marriage on career satisfaction, the subjective component of career success. Friedman and Greenhaus (2000) found that married men were more satisfied with their careers than unmarried men, which was attributed to the higher level of job autonomy reported by married men. They also observed that marriage neither helped nor hindered the career satisfaction of women. With the exception of one study that found married people were more satisfied with their jobs than unmarried people (Judge and Bretz, 1994), a majority of the studies observed no effect of marital status on different subjective dimensions of career success such as career satisfaction and perceived career success (Aryee et al., 1994; Brett et al., 1992; Bretz and Judge, 1994; Judge et al., 1995; Kirchmeyer, 1998; Seibert, Crant, and Kraimer, 1999).

Career withdrawal

The majority of studies have reported no relationship between marital status and turnover intentions (e.g., Rosin and Korabik, 1995; Stroh, Brett, and Reilly, 1996) and absenteeism (Erickson, Nichols, and Ritter, 2000), although lateness may be more prevalent among married than unmarried employees (Blau, 1994). Very little research has examined the influence of family variables on retirement decisions, another form of withdrawal from work. Two studies (Beehr, Glazer, Nielson, and Farmer,

2000; Reitzes, Mutran, and Fernandez, 1998) found no impact of marital status on retirement decisions, although they did observe that having an employed spouse decreased the likelihood of retirement.

Summary

Being married has been shown to be associated with a variety of career-related decisions, although the relationships have been far from consistent. The research suggests that the positive effects of marriage on exposure to career development opportunities, income, and career advancement may be more pronounced for men than women. Conversely, the constraining effects of marriage – on the selection of a career role and on financial rewards – seem more prevalent among women than men. The literature also suggests that spousal employment and attitudes influence a variety of career decisions.

● Dependent Care ●

Career role selection

There is mixed support for the view that mothers limit their job choices to positions that help them cope with their childcare responsibilities. Glass and Camarigg (1992) did not confirm their expectation that full-time employed mothers would select jobs that are compatible with family responsibilities, i.e., jobs that required less effort and that provided greater flexibility. On the other hand, parents have a stronger preference for workplaces that offer greater flexibility and family-supportive cultures than do non-parents (Grover and Crooker, 1995). In addition, women with young children are more likely to be self-employed than those with older children (Connelly, 1992), although Gerson (1993) reported that many highly involved fathers turned toward self-employment for the same reasons: to gain flexibility in time in order to balance their work and family lives.

Work involvement

With the exception of two studies that did not find any relationship between increased parental demands and time spent at work (Parasuraman, Purohit, Godshalk, and Beutell, 1996; Parasuraman et al., 1997), researchers have consistently reported that employees with children work fewer hours a week than those with no children (Brett et al., 1992; Eagle, Icenogle, Marjorie, and Maes, 1998; Gutek, Searle, and Klepa, 1991; Wallace, 1997). Moreover, these effects are more pronounced for women than for men (Friedman and Greenhaus, 2000; Greenberger and O'Neil, 1993; Singh, Greenhaus, Collins, and Parasuraman, 1998). Further, women with pre-school-aged children are more likely to choose part-time employment than women with school-aged children (Drobnic et al., 1999; Herz and Wootton, 1996), even when they have a high status and demanding career of their own (Grant, Simpson, Rong, and Peters-Golden, 1990). Other researchers also reported that mothers are more likely than fathers to adjust their work schedules that may often result in reduced time at work (Galinsky and Bond, 1996; Karambayya and Reilly, 1992).

Another characteristic of family life that affects time involvement in work is the responsibility for elderly parents, spouses, and other relatives. People with existing or potential care-giving responsibilities are likely to cut back on their work hours, rearrange their work schedules, turn down relocation opportunities, and take unpaid leave (Feldman and Bolino, 1998; Galinsky, Bond, and Friedman, 1993; Thyen, Kuhlthau, and Perrin, 1999). It has been suggested that although care-giving can be juggled with regular employment hours, when it becomes very demanding, it results in a reduction of work hours and sometimes complete withdrawal from the workforce (Ettner, 1995).

Research on the effect of childcare responsibilities on psychological involvement in work has produced mixed results. Some studies reported no impact of number of children on career involvement or effort expended at work (Lambert, 1991; Lobel and St. Clair, 1992), whereas one study indicated that women with young children were less psychologically involved in their careers than women with lesser parental demands (Friedman and Greenhaus, 2000).

Career development opportunities

Extensive home and childcare responsibilities have been found to have a negative impact on career development opportunities for women but not men (Friedman and Greenhaus, 2000). It has also been observed that mothers are less geographically mobile in their jobs than fathers (Bielby and Bielby, 1992; Shauman and Xie, 1996). It is possible that some mothers of young children turn down these opportunities because of an anticipated increase in responsibilities, time demands, and pressures. It is also possible that some organizations may not be willing to invest in a group of employees whom they view as being more involved with responsibilities outside of organizational work.

It should not be assumed, however, that men's developmental opportunities are unaffected by the presence of children. Becker and Moen (1999) found that one-third of the dual-career fathers in their sample chose work that was less demanding and also turned down work that involved either substantial travel or relocation. Moreover, studies on relocations (Brett et al., 1992; Shauman and Xie, 1996) found that dual-career male managers with children were more likely than their single-earner counterparts to turn down jobs that required them to relocate.

Career success

Income. Most of the studies reviewed found that income was not affected by parental responsibilities (Bretz and Judge, 1994; Cannings, 1991; Jacobs, 1992; Rosin and Korabik, 1995; Lobel and St. Clair, 1992). Some studies found that the impact of children on income was positive only for men (Friedman and Greenhaus, 2000; Landau and Arthur, 1992). However, this earnings advantage experienced by fathers may be limited to single-earner fathers, who earn more than fathers with employed wives (Brett et al., 1992; Friedman and Greenhaus, 2000; Landau and Arthur, 1992; Schneer and Reitman, 1993).

The impact of children on women's income is mixed. Several studies found that mothers earned less money than women without children (Friedman and Greenhaus, 2000; Jacobs, 1992). However, these findings are clouded by other studies revealing that dual-earner mothers earned as much as other married women and more than unmarried women (Brett et al., 1992; Landau and Arthur, 1992; Schneer and Reitman, 1993, 1995).

Advancement. The impact of children on career advancement seems quite limited. Although Bretz and Judge (1994) observed a positive relationship between number of children and advancement, most of the research has shown no relationship between parental responsibilities and advancement (Aryee et al., 1994; Friedman and Greenhaus, 2000; Kirchmeyer, 1998; Konrad and Cannings, 1997; Melamed, 1996; Shenhav, 1992; Tharenou and Conroy, 1994).

Satisfaction. Most of the research has shown no relationship between parental responsibilities and career satisfaction (Aryee et al., 1994; Bretz and Judge, 1994; Judge et al., 1995; Kirchmeyer, 1998; Lambert, 1991). One exception was the study by Friedman and Greenhaus (2000), which found fathers were more satisfied with their careers than men without children, whereas mothers were less satisfied with their careers than women without children.

Career withdrawal

The impact of family life on withdrawal has been widely studied and has produced mixed results. For example, the presence of children has been found to influence women's decisions to interrupt their careers (Tharenou, 1999), and to leave paid jobs and seek self-employment (Boden, 1999; Carr, 1996). Others also found that the heavy demands placed by pre-school-aged children forced some women to quit employment (Drobnic et al., 1999; Rosin and Korabik, 1990). However, a number of other studies demonstrated that the reasons for withdrawal were the same for both genders, with lack of career opportunities the most important reason why men and women managers quit their jobs or professions (Greenhaus, Collins, Singh, and Parasuraman, 1997; Rosin and Korabik, 1995; Stroh et al., 1996).

The impact of other care-giving responsibilities on turnover decisions has been infrequently investigated. The findings suggest that men and women (but more women than men) are likely to quit work to care for young, ill, or elderly family members (Barker, 1993; Galinsky et al., 1993; Thyen et al., 1999).

Only a handful of studies examined the role of childcare or elder-care responsibilities on other types of withdrawal, and they indicate the importance of gender in these relationships. Mothers are more likely than fathers to miss work, come in late, leave work early, and devote work time to family matters (Blau, 1994; Galinsky and Bond, 1996; Erickson et al., 2000; Greenberger and O'Neil, 1993).

Even though care-giving responsibilities have been suggested to play a role in retirement decisions, it is difficult to draw firm conclusions from the limited research. Nevertheless, the two studies we identified suggested that care-giving responsibilities were positively related to the likelihood of retirement (Beehr et al., 2000; Reitzes et al., 1998).

Summary

Employees who have extensive demands for care-taking may limit their behavioral and psychological involvement in work, experience restricted opportunities for career growth, and may possibly withdraw from overly demanding work environments. Although these effects can occur for men and women, there is some evidence that women's careers are more likely than men's careers to be constrained by dependent care responsibilities.

● Family Involvement ●

In the previous sections, we discussed the impact of structural aspects of family life such as marriage, spousal characteristics, and responsibilities for dependents on career decisions and outcomes. In this section, we examine how behavioral and psychological involvement with family life influences one's career.

Career role selection

We found virtually no research regarding the impact of family involvement on the types of careers, jobs, and occupations that people select. In one study relevant to this issue, Friedman and Greenhaus (2000) found that business professionals who are psychologically and behaviorally focussed on their family lives had considerably lower aspirations for senior management and CEO positions than those who were either career-focussed or career- and family-focussed.

Work involvement

A high level of involvement in one role is often associated with a lower level of involvement with another role (Greenhaus and Parasuraman, 1999). A handful of studies that examined the relationships between time spent in family activities and the number of hours worked found an inverse relationship between the amount of time devoted to each domain (Friedman and Greenhaus, 2000; Frone, Russell, and Cooper, 1992; O'Driscoll, Ilgen, and Hildreth, 1992; Parasuraman et al., 1996). With a few exceptions (Adams, King, and King, 1996; Frone et al., 1992; Williams and Alliger, 1994), an inverse relationship was also observed between psychological involvement in family and psychological involvement in work (Friedman and Greenhaus, 2000; Hammer et al., 1997; Howard, 1992; Parasuraman et al., 1996). We found no evidence that the inverse relationship between family involvement and work involvement is different for men and women.

Career development opportunities

As discussed in previous sections, there is limited research on the impact of family life on career development opportunities. Friedman and Greenhaus (2000) found that family-focussed individuals had a more limited exposure to developmental assignments and had less job autonomy than career- and family-focussed individuals. Moreover, women with extensive family commitments were less likely to receive career-building opportunities than were women with lesser family commitments.

Career success

Income. The few studies that investigated the relationship between family involvement and income have produced mixed findings. For example, Judge and Bretz (1994) found no relationship between time spent on dependent care and household chores and income, whereas two other studies revealed a negative relationship between time spent on dependent care and income (Bretz and Judge, 1994; Judge et al., 1995). However, Cannings (1991) found a negative relationship between time spent on household chores and income for women but not for men. And Friedman and Greenhaus (2000) found no difference in income between family-focussed and career-focussed business professionals.

Advancement. In a series of studies that examined the antecedents of career success, Judge and his colleagues examined the impact of time spent on dependent care and household chores on different indices of career advancement such as job level attained, the number of promotions with one's current employer, and the number of promotions in one's career. They found no impact of time spent on dependent care and household chores on any of the dimensions of career advancement (Bretz and Judge, 1994; Judge and Bretz, 1994; Judge et al., 1995). Similarly, Friedman and Greenhaus (2000) found no difference in the organizational level attained by family-focussed and career-focussed business professionals. In contrast to these findings, Konrad and Cannings (1997) observed that it was men who were penalized for spending time in household labor and not women when it came to the number of promotions and the rank attained in the company.

Career satisfaction. In the same series of studies on career success by Judge and his colleagues, the time spent on household responsibilities and dependent care did not have any effect on individuals' level of career satisfaction (Bretz and Judge, 1994; Judge and Bretz, 1994; Judge et al., 1995). Consistent with these findings, Friedman and Greenhaus (2000) found no difference in career satisfaction between career-focussed and family-focussed business professionals.

Summary

The limited number of studies in the area suggest that employees who are highly involved with their families have lower advancement aspirations and work involvement as compared to less family-involved individuals. However, high family involvement did not hinder career advancement and satisfaction, and its effect on income was inconsistent.

● Family Resources ●

A supportive home environment and satisfactory family relationships may offset some of the negative effects of family demands and responsibilities on work life noted in the preceding sections. Individuals living in a family often draw upon and/or are provided with various supportive resources that directly or indirectly affect their work lives. Family resources include emotional and tangible support provided by one's family members (spouse, children, other relatives) and/or friends. It also includes the availability of financial resources to augment the personal efforts of family members.

Because extensive family responsibilities may limit one's career choices and involvement, different types of tangible and emotional support from one's family can enable the individual to cope more effectively with work-related problems (Adams et al., 1996). For example, Friedman and Greenhaus (2000) found that support from one's partner – in the form of help with children and emotional support – was associated with high income, extensive developmental assignments at work, and high career satisfaction. Emotional and tangible support from one's family can also serve to reduce the extent to which family interferes with work (Adams et al., 1996). When husbands increase their contribution to housework, their wives are able to spend more time at work (Blair and Lichter, 1991; Ishii-Kuntz and Coltrane, 1992; Parasuraman et al., 1997) and demonstrate high job performance (Friedman and Greenhaus, 2000) although this is not always the case (Singh et al., 1998).

Research also shows that emotional support that spouses provide is invaluable in meeting the demands of their work roles (Friedman and Greenhaus, 2000; Greenhaus and Parasuraman, 1994; Rosin, 1990). Spousal support influences women's career aspirations and choices, career priority, and career commitment (Parasuraman and Greenhaus, 1993; Sekaran, 1986). Men also benefit from the emotional support provided to them by their wives by spending more time at work and experiencing greater satisfaction with their careers (Friedman and Greenhaus, 2000). Taken together, these findings generally suggest that the availability of spousal support may enable the recipients to channel greater effort and energy into their work.

Even though children place heavy demands on working parents they can also be a source of help to them. Some recent studies have examined the contributions that children make to family labor. They found that women were likely to increase their time commitment to paid work in response to the household and childcare assistance provided by their children (Blair, 1992; Gill, 1998), although it did not seem to have much of an effect on men's work time.

● Family Role Quality ●

Another important dimension of family life is the quality of the family role. Marital and family satisfaction, quality of family life, family tensions, and distress are frequent indicators of family role quality. Although several studies found that marital quality did not contribute to attendance or satisfaction at work (Aryee et al., 1994; Erickson et al., 2000), other research indicates that stress within the family role is associated with negative emotions at work (Frone et al., 1997).

More commonly, researchers have investigated the relationship between affective reactions in the family role with affective reactions in the work role. These studies have generally revealed positive relationships between family satisfaction and work satisfaction (Duxbury and Higgins, 1991; Friedman and Greenhaus, 2000; Frone et al., 1992; Parasuraman et al., 1996; Williams and Alliger, 1994). Although it is plausible that affect within the family domain spills over into the work role, one study has shown that the relationship between family satisfaction and job satisfaction is non-causal (Frone, Russell, and Cooper, 1994).

● Conclusions and Directions for Future Research ●

The literature reveals a varied array of linkages between family life and career decisions and outcomes. Despite the variations in specific findings, the research strongly suggests that family experiences may either interfere with one's career or may enrich it. Family–career interference occurs when family experiences hinder, limit, or restrict career decisions or outcomes. Family–career enrichment occurs when family experiences strengthen, expand, or enhance career decisions and outcomes.

We believe that some forms of family–career interference can be explained by the concept of accommodation (Lambert, 1990) in which involvement in one role is reduced to accommodate the demands of a more salient or pressing role. We saw that responsibility for dependents – especially children – can restrict the selection of a career role, reduce behavioral and psychological involvement in work, limit one's opportunities for career development, and perhaps trigger withdrawal from a demanding career role. In each of these examples, it is plausible that an individual has limited his or her participation and investment in the work role to accommodate the needs of the family. Indeed, the inverse relationship between family involvement and work involvement we reported provides additional support for accommodation.

The tendency for women's careers to be more substantially constrained by family responsibilities than men's careers may reflect the greater willingness of women than men to make work accommodations for their family. This accommodation may be due to women's personal preferences based on their values or may be due to the absence of support from a spouse or partner. It is also conceivable that employers' inflexibility forces some women to reduce their work hours, interrupt their careers, or seek other forms of employment. Moreover, stereotypes regarding the work commitment of women with children may cause employers to withhold opportunities for continued career growth and development.

Therefore, family–career interference is likely to be produced by a combination of personal values, spouses' attitudes and behavior, and organizational practices. Moreover, although family–career interference of this type may be more evident among women than men, family-involved husbands or fathers also experience career restrictions (Friedman and Greenhaus, 2000).

Another type of family–career interference can be explained by the spillover of emotion from one role to the other. The findings of Frone et al. (1997) show that distress within the family role may produce work distress and can reduce one's performance in the work role. In these instances, difficulties within the family role may produce stress, worry, and preoccupation that interfere with work, heighten work stress, and inhibit job performance.

Family–career enrichment can take several forms as well. Whereas marriage and children may inhibit women's career experiences, there is some evidence that they promote positive experiences at work for men. Marriage or parenthood has been positively related to men's job autonomy, advancement, income, and career satisfaction. A plausible explanation for this enrichment effect is that organizations hold positive stereotypes of married men and fathers (responsible, mature, career-committed) and treat them more favorably than men without spouses or children. Therefore, just as organizational biases may have negative effects on mothers' careers, they may have positive effects on fathers' careers.

Family–career enrichment is also produced by the application of family-derived resources to the work domain (Greenhaus and Parasuraman, 1999; Kanter, 1977). The most frequently studied family resource, social support from one's spouse, can contribute to career enhancement by enabling an individual to devote more time to work and to receive greater opportunities for coaching, job autonomy, developmental assignments, and a more satisfying career. Resources derived from family experiences also include the skills, knowledge, and perspectives that can be effectively applied to work. Although this form of enrichment has been discussed extensively in the literature (Crouter, 1984; Kanter, 1977; Repetti, 1987), there is relatively little empirical research that has examined the dynamics that underlie this process.

Additionally, family role quality can promote positive outcomes in the work domain. Findings regarding the effect of family stress on work stress and negative work behaviors (Frone et al., 1997) also suggest that a low level of family stress has positive consequences for work attitudes and behavior.

Despite the many insights provided by the literature, additional research is needed to achieve a more complete understanding of the impact of family life on careers. As argued elsewhere (Greenhaus and Parasuraman, 1999), research needs to focus more extensively on the ways in which family dynamics enrich life at work. A useful starting point would be an examination of Sieber's (1974) positive outcomes of role accumulation: role privileges, status security, status enhancement, and personality enrichment (Kirchmeyer, 1992). Future research should determine the conditions under which these types of enrichment occur as well as the mechanisms by which family characteristics and experiences promote or inhibit each type of enrichment.

Because resources are a significant source of family–career enrichment, research should explore a variety of economic, social, and psychological resources derived from family life. Moreover, research on social support – the most frequently studied resource – should be expanded to incorporate support from a variety of family members, not just the spouse or partner.

Research should also determine whether family life simultaneously enriches careers in some respects and interferes with careers in other respects. For example, the presence of young children may limit a parent's willingness to work long hours and travel extensively, but may also be associated with the development of interpersonal skills (sensitivity, flexibility, active listening) that can be transferred effectively in the workplace. Therefore, researchers should not view enrichment and interference as mutually exclusive processes, and should design studies that can detect both types of influences.

In order to understand enrichment and interference more richly, however, research needs to go beyond the prediction of career success (earnings, advancement, satisfaction) and incorporate career experiences into models of family–career relationships. Career involvement, participation in developmental activities, career interruptions, and withdrawal from career roles are not only significant in their own right but may also explain the impact of family factors on career success.

Moreover, we need to understand *why* family experiences influence career experiences. Does emotional support from a spouse promote career development opportunities because it enhances the recipient's self-esteem, provides useful advice, or encourages the recipient to be more proactive in career management? Do extensive family commitments reduce women's opportunities for receiving coaching and development because women choose not to pursue these opportunities or because organizations are reluctant to invest in women with extensive family responsibilities? Additional research is required to understand the interplay of personal, family, and organizational factors in explaining enrichment and interference.

We also need to understand *when* family life influences career decisions and outcomes. Although we have concluded that family responsibilities may constrain women's careers, this family penalty is not inevitable (Schneer and Reitman, 1993; Tharenou and Conroy, 1994). Under what conditions do family commitments restrict career growth? Friedman and Greenhaus (2000) found that the negative effects of family commitments on career success were substantially reduced for women who work for supportive employers. Do personal values and family support also determine when family interferes with careers and when it does not?

Just as a broader array of career experiences needs to be examined, so too should a more extensive variety of family variables be explored. Much of the research has focussed on the influence of structural variables (marital status, parenthood, family structure) on work life. Although certainly important, these factors do not capture many of the more subtle characteristics of family life. Not only should multiple indicators of family involvement be examined more frequently, but the effort required to maintain or strengthen relationships with partners, parents, and other relatives should also be explored for its impact on career processes.

In order to examine the kinds of issues discussed in this section, a more varied set of methodologies should be employed in the future. We have learned a great deal from the cross-sectional studies that have dominated the literature, but they can only take us so far. Longitudinal, qualitative, and vignette designs are necessary to gain greater insight into the causal connections among variables.

Virtually every relationship we have discussed to illustrate the impact of family on careers could have been used to illustrate the effect of careers on family life. Does extensive involvement in family reduce career involvement, or does a high level of career involvement restrict one's involvement in the family domain? Does a spouse's help with childcare enable one to work longer hours, or do long work hours require a spouse to pick up the slack at home? Does spousal support encourage one to seek developmental assignments at work, or do challenging assignments and accomplishments elicit more understanding and appreciation from a spouse?

Research designs should also continue to include men and women in the same study so that gender similarities and differences in family–career relationships can be identified and explained. It would also be useful to conduct research at the couple level of analysis to understand how interactions between partners influence the careers of both partners over time. It would be especially helpful to explore enrichment and interference at different stages of the family and career life cycles.

The importance of understanding the interplay between partners in dual-earner relationships should not deter researchers from studying single parents, a growing segment of the workforce. It would be important to determine whether family–career enrichment and interference occur at different rates – or for different reasons – for single parents and parents with partners.

In fact, we should not limit our enquiries to parents, with or without partners. Just as work–family initiatives have evolved into work–life initiatives, we need to turn our attention to how the family, home, and personal experiences of all employees alter their life at work. The research we have reviewed in this chapter provides many insights, but there is much more work to be done.

REFERENCES

Adams, G.A., King, L.A., and King, D.W. (1996). Relationships of job and family involvement, family social support, and work–family conflict with job and life satisfaction. *Journal of Applied Psychology*, 81, 411–20.

Aryee, S., Chay, Y.W., and Tan, H.H. (1994). An examination of the antecedents of subjective career success among a managerial sample in Singapore. *Human Relations*, 47, 489–509.

Barker, K. (1993). Changing assumptions and contingent solutions: The costs and benefits of women working full- and part-time. *Sex Roles*, 28, 47–71.

Becker, P.E., and Moen, P. (1999). Scaling back: Dual-earner couples' work–family strategies. *Journal of Marriage and the Family*, 61, 995–1007.

Beehr, T.A., Glazer, S., Nielson, N.L., and Farmer, S.J. (2000). Work and nonwork predictors of employees' retirement ages. *Journal of Vocational Behavior*, 57, 206–25.

Bellas, M.L. (1992). The effects of marital status and wives' employment on the salaries of faculty men: The (house) wife bonus. *Gender and Society*, 6, 609–22.

Bielby, W.T., and Bielby, D.D. (1992). I will follow him: Family ties, gender role beliefs, and reluctance to relocate for a better job. *American Journal of Sociology*, 97, 1241–67.

Blair, S.L. (1992). Children's participation in household labor: Child socialization versus the need for household labor. *Journal of Youth and Adolescence*, 21, 241–58.

Blair, S.L., and Lichter, D.T. (1991). Measuring the division of household labor. *Journal of Family Issues*, 12, 91–113.

Blau, G. (1994). Developing and testing a taxonomy of lateness behavior. *Journal of Applied Psychology*, 79, 959–70.

Boden, R. J. (1999). Flexible working hours, family responsibilities, and female self-employment: Gender differences in self-employment selection. *The American Journal of Economics and Sociology*, 58, 71–6.

Brett, J.M., Stroh, L.K., and Reilly, A.H. (1992). What is it like being a dual-career manager in the 1990s? In S. Zedeck (ed.). *Work and Family*. San Francisco: Jossey-Bass, pp. 138–67.

Bretz, R.D., and Judge, T.A. (1994). Person-organization fit and theory of work adjustment. *Journal of Vocational Behavior*, 44, 32–54.

Cannings, K. (1991). An interdisciplinary approach to analyzing managerial gender gap. *Human Relations*, 44, 679–95.

Carr, D. (1996). Two paths to self-employment? Women's and men's self-employment in the United States. *Work and Occupations*, 23, 26–53.

Connelly, R. (1992). Self-employment and providing child-care: Employment strategies for women with young children. *Demography*, 29, 17–30.

Cooney, T. M., and Uhlenberg, P. (1991). Changes in work–family connections among highly educated men and women. *Journal of Family Issues*, 12, 69–90.

Crouter, A. C. (1984). Spillover from family to work: The neglected side of the work–family interface. *Human Relations*, 37, 425–42.

Dreher, G.F., and Ash, R.A. (1990). A comparative study of mentoring among men and women in managerial, professional, and technical positions. *Journal of Applied Psychology*, 75, 539–46.

Drobnic, S., Blossfeld, H.P., and Rohwer, G. (1999). Dynamics of women's employment patterns over the family life course: A comparison of the United States and Germany. *Journal of Marriage and the Family*, 61, 133–46

Duxbury, L.E., and Higgins, C.A. (1991). Gender differences in work–family conflict. *Journal of Applied Psychology*, 76, 60–74.

Eagle, B.W., Icenogle, M.L., Marjorie, L., and Maes, J.D. (1998). The importance of employee demographic profiles for understanding experiences of work–family interrole conflicts. *The Journal of Social Psychology*, 138, 690–709.

Eby, L.T., Allen, T.D., and Douthitt, S.S. (1999). The role of nonperformance factors on job-related relocation opportunities: A field study and laboratory experiment. *Organizational Behavior and Human Decision Processes*, 79, 29–55.

Erickson, R.J., Nichols, L., and Ritter, C. (2000). Family influences on absenteeism: Testing an expanded process model. *Journal of Vocational Behavior*, 57, 246–72.

Ettner, S.L. (1995). The impact of parents care of female labor supply decisions. *Demography*, 32, 63–80.

Feldman, D.C., and Bolino, M.C. (1998). Moving on out: When are employees willing to follow their organization during corporate relocation? *Journal of Organizational Behavior*, 19, 275–88.

Friedman, S.D., and Greenhaus, J.H. (2000). *Work and Family – Allies or Enemies? What Happens when Business Professionals Confront Life Choices*. New York: Oxford University Press.

Frone, M.R., Russell, M., and Cooper, M.L. (1992). Antecedents and outcomes of work–family conflict: Testing a model of work–family interface. *Journal of Applied Psychology*, 77, 65–78.

Frone, M.R., Russell, M., and Cooper, M.L. (1994). Relationship between job and family satisfaction: Causal or noncausal covariation. *Journal of Management*, 20, 565–79.

Frone, M.R., Yardley, J.K., and Markel, K.S. (1997). Developing and testing an integrative model of work–family interface. *Journal of Vocational Behavior*, 50, 145–67.

Galinsky, E., and Bond, J.T. (1996). Work and family: The experiences of mothers and fathers in the U.S. labor force. In C. Costello and B.K. Krimgold (eds). *The American Woman, 1996–1997*. New York: Norton, pp. 79–103.

Galinsky, E., Bond, J.T., and Friedman, D.E. (1993). *The Changing Workforce: Highlights of the National Study*. New York: Families and Work Institute.

Gerson, K. (1993). *No Man's Land: Men's Changing Commitments to Family and Work*. New York: Basic Books.

Gill, G.K. (1998). The strategic involvement of children in housework: An Australian case of two-income families. *International Journal of Comparative Sociology*, 39, 301–15.

Gill, H.L., and Haurin, D.R. (1998). Wherever he may go: How wives affect their husband's career decisions. *Social Science Research*, 27, 264–80.

Glass, J., and Camarigg, V. (1992). Gender, parenthood and job–family compatibility. *American Journal of Sociology*, 98, 131–51.

Grant, L., Simpson, L.A., Rong, X.L., and Peters-Golden, H. (1990). Gender, parenthood, and work hours of physicians. *Journal of Marriage and the Family*, 52, 39–50.

Greenberger, E., and O'Neil, R. (1993). Spouse, parent, worker: Role commitments and role-related experiences in the construction of adults' well-being. *Developmental Psychology*, 29, 181–97.

Greenhaus, J.H., Collins, K.M., Singh, R., and Parasuraman, S. (1997). Work and family influences on departure from public accounting. *Journal of Vocational Behavior*, 50, 249–70.

Greenhaus, J.H., and Parasuraman, S. (1994). Work–family conflict, social support, and well-being. In M.J. Davidson and R.J. Burke (eds). *Women in Management: Current Research Issues*. London: Paul Chapman, pp. 213–29.

Greenhaus, J.H., and Parasuraman, S. (1999). Research in work, family, and gender: Current status and future directions. In G.N. Powell (ed.). *Handbook of Gender and Work*. Newbury Park, CA: Sage, 391–412.

Greenhaus, J.H., and Parasuraman, S. (in press). The allocation of time to work and family roles. In D.L. Nelson, and R.J. Burke (eds). *Gender, Work Stress, and Health: Current Research Issues*. Washington, D.C.: American Psychological Association.

Grover, S.L., and Crooker, K.J. (1995). Who appreciates family-responsive human resource policies? The impact of family friendly policies on the organizational attachment of parents and non-parents. *Personnel Psychology*, 48, 271–89.

Gutek, B.A., Searle, S., and Klepa, L. (1991). Rational versus gender role explanations for work–family conflict. *Journal of Applied Psychology*, 76, 560–8.

Hammer, L.B., Allen, E., and Grigsby, T.D. (1997). Work–family conflict in dual earner couples: Within-individual and crossover effects of work and family. *Journal of Vocational Behavior*, 50, 185–203.

Herz, D.E., and Wootton, B.H. (1996). Women in the workforce. In C. Costello and B.K. Krimgold (eds). *The American Woman, 1996–1997*. New York: Norton, pp. 79–103.

Howard, A. (1992). Work and family crossroads spanning the career. In S. Zedeck (ed.). *Work, Families and Organizations*. San Francisco: Jossey-Bass, pp. 70–137.

Ishii-Kuntz, M., and Coltrane, S. (1992). Predicting the share of household labor. *Sociological Perspectives*, 35, 629–47.

Jacobs, J.A. (1992). Women's entry into management. *Administrative Science Quarterly*, 37, 282–301.

Judge, T.A., and Bretz, R.D. (1994). Political influence processes and career success. *Journal of Management*, 20, 43–65.

Judge, T.A., Cable, D.M., Boudreau, J.W., and Bretz, R.D. (1995). An empirical investigation of the predictors of executive career success. *Personnel Psychology*, 48, 485–519.

Kanter, R.M. (1977). *Work and Family in the United States: A Critical Review and Agenda for Research and Policy* (Social Science Frontiers No. 9). New York: Russell Sage.

Karambayya, R., and Reilly, A.H. (1992). Dual-earner couples: Attitudes and actions in restructuring work for family. *Journal of Organizational Behavior*, 13, 585–601.

Kirchmeyer, C. (1992). Nonwork participation and work attitudes: A test of scarcity vs. expansion models of personal resources. *Human Relations*, 45, 775–95.

Kirchmeyer, C. (1998). Determinants of managerial career success: Evidence and explanation of male/female differences. *Journal of Management*, 24, 6, 673–92.

Konrad, A.M., and Cannings, K. (1997). The effects of gender role congruence and statistical discrimination on managerial advancement. *Human Relations*, 50, 1305–28.

Korenman, S., and Neumark, D. (1991). Does marriage really make men more productive? *Journal of Human Resources*, 26, 283–307.

Lambert, S.J. (1990). Processes linking work and family: A critical review and research agenda. *Human Relations*, 43, 239–57.

Lambert, S.J. (1991). The combined effects of job and family characteristics on the job satisfaction, job involvement, and intrinsic motivation of men and women workers. *Journal of Organizational Behavior*, 12, 341–63.

Landau, J., and Arthur, M.B. (1992). The relationship of marital status, spouse's career status, and gender to salary level. *Sex Roles*, 27, 665–81.

Lobel, S.A., and St. Clair, L. (1992). Effects of family responsibilities, gender, and career identity salience on performance outcomes. *Academy of Management Journal*, 35, 1057–69.

Melamed, T. (1996). Career success: An assessment of a gender-specific model. *Journal of Occupational and Organizational Psychology*, 69, 217–42.

O'Driscoll, M.P., Ilgen, D.R., and Hildreth, K. (1992). Time devoted to job and off-job activities, interrole conflict, and affective experiences. *Journal of Applied Psychology*, 77, 272–9.

Parasuraman, S., and Greenhaus, J.H. (1993). Personal portrait: The lifestyle of the woman manager. In E. A. Fagenson (ed.). *Women in Management: Trends, Issues, and Challenges in Managerial Diversity* (Vol. 4). Newbury Park, CA: Sage, pp. 186–211.

Parasuraman, S., Greenhaus, J.H., Rabinowitz, S., Bedeian, A.G., and Mossholder, K.W. (1989). Work and family variables as mediators of the relationship between wives' employment and husbands' well-being. *Academy of Management Journal*, 32, 185–201.

Parasuraman, S., Purohit, Y.S., Godshalk, V.M., and Beutell, N.J. (1996). Work and family variables, entrepreneurial career success, and psychological well-being. *Journal of Vocational Behavior*, 43, 198–208.

Parasuraman, S., Singh, R., and Greenhaus, J.H. (1997). The influence of self and partner family variables on career development opportunities of professional women and men. In P. Tharenou (ed.). *Best Paper and Abstract Proceedings of the Australian Industrial and Organizational Psychology Conference*. Melbourne: Australian Psychological Society, pp. 125–9.

Philliber, W.W., and Vannoy-Hiller, D. (1990). The effect of husband's occupational attainment on wife's achievement. *Journal of Marriage and the Family*, 52, 323–30.

Reitzes, D.C., Mutran, E.J., and Fernandez, M.E. (1998). The decision to retire: A career perspective. *Social Science Quarterly*, 79, 607–20.

Repetti, R.L. (1987). Linkages between work and family roles. In S. Oskamp (ed.). *Family Processes and Problems: Social Psychological Aspects*. Newbury Park, CA: Sage, pp. 98–127.

Rosin, H. (1990). The effects of dual-career participation on men: some determinants of variation in career and personal satisfaction. *Human Relations*, 43, 169–82.

Rosin, H., and Korabik, K. (1990). Marital and family correlates of women managers' attrition from organizations. *Journal of Vocational Behavior*, 37, 104–20.

Rosin, H. and Korabik, K. (1995). Organizational experiences and propensity to leave: A multivariate investigation of men and women managers. *Journal of Vocational Behavior*, 46, 1–16.

Schneer, J., and Reitman, F. (1993). The effects of alternate family structures on managerial career paths. *Academy of Management Journal*, 36, 830–43.

Schneer, J., and Reitman, F. (1995). The impact of gender as managerial careers unfold. *Journal of Vocational Behavior*, 47, 290–315.

Seibert, S.E., Crant, J.M., and Kraimer, M.L. (1999). Proactive personality and career success. *Journal of Applied Psychology*, 84, 416–27.

Sekaran, U. (1986). *Dual-Career Families*. San Francisco: Jossey-Bass.

Shauman, K.A., and Xie, Y. (1996). Geographic mobility of scientists: Sex differences and family constraints. *Demography*, 33, 455–68.

Shenhav, Y. (1992). Entrance of blacks and women into managerial positions in scientific and engineering occupations. *Academy of Management Journal*, 35, 889–901.

Sieber, S.D. (1974). Toward a theory of role accumulation. *American Sociological Review*, 39, 567–78.

Singh, R., Greenhaus, J.H., Collins, K.M., and Parasuraman, S. (1998). *The Influence of Family Responsibilities, Gender and Social Support on the Career Involvement of Professionals.* Proceedings of the 35th Annual Meeting of the Eastern Academy of Management, pp. 267–70.

Spitze, G., and Loscocco, K. (1999). Women's position in the household. *Quarterly Review of Economics and Finance*, 39, 647–61.

Stroh, L.K., Brett, J.M., and Reilly, A.H. (1996). Family structure, glass ceiling, and traditional explanations for the differential rate of turnover of female and male managers. *Journal of Vocational Behavior*, 49, 99–118.

Stroh, L.K., and Reilly, A.H. (1999). Gender and careers: Present experiences and emerging trends. In G. N. Powell (ed.). *Handbook of Gender and Work*. Newbury Park, CA: Sage, pp. 307–24.

Tharenou, P. (1999). Is there a link between family structures and women's and men's managerial advancement? *Journal of Organizational Behavior*, 20, 837–63.

Tharenou, P., and Conroy, D.K. (1994). Men and women managers' advancement. *Applied Psychology: An International Review*, 43, 5–31.

Thyen, U., Kuhlthau, K., and Perrin, J.M. (1999). Employment, child care, and mental health of mothers caring for children assisted by technology. *Pediatrics*, 103, 1235–49.

Waite, L.J. (1995). Does marriage matter? *Demography*, 32, 483–507.

Wallace, J.E (1997). It's about time: A study of hours worked and work spillover among law firm lawyers. *Journal of Vocational Behavior*, 50, 227–48.

Whitely, W., Dougherty, T.W., and Dreher, G.F. (1991). Relationship of career mentoring and socio-economic origin to managers' and professionals' early career progress. *Academy of Management Journal*, 34, 331–51.

Williams, K.J., and Alliger, G.M. (1994). Role stressors, mood spillover, and perceptions of work–family conflict in employed parents. *Academy of Management Journal*, 37, 837–68.

Changes to Jobs and Work

6

Contingent Work Contracts: Practice and Theory

DANIEL G. GALLAGHER

It should come as no surprise, to even the most casual observer of international trends in human resource practices, that there has been a gradual restructuring of the fundamental nature of employment contracts. Accordingly, within the lexicon of workology and the human resources vocabulary, terms and practices such as "ongoing" and "regular jobs" are gradually being displaced with increasingly frequent references to "alternative," "non standard," and "atypical" work arrangements (Carré, Ferber, Golden and Herzenberg, 2000; De Grip, Hoevenberg, and Willens, 1997; Zeytinoğlu 1999a). In particular, "contingent employment" or "contingent work contracts" have become a popular label for employment arrangements which fit the alleged post-Fordist era's organizational goals of "flexibility" or connote a workplace status which is viewed as "peripheral," "marginal(ized)," "distanced," or "external" to the core workforce of an organization (e.g., Hartley, 1995; Marin, 2000; Pfeffer and Baron, 1988; Treu, 1992). The nomenclature itself suggests that a divide exists between organizational "insiders" and a reserve army (Rifkin, 1995) of scruffy contingent "outsiders" or "visitors" who are enlisted and discharged as the needs of the employer organization dictate. Government, popular, and scholarly publications are fairly consistent in their observations that the phenomenon of contingent work is a growing share of the employment profile on an international basis (Delsen, 1999; Nollen, 1999). However, it may be argued that our understanding of contingent work is confused by misleading stereotypical images of contingent workers. Furthermore, contingent work may not be a monolithic or catchall category for workers who are employed anywhere outside an organization's "core" or "central" workforce. It is perhaps more realistic to suggest that contingent employment contracts come in a variety of forms, and that the types of workers who perform such work are also diverse in their skill levels and motivations. Similarly, it can be argued that from the perspective of employer organizations, there may be considerable diversity in the motivations for entering into contingent contracts, how such contracts are managed, and the results that are achieved.

The broad objective of this chapter is to address a number of fundamental issues associated with contingent work arrangements and to assist both academics and practitioners in better understanding the implications of contingent work from organizational and individual worker perspectives. As part of this task, attention will first be directed to examining and defining the meaning of the term "contingent work." Illustrations will be offered of the extent to which various "alternative" employment arrangements fit within the realm of contingent work. Second, popularly cited reasons for the growth of contingent work will be noted. Of particular concern will be the extent to which contingent work is driven by employer interests or reflects the employment preferences of individual workers. Third, discussion will be directed toward consideration of whether the structure of contingent work contracts fits within the broader theoretical frameworks which have been developed and applied in the context of more permanent employer–employee relationships. Alternatively, there is a need to consider if the emergence of contingent working arrangements calls for behavioral or psychological theories of employment which can be generalizable across differing forms of work arrangements. Finally, the chapter will conclude with a brief discussion of the emerging research and practical issues associated with the growth of contingent employment contracts. An effort will made to identify future issues which may be important to our understanding of the potential impacts of contingent employment at the individual and organizational levels.

● Defining Contingent Work ●

The ability to systematically analyze research on individual and organizational experiences with contingent work, as well as efforts to address a broad range of theoretical and public policy issues, is complicated by the fact that there is no clear or universally accepted definition of the term "contingent work." In one sense, the term "contingent" has been associated with employment arrangements which operate on a "conditional" or "as-needed" basis (Feldman, 1995). From a technical perspective, economists would argue that the necessity for some type of demand function makes all employment contracts conditional in nature. However, a step toward narrowing the definition rests in the observation that contingent work is frequently referenced in the context of employment which is either "temporary" or "transitory" in nature. One frequently referenced definition of contingent work has been formulated by Polivka and Nardone (1989) as part of the US Department of Labor's early efforts to measure and analyze the growth of "alternative employment" arrangements. Specifically, Polivka and Nardone initially defined contingent work as those situations where workers "do not have *explicit* or *implicit* contracts for long-term employment and one in which the minimum hours can vary in a non-systematic manner" (1989: 11).

Such a definition is helpful but also opens the door for further consideration. Most notably, how is "long-term" defined? For accounting purposes, it is entirely possible to set a numerical definition or limit. But from both worker and organizational perspectives, the meaning of the words "long-term" may have fundamental differences to people and vary by organizational circumstances. For such reason, contingent work has been increasing referenced in the context of the absence of an *ongoing* employment relationship rather than as "long-term" in nature (Hipple, 1998). Second, Polivka and Nardone's (1989) effort at defining contingent work realized the important point that contracts may be both empathic (e.g., "explicit" verbal or written) or involve an element of individualized "perception" (e.g., "implicit" understandings). The introduction of the element of perception into contractual definitions suggests the possibility that equally situated individuals could reach different understandings about the perceived permanency of their relationship with an employer organization. Such potential ambiguity may complicate the accuracy and interpretation of survey-based efforts to measure the number or extent of contingent workers. However, as reflected in much of the psychological contract research (Rousseau, 1995), how the individual perceives the arrangement or "the deal" may be more important to understanding the attitudes and behaviors of workers than the ability to precisely slot workers into well-defined employment categories (McLean Parks, Kidder, and Gallagher, 1998).

In addition to the presence or absence of an "ongoing" relationship, consideration of the degree to which *minimum hours can vary in a non-systematic manner* is also a very important definitional component of contingent work. For purposes of illustration, an individual worker could have an agreement with a local school district or school board that they will work as a substitute teacher and be called in to work on an as-needed basis. There may be a long-standing or "ongoing" relationship between the teacher and the school, but there is no guarantee of work hours or a reasonably predictable schedule. In essence, the level and regularity of work is entirely contingent on the variable needs of the employer.

For the purpose of establishing greater clarity and meaning to the concept of "contingent work," it will be demonstrated throughout this chapter that contingent work can best be exemplified in the form of three basic types of employment arrangements.

First, and perhaps one of the most commonly recognized employment arrangements, which fits the noted parameters of contingent work, is fixed-term employment established through the use of an intermediary organization such as a "temporary-help service firm" or "temporary staffing agency" (e.g., Adecco, Manpower, Accutemps, Career Staff, etc.). Through the use of temporary employment agencies, an organization directly contracts labor for either a fixed period of time or until the completion of a particular event or project. Within virtually all of these arrangements there is a contractually explicit understanding that the employment is of a fixed duration. In many countries there may also be statutory limitations on how long a particular worker may be "dispatched" by the temporary-help firm to the user organization. Furthermore, the contractual arrangement which the worker has with the temporary-help firm is of a fixed duration and dependent upon the availability of assignments for which the worker may be qualified.

Two trends exist within the temporary-help services industry which are especially important to note. First, although the percentage of workers actually hired through temp firms is a very small share of total employment, the temporary-help services industry and the employment of "agency temps" has been the fastest growing segment of the workforce in most countries in the past decade (Delsen, 1999; Druker and Stanworth, 2000; Nollen, 1999). Secondly, the image of "temporary" workers as a legion of unskilled and semi-skilled day laborers, receptionists, and file clerks is no longer universally applicable. The temporary-help industry has moved increasingly toward contracting more professional or "elite" workers such as accountants, engineers, information technology experts, nurses, and other medical or scientific professionals (Carnoy, Castells, and Benner, 1997).

In contrast to using temporary-help agencies, a significantly larger share of temporary or contingent workers are actual hired through "direct-hire" or "in-house" arrangements with the immediate employer organization. In practice, direct-hire contingents may have an ongoing relationship with a single employer organization, perhaps with an implicit or explicit understanding that a more permanent contract may result, but there is the general absence of a "systematic" or "predictable" work schedule. A variation on the direct hiring of temporary workers is the use of what can also be referred to as "zero-hour" workers. Rather than assuming that a work week will be of a specified number of hours, "zero-hour" contracts begin with the contractual principle that working hours will be offered only when a definite demand exists for such labor.

A third major and increasingly popular form of contingent work arrangement rests in the organizational use of "independent contractors." Within most countries, "independent contractors" or "freelance" workers are legally defined as self-employed individuals who contract or sell their services to a client organization on a fixed-term or project basis. An increasingly common illustration of an independent contractor arrangement would be a situation where an organization contracts with a self-employed information technology (IT) specialist to install a new computer-based messaging system within an office. As in the case of most all independent contractor arrangements, the duration of the contract is normally tied explicitly to the completion of a specific project. Once the project is completed, the contractual relationship is terminated unless a decision is made by both parties to enter into a subsequent contract. Typically, independent contractor or freelance arrangements assume that the worker has considerable discretion and independence as to how the work is performed and the emphasis is often on outcomes rather than process. Independent contractors are also clearly distinct from professionals who may offer similar types of services but who are also employees of a consulting firm or organization.

Collectively these three prominent forms of work arrangements suggest that contingent work is not a totally new phenomenon, but perhaps the notoriety exists in the rate of growth which all three types of work arrangements have experienced. Also interesting to note is that "contingent work" is a fairly new term within the context of human resources, but the temporary-help firm, direct-hire, and independent contractor work arrangements are not. In fact, some writers have appropriately observed that in most pre-industrial societies, casual and temporary employment contract relationships had been the norm rather than the exception (Cappelli, 1999). However, in the context of a more contemporary definition of "contingent work," all three of the above noted arrangements can be characterized as being either without an explicit or implicit promise of "ongoing" employment or a consistent schedule of minimum and predictable hours of work.

Although it can be argued that contingent work is not a narrowly defined construct, there is a corresponding problem of defining most alternative contractual work arrangements as contingent. Perhaps a good illustration of this point is the question as to whether or not "part-time" work is a representative form of "contingent" work (Barling and Gallagher, 1996; Gallie, White, Cheng, and Tomlinson, 1998). In most respects, part-time work has more in common with traditional employment contracts than it does with most of the previously noted forms of contingent work. Most notably, the majority of workers on "part-time" work schedules are immediately distinguishable from "full-time" workers on the basis of the number of scheduled hours which they work in a week. But for most part-time workers, their employment contract is based on an expectation of an "ongoing" and identifiable employer–employee relationship. It is not unusual to find employees who have a long tenure as part-time or "key-time" workers within an organization. Furthermore, in many service industries and the retail trade, part-time work may actually be more "traditional" and the major form of employment contract within an organization. Part-time workers, in some industries, may very well be the "core" workforce of the organization. In addition, although the number of hours may be less than their full-time counterparts, part-time work schedules are often definitive and predictable from both the worker and employer perspectives. Although there is some argument that part-time workers are relatively disadvantaged compared to the benefits, training, and career opportunities provided to full-time workers (Zeytinoğlu, 1991), the part-time contract is neither structurally nor theoretically distinct from the "traditional full-time or regular" employment arrangement. However, it could reasonably be argued that part-time workers, who are hired on a seasonal basis (e.g., ski resorts, summer jobs), could be defined as contingents since their contracts are often defined in terms of explicit starting and termination dates. Similar to other forms of contingent employment, seasonal work often does not include an implicit or explicit understanding that the relationship will be ongoing in nature.

In the same sense that the inclusion of part-time workers might inappropriately expand both the definition and number of contingent workers, the inclusion of other forms of alternative work arrangements, as being within the realm of contingent employment, may be equally misleading. Other contractual arrangements such as "leased workforces," "outsourced," and "subcontracting" have been, to varying degrees, thrown into the cauldron of alternative or non-standard employment contracts. But it is extremely important not to confuse contingent work with other forms of employment which provide flexibility in staffing or are outside the commonly held view of regular employment.

In particular, staffing arrangements such as employee leasing, outsourcing, and subcontracting are distinctive from contingent employment in that these alternative staffing arrangements involve an ongoing employer–employee relationship. For example, in the case of outsourcing or subcontracting arrangements, a client or customer organization achieves flexibility by contracting out services or production to a third-party organization. However, employees within the third-party organization have a more "traditional" arrangement in that they have a clear and identifiable employer and the usual expectation of an ongoing relationship subject to satisfactory individual and organizational performance. Even in the case of more complicated "employee leasing" arrangements, where there is often an intermediary organization, the employment arrangement is again long-term in expectation and with a single employer.

A related point that does deserve recognition and future attention is the issue of "dependent employment" (International Labour Office, 2000; Martin, 2000). For example, in the case of independent contractors, it can be argued that the ability of workers to be truly "independent" or effectively outside a traditional employment model may be seriously limited if the contract worker is reliant for employment upon a single client organization. Also as noted by Greene (2000), many workers who move from employee to independent contractor status, within the same organization, may actually be moving to the status of dependent contractor if their employment prospects are tied to a single client. The ILO has referred to such contingent arrangements as being "objectively ambiguous" since independence may be limited by the lack of alternative clients. Similarly, employment in outsourcing and subcontracting arrangements, which overly rely upon serving a single client organization through the employment of prior employees of the organization, could represent a form of "spurious externalization" where the true employment status may be more akin to contingent than traditional (International Labour Office, 2000).

Within the context of this discussion, the goal is to avoid utilizing such broad definitions of contingent employment as to make the concept theoretically and empirically meaningless. For practical and illustrative purposes, contingent employment will be defined and measured in terms of the extent to which the work arrangement implies or offers "ongoing" employment and provides hours of employment in a systematic way or on a predictable basis. Furthermore, this focus and subsequent discussion of contingent work will strive to avoid any misleading suggestions that contingent workers are necessarily outside an organization's "core" workforce or that contingent work is automatically synonymous with peripheral or marginal status.

• Why Contingent Work? •

With the realization that there is not a universally accepted definition of either contingent work or alternative work arrangements, considerable caution should be exercised in the interpretation of data pertaining to the actual growth in employment outside of the traditional employer–employee relationship. However, there is unquestionable evidence that contingent work arrangements are becoming a growing share of the new workforce. For example, in a study of 14 European countries, Brewster, Mayne, and Tregaskis (1997) found that "non-permanent" or "contingent" contracts ranged from one-third of the working population in Spain to a low of 7.5 percent in countries such as Belgium and the UK. Within Canada and the US approximately 10–12 percent of the workforce could be characterized as contingent (Cohany, 1998; Zeytinoğlu, 1999b). Furthermore, it is interesting to note that at the organizational level, Brewster et al. (1997) found that four out of every five employers in their European study used non-permanent workers. A recent and in-depth analysis of employment practices in Britain by Cully, Woodland, O'Reilly, and Dix (1999) also indicated that close to one-half of British firms utilized workers on direct-hire fixed-term contracts. In most industrialized economies a disproportionate share of "new job" creation in the last decade has been in the form of contingent contract arrangements (Delsen, 1999; Nollen, 1999).

To date, there exists a considerable volume of literature which has sought to document and explain the growth of contingent work arrangements. In a very broad sense, efforts to explain this growth have looked at the existence and relative importance of demand versus supply-based factors. Demand-side explanations have emphasized the role of changing market forces which influence the desire of employers to increase their reliance on contingent or temporary workers. For example, through the utilization of time-series data pertaining to the growth of temporary employment in the US, Golden and Appelbaum (1992) found that the demand for temporary workers was closely associated with three major factors: cyclical fluctuations in output, increased foreign competition, and the magnitude of non-wage labor costs. These results appear to fit in well with a significant share of the prescriptive and survey-based literature which indicate that employer organizations are seeking increased "flexibility" in staffing practices as a means of addressing competitive market practices (e.g., Laird and Williams, 1996). Of particular interest is the growing emphasis which organizations appear to have placed on both the "numerical" and "functional" aspects of employment flexibility (Cully et al., 1999; Nollen and Axel, 1996; Sparrow, 1998). The issue of numerical flexibility centers around the ability of a employer organization to expand or contract the size of its workforce in order to quickly adjust to cyclical variations in market demand. In this regard, contingent or short-term contracts allow employers to restructure a greater share of their workforce from a "fixed" to a "variable" cost.

There also exists some argumentation that employer preferences for contingent contracts and flexibilization is driven by government policy. In particular, a number of researchers contend that government policies, which are restrictive on the ability of employers to lay off or discharge workers and impose high social insurance associated with the employment of permanent workers, will encourage employers to seek out strategies for employing workers outside the purview of extensive government regulation (e.g., Alba-Ramirez, 1998; Segal and Sullivan, 1997). In contrast, there are some studies which suggest that the role of government regulation may have a negligible impact on the use of contingent and alternative employment arrangements (e.g., Brewster et al., 1997). Such research is generally suggestive of contingent and short-term employment being more sensitive to market forces (i.e., business cycles) than government regulation.

As noted, research also points to an increased employer emphasis on contingent work for the reason of functional flexibility. This flexibility is primarily associated with the desire of employers to achieve a balance between the changing skill needs of the organization and the skills possessed by its workforce. In environments where technology is rapidly changing, finding a match between new functions and the skills of regular workers may be difficult. For many organizations, contingent work arrangements represent an efficient way to address the need to secure the necessary skills which are absent or in short supply within a firm's internal workforce. Research exists to suggest that firms are most likely to turn to contingent "independent contractor" or "temporary-help agencies" when they need workers with specific technical skills (Nishikawa, 2000). Such a finding fits well with the previously noted observation that there is a growing cadre of "elite" or "professional" temporaries and independent contractors who are attractive to employers for their ability to provide technical skills. In addition, there are some excellent studies which have also argued the position that the use of outside "independent contractors" and "consultants" (and even outsourcing arrangements) represents an effective mechanism by which the intellectual capital of organizations can be enhanced by exposure to extra-organizational trends and practices (Greer, Youngblood, and Gray, 1999; Matusik and Hill, 1998).

A few studies have also enhanced the understanding of the growth of contingent work arrangements by seeking to identify firm characteristics and organizational practices which either contribute to or retard the use of contingent workers. Davis-Blake and Uzzi (1993) examined the relationship between firm-level characteristics and the use of temporary workers and independent contractors. Although some criticism may be raised over the construction of the dependent variables of interest, the results of the research are still informative. In general, the research found that firm-specific training, government oversight, bureaucratized employment practices, establishment size, and requirements for high levels of information or technical skills had negative effects on the use of temporary workers. In addition, the results predictably indicated that the degree of variability in employment demand is positively associated with the use of temporary workers. However, with regard to the use of independent contractors the results indicated that in contrast to the identified correlates of temporary worker usage, bureaucratized employment practices, establishment size, and being part of a multi-site establishment had positive effects on the use of "independent contractors." This type of study is important, not only for the effort to theoretically and empirically link different firm and job characteristics with the usage of contingent workers, but the finding that different forms of contingent employment may have different firm-level determinants. A similar study by Uzzi and Barsness (1998) among British establishments found that the "intensity" of "fixed-term contract" use was positively related to organizational size. In terms of organizational control mechanisms, Uzzi and Barsness found that organizations which were capable of systematically measuring and monitoring performance were more inclined to employ temporary workers. They also found that there was a greater use of fixed-term hires in firms which had implemented major changes in job-related computer technology. The role of unionization was also examined with regard to the use of contingent workers in British firms. The findings indicated that there existed a non-linear relationship between the percentage of a firm's workforce which is unionized and the use of contingent workers. Equally revealing was the related finding that the level of union–management conflict was positively related to the use of contingent workers (Uzzi and Barsness, 1998).

A somewhat more controversial aspect of the investigation of factors which have contributed to the growth of contingent work contracts is the role of "supply-side" influences. Based on analysis of time-series data pertaining to the level of employment in the temporary-help industry within the US, research by Laird and Williams (1996) was critical of prior economic models of contingent employment for the reason that such studies tended to underestimate the importance of labor supply. Laird and Williams argued that although the long-run growth of temporary-help employment was not well predicted by demand and supply variables, short-run fluctuations in temporary employment were a function of the continued growth of married women entering and remaining in the labor force.

As will be discussed elsewhere in this chapter, consideration of supply-side aspects of contingent work also suggests the need for discussion of the extent to which the undertaking of such work is a preferred choice or an involuntary response to a lack of alternatives.

The need to develop even further insights into the nature and relative weight of both demand- and supply-side factors which contribute to the growth of contingent employment contracts is important because they can shed more light on the underlying motivations as to why employer organizations use contingent workers and why individuals are willing to work under this type of arrangement. Such information is important because the reasons for using contingent workers may have an influence on the ways in which an organization manages its workforce and the type of contingent arrangement (temporary-help firm, direct-hire, or independent contractor) it utilizes. As will be discussed, an organization's motivation for using contingents may influence organization-based human resource management strategies, implementation, and outcomes (Lautsch, 1999). Alternatively, worker motivations for seeking or accepting contingent work arrangements may influence or moderate their work and organization-related attitudes and behaviors.

● In Search of a Theoretical Framework ●

Although the lion's share of existing literature on the topic of contingent work has focussed on the organizational motivations and environmental influences which have contributed to the growth of contingent work arrangements, there has been a limited but emerging number of empirical studies which have sought to examine the impact of contingent employment at the individual worker level. Among the most frequently addressed issues are the examination of multiple dimensions of job satisfaction (e.g., Ellingson, Gruys and Sackett, 1998; Krausz, Brandwein, and Fox, 1995) and the extent to which transitory contingent work assignments are associated with a higher level of role conflict, ambiguity, and stress (e.g., Krausz et al., 1995; Sverke, Gallagher, and Hellgren, 1999). There have also been a number of studies which have sought to ascertain the extent to which contingent workers evidence commitment to the organization(s) for which they work (e.g., Van Dyne and Ang, 1998). In addition, a few studies have even sought to examine the extent to which commitment is associated with organizational citizenship or other forms of work-related behaviors (e.g., Pearce, 1993; Van Dyne and Ang, 1998). In many respects, the growing attention which has been focussed on these types of issues reflects a natural curiosity by researchers concerning how contingent workers measure up relative to the attitudes and behaviors of traditional employees.

Although much of the emerging research examining contingent workers is, in fact, anchored in popular behavioral or psychological theories of work, there should be some skepticism over the wholesale applicability of existing theory to the contingent work arrangement. Such a concern was raised more than a decade ago by Pfeffer and

Baron (1988), with their suggestion that existing organization theory was primarily developed when organizational models of bureaucratic control were prevalent. Similarly, Brewster et al. (1997), Ho and Ang (1998), and Kochan, Smith, Wells, and Rebitzer (1994) have noted that much of our academic knowledge, organizational strategies, and public employment policy are based on the assumption of a stable and ongoing "employer–employee" relationship. Implicit within the prevailing view of the employment relationship is an understanding that workers hold varying levels of attachment to a "single" employer, and that work roles, attitudes, and behaviors are "nested" within the company (organization), the department, and the work group (March and Simon, 1958). Furthermore, within the context of the employer organization there exist a number of constituencies or coalitions, such as management, co-workers, immediate supervisor, and client to which employees of the organization may hold varying degrees of commitment (Reichers, 1985; Meyer and Allen, 1997). As noted by Gallagher and McLean Parks (in press), the choice of the term "employee" is itself important since it implies an identification of joint responsibility between the individual and the organization.

Research by Beard and Edwards (1995) also provides some recognition of the possible need to re-examine the framework in which contingent workers view and react to their work status. In particular, they suggested that understanding the job-related attitudes (e.g., satisfaction, involvement, commitment) and the overall mental and physical well-being of contingent workers may be a function of the "psychological experience" of contingent work. Most notably, Beard and Edwards point out five key areas in which the contingent work experience may differ from "core" work, including: (1) *job insecurity*; (2) *predictability* in terms of the knowledge of both the conditions under which an event will occur and the expected effects; (3) *control* over how and when the work is performed; (4) the nature of the *psychological contract*; and (5) the *social comparison process* with referent non-contingent workers. Although all five areas were developed in terms of explaining the possible effects on job-related attitudes, the application of psychological contract theory to the understanding of contingent work is particularly interesting. Most notably, Beard and Edwards suggest that in contingent work relationships the psychological contract is "transactional" in form and based upon an "asymmetrical" power balance which clearly favors the employer. Although, both psychological contract and social exchange theories have received increasing attention as a basis for contingent work research, the applications developed by Beard and Edwards also reflect the common and narrow stereotype of contingent workers being in highly insecure positions with little control, and feeling relatively disadvantaged compared to the permanent employees with whom they work. However, it has been argued in this chapter that contingent work arrangements may exist in a variety of forms and may vary in the level of knowledge or skills held by contingent workers. A comparison of contingent employment arrangements offers potential recognition of the fact that the structure of contingent work not only differs from traditional employer–employee arrangements, but also differs among types of contingent work arrangements. These structural differences not only point to questions about the applicability of bureaucratically based models of behavior, but also to the extent to which developing or reformulated theories of contingent employment can be generalizable across types of contingent employment arrangements.

For example, from the perspective of the contingent or temporary worker who is dispatched to a "job" by a temporary-help firm (e.g., Manpower, Adecco, Randstad, etc.), the existence of an identifiable "employer" organization may be less clear-cut than is assumed under existing organizational studies. Most notably, contingent workers under this type of employment arrangement can be viewed as having a "multiple agency relationship" where they hold "simultaneous" obligations to more than one entity (McLean Parks et al., 1998). Within this context, the meaning and significance of "employer" status and responsibility become somewhat ambiguous. For example, although the legal status of employer may rest with the temporary-help firm, the "organizational" context where the work is being performed (e.g., supervision, co-workers, working conditions) may rest with the "client" organization. The issue of potential theoretical ambiguity associated with such a "triangular" (worker–agency–client) employment relationship can be demonstrated in the case of organizational commitment. As noted in a number of studies, antecedents and correlates of organizational commitment include consideration of role status (e.g., ambiguity conflict), job characteristics (e.g., skill, task autonomy, challenge, etc.), group–leader relations (e.g., leadership styles, group cohesiveness), and job satisfaction (e.g., intrinsic, extrinsic, promotion, pay, etc.) (Meyer and Allen, 1997). However, in the temporary-help firm–client relationship, control over those factors, which may contribute to organizational commitment-building, are outside of the sole control of a single organization. For example, although the temporary-help firm may control assignments and pay levels, other factors which contribute to commitment such as the level of autonomy, supervision, and co-workers' experiences are largely within the control of the client organization.

Contingent work assignments which are established through temporary-help agencies also raise theoretical and practical questions about the meaning of something as apparently straightforward as the notion of a "job" or perceived job satisfaction. For example, workers dispatched thorough temporary-help firms may have dissimilar interpretations of survey terminology such as "my job." It is conceivable that some temporary agency-based contingent workers may perceive their job as being that of a "temporary" worker, while others may identify their "job" as being the tasks that they are currently performing for the client organization. In the latter case, attitudes which a worker holds toward their "job" have the potential of dramatically changing as the contingent worker moves from one client organization to another. For contingent workers, job perceptions (e.g., job satisfaction) may be variable and reflective of particular client assignments. Alternatively, some contingent workers, particularly those in more elite assignments (e.g., accountants, nurses, engineers, etc.), may equate their "job" attitudes in the context of a more stable professional or occupational context.

In contrast, it may be reasonable to assert that direct-hire contingents appear to have employment relationships which are structurally more similar to traditional employment models. In comparison to Beard and Edwards' (1995) anticipated psychological experience of insecurity and inevitable termination, the direct-hire or in-house contingent worker–employer relationship can take on the form of an ongoing relationship. However, direct-hire arrangements do, in fact, create the curious situation where a distinction can be made between an ongoing "on-call" relationship and an ongoing employment relationship. In addition, within many direct-hire or

roster-based contingent arrangements, it may also be the case that direct-hire workers are deployed in assorted capacities or to various units within the organization,
which potentially increases the number and complexity of nested work relationships
(Barsness, 1996; Gallagher and McLean Parks, in press).

For many individuals, work as an in-house temporary may be seen as a means of
obtaining more permanent employment with the employer. Under such expectations,
it may be possible to suggest that the relationship between the worker and the organization may become less "transactional" and more "relational" in nature. More
specifically, some direct-hire contingent workers may begin to view the arrangement
as more open-ended and may be willing to participate in extra-role behaviors which
may not be immediately rewarded under the terms of the contract (e.g., Van Dyne
and Ang, 1998). Such behavior may be based on the expectation that positive behaviors
as an in-house contingent will eventually be reciprocated by the organization through
an offer of a more traditional employment contract.

The above-noted point not only raises the issue of understanding the intent of
contingent workers, but also the importance of "volition." Emerging empirical studies have found that contingent workers who were "voluntarily" employed as temporaries had significantly higher levels of both intrinsic and overall job satisfaction
compared with individuals who were "involuntarily" working as temporaries due to
the lack of more permanent options (Krausz et al., 1995). More recently, Krausz (in
press) found that not only did a voluntary vs. involuntary work status affect job-
related attitudes, but contingent workers who viewed temporary work as a long-
term preference had significantly higher levels of overall intrinsic and extrinsic job
satisfaction compared with workers who undertook temporary assignments as a
"short-term" arrangement or were unable to secure permanent employment (i.e.,
involuntary temps). From a theoretical perspective these findings are particularly
important to understanding contingent work because, similar to research on part-
time work (e.g., Barling and Gallagher, 1996), it affirms the view that volition is
associated with work-related attitudes. Such findings also fit well with prior research
on "status congruency" (Deery and Mahony, 1994; Krausz et al., 1995; Walsh and
Deery, 1999) which argues that job-related satisfaction reflects the degree of match
between preferred and actual work arrangements. Similarly, it might be argued that
the degree of violation may be closely tied to an occupation or profession. Most
notably, among "elite" temps (e.g., accountants, engineers) and certain categories of
direct-hire temporaries (e.g., nurses), the choice to work in a temporary or contingent arrangement may be more a function of individual choice than of a lack of
permanent opportunities.

Efforts to apply existing behavioral frameworks, developed in the context of identifiable employer – employee relationships to the world of contingent employment,
can become even more complex when attention is directed toward the growing number
of contingent workers who are employed as "independent contractors." As previously noted, independent contractors are technically self-employed and provide a
"client" organization with their services for a specific project or task. In contrast to
the Beard and Edwards (1995) characterization of temporary work as having low
worker predictability and control, independent contractors may have substantial input concerning when, where, and how the work is performed.

Independent contractor arrangements also vary from other forms of contingent work in that they may have contractual relationships with more than one "client" organization at a particular point in time (London, 1998). Unlike "multiple agency" situations, found in temporary-help firm arrangements, the fulfillment of obligations to one client does not represent a simultaneous fulfillment of responsibilities to other clients. However, the question may arise as to whether or not the nature of the psychological contract differs between the independent contractor and each client organization. In particular, although it is reasonable to assert that most contractual arrangements between independent contractors and clients are clearly delineated transactional statements of mutual obligations and responsibilities, it is possible to suggest that a desire to establish a repeat or "ongoing" series of contractual arrangements may lead contractors to establish more pliable or relational contracts. Furthermore, independent contractors may evidence differing levels of attachment to client organizations depending on the importance or dependency that the contractor places on a specific client relationship. Along similar lines, questions pertaining to job-related satisfaction, motivation, and commitment for independent contractors may be complicated since such workers are simultaneously performing different roles, which are nested in different client organizations and work environments.

In summary, the growth of contingent work raises a broad range of issues concerning the applicability of behavioral theories, developed in the context of ongoing employment relationships, to the reality in the world of more temporary and flexible contractual arrangements. The challenge that lies ahead is the task of determining the extent to which the theoretical underpinnings, which have guided our understanding of employment relationships, can be fully or partially transferred to contingent work arrangements. The growth of contingent work fits well with the point raised only a decade ago by Pfeffer and Baron (1988), that there is a continuum of organization inclusiveness in labor contracts and that much of this variety is overlooked by theory. Within this section, frequent reference has been made to the applicability of psychological contract theory and research to the world of contingent employment. This is not to suggest that psychological contracts represent the definitive framework for the study of contingent employment. However, the more salient point rests in the fact that the task of further developing a theoretical or behavioral foundation, in which to better explain the attitudes and behaviors of contingent workers, cannot be based on the view that there is a uniform, or for that matter, typical form of contingent employment. A more encompassing theoretical and analytical framework requires recognition of the diversity along the continuum of contingent work arrangements.

● Research and Practice: Future Issues ●

As noted throughout this chapter, the literature is replete with descriptive and prescriptive writings which have sought to explain the market, governmental, and strategic factors which have contributed to the increased utilization of contingent employment contracts. In addition, there is a litany of ascribed benefits which contingent contracts may have for organizational flexibility and efficiency. There is an increasing number of writings which have also sought to expose the past and continuing presence of a "dark side" to the world of contingent and short- term employment contracts (e.g., Nollen, 1996; Parker, 1994; Rogers, 1995). But as also suggested earlier in this chapter, it is important to realize that contingent work is not a monolithic concept. It exists in different contractual forms, and both organizations and workers may be driven by differing motivations for entering into contingent work contracts.

The emerging behavioral research, which is focussed on many of the previously mentioned attitudes and behaviors observed among contingent workers, is both instructive but subject to limitations. Most notably the limitations rest, in part, not with the individual contribution but in the fact that when many of these recent studies are viewed collectively, a rather unclear and, at times, contradictory image takes shape. These fuzzy outcomes reflect obvious differences in the definition and operationalization of the dependent variables of interest, as well as a number of other complicating factors. Within some studies, the focus on analysis has been on contrasting contingent with traditional workers, while other studies have focussed on differences within the contingent workforce. Furthermore, the type or characterization of what is being viewed as contingent employment varies dramatically from study to study. Despite these limitations, there are a number of avenues for future research which may warrant even greater attention.

Measurement

An examination of the many measurements used in recent empirical studies and broader discussions of the structure of various contingent work arrangements emphasizes the need for future research to give greater attention to the relevancy and design of particular behavioral constructs (Gallagher and McLean Parks, in press). One of the best possible illustrations of this concern is the measurement of commitment to the "employer" organization within the context of contingent work. Not only may there be questions about who the employer is, but also about the psychometric properties of the items which have been used to create such measures. For example, a number of recent studies have taken commonly utilized measures of organizational commitment (Mowday, Porter, and Steers, 1982; Meyer and Allen, 1997) and modified the "object" of commitment to apply to both temporary-help firms and "client" organizations. Obviously, the wholesale application of affective commitment scales, which are partially anchored in terminology such as "a sense of belonging to *my* organization," to temporary-help firms or clients has an element of ambiguity for dispatched or self-employed independent contractors. Similarly, the applicability of measures of continuance commitment, which address the difficulty of leaving the (my) organization, may in fact be more of a form of "normative" commitment which a temporary worker holds to the temporary-help firm than "continuance" commitment to the client. In the case of self-employed independent contractors, the meaning of employer commitment may be irrelevant or possibly have more significance in terms of "occupational" or "professional" commitment. In sum, it is suggested that before the agenda gets overextended, researchers should refocus attention on the need to reassess the validity of constructs which are being applied to contingent worker research but developed in the context of the traditional ongoing employer–employee relationship.

Trust

The growing introduction of contingent employment contracts into organizations which have primarily structured the employment relationship on the basis of permanent or more ongoing contractual arrangements also raises questions concerning the potential impact which the utilization of contingent workers has on managerial practices.

One issue, which may be in need of greater understanding, is related to the possible impact which the introduction of contingent work arrangements has upon the "trust" or faith in the perceived fairness which more traditional or permanent employees hold toward their employer organization (Pearce, 1993). Such a question may be of particular importance in light of suggestions that worker perceptions of organizational trust are associated with performance levels. Although the issue of the relationship between the use of contingent workers and organizational trust has received limited attention, there is some evidence to suggest that the use of contingent workers is associated with lower levels of trust and perceived organization fairness (Lautsch, 1999; Morishima and Feuille, 2000; Pearce, 1993) and higher levels of perceived insecurity among permanent workers (Kochan et al., 1994). Clearly a need exists to more definitively address the spillover effect that the use of contingent workers may have on permanent workers. However, it would also be important to determine if perceived shifts of organizational trust and fairness were related to changes in the nature of the psychological contract which the permanent worker holds with the employer organization (e.g., Ho and Ang, 1998; Sparrow and Cooper, 1998). Furthermore, it is conceivable to speculate that the process by which an organization introduces contingent workers may affect both employee trust and the nature of the psychological contract. For example, utilizing contingent work as a strategy for expansion may have fundamentally different implications than when permanent jobs are replaced with contingent workers. As noted by Schalk and Freese (1999), the level of distrust and resulting insecurity associated with the introduction of change in the form of contingent workers may have implications for the extent to which current workers seek to either "balance," "revise," or totally "abandon" their existing psychological contract with their employer organization.

Management strategies

For research on the issue of contingent work to have value, it should ultimately be transferable into suggestions as to how organizations can more effectively utilize workforces which consist of both permanent and contingent workers. In particular, a number of studies have noted that the role of managers and the skills they require may be substantially different in organizations that place greater reliance on an externalized or contingent-based workforce (e.g., Feldman, 1995; Pfeffer and Baron,

1988; Smither, 1995). Recent research by Lautsch (1999) has suggested that organizations may follow different strategies in regard to the degree to which distinctions are made between permanent and contingent workers in practices pertaining to pay and task differentiation, supervision, skill development, and the movement of workers from temporary to permanent status, and that such distinctions in treatment may be a function of the strategic objectives associated with the motivation to use contingent workers. For example, Lautsch found that organizations which utilized contingent workers to contain costs were likely to follow management practices which tended to separate contingent from permanent workers and maintain a moderate to high level of differential between the two groups of workers in terms of pay, task assignments, and closeness of supervision. Conversely, firms which were motivated to use contingent workers for the primary reason of gaining staffing flexibility were more inclined to follow management practices minimizing wage differentials as well as placing greater parity between permanent and contingent workers in terms of tasks, supervision, and skill development (Lautsch, 1999; Morishima and Feuille, 2000).

Teams and team-building

There is also a growing level of research and practitioner interest in the development and success of team-based approaches to the performance of organizational tasks. Once again, one might question the extent to which the utilization of workers on contingent employment contracts hinders or contributes to such broader organizational goals as team-building. Unfortunately, very little empirical evidence exists that deals with the impact of contingent workers on team formation and effectiveness. As noted, there is considerable speculation that organizations may be extremely reluctant to assign contingent workers to perform tasks that both require extensive task integration with other units or employees, and have a strong bias toward excluding contingent workers from sensitive or proprietary information or data (Matusik and Hill, 1998; Pearce, 1993). In fact, some argument exists that the inclusion of contingents as organizational team members may be dysfunctional for the reason that contingents are not as internally networked within organizations as permanent employees (Barsness, 1996; Nollen and Axel, 1996). On the other side of the coin, there is some empirical evidence to support the observation that the use of contingent workers does not necessary negatively affect team performance. In fact, Barsness (1996) found that among direct-hire nurses in the health-care industry, the clear structure and professional qualifications of "service-based" teams more readily accommodated the integration of contingent workers. By contrast, the integration of contingents (professional or otherwise) into a team environment could be more difficult in project-based teams or where member's tasks were less clearly defined (Barsness, 1996).

Ironically, Matusik and Hill (1998) made a rather compelling argument that the integration of independent contractors (consultants) into organization-based work teams represented an outstanding opportunity for firms to promote the creation of new knowledge. The inclusion of skilled contingents served as a means of integrating externally developed public knowledge and practices into the organization. However, the success of knowledge transfer and subsequent new private knowledge creation within a firm may, in part, be a function of the ability of a firm to proactively manage the interface between contingent and traditional employees. The issue of maximizing the potential contribution of contingent workers to an organization again appears to be dependent upon the extent to which management seeks to develop strategies which integrate rather than segregate contingents (Gerber, 1999; Matusik and Hill, 1998). In many respects, future research in the area of contingent employment should give attention to organization-based factors which encourage or discourage the integration of contingents.

Human resource development

Closely tied into the issues of knowledge transfer and strategies for managing contingent workers are questions concerning how and to what extent contingent workers are able to develop and upgrade their human capital. Within the context of traditional employment relationships, employer organizations frequently undertook the responsibility for providing employees with varying degrees of firm-specific and generalizable training. Also within many companies, an emphasis was placed on the development of skills which contributed to employee advancement and promotion. For workers employed in contingent or short-term arrangements, it appears that the motivation of employing organizations to provide other than the most basic of training and orientation may be limited. Particularly in the case of workers hired through temporary employment agencies and independent contractor arrangements, the employer or client organization often expects that the contingent worker already possesses the needed skills to perform the job for which they have been hired. This is especially true in the case of independent contractors who are often hired for the specific reason that the organization internally lacks the skills for which the contingent is hired. In the case of workers hired through temporary-help firms, the training responsibility may be a function of professional level. For example, for high-skilled temporaries such as nurses, accountants, translators, etc., training and knowledge development is likely to be acquired external to the temporary-help firm or the client organization. In the case of less skilled contingent occupations, temporary employment firms may play a greater role in the training and actual development of workers by providing them specific job-skill training.

Among those professionals who work in contingent arrangements, a major task is to not only retain employment but also maintain their *employability* (Arthur and Rousseau, 1996; Carnoy et al., 1997; Kanter, 1995). What then becomes a crucial issue is how highly skilled contingents are able to continually upgrade their human capital. As noted by Matusik and Hill (1998), knowledge transfer in a concluding relationship can be bi-directional. However, the extent to which contingents are able to access new information and skills again returns to the question of the willingness of the client organization to allow contingents to be integrated into client-based work teams and exposed to developing knowledge (Castaneda, 1999). Among independent contractors, there are also issues concerning the extent to which the search for new information or knowledge is dependent upon the development of informal networking arrangements with other independent contractors (Carnoy et al., 1997).

In the future, it would appear that more research is needed in understanding the means by which contingent workers are able to develop and update their employability. And once again, it appears reasonable to suggest that the source and process of skill development may not only be a function of occupation skill level but also the form of the contingent work arrangement. In the case of contingents hired through temporary-help firms, there may be a joint employer relationship between the client and temporary firm which dictates the need for coordination between the training efforts of the temporary firm and the skills needs of the client organization. From a broader macro-organizational perspective, this may suggest the importance of understanding the conditions under which client or provider organizations are able to develop strategic partnerships pertaining to the training and effective placement of contingent workers.

● Conclusion ●

The goal of this chapter has not been to overcomplicate our understanding of contingent work arrangements. However, a simple reality exists in the fact that contingent work arrangements are, in fact, both diverse in their form as well as in the underlying motivations as to why employer organizations utilize such employment contracts. Further, contingent work certainly fails to fit the narrow stereotyped image of unskilled day-laborers and office support staff. From an academic perspective, there still remain a substantial number of issues which deserve further consideration. As suggested throughout this chapter, one broad but central question relates to the applicability of existing theories of organizational behavior and industrial psychology, which were primarily developed in the context of ongoing and identifiable employer–employee relationships, to contingent work arrangements. Ultimately, the future of contingent research needs more *a priori* consideration of theory application and hypothesis testing rather than *post hoc* utilization of theory to explain unexpected results. Furthermore, much more needs to be known about the practical side of how organizations manage and utilize contingent workers, most notably, the extent to which contingent workers are either integrated into the organization or segregated into forms of organizational "apartheid" (Gerber, 1999) and how such practices impact the ability of the organization to realize the goals associated with the utilization of contingent arrangements, as well as the implications for the future employability of individuals who have voluntarily or involuntary chosen to work in contingent arrangements.

The challenge of contingent work is that there currently exist more questions than answers. But as contingent work arrangements continue to grow worldwide, the opportunities for identifying and examining many of the emerging questions become greater for both researchers and practitioners.

REFERENCES

Alba-Ramirez, A. (1998). How temporary is temporary employment in Spain? *Journal of Labor Research*, 19, 695–710.

Arthur, M.B., and Rousseau, D.M. (1996) (eds). *The Boundaryless Career: A New Employment Principle for a New Organizational Era*. Oxford: Oxford University Press.

Barling, J., and Gallagher, D.G. (1996). Part-time employment. In C.L. Cooper and I.T. Robertson (eds). *International Review of Industrial and Organizational Psychology*, 11, 243–77. Chichester: Wiley.

Barsness, Z.I. (1996). Just-in-time workers and the team based organization: Employee orientation, internal group process and work group effectiveness. Paper presented at the Academy of Management Meeting, August, 1996, Cincinnati, Ohio.

Beard, K.M., and Edwards, J.R. (1995). Employees at risk: Contingent work and the experience of contingent workers. In C.L. Cooper and D.M. Rousseau (eds). *Trends in Organizational Behavior* 2. Chichester: Wiley, pp. 109–26.

Brewster, C., Mayne, L., and Tregaskis, O. (1997). Flexible working in Europe: A review of the evidence. *Management International Review*, 37, 85–103.

Brewster, C., and Tregaskis, O. (1997). The non-permanent workforce. *Flexible Working*, 2, 6–8.

Cappelli, P. (1999). *The New Deal at Work*. Boston, MA: Harvard Business School Press.

Carnoy, M., Castells, M., and Benner, C. (1997). Labour markets and employment practices in the age of flexibility: A case study of Silicon Valley. *International Labour Review*, 136, 27–48.

Carré, F., Ferber, M.A., Golden, L., and Herzenberg, S.L. (eds) (2000). *Nonstandard Work*. Champaign, ILL: Industrial Relations Research Association.

Castaneda, L.W. (1999). Social networks in the open labor market: An exploration of independent contractors' careers. Paper presented at the Academy of Management Meeting, August, 1999, Chicago, IL.

Cohany, S. (1998). Workers in alternative employment arrangements: A second look. *Monthly Labor Review*, 121, November, 3–21.

Cully, M., Woodland, S., O'Reilly, A., and Dix, G. (1999). *Britain at Work*. London: Routledge.

Dale, A., and Bamford, C. (1988). Temporary workers: Cause for concern or complacency? *Work, Employment and Society*, 2, 191–209.

Davis-Blake, A., and Uzzi, B. (1993). Determinants of employment externalization: A study of temporary workers and independent contractors. *Administrative Science Quarterly*, 38, 195–223.

Deery, S.J., and Mahony, A. (1994). Temporal flexibility: Management strategies and employee preferences in the retail industry. *Journal of Industrial Relations*, 36, 332–52.

De Grip, A., Hoevenberg, J., and Willems, E. (1997). Atypical employment in the European Union. *International Labor Review*, 136, 49–71.

Delsen, L. (1999). Changing work relations in the European Union. In I.U. Zeytinoğlu (ed.). *Changing Work Relationships in Industrialized Economies*. Amsterdam: John Benjamins Publishing, pp. 99–114.

Druker, J., and Stanworth, C. (2000). Labour market change and the contingent workforce: The use of employment agencies. *Proceedings of the 12th World Congress of the International Industrial Relations Research Association*. Tokyo, Japan, 1, 120–30.

Ellingson, J.E., Gruys, M. L., and Sackett, P. (1998). Factors related to the satisfaction and performance of temporary employees. *Journal of Applied Psychology*, 83, 913–21.

Feldman, D.C. (1995). Managing part-time and temporary employment relationships: Individual needs and organizational demands. In M. London (ed.). *Employees, Careers, and Job Creation*. San Francisco: Jossey-Bass, pp. 121–41.

Feldman, D.C., Doerpinghaus, H.I., and Turnley, W.H. (1994). Managing temporary workers: A permanent HRM challenge. *Organizational Dynamics*, Autumn, 49–63.

Gallagher, D.G., and McLean Parks, J. (in press). I pledge thee my troth . . . contingently:

Commitment and the contingent work relationship. *Human Resource Management Review*.

Gallagher, D.G., and Sverke, M. (2000). Contingent employment contracts: Are existing theories still relevant? *Proceedings of the 12th World Congress of the International Industrial Relations Research Association*. Tokyo, Japan, 1, 131–40.

Gallie, D., White, M., Cheng, Y., and Tomlinson, M. (1998). *Restructuring the Employment Relationship*. Oxford: Oxford University Press.

Gerber, S.Z. (1999). Independent contractors: The impact of perceived fair treatment on measures of commitment, organizational citizenship behavior and intent to stay. Paper presented at the Academy of Management Meeting, August, 1999, Chicago, IL.

Golden, L., and Appelbaum, E. (1992). What was driving the 1982–88 boom in temporary employment. *American Journal of Economics and Sociology*, 51, 473–93.

Greene, B. (2000). Independent contractors: An attractive option? University of Otago, Dunedin, New Zealand. Unpublished research paper.

Greer, C.R., Youngblood, S.A., and Gray, D.A. (1999). Human resource management outsourcing: The make or buy decision. *Academy of Management Executive*, 13, 85–96.

Hartley, J. (1995). Challenge and change in employment relations. In L. Tetrick and J. Barling (eds). *Changing Employment Relations: Behavioral and Social Perspective*. Washington, D.C.: American Psychological Association, pp. 3–30.

Hipple, S. (1998). Contingent work: Results from the second survey. *Monthly Labor Review*, November, 22–35.

Ho, V.T., and Ang, S. (1998). Spillover of psychological contract: When employees become contract labor in an outsourcing context. Paper presented at the Academy of Management Meeting, August, 1998, San Diego, CA.

International Labour Office (2000). *Meeting of Experts on Workers in Situations Needing Protection*. MEWNP/2000. Geneva: International Labour Office.

Kanter, R.M. (1995). Nice work if you can get it: The software industry as a model for tomorrow's jobs. *American Prospect*, 23, 52–9.

Kochan, T.A., Smith, M., Wells, J.C., and Rebitzer, J.B. (1994). Human resource strategies and contingent workers: The case of safety and health in the petrochemical industry. *Human Resource Management*, 33, 55–77.

Krausz, M. (in press). Effects of short and long term preference for temporary work upon psychological outcomes. *International Journal of Manpower*.

Krausz, M., Bizman, A., and Braslavsky, D. (in press). Effects of attachment on preferences for and satisfaction with different employment contracts: An exploratory study. *Journal of Business and Psychology*.

Krausz, M., Brandwein, T., and Fox, S. (1995). Work attitudes and emotional responses of permanent, voluntary, and involuntary temporary-help employees: An exploratory study. *Applied Psychology: An International Review*, 44, 217–32.

Laird, K., and Williams, N. (1996). Employment growth in the temporary help supply industry. *Journal of Labor Research*, 17, 663–81.

Lautsch, B.A. (1999). Boundary labor markets: A grounded theory of contingent work. Working paper, Simon Fraser University, Burnaby, British Columbia, Canada.

London, M. (1998). *Career Barriers: How People Experience, Overcome and Avoid Failure*. Mahwah, NJ: Lawrence Erlbaum Associates.

March, J., and Simon, H. (1958). *Organizations*. New York: Wiley.

Marin, E. (2000). The perspectives for a new and comprehensive vision of the protection of workers. *Proceedings of the 12th World Congress of the International Industrial Relations Research Association*, Tokyo, Japan, 1, 151–9.

Matusik, S.F., and Hill, C.W.L. (1998). The utilization of contingent work, knowledge creation, and competitive advantage. *Academy of Management Review*, 23, 680–97.

McLean Parks, J., Kidder, D. L., and Gallagher, D.G. (1998). Fitting square pegs into round holes: Mapping the domain of contingent work arrangements onto the psychological contract. *Journal of Organizational Behavior*, 19, 697–730.

Meyer, J.P., and Allen, N.J. (1997). *Commitment in the Workplace: Theory, Research, and Application*. Thousand Oaks, CA: Sage Publications.

Morishima, M., and Feuille, P. (2000), Effects of the use of contingent workers on regular status workers: A Japanese–US comparison. Paper presented at the 12th World Congress of the International Industrial Relations Research Association, May, 2000, Tokyo, Japan.

Mowday, R.T., Porter, L.W., and Steers, R.M. (1982). *Employee–Organizational Linkages: The Psychology of Commitment, Absenteeism & Turnover*. New York: Academic Press.

Nishikawa, M. (2000). Diversification in the use of atypical workers at the Japanese establishments. *Proceedings of the 12th World Congress of the International Industrial Relations Research Association*. Tokyo, Japan, 1, 160–8.

Nollen, S.D. (1996). Negative aspects of temporary employment. *Journal of Labor Research*, 17, 567–81.

Nollen, S.D. (1999). Flexible work arrangements. In I.U. Zeytinoğlu (ed.). *Changing Work Relationships in Industrialized Economies*. Amsterdam: John Benjamins Publishing.

Nollen, S.D., and Axel, H. (1996). *Managing Contingent Workers*. New York: American Management Association.

Parker, R.E. (1994). *Flesh Peddlers and Warm Bodies: The Temporary Help Industry and its Workers*. New Brunswick, NJ: Rutgers University Press.

Pearce, J.L. (1993). Toward an organizational behavior of contract laborers: Their psychological involvement and effects on employee coworkers. *Academy of Management Journal*, 36, 1082–96.

Pfeffer, J., and Baron, N. (1988). Taking the work back out: Recent trends in the structures of employment. In B.M. Staw and L.L. Cummings (eds). *Research in Organizational Behavior*, 10, 257–303.

Polivka, A.E., Cohany, S.R., and Hipple, S. (2000). Definition, composition, and economic consequences of the nonstandard workforce. In F. Carré, M.A. Ferber, L. Golden, and S.A. Herzenberg (eds). *Nonstandard Work*. Champaign, IL: Industrial Relations Research Association, pp. 41–94.

Polivka, A.E., and Nardone, T. (1989). The definition of contingent work. *Monthly Labor Review*, 112, 9–16.

Reichers, A.E. (1985). A review and reconceptualization of organizational commitment. *Academy of Management Review*, 10, 465–76.

Rifkin, J. (1995). *The End of Work*. New York: Putnam.

Rogers, J.K. (1995). Just a temp: Experience and structure of alienation in temporary clerical employment. *Work and Occupations*, 22, 137–66.

Rousseau, D.M. (1995). *Psychological Contracts in Organizations: Understanding Written and Unwritten Agreements*. Thousand Oaks, CA: Sage Publications.

Schalk, R., and Freese, C. (1999). The impact of organizational changes on the psychological contract and attitudes toward work in four health care organizations. In K. Iskasson, C. Hogstedt, C. Eriksson, and T. Theorell (eds). *Health Effects of the New Labour Market*. New York: Kluwer Academic, pp. 129–44.

Segal, L.M., and Sullivan, D.G. (1997). The growth of temporary services work. *Journal of Economics Perspectives*, 11, 117–36.

Smither, J.W. (1995). Creating an internal contingent workforce: Managing the resource link. In M. London (ed.). *Employees, Careers, and Job Creation*. San Francisco: Jossey-Bass, pp. 121–41.

Sparrow, P. (1998). The pursuit of multiple and parallel organizational flexibilities: Reconstituting jobs. *European Journal of Work and Organizational Psychology*, 7, 79–95.

Sparrow, P., and Cooper, C. (1998). New organizational forms: The strategic relevance of future psychological contract scenarios. Sheffield University Management School Discussion Paper 97.16. Sheffield, England: February 1998.

Sverke, M., Gallagher, D.G., and Hellgren, J. (1999). Alternative work arrangements: Job stress, well-being, and work attitudes among employees with different employment contracts. In K. Iskasson, C. Hogstedt, C. Eriksson, and T. Theorell (eds). *Health Effects of the New Labour Market*. New York: Kluwer Academic, pp. 145–68.

Treu, T. (1992). Labour flexibility in Europe. *International Labour Review*, 131, 497–512.

Uzzi, D., and Barsness, Z.I. (1998). Contingent employment in British establishments: Organizational determinants of the use of fixed-term hires and part-time workers. *Social Forces*, 76, 967–1007.

Van Dyne, L., and Ang, S. (1998). Organizational citizenship behavior of contingent workers in Singapore. *Academy of Management Journal*, 41, 692–703.

von Hippel, C., Mangum, S.L., Greenberger, D.B., Heneman, R.L., and Skoglind, J.D. (1997). Temporary employment: Can organizations and employers both win? *Academy of Management Executive*, 11, 93–104.

Vosko, L. (2000). *Temporary Work: The General Rise of a Precarious Employment Relationship*. Toronto: University of Toronto Press.

Walsh, J., and Deery, S. (1999). Understanding the peripheral workforce: Evidence from the service sector. *Human Resource Management Journal*, 9, 50–63.

Zeytinoğlu, I.U. (1991). A study of part-time workers covered by collective agreements: Why do employers hire them? *Relations Industrielles / Industrial Relations*, 46, 401–18.

Zeytinoğlu, I.U. (1999a) (ed.). *Changing Work Relationships in Industrialized Economies*. Amsterdam: John Benjamins Publishing.

Zeytinoğlu, I.U. (1999b). Flexible work arrangements: An overview of development in Canada. In I.U. Zeytinoğlu (ed.). *Changing Work Relationships in Industrialized Economies*. Amsterdam: John Benjamins Publishing, pp. 41–58.

7

Reduced-Load Work Arrangements: The Changing Nature of Professional and Managerial Work[1]

MARY DEAN LEE, PIERRE-GUY HOURQUET, AND
SHELLEY M. MACDERMID

Professional and managerial careers are currently going through upheaval and a process of differentiation and evolution, as a result of a multitude of convergent forces at work in North American society. At the organizational level, the productivity crisis and increased global competition have led to recurrent waves of downsizing and delayering which have reduced the sheer number of managerial jobs and dismantled traditional internal promotion opportunities (Osterman, 1996). Firms have also been experimenting with new employment relationships and organizational structures that provide greater flexibility to adapt to shifting market contingencies (Arthur and Rousseau, 1996; Sullivan, 1999). At the same time, the economy's shift to the Information Age and the critical role of knowledge workers, often in short supply, and an expected shortfall of qualified middle-level managers over the next ten years has led to a war for talent (Capelli, 2000). Recruitment and retention issues are pushing some firms to rethink previous decisions to abandon traditional internal promotion systems (*Business Week*, 2000; Gunz, Evans, and Jalland, 2000), and other firms are clearly seeking to adapt to the seller's market by offering whatever the desired potential employees want in terms of working conditions, benefits, compensation, etc. (Capelli, 2000).

Another force which has strongly shaken traditional professional and managerial careers is demographic change, which has affected who is pursuing professional and managerial careers and the scope of other responsibilities these individuals must juggle. There has been a sharp increase in rates of women's paid employment, especially those with pre-school-age children. In particular, there has been a dramatic increase in the percentage of women in high-status professions, like medicine, law, accounting, engineering, management. At the same time there has been a decline in the prevalence of the traditional family structure, and in fact more than half the labor force is from a dual-earner household. So both men and women have experienced increased demands at home, in that men are sharing more in the family work, on top of their paid employment; women are still doing the majority of family work but on top of part-time or full-time jobs. A survey of time use among Canadians between the ages of 25 and 44 (Women in the Labour Force, 1994) found that on average, men were doing 48.6 hours of paid work per week and 22.8 hours per week of unpaid work; women were doing 38.8 hours of paid work per week and 34.4 hours of unpaid work.

A third force of change has been a gradual increase in actual hours worked per week among men and women across all occupational categories in North America (Babbar and Aspelin, 1998; Bond, Galinsky, and Swanberg, 1998). This trend has been more pronounced among white-collar, salaried professionals and managers, whose hours are determined by work unit norms or informal expectations of unofficial "overtime" rather than a fixed schedule (Eastman, 1998; Perlow, 1998). The fact that this increase in work demands has coincided with changing family structures has been described as having created somewhat of a collision course (Bailyn, 1993), because demands have been going up both at work and at home, but there are no additional hours in the day or week!

Finally, a shift in social norms and individual attitudes has begun to be noticed and documented involving increased employee concern about having adequate time for non-work commitments and interests. Several studies have recently found that among the job factors men and women consider most important in taking a new job, compatibility with family life in terms of workload and scheduling flexibility has become more important than in the past and equally important for young men and women (Friedman and Greenhaus, 2000; *Perspectives*, 2000).

Given the convergence of these various forces, it is not surprising that a new phenomenon has emerged among professionals: they are negotiating alternative work arrangements which involve working *less* – through job sharing, reduced load, or reduced hours – in order to escape the time crunch. This kind of work is distinct from involuntary temporary, or contingent, part-time work, which usually offers limited compensation and opportunities for advancement. A number of studies have begun to document the experiences of a variety of professionals in these kinds of work arrangements – in medicine, accounting, law, engineering (Barnett and Gareis, 2000; Clark, 1998; Epstein, Seron, Oglensky, and Saute,1998; Lee, Engler, and Wright, in press; Levy, Flynn, and Kellogg, 1998; Meiksins and Whalley, 1996). And more and more corporations are allowing non-standard, reduced-load work arrangements across a wide variety of types of jobs, in order to accommodate valued employees (Catalyst, 1997; Lee, MacDermid, Williams, Buck, Schreiber, Borelli, Leiba-O'Sullivan, Smith, Bernstein, and Dohring, 1999). However, there has been little systematic investigation of what kinds of terms and conditions surround these alternative work arrangements and how well they are working out, from the perspective of the individual employees, as well as their employers. The two overarching objectives of this study then, were: (1) to begin to document the variety of kinds of reduced-load work arrangements among corporate professionals and managers; and (2) to examine outcomes in order to generate a theoretical framework for explaining under what conditions these new ways of working, and others like them, are likely to be mutually beneficial, from both the individual and organizational perspectives.

● Method ●

Sample and procedures

Results reported in this chapter come from an exploratory study of 82 cases of reduced-load work arrangements involving 46 managers and 36 professionals, all of whom were currently or had recently worked on a reduced-load basis for at least six months. Managers were distinguished from professionals by having responsibility for three or more direct reports. Reduced-load work was defined as voluntarily working 50–90 percent of a full-time equivalent job, with an accompanying proportional reduction in compensation.

Because reduced-load work is still relatively rare among professionals and managers in corporations, participants were recruited using personal contacts with human resources and work/life administrators, "cold calls" to employers, and direct mail solicitations to members of organizations. As a result, the sample is diverse but not representative. The work arrangements were located in 45 employers throughout North America, in industries including manufacturing, financial services, natural resources, telecommunications, and professional and managerial services. The employers included were disproportionately large, with workforces ranging from 170 to 240,000 employees. The median workforce size was 34,200 employees.

We interviewed 86 managers and professionals working in 82 part-time work arrangements (four were job shares). Most of these individuals were women (N = 77), and most were married (N = 78) and parents (N = 80) of relatively young children (average age of youngest child = 4.7 years). On average, the reduced-load arrangements had been in existence 4.2 years and involved .72 of a full-time equivalent job. The average number of hours worked each week was 32, about 18 hours less than had been worked on a full-time basis. Pro-rated to a full-time equivalent, salaries ranged from US$31,111 to $175,000, with an average of $79,441 at the time of data collection, 1996–8.

Multiple sources of data and methods of collection were used. We conducted face-to-face interviews with each manager or professional, as well as his or her spouse or partner, senior manager, a peer co-worker, and a human resources representative. Interviews with the target respondent lasted about 1.5 hours; other interviews lasted about 45 minutes. In all, 376 interviews were conducted, each transcribed verbatim for analysis. Each complete case generated about 100 pages of single-spaced transcripts.

Interviews were semi-structured and included the following topics: (1) how and why the reduced-load work arrangement came about; (2) how the job was restructured or created to accommodate the reduced-load schedule; (3) perceptions of the challenges and difficulties involved in restructuring the job; (4) costs and benefits of reduced-load work arrangements from multiple perspectives; and (5) factors important in making the reduced-load work arrangements successful or unsuccessful.

Finally, the subordinates of all managers in the sample were asked to complete a brief quantitative survey assessing their manager's effectiveness. Of the 253 direct reports of the managers in the study, 218 were sent questionnaires to complete anonymously and return directly to the researchers in a pre-stamped, self-addressed envelope. Overall, 72 percent (N = 153) of the questionnaires were returned.

Analyses and measures

Except for the survey of direct reports, data analyses were primarily qualitative. Rather than quantifying respondents' answers, qualitative methods analyze the actual content of what people say and how they say it. Most analyses for this study used a form of "axial coding," where interviewers combed through the transcripts for each case to extract any information relevant to several pre-selected issues (Miles and Huberman, 1994). These included the outcomes, costs and benefits of the reduced load, and the factors which facilitated and hindered its success. The results of the axial coding were compiled in "analytic memos" written for each case by the researcher who conducted the interviews. Material extracted from the transcripts was organized according to respondent (e.g. spouse, co-worker, boss, etc.).

The analytic memos provided long lists of examples and quotes related to each of the key issues, which were then aggregated across cases. As this occurred, clusters of similar ideas or themes became evident within the compiled lists, and it became possible to see how prevalent each theme was across all the cases in the data set. For example, we examined closely recurrent themes around individual and organizational outcomes or consequences of the reduced-load work arrangements.

The final section of the analytic memo mentioned subtexts, notable consistencies or inconsistencies across stakeholders within each case, and data that seemed puzzling. Finally, the interviewer in charge of each case provided an overview of the case outcomes through a series of ratings of the costs, benefits, and overall success of the case, taking into account the perspectives of all stakeholders. The ratings did not reflect the interviewer's personal opinion; rather, they were intended to summarize respondents' perceptions of costs and benefits. Using a scale from 1 to 7 (1 = low), interviewers first rated separately the costs and benefits of the reduced-load work arrangement from three perspectives – the target individual, the family, and the organization – generating a total of six ratings. By subtracting costs from benefits in each domain, three "net benefit" scores were created for the individual, the family, and the organizational domains. These ratings were then examined carefully, along with an overall review of all field notes, in order to assign a "Global Success" rating to each case.

The Global Success rating was designed to be a summary measure allowing us to make comparisons across cases on the overall success of the reduced-load work arrangement, from multiple perspectives. The interviewers considered the following criteria simultaneously, taking into account the perspectives of all stakeholders: (1) the extent to which individual professionals or managers were happy with their work arrangements, including from a long-term career perspective; (2) the extent to which the senior manager and co-workers reported positive outcomes; and (3) the extent to which the spouse or partner and target individual reported positive effects on children, family life, and/or the couple relationship. A rating of "1" indicated consistently negative outcomes reported across stakeholders and a "9" indicated consistently positive outcomes. Two researchers rated each case, and any differences were discussed and resolved. After the ratings were complete, three groups were created: High (scores of 7–9), Moderate (5–6), and Low (1–4) success.

For purposes of examining in more depth under what conditions reduced-load work arrangements resulted in mutually beneficial outcomes for both organizations and individuals, two sub-groups were created in the sample based on the "net benefit" ratings described above. The first group consisted of cases where the ratings of both organizational and individual net benefits were above the mean. This group was labeled HiHi. The second group consisted of cases in which the ratings of both organizational and individual net benefits were below the mean. This group was labeled LoLo.

● Results ●

First of all we provide a brief summary of findings related to the terms and conditions, as well as the overall success of the reduced-load arrangements studied. Secondly, we summarize emergent dominant themes in the qualitative data on individual and organizational outcomes. Thirdly, we examine closely the cases where mutually beneficial outcomes were achieved and not achieved, from an organizational and individual perspective. These cases are then interpreted as illustrating the importance of ongoing processes, drawing on two perspectives that represent the individual as an active and dynamic force in social contexts. Weick's (2000) enactment model of organizing and Ibarra's (1999) proposition that individuals experiment with "provisional selves" in career transitions serve as interpretive frameworks for explaining differences in individual and organizational outcomes.

Terms and conditions of reduced-load work arrangements

A complete report of the study findings can be obtained from either the first or third author of this chapter (Lee et al., 1999). Other published papers focus on various aspects of the study (e.g., Buck, Lee, MacDermid, and Smith, 2000; Lee, MacDermid, and Buck, 2000; MacDermid, Lee, Buck, and Williams, in press; Lee, MacDermid and Buck, in press).

Impetus and context. The most typical reason professionals and managers in this study gave for pursuing a reduced-load work arrangement was to spend more time with children or improve the quality of family life. They expressed a deep and continuing commitment to their careers, but an equally important commitment to their work at home in the family context. Those without children requested to work less in order to have time to pursue hobbies, religious activities, or community service, or in response to concerns about their health.

About 15 percent of the respondents changed employers in order to achieve a reduction in workload, usually because they had been unable to arrange a part-time position with a previous employer. In 72 percent of the cases individuals stayed with the same employer and either moved into a new or pre-existing part-time job, or negotiated a formal reconfiguration of their previous job. In the remainder of cases individuals continued to carry out essentially the same responsibilities but in less time, with varying levels of agreement between the senior manager and professional about how the same job was to be accomplished under formally "reduced load" and reduced compensation conditions.

Although 40 percent of the firms in the sample had well-developed and well-publicized policies, guidelines, or programs that specifically included the opportunity to work on a reduced-load basis, the actual negotiations took place in almost every case at the level of the work unit between the professional wanting to work less and his or her senior manager. Even with a formal policy on the books, it was the senior manager's responsibility to make sure there would be no negative business impact of initiating an alternative work arrangement.

Employer response.   Since there was no formal policy allowing reduced-load work at the professional level in over half the cases, it was important to ascertain why employers accommodated requests for alternative work arrangements. The most common rationale given had to do with retention. The senior managers talked about the fact that these individuals had strong performance records and/or had very specific skill sets in high demand and short supply. The firm could not afford to take the chance of losing these employees if it wanted to remain competitive. A second reason given was maintaining the firm's commitment to development of "high potential" employees. In 20 percent of the managerial cases these individuals had been identified as "fast trackers" when first entering the company, meaning they were viewed as having the potential to progress to the top rank of the company. Accordingly, these companies had invested heavily in training and development activities for these individuals, including frequent new job assignments in different areas of the firm, as well as mentoring relationships and more traditional training and development experiences. These employers had made a commitment to these employees for the long term (30–40 years), and they were not ready to toss in the towel for what they viewed as a likely short-term blip in an ultimately high-powered career trajectory.

There were two other kinds of rationale most commonly given to explain a positive employer response. The first had to do with Diversity in general. In a quarter of the firms there was a high level of commitment to Diversity and an explicit goal to increase the percentage of women at middle and upper levels of management. In one firm, for example, several different stakeholders indicated that the company had recently discovered it was losing a disproportionate number of senior, seasoned women managers just as they were ready to move into the most senior ranks of the company. In this firm there was a strongly held belief expressed by several senior managers interviewed, that by allowing reduced-load work arrangements, the company could perhaps stem the tide of talented women leaving and thus also increase their success in achieving Diversity goals.

A final recurrent theme in reasons for accommodating requests for reduced load was the fact that, in one-quarter of the firms, unusual work schedules had either always been part and parcel of the way work was allocated and distributed, or had recently proliferated in response to changing conditions in the external environment. For example, in these firms stakeholders often reported that the company had been experimenting with flex-time, telecommuting, compressed work weeks, work in multiple sites, use of subcontracting employees alongside permanent employees on project teams, etc. for many years. These practices then resulted in less resistance to yet another different way of working – reduced load. Respondents in these cases described their employers as being more results-oriented and putting less emphasis on "face" time, which made reduced-load work seem less of a big deal.

Duration and schedule of work. As reported earlier, the professionals and managers interviewed for this study worked in jobs structured on average at 72 percent of a full-time equivalent job. The most common degrees of reduction were 60 percent and 80 percent, which accounted for $\frac{3}{5}$ of the total sample. Their average number of hours actually worked was 32 hours per week, which of course represents more than 72 percent of 40 hours. However, in most organizations professionals are expected to work more than the official full-time work week, and most of the individuals in this study indicated they expected to work more than the official number of hours according to their percentage reduction. But in general the perception was that there was a limit to how much "overtime" was appropriate without being remunerated, whether through compensatory time off or additional pay. In many cases these professionals had an explicit mechanism for adjusting their own compensation according to the varying cycles of business throughout a given year. In other cases it was clear that it was up to the professionals themselves to make sure they were working an appropriate number of hours given their reduced load and reduced compensation. If they worked "too many" hours during a given period, they attempted to work less during other periods.

The actual logistics of work hours and places were highly variable and fluid over time. Less than half of the individuals on reduced load worked the same schedule throughout a given year (e.g., Monday to Thursday). Some worked different schedules at different times of the year; others varied their schedule on a weekly basis as a function of the needs of the business and/or children. Some worked in the office every day, just for fewer hours; others worked some days in the office and some at home. Most of these individuals had the capacity to work from home, and often the company was paying for the appropriate technological support to allow them to do this. Some drew more rigid boundaries around being disturbed on their day off. Others checked voice mail and e-mail throughout the week.

As over half of the individuals in reduced-load work arrangements in the study had been working this way over four years, it is not surprising that most of them had experienced working in more than one part-time position. Furthermore, many described an ongoing process of experimentation and adaptation in order to find the appropriate amount of work and best schedule from a time and place perspective, considering both work unit demands and family circumstances. In this sense, because of ongoing fine-tuning and adjustments made, reduced-load work in this study appeared to be more like "customized" work rather than "part-time" work. It was more fluid than fixed, and the logistical details emerged out of a continuous process of interaction and mutual negotiation with bosses, clients, co-workers, direct reports, spouses, and childcare providers.

Compensation structure.   In 90 percent of the cases studied individuals were paid a salary pro-rated according to the percentage of load reduction, and their benefits were either continued as if they were still full-time, or were also pro-rated. There was great variation in how firms handled bonuses in these cases. Some didn't allow reduced-load professionals to qualify for bonuses at all; others pro-rated the bonuses; and others kept bonuses intact. Other managerial perks were also handled in different ways. For example, in some cases individuals were not allowed to buy stock options while on reduced load. Some kept their company cars, while others had to give up prestigious offices.

Types of jobs.   There was a wide range of types of jobs being done on a reduced-load basis, and there was no agreement among stakeholders about specific jobs that absolutely could not be restructured to accommodate someone wanting to work less. Individuals in "independent contributor" jobs, without responsibility for the work of others, were most likely to work in the areas of Finance, Human Resources and Corporate Communications, or Research and Development. However, 25 percent were in Information Systems, Production/Operations, and Marketing. Some examples of job titles included: Assistant Brand Manager, Software Engineer, Principal Research Scientist, Manager of International Business Development, Vice-President, Finance.

   Those who had responsibility for direct reports were in one of three different types of managerial jobs: managing professionals in a support function, line managers, and project managers. About half were managing professionals, which meant that they had direct reports who were usually highly competent and needed little direct supervision. Sample job titles included Director of Finance and Vice-President, Human Resources. The critical interface with others in this kind of managerial job was not downward, but lateral and upward. Line managers comprised two-fifths of the managers in the study. They were in functional areas linked directly to production and operations, or delivery of product/services to customers. Sample job titles included Manager, Export Operations, Sales Manager, Branch Manager. These managers described their jobs as primarily involving organizing and coordinating the work of their group, as well as assuring they had the right mix of people, in terms of skills and expertise. This meant devoting attention to selection, training, coaching, mentoring, monitoring, and assessing employees. These managers were held accountable for financial or other deliverables on a monthly or quarterly basis, and they operated under critical time deadlines on a regular basis. The remainder of the managers worked as leaders of project teams composed of professionals, and they functioned more as matrix managers than traditional hierarchical managers. Their work involved a great deal of lateral interface across different areas, seeking consultation and gaining cooperation on the basis of their expertise and interpersonal skills rather than their rank.

Success

Overall we found a high level of success in the reduced-load arrangements observed, based on interviewers' Global Success ratings explained earlier. Sixty-two percent of the cases were in the High success group (with ratings of 7–9), 31 percent in the Moderate group (with ratings of 5–6), and 7 percent in the Low group (with ratings of 1–4). The subordinates of the managers on reduced load rated their managers' effectiveness 7.2 on average, on a scale from 1 to 9. Target individuals on reduced load had gained an average of 18 hours per week by working reduced load, and 91 percent were happier and more satisfied with the balance between home and work. Ninety percent also reported positive effects on their children – better relationships and more time with them.

For most of the managers and professionals working reduced load, and their colleagues and families, this way of working was not a temporary "blip" in their career, but rather a longer-term adaptation. The average length of time on reduced load was four years, and only 10 percent of the sample planned to return to full-time within the next three years. The costs of working reduced load were considered temporary and "worth it." Two-thirds of respondents reported believing that their career progress had been slowed, not stopped, and their bosses agreed. In two-thirds of the cases the bosses believed that the target individuals could immediately resume their former progress if they were to return to full-time work. Thirty-five percent of our respondents had actually been promoted while on reduced load.

Finally, respondents attributed the success of their reduced-load arrangements to a variety of factors, including individual characteristics or strategies as well as contextual factors. There was consensus that success did not depend on the presence of just one or two variables, but rather on a convergence of multiple ingredients. It was clear from interviews with bosses and co-workers that these individuals were highly skilled and had strong "track records." They were also described as working in a very organized and highly focussed manner and as being very flexible in responding to work demands. Competent and supportive peers or direct reports also ranked high among factors listed as critical. A supportive organizational culture, or the existence of company-wide work/life policies and programs, were also seen as helpful, but not essential for success. Thus, respondents tended to weave tales of concurrent forces and synergy operating when the reduced-load arrangement was truly successful.

Positive and negative outcomes of reduced-load work

Respondents tended to talk about a variety of outcomes, or consequences of working reduced load, mostly positive, but including some negatives. We will highlight here recurrent themes first from a personal and career perspective and secondly from an organizational perspective.

<u>**Personal and career outcomes.**</u>   As mentioned previously, enhanced personal well-being was reported in 91 percent of all cases. At a psychological level this involved a feeling of greater happiness and/or greater balance between work and home. The target individuals described themselves as more energetic, more creative, more focussed, more fresh. Some described specific improvements in quality of life, for example "having the time, energy and mindset to enjoy my kids when I'm with them." Others emphasized the advantages of gaining an extra day in their schedule. They liked being able to get a lot of errands or chores out of the way on their "day off," so that the weekend was free for more relaxation and fun with the whole family. They talked about being pleased to be able to live more in accordance with their personal priorities and to feel successful both at home and at work.

At a more physical level, enhanced personal well-being meant relief from the hectic pace of life, a decrease in stress, less fatigue, and fewer health problems such as headaches, eye strain, neck pain, high blood pressure, hair loss, etc. In half of the cases individuals described specific improvements in overall health or physical well-being which they felt had been achieved because of the reduced-load work arrangement.

The third dominant theme in positive outcomes, from strictly a personal point of view, was enhanced satisfaction with life due to time gained for self. The most common investment of additional time was in self-development kinds of activities, for example taking jazz piano lessons, attending fitness classes, playing tennis, hobbies, continuing education. In other cases these activities were more clearly leisure-oriented, for example shopping, sleeping in, reading, gardening. Another set of activities involved connecting with social networks, for example socializing with friends, neighbors, family, and children's friends and their families. Finally, there were also many cases where these individuals chose to use their extra time to volunteer in community activities, for example coaching children's sports teams, teaching Bible School, etc.

As for negative personal outcomes, the biggest problem reported, in about a third of the cases, was that these individuals felt conflicted at times – they were still quite busy and struggled to get time for themselves. They reported that it was a constant challenge to contain the workload and resist pressure to either return to full-time, or to actually do a full-time job in less time.

From a career point of view, in 70 of the 82 cases (85 percent) respondents felt quite positive about the implications of working part-time for their jobs and careers. They liked their jobs and felt that they were doing interesting, challenging work. They also reported that they were performing well and in general receiving the recognition they deserved for their accomplishments. Some even believed that their performance had improved since they had begun working *less*, because they came to work less exhausted and brought more positive, creative energy to problem-solving, new initiatives, managing a team, etc. Senior managers of these individuals made the same observation in a number of cases. There was also a consensus that these individuals working on a reduced-load basis tended to work in a very focussed, concentrated manner and were therefore unusually efficient in getting their work done.

As for perspectives on career outcomes, there was a complex array of feelings, both positive and negative. In 56 out of 82 cases (68 percent) respondents believed that their part-time work arrangements would have no long-term impact on their careers, and their bosses agreed. That is, the consensus was that once these individuals returned to full-time, they could still rise to the very highest levels in the company. They felt well respected by their colleagues, and they observed that their employer was continuing to invest in their long-term professional growth and development. For some this manifested in actual promotions while on reduced load (29 of the 82, or 35 percent of the total sample); others had experienced lateral job moves, or were assigned to high-profile task forces, or were given prestigious training and development opportunities, etc. However, in most of these cases (74 percent) these individuals believed their rate of career advancement was slower because of their choice to work on a reduced-load basis, and they described the kinds of tradeoffs they had made. For example, several mentioned the difficulty they had experienced watching members of their cohort advance beyond them. Others realized there were missed developmental opportunities in terms of not being offered extra projects or interesting, highly time-consuming, short-term assignments. However, as these individuals acknowledged the tradeoffs they were making, they were also quite adamant that they were happy or at peace with making family or personal life a priority at this point in their lives.

There were also a couple of recurrent themes that clearly represented some negative aspects in terms of career outcomes, but they were mentioned in less than half the cases. In approximately one-third of the cases, the individuals working less felt that others in the organization viewed them differently because of their alternative work arrangement. They sensed that others questioned their commitment, motivation, and dedication. In about a quarter of the cases, the individuals expressed frustration about the fact that they felt pressure to return to full-time, or else felt they had to expend a great deal of energy fiercely guarding and protecting their day off.

Organizational outcomes.   The main organizational outcomes that were mentioned by respondents included some related to specific individuals and work units, and others related to broader organizational goals. In 66 out of 82 cases (80 percent) there was consensus among stakeholders interviewed that the individual's performance in relation to the work unit had either remained at a high level or actually improved. Performance *improvement* was generally explained as arising from: (a) individuals working more effectively and creatively as a result of a rich, external life outside of work and personal fulfillment in multiple roles; or (b) individuals working harder and with more commitment and loyalty as a result of the organization's supporting their need for work/life balance; or (c) productivity gains realized because these individuals tended to deliver the same quality and close to the same amount of work over fewer hours at reduced pay. In addition, 70 percent of the senior managers were rated by the interviewers as highly supportive of the reduced-load arrangement. This was especially impressive considering that only 40 percent were the senior managers who originally negotiated with the individuals to establish the work arrangement in the first place.

Other positive outcome themes from an organizational perspective included more general benefits to the organization of offering alternative work arrangements. For example, in over 80 percent of the cases there was some mention of the fact that allowing reduced-load work helped the employer attract or retain valued talent and expertise. Respondents often then outlined specific cost savings associated with retention of professionals with significant experience in the firm. In addition, in some firms there was specific mention of how alternative work arrangement policies and programs were helping with achievement of Diversity goals, in particular with respect to the representation of women at higher managerial levels in the firm. Finally, in over half the cases it was mentioned that a benefit accruing to the employer was an enhanced image, both internally as well as externally. Offering reduced-load work arrangements was viewed as improving morale within the organization, and it also attracted positive attention from the community and media. Some even believed their employers were gaining a competitive edge in recruitment and retention as a result of their generous work–life policies and programs.

On a negative note, in 40 percent of the cases, the senior managers complained of scheduling "hassles" around the reduced-load work arrangements. Twenty-five percent of the co-workers interviewed were rated as definitely *not* supportive of the reduced-load arrangement, based on their description of negative outcomes from their own personal perspective, or from the perspective of the work group. For example, some co-workers felt that some of the work removed from the reduced-load professional wound up on their plate, without appropriate adjustments made in workload or compensation. Or, in emergency situations on the reduced-load professional's day off, co-workers felt they got stuck covering for them with customers, clients, or senior executives.

Comparison of outcomes by subgroups: HiHi vs. LoLo

<u>HiHi.</u>   This group of cases represents the ideal outcome, where both the organization and the individual working less reap substantial benefits from the reduced-load work arrangement. The cases in this group were mostly managers (six of nine) working in a wide range of types of jobs and companies. The predominant themes in the qualitative data on organizational outcomes were consistent with those in the total sample already highlighted. There was consensus that these individuals were performing very well, and in two cases outstanding performance awards had recently been won. In all cases stakeholders mentioned the positive effects of reduced-load work arrangements from the perspective of recruitment and retention of top talent. Some even pointed out money saved through avoiding turnover, and not losing sunk-costs training investments.

In more than half the cases we also heard about positive effects of reduced load on innovation and organizational adaptation to change. Stakeholders mentioned that alternative work arrangements stimulate openness and creativity and result in managers considering more options in terms of the allocation and distribution of work. In a majority of cases stakeholders also talked about the positive public relations impact of offering alternative work arrangements, both internally and externally. For example, they mentioned that successful reduced-load work had led to gradually changing attitudes toward different ways of working, as well as resulting in these individuals serving as role models or as an inspiration to others to negotiate what they needed to balance work and life commitments in changing times. On the other hand, in a majority of cases the target individuals also said that they felt there was mixed acceptance of reduced-load work within the corporation. And in five of the nine cases there was at least one stakeholder who reported he or she thought that those working on reduced load were delivering more than the official percentage of full-time being worked, and that there was unfairness there, in the sense that the company was getting more than it paid for.

As for personal outcomes, the individuals in these cases were similar to the overall sample in being happier and more satisfied with their lives, being able to fulfill the two main priorities in their lives. A majority also mentioned specifically valuing the added flexibility, freedom or control they had gained through the reduced load, and liking being able to add more diverse activities to their lives. In seven of nine cases these individuals felt their career progress had slowed, but they were comfortable with those tradeoffs. Furthermore, six mentioned being very satisfied with their careers and their feeling that they were continuing to advance with either minimal or no impact of the reduced load. In 100 percent of these cases the individuals reported really liking the work they did, and continuing to be challenged in spite of the reduced load.

<u>LoLo.</u> There were nine cases in this sub-group, four professionals and five managerial; one was a job share. The cases involved a wide range of types of jobs as well as types of companies. Emergent themes in the qualitative data on organizational outcomes in these cases indicated that there were clear performance deficiencies or incapacity to meet career progression criteria in all five of the managerial cases. And in fact in two of the five the reduced-load work arrangement had been terminated before the actual interviews took place. In the other three managerial cases the arrangements were continuing under one of two conditions. In the first scenario individual performance was clearly borderline or problematic, but the individual was doing contortions to try to make the reduced load work by working longer hours than appropriate and paying a price in the personal/family realm. Alternatively, in one case, the individual was not engaging in extreme measures and viewed the company as at least half-responsible for the ineffectiveness of the arrangement. The senior manager and human resource manager comments suggested that the company had decided to "live with" a less than ideal situation because of the high value-added person in terms of her skills and expertise. Also, the company was highly committed to its work–life programs and policies also, and so wanted to maintain its image as a progressive employer. Meanwhile, it looks like the company is biding its time until it can move that individual to a more positive situation.

In the professional cases there were no individual performance problems from an organizational point of view. The organizational costs of allowing the reduced-load work were related to the firm's needing these individuals to work full-time because of their unique skill sets and experience. These employers had accommodated these individuals because having them part-time was better than not having them at all, but there was a clear preference to get them back full-time. Two of the four professionals on reduced load in this sub-group reported experiencing pressure to terminate the reduced-load arrangement.

As for personal and career outcomes, this sub-group contrasts dramatically with the sample as a whole. The majority of these individuals did **not** express feelings of enhanced well-being or increased satisfaction with life. Five of the nine did talk about appreciating the chance to continue in their career, even if not at full speed, while also devoting time to family. But the emphasis was more on the importance of continuing in the career rather than on the importance of spending more time with children. A majority of this sub-group also reported health problems and increased stress as a result of the reduced-load work arrangement, rather than positive improvements in physical health. Across both the managerial and professional cases there was a recurring theme of decreasing job satisfaction among these individuals. This was coming from either a lack of challenge or development, or from a personal sense of not really achieving at the level of their own expectations and/or not meeting organizational goals.

Finally, it should be noted that in four cases, one of the positive outcomes mentioned was that these individuals felt they could stay on reduced load as long as they wanted. However, in three of the remaining five cases the organization had tried to or succeeded in terminating the reduced-load arrangement, against the wishes of the incumbent. In another case the individual had tried to terminate her reduced load and had not been able to get agreement from the firm; and in the remaining case, the senior manager indicated a strong *desire* to terminate the part-time work. So the security of the reduced-load arrangement was definitely an issue in this sub-group.

• Discussion •

Organizational sense-making and identity theory: an interpretive framework

Comparing and contrasting cases according to accrual of benefits on the organization and individual sides did not yield any clear patterns in terms of specific critical individual or organizational characteristics. For example, no particular type of job or type of company tended to yield more mutually beneficial reduced-load work arrangements; nor did boss support alone appear to make a difference. Furthermore, the degree of load reduction and tenure on reduced load were also not related to outcomes. However, the narrative accounts of the evolution of the cases in each of the two sub-groups representing contrasts in outcomes, pointed strongly to the importance of processes of mutual adaptation in work roles and identity, both in the workplace and in the family or non-work domain.

Processes of mutual adaptation in work roles and identity have been studied by those interesting in organizing, or how people "produce and acquire a sense of order that allows them to coordinate their actions in ways that have mutual relevance" (Weick, 2000: 26), as well as those interested in career transitions and socialization (Schein, 1978; Nicholson, 1984; Ibarra, 1999). Weick is interested more in the phenomenon of organizations and in how individual enactment can have an enormous influence on "organizing." He posits that organizing begins with moments of behavioral commitment, enactment, action. Negotiation of reduced-load work indeed represents a good example of such action. Weick suggests that organizing then follows from action, through justification of those commitments in "concrete communicative interaction" between the implicated parties, which is essentially a process of sense-making that leads to social order and structure. Using this framework to examine reduced-load work arrangements, it is clear they are not just about employees invoking work–life benefits policies to get more time with their families. Rather, they represent an example of action taken by individuals to lower their workload, which is followed by the subsequent responses of bosses, clients, co-workers. How things unfold and evolve over time then creates a cumulative pattern of mutual adjustment and organizational sense-making. Weick's unique perspective is that through individual actions organizations evolve and are shaped by individual members. He proposes that choices are made first and then streams of people, solutions, and problems become organized to justify choices. This framework can help us interpret the phenomenon of reduced-load work in a broader context.

On the other hand a different stream of research on mutual adaptation to change is that which has looked at career transitions and socialization into new work roles. However, this research has examined exclusively career transitions *within* a work context. A great deal of attention has been devoted to identity changes that accompany career transitions. Socialization into new work roles has been deeply analyzed and is generally viewed as a negotiated adaptation where individuals incrementally strive to improve the fit between themselves and their work environment. There is consensus that over time individuals adjust their self-conceptions as they gain experience in new roles, and eventually a new identity emerges (Ibarra, 1999). However, these ideas have not been applied to deepening our understanding of what happens when individuals experience work role transitions or career transitions involving new role demands *outside* the workplace.

Ibarra notes that identity has long been seen as socially constructed – as we observe our own behavior and others' reactions to it, followed by incremental modifications in our views as we respond. She uses Gecas's (1982) definition of identity as involving various meanings attached to a person by self and others. These self-conceptions are grounded in individuals' social roles and group memberships as well as personal attributes displayed or observed by others. Ibarra (1999) proposes that when individuals go through career transitions, they have an opportunity to renegotiate both private and public views of the self. She suggests they develop "provisional selves" in these periods of their lives, where they identify role models, experiment with unfamiliar behaviors, and engage in vigorous self-evaluation, all of which is really part of the process of the ongoing construction of identity.

Taking these concepts related to the ongoing construction of identity in a social context and applying them to the phenomenon of reduced-load work arrangements, it is clear that for most individuals studied working less was part of an experiment involving adjustment to new work roles *outside* the workplace, i.e. being a parent, as well as adjustment of responsibilities at work. There was a great deal of variation in the extent to which individuals actively and self-consciously engaged in a process of expanding their self-conceptions to incorporate who they were in their new social roles outside of work. The opportunity to negotiate a reduced-load work arrangement provided the individual more space to experiment with enactment of the new role of parent, and to observe and learn from interactions with others in the expanded social network resulting from working less. For example, target individuals reported that when they were working full-time, they rarely had time to interact socially with the parents of their children's friends or other working parents in the neighborhood. Working reduced load provided more opportunities to get to know others in similar situations and to observe how they managed to combine career and family.

If we examine the LoLo sub-group of cases where there were low net organizational and low net individual benefits associated with the reduced load, a number of observations can be made. First of all, in five of nine cases there were performance deficiencies, and in two of the five the reduced load had already been terminated unilaterally by the organization as a result. The target individuals involved in those cases did not agree with the perception that there was a negative effect of the reduced load on the work unit, and they were very upset about the termination. They were still allowed to work on a part-time basis, but in less interesting and challenging jobs. In the remaining cases where there were performance problems reported, the senior managers involved were reluctant to take action out of their fear of losing these highly talented and experienced professionals. The other cases, where performance was fine, were still problematic from the organization's point of view for the same reason. These employees added value in key areas, and the firm needed them to work full-time. However, a decision was reached that it was better to have them part-time than not at all. In spite of this compromise, there was no ongoing process of negotiation, or cumulative pattern of adaptation where the organization and the individual were engaged in trying to develop more effective coordination mechanisms that were mutually beneficial. The process of experimentation with different work structures and provisional selves in a major career–life transition appeared to have been cut short, or arrested, and a static truce was struck.

This state of affairs was not good for the organization or the individual. The individuals in this sub-group tended to complain of increased rather than decreased stress and health problems. Except for one case, they also did not express enthusiasm for the additional time they had gained for being with family. In fact, they seemed to be in internal conflict over their decision to work less, because they were making a career sacrifice and yet not feeling any satisfaction about where they had shifted their attention – to home and family. They also reported decreasing job satisfaction, which was related either to a lack of challenge and professional development, or to their personal frustration at not being able to achieve at the level of their own expectations or expectations of their employers.

The two examples below from the LoLo sub-group illustrate how the process of mutual adaptation can be arrested and result in dysfunctional outcomes.

> Jane was a fast-track manager at her company and had returned quickly from two maternity leaves. According to her, at that time she was driven to reach the top ranks in the organization and was totally focussed on her career. She only considered a reduced-load arrangement several years later after it was discovered that one of her children had "special needs" as a result of a congenital condition, right around the

time she also realized her marriage was in trouble. After her husband left, she felt compelled to negotiate a reduced load even though her own personal desire was to simply keep striving for the top. She had not come to terms with or adjusted her sense of self to incorporate the new role she was playing in the family. She did not want to revise her identity as a "high potential" manager motivated primarily by her desire for career success. Yet her family situation demanded a change. At the time of the interview she was obviously still coming to terms with the career transition going on and struggling with construction of a new identity.

Sue was a project manager at corporate headquarters in a work unit jointly staffed by finance and information systems professionals. She had also taken a minimum maternity leave with her first child, but when she found out she was having twins the second time around opted to return to a reduced-load arrangement. At that time she was moved to a different work unit and yet officially still reported to her old boss, even though the new boss was more implicated in the project she was managing. Although there were complaints about communication glitches with her direct reports, her unofficial boss was not acting to try to address the problem. She knew she should suggest a change in reporting relationships, but was holding back because of the uncertainties involved in doing so. So a flawed work assignment continued, and neither the organization nor the individual was satisfied.

In both of these cases the individuals were initially carrying out cumulative patterns of adjustment and adaptation as they interacted with their bosses to establish acceptable new work structures. However, in both cases these individuals were reluctant to really leave behind in any way their previous identities as high-powered, career-oriented professionals. This then created a great deal of strain, and they went into holding positions trying to return to a former identity at work that was not really compatible with a new emerging identity that incorporated an expanded role in the family context. The dynamic process of the work structure responding to the changing needs of the individual in the overall context of business needs was interrupted, as the mutual accommodation between the individuals, their bosses, co-workers, and direct reports failed to continue. In addition, in the family context, choices around identity were constrained by an absent husband in one case and a traditional marriage ideology in the other, with a husband whose job required a great deal of travel and long work hours.

Now turning to cases where there were mutual benefits to the organization and the individual, there is evidence of cumulative patterns of adaptation at work and enactment of "provisional selves" in both work and non-work domains. The case of a partner in an accounting firm provides an illustration.

Carol had been on reduced load for 12 years at the time she was interviewed and was promoted to partner during that period. Her decision to go on reduced load came after she had initially rejected her supervisor's suggestion that she might want to consider a phased return to full-time work after her maternity leave. She was opposed to the idea while still pregnant, had no plan for complying, but changed her mind after her son was born. As she experienced the transition to being a parent as well as a professional, the chance to negotiate a change in her work role became more interesting. The maternity leave interruption of her career track provided an occasion for improvisation and learning. But the reduced-load arrangement was not static once in place. When she first began the reduced load, the pace of business in the industry was slow and she could really work 80 percent. However, she was then due to come up for partner and was told she could not be considered on part-time. But when she questioned this and pushed back, her boss backed off and championed her. Eventually, after she received the promotion, however, she was required to sign an agreement that she would return to full-time after one year. Her boss assured her that this agreement would never see the light of day. Meanwhile, as the pace of business increased, Carol found it harder and harder to contain her workload and decided to negotiate an increase in her load and compensation to 90 percent. The way Carol has used her time off has also evolved over time. Initially she would spend her day off at home with her children and give the Nanny a day off. Then she became volunteer at the children's school and accompanied them on school trips or outings. Now that her children are older she uses her time off to play tennis, go shopping, get a haircut, relax.

Among the HiHi cases over half of the target individuals had experienced more than one reduced-load job, and all of them had experimented with different schedules and allocations of work time to the office versus home. The reduced-load work arrangement was a process of customizing work to maximize the fit between the individual and the work unit. It should also be noted that among the HiHi cases all but one involved marriages that were rated as egalitarian as opposed to traditional or post-traditional. This rating meant that in those families the spouses of the target individuals took significant responsibility for children and/or division of labor in the family did not fall along traditional gender lines. The fact that these target individuals had partners with whom they could negotiate and trade off responsibilities in the family domain meant they also were less constrained in their construction of new identities as they adapted to being parents and professionals.

An identity and organizational sense-making framework for analyzing outcomes of reduced-load work arrangements is appropriate given the interest in what happens to both individuals and organizations. Furthermore, the pinpointing of the importance of a process of mutual negotiation of identity and work structures in both the workplace and the home or community leaves open the possibility of all kinds of new ways of working and being. However, further research is needed to increase our understanding of how these career transitions that involve expanding self-conceptions in different domains proceed. And more investigation is needed to figure out why and when the "committed interacts" in organizations break down, because these are critical to the ongoing cumulative pattern of adaptation that allows and supports new ways of working for individuals and ongoing learning for organizations. The findings from this study suggest that reduced-load work is an emergent, ad hoc, trial-and-error phenomenon unlikely to be a permanent fixture in organizational landscapes in the future. What *is* likely to be found more frequently in organizations in the future, if the professionals studied here are any indication, is more customized work arrangements, and work arrangements that are constantly in flux and changing according to individual and business needs.

NOTE

1 We are deeply indebted to over 350 men and women who shared their time and insights with us. Other members of the research team were: Margaret L. Williams, Michelle Buck, Carol Schreiber, Leslie Borrelli, Sharon Leiba-O'Sullivan, Minda Bernstein, Stephen Smith, and Pamela Dohring. This research was made possible by financial support from the Alfred P. Sloan Foundation and the Social Sciences and Humanities Research Council of Canada.

REFERENCES

Arthur, M.B., and Rousseau, D.M. (1996). *The Boundaryless Career.* New York: Oxford University Press.

Babbar, S., and Aspelin, D.J. (1998). The overtime rebellion: Symptom of a bigger problem? *Academy of Management Executive*, 12, 1, 68–76.

Bailyn, L. (1993). *Breaking the Mold.* New York: Free Press.

Barnett, R.C., and Gareis, K.C. (2000). Reduced-hours employment. *Work and Occupations*, 27, 2, 168–87.

Bond, J.J., Galinsky, E., and Swanberg, J.E. (1998). *The 1997 National Study of the Changing Workforce.* New York: Families and Work Institute.

Buck, M.L., Lee, M.D., MacDermid, S.M., and Smith, S. (2000). Reduced load work and the experience of time among professionals and managers: Implications for personal and organizational life. In C.L. Cooper and D. Rousseau (eds). *Trends in Organizational Behavior.* New York: John Wiley.

Business Week. (2000, August 28). The 21st century corporation.

Capelli, P. (2000). A market-driven approach to retaining talent. *Harvard Business Review*, January–February, 103–11.

Catalyst. (1997). *A New Approach to Flexibility: Managing the Work/Time Equation.* New York.

Clark, V.S. (1998). *Making Sense of Part-Time Professional Work Arrangements.* Doctoral dissertation. Vancouver, CA: The University of British Columbia.

Eastman, W. (1998). Working for position: Women, men, and managerial work hours. *Industrial Relations*, 37, 1, 51–66.

Epstein, C.F., Seron, C., Oglensky, B., and Saute, R. (1998). *The Part-Time Paradox.* New York: Routledge.

Friedman, S., and Greenhaus, J. (2000). *Work and Family: Allies or Enemies.* New York: Oxford University Press.

Gecas, V. (1982). The self-concept. *Annual Review of Sociology*, 8, 1–33. Palo Alto, CA: Annual Reviews.

Gunz, H., Evans, M., and Jalland, M. (2000). Career boundaries in a "boundaryless" world. In M. Peiperl, M. Arthur, R. Goffee, and T. Morris (eds). *Career Frontiers.* New York: Oxford University Press, pp. 24–53.

Ibarra, H. (1999). Provisional selves: Experimenting with image and identity in professional adaptation. *Administrative Science Quarterly*, 44, 4, 764–91.

Lee, M.D., Engler, L., and Wright, L. (in press). Exploring the boundaries in professional careers: Reduced load work arrangements in law, medicine, and accounting. In R. Burke and D. Nelson (eds). *Current Trends in Research on Women in Management.*

Lee, M.D., MacDermid, S.M., and Buck, M.L. (2000). Organizational paradigms of reduced load work: Accommodation, elaboration, transformation. *Academy of Management Journal*, 43, 6, 1211–26.

Lee, M.D., MacDermid, S.M., and Buck, M.L. (in press). Reduced work arrangements: Response to stress or quest for integrity of functioning. In D. Nelson and R. Burke (eds). *Gender, Work Stress, and Health*. Washington, D.C.: American Psychological Association.

Lee, M.D., MacDermid, S.M., Williams, M., Buck, M.L., Schreiber, C., Borrelli, L., Leiba-O'Sullivan, S., Smith, S., Bernstein, M., and Dohring, P. (1999). Reconceptualizing professional and managerial careers. Technical Report prepared for the Alfred P. Sloan Foundation, New York.

Levy, E.S., Flynn, P.M., and Kellogg, D.M. (1998). Customized work arrangements in the accounting profession: An uncertain future. Executive Summary of Final Report to the Alfred P. Sloan Foundation, New York.

MacDermid, S.M., Lee, M.D., Buck, M.L., and Williams, M.L. (in press). Alternate work arrangements among professionals and managers: Rethinking career development and success. *Journal of Management Development*.

Meiksins, P., and Whalley, P. (1996). Technical working and reduced work. Paper presented at the Annual Meeting of the American Sociological Association. Washington, D.C.

Miles, M.B., and Huberman, A.M. (1994). *Qualitative Data Analysis: An Expanded Sourcebook*. Thousand Oaks, CA: Sage.

Nicholson, N. (1984). A theory of work role transitions. *Administrative Science Quarterly*, 29, 172–91.

Osterman, R. (1996). *Broken Ladders*. New York: Oxford University Press.

Perlow, L.A. (1998). Boundary control: The social ordering of work and family time in a high tech corporation. *Administrative Science Quarterly*, 43, 235–56.

Perspectives (2000, Spring). Work–life survey results released. Cambridge, MA: Harvard University: Radcliffe Public Policy Center, pp. 1–2.

Schein, E.H. (1978). *Career Dynamics: Matching Individual and Organizational Needs*. Reading, MA: Addison-Wesley.

Sullivan, S.E. (1999). The changing nature of careers: A review and research agenda. *Journal of Management*, 25, 3, 457–84.

Weick, K.E. (1979). *The Social Psychology of Organizing*. Reading, MA: Addison-Wesley.

Weick, K.E. (2000). *Making Sense of the Organization*. Oxford: Blackwell Publishers.

Women in the Labour Force (1994) (ed.). Ottawa: Statistics Canada, Catalogue No. 75–507E, 5.

8

Telework: A Primer for the Millennium Introduction

LINDA DUXBURY AND CHRISTOPHER HIGGINS

This chapter focusses on telework, operationalized in this chapter to include work performed by individuals who are employed by an organization but who work at home or at a telecenter for some portion of their working time during regular business hours. It does not talk about the experiences of others who may work at home (i.e. self-employed workers, homemakers, farmers) – these people work at home, but do not commute regularly to work.

Telework is part of a general trend towards remote work. While it can be seen as an "information age" phenomenon (Shore, 2000) which is being fueled by the growth of knowledge work and the rapid advance of technology, the trend in this is consistent with predictions made by futurist Alvin Toffler (1980) in his book *The Third Wave*, who noted that: "Work is not necessarily going to take place in offices or factories. It's going to take place everywhere, anytime".

At the present time there is a lot of controversy in both academic and practitioner literatures with respect to how telework affects organizations and employees. At one extreme, telecommuting is considered a flexible work arrangement that will solve a multitude of problems. A number of books and articles (see McCloskey and Igbaria (1998) for a list of relevant references) suggest that telework will increase job satisfaction and productivity, reduce employee stress and lead to a cleaner environment. At the other extreme, authors have implicated telework in the etiology of a number of negative consequences including loneliness, isolation, exploitation, increased stress, and limited career advancement (again, see McCloskey and Igbaria (1998) for a list of relevant references).

When writing this chapter we tried to strike a balance between what human resource practitioners, managers, and employees would like to know about telework and what researchers in the area would see as critical. Our search for useful material reached beyond the empirical literature to include recent articles found on the web. The results of the web search (which are summarized in table 8.1) indicate the magnitude of the task before us. There were 73,480 hits using the word "telework," 13,000 hits using the keywords "telework research," and 7,250 hits using the keywords "telework benefits."

Table 8.1   Web search on topic of telework

A web search using Google produced the following results:

Item searched	No. of hits
telework	73,480
telework: research	13,000
telework: benefits	7,250
telework: Europe	6,800
telework: Canada	6,740
telework: business case	4,830
telework: USA	4,230
telework: Ireland	3,999
telework: Germany	3,890
telework: case studies	3,500
telework: Japan	2,460
telework: EEC	2,210
telework: Australia	2,140
telework: Finland	1,910
telework: England	1,790
telework: Asia	1,670
telework: Portugal	1,570
telework: Denmark	1,270
telework: India	1,090
telework: China	997
telework: Singapore	891
telework: disadvantages	288
telework: Hong Kong	685
telework: Korea	578
telework: drawbacks	245

Reviewing the empirical literature was equally daunting. For example, Bailey and Kurkland (2000) in a recent review of the academic literature pertaining to telework searched library databases like ABI/Inform and PsychoInfo using the following keywords: telework, telecommuting, remote work. They identified 75 published field studies and more than 50 other articles or book chapters in a wide range of disciplines. The academic articles took the form of essays on topics such as the future of teleworking (Handy and Mokhtarian, 1995), methodological issues (Kraut, 1988; Mokhtarian et al., 1995; Mokhtarian, 1991), legal and union issues (e.g., DiMartino and Wirth, 1990), gender issues (Holcomb, 1991; Huws, 1991), and considerations of time and space (Perin, 1998). Other current extensive reviews of the academic telework literature conducted by McCloskey and Igbaria (1998) and Haddon and Lewis (1994) obtained similar results.

This chapter marries the practitioner and academic literatures to provide an overview of the current thinking with respect to this work arrangement. It looks beyond an enumeration of telework's advantages and disadvantages to also include material on the definition of telework, telework intensity (i.e., how many teleworkers there are), factors supporting and inhibiting the growth of telework, an enumeration of the characteristics of people who do telework and who could telework, factors associated with the implementation of a successful telework program, how best practice companies have implemented telework, the impact of telework on work–life balance, and an evaluation of the empirical research in the area.

● Telework: What Is It? ●

One of the problems encountered in the study of telecommuting is the lack of a generally accepted definition of the phenomena (Hartman, Stoner, and Arora, 1992). The term telecommuting was coined by Jack Nilles who is often referred to as the "father of telework." Nilles defined telework (or alternatively telecommuting) as a work arrangement that entails working outside the conventional workplace and communicating with it by way of telecommunications or computer-based technology. Many other researchers have used this definition of telework (Nilles, 1994; Olson and Primps, 1984; Bailey and Kurkland, 2000).

Telecommuting is the term most widely used in North America while telework is the expression most commonly used in Europe (European Telework, 2000). The term telework has been popularized in Europe through its use by the European Commission which has sponsored considerable research in this field as a way to develop economic activity and create work opportunities in rural areas and places with economic problems (European Telework, 2000).

Unfortunately, over time, others have twisted the definition of telework to suit their own needs with the result that there is now a lot of confusion over what exactly is meant by the term. As both McCloskey and Igbaria (1998) and Bailey and Kurkland (2000) point out, the definition of telework across studies in both the practitioner and empirical literatures is inconsistent. The terms home work, home-based work, off-site work, remote work, telework, and telecommuting have been used interchangeably in the literature (Shamir, 1992). These terms should not be used interchangeably, however, since they do not refer to the same phenomenon.

Variations in the definitions of telework can be found around the following themes (McCloskey and Igbaria, 1998; Duxbury et al., 1998):

- *Technology*. The question here is whether or not, to be considered a teleworker, an employee just has to work remotely or must also have to use a computer, or a computer *and* electronic data transfer.
- *Location*. The confusion here revolves around whether the term telework is restricted to someone who works only from their employer's premises and their own home or whether a teleworker can also be considered as someone who does their work in a variety of locations (including the home) or from a satellite work center.
- *Employment relationship*. The main concern here is whether self-employed people should be considered teleworkers or can you only be considered a teleworker if you work for an organization.

- *Structure*. This debate focuses on whether people who work at home outside of regular work hours are teleworkers or whether teleworkers must, by definition, work at home during regular office hours.

Distinctions are also make in the literature between informal, illicit or "guerrilla" telework (the individual and his or her immediate manager see the benefits of teleworking and adopt the practice without corporate approval) and formalized telework programs (i.e., the company recognizes and supports telework through the use of policies and programs). While there is no consensus with respect to whether all types of remote work should be lumped together and considered telework, all agree that telework is, by definition, remote work (Shamir, 1992).

To help the reader make some sense of the various terms used in conjunction with discussions on telework, a glossary with the most common terms is included at the end of this chapter. In this chapter we view telework as a unique alternative work arrangement in which organizational employees regularly work at home or at a remote site one or more complete workdays a week in lieu of working in the office (Hartman et al., 1992).

● Telework Today ●

Telework intensity

The workforce of the new millennium is being turned upside down by a number of drivers and trends including the information revolution, corporate restructuring and downsizing, a shortage of qualified labour, growing market competition and global expansion (Ceridian, 2000). These trends are resulting in fundamental changes in how employees are working together. More and more, employees are becoming part of a "boundaryless workforce." Many predict that this metamorphosis in the loci of the workplace (from the office to the home) will become even more prevalent in the future, fueled by the coming ubiquity of the Internet, vastly improved connectivity, and fundamental changes in the very nature of work (Ceridian, 2000; Nie, 1999).

According to the popular press, "virtual" employees are now "part of the mainstream" (Reingold, 2000). The following section of the chapter seeks to determine if the data currently available supports this contention by examining the following questions: how many people currently telework? how many people do we expect to telework within the next couple of years? what are the characteristics of employees who telework?

HOW MANY PEOPLE TELEWORK?

Determining an answer to this question has never been easy. Teleworkers are difficult to count and estimates vary substantially from source to source for methodological reasons (i.e. how the sampling was obtained, the definition of teleworker employed). Much of the data quoted in the literature is also several years old, a fatal flaw in a world where the speed and cost of computation and connectivity change by the month

(Nie, 1999).[1] Some current estimates of the teleworking populations for the United States, Canada and Europe are presented below.

TELEWORK INTENSITY: THE UNITED STATES

High-end estimates include the one offered by Internet survey company Cyber Dialogue, which claims that there are currently some 15.7 million wage and salary workers (14 percent of the US workforce) spending at least part of their work week telecommuting from home – up they say from 4 million in 1990. Nie (1999) points out, however, that this estimate is likely to be high due to the sampling methodology used.

At the other end of the spectrum are numbers offered by the US Bureau of Labor Statistics (BLS). The agency's most recent analysis reported that there were 10.1 million telecommuters and home office workers in 1997. This translates to about 8 percent of the US labor force. Nie (1999) points out that this estimate is probably about a million "short" because of the ambiguity of the telecommuting question used to collect data.

Also useful are repeated estimates over time from the same source. Telework America produces a series describing the growth and characteristics of telework in the United States. In July 2000 Telework America conducted 1,877 in-depth telephone interviews. These interviews constituted a random sample of households proportionally allocated throughout the United States. This analysis (Telework America 2000, 2000) determined that in 2000 there were 16.5 million regularly employed teleworkers in the US who telework at least one day per month and 9.3 million US teleworkers who telework at least one full day per week.

When all the available data are considered, it seems safe to conclude that between 8 percent and 10 percent of the US workforce teleworks at least one full day per week (i.e., Dannhauser (1999) reported that 9 percent of the US workforce telecommutes, Shore (2000) estimates 10 percent, BLS says approximately 8 percent and Cyber Dialogue figures 14 percent). Millions more employees do work away from the office on an occasional basis (Bailey and Kurkland, 2000). While only one in ten North American employees may telework, the potential impact of this work arrangement is much greater if one factors in the larger numbers of managers, co-workers, and clients associated with teleworking individuals.

TELEWORK INTENSITY: EUROPEAN UNION

In 1999, 15 European Union countries conducted telework surveys (Telework America 2000, 2000). In 1999 these countries had 6 million regular teleworkers (i.e., defined as employees who teleworked at least one full day per week). According to this study, the world leader in the number of regular teleworkers, as a fraction of the workplace is Finland (10.8 percent) followed by the Netherlands (8.3 percent) and Sweden (8.0 percent). If the number of employees who telework less than one full day per week is added to these totals, the EU countries had 9 million teleworkers in 1999 (Telework America 2000, 2000).

Telework intensity: Canada

Statistics from Canada show that in 1997 there were 1 million teleworkers across Canada, up from 600,000 in 1993 (TBS, 2000). Predictions are that in 2010, given the current rate of grown, there will be 1,500,000 teleworkers in Canada.

THE GROWTH OF TELEWORK

A review of the available data would suggest that not only is telework becoming more mainstream as a work arrangement, the demand for telework will likely increase as: (1) technological advances make it easier for employees to work and communicate with others any time, anywhere, and (2) the number of employees working in the knowledge sector continues to grow (AT&T, 2000d).

The Telework America (Telework America 2000, 2000) study, for example, reported that between 1999 and 2000 the number of teleworkers grew by 20.6 percent Furthermore, their forecasting models suggest that if current growth rates continue there should be 30 million US teleworkers by the year 2004 and 40 million by 2010 (Telework America 2000, 2000). This forecasting model also predicts that the number of teleworkers in EU countries will hit 30 million by the end of 2004 and arrive at 40 million three years ahead of the US (i.e. by 2007).

A more conservative estimate of the growth of telework can be obtained from the BLS's tally of job-related home workers (based on their 1998 Current Population Survey). According to the BLS, between 1991 and 1997 fewer people took work home to do on their own time while the number of employees who said they did some telecommuting from home and got paid for it exploded, up from 1.9 million in 1991 to 3.6 million in 1997 – an 89 percent increase. (Dannhauser, 1999).

Shore (2000) provides yet another estimate of the growth of telework over the last decade. His data, culled from a number of different sources, suggests that the number of teleworkers has grown from 3.4 million people in 1990 to 23.6 million people in the year 2000 (see table 8.2). Nie (1999) points out that this trend towards greater telework intensity will surely continue and accelerate during the next decade since the types of jobs likely to grow the fastest in the next five years are those most compatible with teleworking (i.e. computer software design, engineering, and many other information services jobs).

Not only is the number of people teleworking growing, there would also appear to be a pent-up demand for telework in today's workforce. Telework America, for example, projects that by the year 2004 there may be as many as 30 million regular teleworkers (Telework America 2000, 2000). They arrive at this estimate by extrapolating from the following findings:

- 39 percent of those who currently do not telework are interested in teleworking, and
- 13 percent of these workers would consider the ability to telework an important influence when making a decision to accept another job.

Table 8.2   Growth of telework in the USA (as cited in Shore, 2000)

Year	No. (millions) teleworking in USA	Source
1990	3.4	Find/SVP
1994	9.1	Find/SVP
1997	11.1	Find/SVP
1998	15.7	Cyber Dialogue
1999	19.6	ITAC/AT&T
2000	23.6	ITAC/AT&T

An ITAC study funded by AT&T obtained similar findings. They observed that within the US:

- 26 percent of workers who currently don't telework (a total of 23 million workers) have jobs that would allow them to work at home, and
- 60 percent of those whose jobs would allow them to telework report that they would be interested in doing so (AT&T, 2000d).

A study in late 1998 by Canadian polling firm EKOS (TBS, 2000) observed the same phenomena occurring in Canada. They reported that:

- 58 percent of Canadian employees wanted to telework,
- 50 percent felt that their jobs were at least partly teleworkable,
- 29 percent expected to telework within the next year,
- 63 percent expected to telework at some point during their career,
- 43 percent would quit their job if another employer offered them an equivalent job and permitted them to telework,
- 33 percent would choose telework over a 10 percent raise, and
- 77 percent believed that new technology makes telework more possible.

FORCES DRIVING THE GROWTH OF TELEWORK

The data presented above indicates that the number of employees teleworking is expected to grow substantially within the next decade. The literature helps us understand what is driving this growth. Studies in Europe (European Telework, 2000), identify the following factors:

- the reduced cost and increased performance of computers and telecommunications,
- the ready availability of tools and services that support work away from the office (i.e., the internet, open electronic networking),
- increasing willingness by employers and employees to explore innovative ways to achieve business and personal goals,

- increasing pressure on industry to reduce costs while improving the levels of customer service,
- increasing concern about the environment and especially the impact of roads and cars,
- the emergence of a networked economy, and
- the shift from "paid employment" to work opportunities.

A similar list has been compiled by American researchers. Shore (2000), for example, identified the following factors which are believed to encourage the use of telework arrangements within the North American context:

- technology is making it easier for people to work any time, anywhere (i.e. internet growth has created a demand for PCs and provided an incentive to set up a home office; office technology such as cellphones, notebook computers etc. equip employees to work any time, any place),
- changes in worker values mean that more employees are seeking job opportunities that allow for flexibility in work schedule and work location, and give health/financial benefits (i.e. some employees are making their acceptance of a new job conditional on pre-approval to telework).

BARRIERS TO THE ADOPTION OF TELEWORK

Despite these many inducements for telework, it has yet to become as popular as futurists predicted (e.g., Huws, 1991; Kraut, 1989; Bailey and Kurkland, 2000). Although there are fewer studies that look at why adoption and diffusion of telework has been slower than expected, managerial resistance and lack of managerial interest in telework are widely reported to be the main barriers (European Telework, 2000). Studies supporting this conclusion are numerous.

Huws and her colleagues (1991), for example, polled over 4,000 European managers and concluded that telework is "still very much a minority interest" among European managers. Major barriers to telework identified by Huws et al. include the following:

- there was no need for the change,
- coordinating the program was difficult,
- the anticipated costs of implementing and managing telework programs were too high, and
- they perceive it will be hard to control and coordinate work done outside the office.

The ITAC study (AT&T, 2000d) concluded that the main obstacle to telework appears to be the employer (particularly the individual's immediate manager) rather than the employee. They found 40 percent of those who wanted and could work from home said that their employer would not allow it. Other studies report that while many managers will say they believe that telework is a good idea in theory, they have concerns about whether it will work for them. Much of a manager's concern may come down to a matter of trust (or lack thereof) and resistance to "managing at a distance" (i.e., relying on employees to self-manage their workday location: Shore, 2000; Harrington and Ruppel, 1999). Many managers say "My staff aren't ready for telework" when what they really mean is "I'm not ready for telework."

AT&T (2000a) espouses a slightly different view of the situation. They perceive that the greatest obstacles to telework will be psychological, social, and cultural, not technical or economic, and note the following: "Today, the biggest obstacles to telework are employers who are afraid of lack of control and employees who are afraid of isolation or being fired." Nilles (European Telework, 2000) offers yet another explanation on why telework is not growing as quickly as it might. He coined the phrase "edifice complex" in reference to the fact that many corporations equate the size and design of their office complex with their worth and prestige. He went on to note that this "edifice complex" often acts as a barrier to the adoption of work at home (European Telework, 2000). Other barriers to telework can be found later in this chapter in conjunction with our discussion of the perceived disadvantages of telework arrangements.

Who does telework?

Is telework really mainstream? That question can be partially answered by examining the demographic characteristics of those who telework. Given the difficulties in surveying teleworkers, obtaining a definitive answer to the question of who teleworks may prove impossible (Bailey and Kurkland, 2000). The following conclusions can, however, be drawn from the data that is available.

First, it would appear that most telecommuters use this arrangement on an informal (i.e. deals worked out with one's own immediate boss), part-time (i.e., work some days at home and some days at the office) basis. Data from a number of large studies indicate that most people who telework do so only a few days a month (Bailey and Kurkland, 2000). A 1997 AT&T survey of 17,000 teleworkers, for example, found that teleworkers in the US spent an average of 11 days a month working from home. Telework America, on the other hand, reported that teleworkers work remotely 20 hours per week on average (Telework America 2000, 2000).

The study done by Telework America (Telework America 2000, 2000) provides one of the most comprehensive descriptions of who teleworks. According to this study teleworkers:

- are predominantly male (65 percent of the teleworkers in this study were male),
- tend to be older, more seasoned employees who often see teleworking as an attractive way to improve family life while maintaining their careers,
- are slightly more prone to be urban area dwellers rather than live in rural areas or small towns,
- are more likely to have local rather than remote supervision (60 percent of the teleworkers in this sample had a local supervisor while 20 percent were supervised by someone remotely),
- are more likely to work at home on an intermittent or part-time basis than full-time,

- commute to work on days they are not teleworking,
- have longer commutes than their counterparts who do not telework (i.e., the one-way commute distance for the teleworkers in this sample averaged 19.7 miles and took 63 minutes round trip. This is substantially longer than the 13.3-mile, 34-minute commute reported by non-teleworkers),
- tend to be heavier users of computer technology than workers in general. The average ownership pattern for teleworkers is one PC for work and another for non-work purposes. This contrasts with an average of 0.8 PCs for work and 0.5 for non-work for non-teleworkers.

These findings are consistent with the work of Finnish researchers who found that telecommuters were primarily high-income, high-educated, male, independent professionals (Luukinen, 1996).

In contrast to the Telework America and Finnish studies, Cyber Dialogue's (2000) data showed that the likelihood of teleworking was not associated with gender (51 percent women, 49 percent men). The typical teleworker in this sample was in their mid-forties, and well paid (medium household income of $45,200). These demographic figures differ only slightly from those reported by the consulting firm LINK Resources (US Department of Transportation, 1993) more than five years earlier and are also consistent with those reported by Mokhtarian and her colleagues in publications on their studies in Southern California (Mannering and Mokhtarian, 1995; Mokhtarian and Salomon, 1996a, 1996b).

According to Bailey and Kurkland (2000) the gender differences in the various samples may reflect differences in the occupation of the teleworker along clerical/professional lines. Their review of the literature would suggest that full-time teleworkers are more likely to be younger, male, highly paid professionals while part-time teleworkers are predominantly older, lower-paid female clerical workers.

Recent studies in this area also give us some insight into where teleworkers can be found. Within the US, telework is not limited to certain industries although high-tech companies probably lead the way (Shore, 2000). Teleworking is most common in the high-tech, manufacturing, business services, banking, insurance, transport, and communications industries (Telework America 2000, 2000). However, every industrial sector in the US has teleworkers. Half of all American teleworkers work for organizations with at least 1,500 employees. The rest work for medium- and small-sized organizations. Telework is also international in nature as employees in many countries use this work arrangement (Shore, 2000; table 8.1).

Finally, it is interesting to examine issues such as "What do teleworkers do when they are working from home?" and "What tools do they use to do this work?" Again, the recent study by Telework America gives us an indication. The primary telework activity appears to be computer-related work (makes up 55 percent of all activities done at home) followed by telephoning, reading, and face-to-face meetings (7 percent of the time) (Telework America 2000, 2000). Not surprisingly, given the above information, the top three non-computer technologies in use by teleworkers are, in decreasing order of importance, the telephone, pagers, and fax. This study also observed that while half the teleworkers in their sample use e-mail at least three hours per week, the average e-mail use is seven hours because of some heavy users (Telework

America 2000, 2000). Slightly more than 75 percent of teleworkers have analog modems to connect them to their employers and/or the internet (Telework America 2000, 2000).

Who could telework?

Numerous practitioners and academics have attempted to identify the traits of employees who could telework if they so desired and the factors that predict who will telework (Bailey and Kurkland, 2000). According to Bailey and Kurkland (2000) prime candidates for telework include knowledge workers, information workers, and sales and marketing personnel. Nie (1999) puts it more succinctly. He says telework is possible:

- when what one builds or processes is digital rather than material,
- when remote coordination is possible (even if not preferable), and
- when expertise and intellectual resources can be easily shared at a distance.

Efforts to determine which factors are predictive of who will telework have spawned some of the most rigorous telework research to date, most of it within the transportation literature (Bailey and Kurkland, 2000). Models created by Mokhtarian and her colleagues (Mannering and Mokhtarian, 1995; Mokhtarian and Salomon, 1996b, 1997) indicate that work-related factors are most predictive of an individual's choice to work remotely. Work factors that were powerful predictors of use of telework include manager's willingness, need for workplace interactions, and self-perceived job suitability. A number of personal and household attitudes also appear predictive including lack of personal discipline, household distractions, preference to work with a team, family orientation, and workaholism. Technology factors (e.g. computer availability) also appear in some models.

Other research by these authors has shown that idiosyncratic details of individual jobs, not general job traits, are more likely to determine whether a specific individual can telework (Bailey and Kurkland, 2000; Mokhtarian, 1998). Mokhtarian (1998) found, for example, that employees' self-perceived job unsuitability significantly constrained their choice to telework. In other words, based on firsthand knowledge of what their work entailed, individuals chose not to telework because they thought their job could not be performed well away from the office. In short, perceptions of job suitability based on intimate knowledge of specific jobs rather than global job categories may best determine who can telework (Bailey and Kurkland, 2000; Mokhtarian, 1998).

Other research indicates that status and power may interfere with assessments of who can telework based solely on perceptions of job suitability. Several studies have found that clerical workers may face greater opposition from management to their requests to work at home than do their counterparts in professional positions (e.g., Huws, Korte, and Robinson, 1990; Olson and Primps, 1984).

● The Advantages and Disadvantages of Telework Arrangements ●

Comprehensive studies on telework date back to the 1970s (i.e., Nilles et al., 1976). Unfortunately, despite a long history and extensive publicity, much of the discussion of remote work and telework has been at a fairly superficial level (Westfall, 1998). A common theme in the telework literature over the past several decades has been an uncritical enumeration of the advantages of this work arrangement (see the number of websites dealing just with the advantages of telework). There is also a large body of literature which debates the pros and cons of telework arrangements (e.g., Nilles et al., 1976; DiMartino and Wirth, 1990; Gerson and Kraut, 1988; Huws, Korte, and Robinson, 1990; Korte, Robinson, and Steinle, 1988; Kraut, 1987, 1988, 1989; AT&T, 2000a, 2000b; Telework America 2000, 2000; Shore, 2000; European Telework, 2000). Reviewing this literature one is struck by how little the contents of the list have changed over time. One also forms the impression that those who are trying to "sell" this work arrangement are making an attempt to appeal to all stakeholders (i.e., organizations, employees, and society itself).

The following section discusses the advantages of telework. This is followed by a discourse on the disadvantages of telework. In both cases, three perspectives are given: the employee, the organization, and society itself. This approach is consistent with the research which indicates that telecommuting has grown due to the demands of three constituents:

- *employees* (i.e., changes in family structures make work–life balance more of an issue, changes in attitudes and values),
- *organizational demands* (i.e., recruiting needs, legislative requirements, plans for disaster),
- *societal demand* (i.e., environmental concerns).

The lists presented in these sections were compiled by examining a number of key articles, books and websites. We also reviewed several studies which had obtained and analyzed the views of experienced teleworkers and of managers who had experience in working with teleworkers (e.g., Telework America 2000, 2000; European Telework, 2000; AT&T 2000b). It is our belief that the lists of advantages/disadvantages presented in this section is fairly exhaustive (i.e., although we looked at over 50 sources, no new items were added beyond those obtained from the first ten sources!).

The advantages of telework

THE BENEFITS OF TELEWORK ARRANGEMENTS: THE EMPLOYEE

The list of employee benefits discussed in this section (see table 8.3) was generated from numerous sources (i.e., European Telework, 2000; Shamir and Salomon, 1985; AT&T, 2000a, 2000d; Bailey and Kurkland, 2000; Nie, 1999; Mokhtarian and Salomon, 1997; Stanek and Mokhtarian, 1998; Mannering and Mokhtarian, 1995;

Table 8.3 Benefits for employees

- Reduced commuting time
- Increased ability to manage work and family responsibilities
- Reduced job-related costs
- Improved work opportunities
- Positive impacts on family life
- Increased ability to participate in the local community
- Flexible hours/schedule flexibility
- Better work environment (i.e. fewer interruptions, greater autonomy; greater efficiency)
- Higher levels of perceived control
- Improved quality of life

Shore, 2000; TBS, 2000; Dannhauser, 1999; Huws et al., 1990; Gordon and Kelly, 1986; Haddon and Lewis, 1994). Telework is believed to benefit employees in the following ways:

1. *Reduced travel time*. The European Telework Association reports that a teleworker who works two days a week at home saves eight hours per month or 96 hours per year (the equivalent of 2.5 work weeks). The advantage escalates for those employees who commute more than one hour per day. Studies done in the US (e.g., AT&T, 2000d) support these findings. They report that teleworkers save nearly an hour of commute time per day working from home. Based on this sort of evidence Nie (1999) concluded that telecommuting can be considered "a gift of up to several hours per day" for employees using this arrangement (Nie, 1999).

Reducing commute time was traditionally considered to be the primary reason many teleworkers adopted this arrangement. The empirical work in this area does not support this assumption. As Bailey and Kurkland (2000: 10) note, "travel reduction has not proved to be the strong motivator for telework that early forecasters surmised." Transportation studies of telework indicate that neither time to commute nor the distance of the commute is predictive of: (1) the preference of employees to telework rather than work in the office (Mokhtarian and Salomon, 1997; Stanek and Mokhtarian, 1998), or (2) the frequency of teleworking (Mannering and Mokhtarian, 1995). This finding is consistent with the fact that most research in this area indicates that the majority of teleworkers use at least part of this "extra time" to get more work done as opposed to having a more relaxed lifestyle (the portrait painted by the media).

2. *Better balance of work and family*. A second highly touted motivation for telework is the ability to balance work and family duties, particularly among women with small children at home. Telework has been heralded as a strategy to respond to employees' needs for a healthy work–life balance. Women in particular appear to be attracted to this work arrangement because they perceive that it will help them juggle competing work and family demands (Duxbury et al., 1998; Huws et al., 1990).

The research evidence available to date does not, however, support the hypothesis that the desire for balance will drive women to telework. Women do not dominate telework populations. Large studies indicate that either the population is nearly evenly split between men and women (Cyber Dialogue, 2000; Mannering and Mokhtarian, 1995; Mokhtarian and Salomon, 1996a, 1996b, 1997) or that more men than women telework (Duxbury et al., 1998; Luukinen, 1996). Other research suggests that interest in telework is stronger among couples with no children than among parents (Huws et al., 1991). The actual impact of telework on work–life balance is explored in further detail later in this chapter.

3. *Reduction in work-related costs*. Telework can help reduce work-related expenses linked to transportation, parking, food, and clothing.

4. *Improved work opportunities*. With telework, employees have the opportunity to take advantage of job opportunities which are outside of what could be considered a " reasonable commuting distance."

5. *Positive impacts on family life*. An effective telework and flexible working program reduces the need for job relocation (i.e. employee can take a job in a different city without having to move and "uproot" their family). It has also been noted that telework is one of the first social transformations in centuries that pulls working fathers and mothers back into the home rather than pushing them out for longer and longer periods of time. As such, it has the potential to strengthen the nuclear family.

6. *Participation in the local community*. For many people being "on the spot" to participate in community activities at a time when commuters are still en route is a key advantage of teleworking.

7. *Flexible hours*.   Many employees appreciate the opportunity telework gives them to tailor their workday to their individual biorhythms (i.e. some people are more creative in the morning, others late at night). Typical commuting patterns and office hours condemn everyone to work roughly the same timetable while a flexible telework approach can mean that employees have some freedom to start and stop work according to what works best and to accommodate other demands on their time. For example, the recent study of teleworkers funded by AT&T (AT&T, 2000d) reported that:

- 40 percent of teleworkers say they can schedule multiple personal tasks and errands during the days they work from home allowing them to combine work and personal life in a more fluid manner,
- 25 percent of teleworkers find they can schedule work before or after standard working hours if they need to use that time for personal or family needs (AT&T, 2000d).

8. *Better work environment* (i.e. freedom from interruptions at work; increased efficiency). After an in-depth evaluation of the telework literature, Bailey and Kurkland (2000) concluded that the motivation for telework among individuals is quite simple – they wish to avoid workplace interruptions. Other studies have shown that telework

arrangements optimize productivity which in turn leads to improvements in employee performance, satisfaction, motivation, and morale. It also has been linked to improved quality of life.

9. *Increased sense of control.* Teleworkers usually report an increased feeling of control over their lives, a key factor in reducing perceived stress. As Dannhauser (1999) notes, "There is a shifting sense of values. Dollars are nice but you can't replace time with dollars. So people are setting up at home to be masters of the time they have" (Dannhauser, 1999).

THE BENEFITS OF TELEWORK ARRANGEMENTS: SOCIETY

Telework came into vogue in the 1970s as an oil crisis gave rise to concerns of gasoline consumption, long work commutes, and traffic congestion in major metropolitan areas (Bailey and Kurkland, 2000). Since this time period telework has been heralded as a strategy to help reduce the number of cars on the road with a concomitant reduction in air pollution and traffic congestion (Handy and Mokhtarian, 1995; Novaco et al., 1991; Bailey and Kurkland, 2000). A review of a number of current articles in this area (i.e., Handy and Mokhtarian, 1995; Novaco et al., 1991; Bailey and Kurkland, 2000; Telework America 2000, 2000; European Telework, 2000; Shore, 2000; TBS, 2000; AT&T, 2000a; Ritter and Thompson, 1994; McCloskey and Igbaria, 1998; Huws et al., 1990; Gordon and Kelly, 1986; Haddon and Lewis, 1994) reveals that the social benefits of telework mentioned in the literature (see table 8.4) still focus largely on its positive impacts on the environment. Telework is believed to benefit society in the following ways:

1. *Reduced traffic congestion/fewer traffic accidents/shorter commutes.* We have all observed how much smoother traffic flows in the summer when about 10 percent of employees are away any given week on summer holidays. The same effect can be observed when 10 percent of the population stays home teleworking. Fewer cars on the road means fewer accidents and shorter commute times.

2. *Benefits to the environment.* With the new millennium, public concern for the environment has reached an all-time high. Telecommuting allows for the reduction in the number of people commuting to work which contributes to less traffic congestion. This in turn reduces fossil fuel emissions, conserves energy, and benefits the

Table 8.4   Benefits for society

- Reduced traffic congestion/fewer traffic accidents/shorter commutes
- Benefits to the environment (i.e. reduced air pollution, increased conservation of energy)
- Wider employment/work opportunities
- Access to work for people with specific difficulties
- Safer communities

environment by reducing air pollution. The United States Office of Personnel Management estimates that the current trends towards telecommuting will save approximately 1.5 billion gallons of motor fuel by the year 2000 (TBS, 2000).

Telework also has an impact on such global problems as greenhouse gas emissions. Countries who have agreed to reduce greenhouse gases are focussing on environmentally responsible transportation as transportation is a main source of this problem. For example, in Los Angeles 205 million miles and 47,000 tons of pollutants could be eliminated each year if 5 percent of commuters telecommuted one day per week (Ritter and Thompson, 1994; McCloskey and Igbaria, 1998).

3. *Wider employment/work opportunities.* Telework can potentially enable people in an area of high unemployment to have access to work opportunities that occur elsewhere. Telework has also been linked to economic regeneration and enhancement of rural economies.

4. *Access to work for people with specific difficulties.* Telework provides employment opportunities for groups such as the disabled who are not able to travel or work to a normal 9 to 5 working day. This arrangement could also benefit single parents and employees with responsibility for an elderly of sick relative.

5. *Safer communities.* Telework means more adults at home during the day in urban and suburban neighborhoods. This impacts on home security and can reduce some of the problems associated with "latch-key" children and elder care.

THE BENEFITS OF TELEWORK ARRANGEMENTS: THE ORGANIZATION

A review of the literature would suggest that although the personal and societal impacts of telework are important, implementation of telework is largely driven by considerations within organizations (Westfall, 1998). When considering implementation of a telework program, most employers focus on bottom-line impacts including productivity improvements, space savings, and links with employee retention and/or recruiting. From an organizational perspective, telework should be justified if the costs are balanced by the benefits. If these bottom-line impacts cannot be found, then there is little hope that telework will be implemented. Fortunately, a review of the available literature (Egan, 1997; Matthes, 1992; Telework America 2000, 2000; AT&T, 2000a, 2000b, 2000d; Ceridian, 2000; NetWorld Fusion, 2000; Robertson, 1997; Boyd, 2000; Shore, 2000; Dannhauser, 1999; Nie, 1999; McCloskey and Igbaria, 1998; Westfall, 1998; TBS, 2000; McCloskey and Igbaria, 1998; Huws et al., 1990; Gordon and Kelly, 1986; Haddon and Lewis, 1994) links telework to an improved bottom line. For example, the recent ITAC study predicts that US employers could potentially save an aggregate $441 billion dollars through implementing telework programs (AT&T, 2000d). This section looks first at evidence suggesting that telework will improve an organization's bottom line. Only those benefits where cost savings had been quantified in some manner were included in this part of the discussion. This is followed by an examination of the more intangible organizational benefits that accompany telework. A summary of the benefits covered in this section is given in table 8.5.

Table 8.5   Benefits for employers

- Positive impact on bottom line
  - increased productivity
  - reduced office space costs
  - reduced overhead
  - reduced absenteeism and tardiness
  - enhanced recruiting and retention
    - expand labour pools
    - reduce turnover
    - skills retention
- Improved motivation
- Increased time available to work
  - reduced non-productive time in office
  - enhanced peak performance (by working at times that are most productive)
  - work with fewer interruptions
- Organizational flexibility
- Flexible staffing
- Resilience
- Enhanced customer service
  - expanded service hours
  - improved response time to customer enquiries and requests
- Schedule flexibility
- Tax incentives
- Compliance with legislation

TELEWORK AND THE BOTTOM LINE

1.   *Increased productivity.* Published references to telecommuting assert, almost without exception, that telecommuting increases productivity (Westfall, 1998). Huws et al. (1990: 44) describe this as a "surprising degree of unanimity." This assertion is offered so frequently and by such a variety of sources that it has now entered the realm of conventional wisdom (Westfall, 1998). But what data is there available to support this assertion?

According to Telework America 2000 (2000) the self-reported productivity improvement of home-based teleworkers averages 15 percent. This translates to an average annual bottom-line impact of $9,712 per teleworker. With 16.5 million teleworkers in the US, this works out to an annual national impact exceeding $160 billion (Telework America 2000, 2000). AT&T (2000d) claim that employers can expect an average $5,500 in productivity gains yearly per teleworker while the Gartner Group estimates that telecommuting improves employee productivity by 10 to 40 percent (Nie, 1999)

Boyd (2000) notes that both employees who telework and their supervisors state that they are more effective at home than when they work out of the office. He attributes this increase in productivity to a reduction in interruptions, and notes that while the social aspects of work are important to employees, there are times when these activities detract from their work. Positions that telecommute one to three days per week find that they can be more effective when at home but still maintain social relationships back at the office. Dannhauser (1999) found that nearly three-quarters of his sample of teleworkers reported feeling more productive working at home than at the office, saying that they accomplished "at least 30 percent more work in the same amount of time." Finally, Telework America (Telework America 2000, 2000) reports that teleworkers and their managers both consistently report significant productivity gains under telework arrangements.

Overall, then it would appear that telework is linked to greater perceived productivity. While productivity increases of 40 percent have been reported, a range of 10 to 30 percent is probably more typical across a large-scale program. This increased productivity is typically associated with a reduction in both travel times and the interruptions of an office environment.

2. *Reduced office space and overhead costs.* The literature also reports that organizations with extensive telework programs are more able to reduce overhead expenses typically associated with premises costs, office overheads, occupancy costs, space and furnishing requirements for employees. These savings can be gained in a number of ways. First, depending on employees' schedules, teleworkers could share office space at the designated workplace (i.e. hotelling). Second, as Nie (1999) points out, it is substantially less expensive to set up a worker at home than it is to do so in a centralized office. Finally, organizations have reported up to 30 percent reductions in overheads (Boyd, 2000).

While it is hard to determine exactly how much space is saved at their employer's facilities as a result of teleworking, Telework 2000 (2000) provides the following estimate. They determined that 17 percent of employee-teleworkers (12 percent of all home-based teleworkers or 1.6 million teleworkers) share their workspace with at least one other person at the employer's facility. Assuming that each teleworker shares their space with only one other person, this is a direct reduction of 1.6 million office spaces nationally.

Robertson (1997) assumes that an organization that uses 40,000 square feet to accommodate its 200 employees (i.e. 200 work stations), 10 percent of whom perform mobile work and 10 percent of whom telework, can achieve savings of $115,000 per year if they can share workstations as follows:

- one workstation between four mobile workers
- one workstation between three teleworkers

These saving are based on operating costs per square foot of office space of approximately $25.

A thorough economic analysis of telework by Westfall (1998) resulted in the following key conclusions with respect to the economic viability of telework:

- to make telework economically viable it is essential to capture the potential occupancy costs savings associated with work at home;

- if these savings can be attained, telecommuting is justifiable on a one-day basis for employees earning around $5,000 per year and for annual salaries slightly over $20,000 on a two-day basis;
- telecommuting can be justified for a relatively large proportion of the workforce if it is implemented in the form of a virtual workplace where potential occupancy costs savings are captured.

An additional inducement is that telework arrangements also allow companies to grow without expanding office space (NetWorld Fusion, 2000). This is a big plus in communities where real estate is expensive.

3. *Reduced absenteeism.* There appears to be a reduction in absenteeism associated with telework arrangements. Teleworkers have been found to be less likely to use sick days for their own minor illnesses and report reduced absence due to stress. In addition, employees who may feel too ill to commute to the office and work a full day may feel well enough to complete a partial day of work at home. It also reduces absenteeism for family-related reasons. The recent AT&T (2000d) study indicates that employers can save 63 percent of the costs associated with absenteeism by allowing telework.

4. *Increased ability to recruit and retain skilled employees.* Demographic data suggests that the first decade of the new millennium can be characterized as an employees' market (AT&T, 2000d). With the economic boom, more people who want to work, do work and the pool of potential employees is low (AT&T, 2000d; Dannhauser, 1999; Nie, 1999). The next generation of workers will be much smaller than the current workforce. As older workers who are experienced and trained retire, the smaller pool of younger workers is resulting in a shortage of needed employees (McCloskey and Igbaria, 1998; Perin, 1991). This means that employers have to offer incentives to attract employees and to keep top people from jumping ship. While employees want good pay, money isn't everything and in these "increasingly quality-of-life conscious times" employees are looking beyond financial rewards to other benefits like flexibility and time with family when deciding whether to take or keep a job (AT&T, 2000d). Research would indicate that the current generation want to live in pleasant surroundings, participate in leisure activities, and have time to spend with their families. They also seek work arrangements that allow them to meet these needs (McCloskey and Igbaria, 1998). As such, employees who are interested in recruiting and retaining quality employees in this market need to consider flexible work options (McCloskey and Igbaria, 1998).

A review of the available literature would suggest that telework arrangements have become more attractive as the strong economy means that employers must make accommodations to attract the best and the brightest workers (Ceridian, 2000). Telework appears to gives organizations a competitive edge at recruiting and retaining staff whose knowledge and skills are critical to the success of the organization. It can also widen the pool of potential employees as it offers flexibility to individuals who, otherwise, would have difficulty working (i.e., employees with commuting difficulties, employees with dependants, those who are recovering from illness or who have disabilities). The following data culled from the recent International Telework Association (ITAC) study (AT&T, 2000d) makes a strong case for establishing recruitment and retention as one of the major benefits of telework arrangements.

- Telework rates highly on the list of desired employer traits. Over half of those who currently telework say that the possibility of working at home some of the time is important/extremely important in choosing their employer.
- 10.4 million Americans who would like to work at home believe their employers wouldn't let them. This suggests that employers who offer telework can better attract and retain workers.

Other research showing that employees who have experienced the benefits of telecommuting programs tend to prefer these work arrangements and seek out similar opportunities elsewhere supports these findings (Boyd, 2000). The Ceridian (2000) and NetWorld Fusion (2000) studies of employers also demonstrate a strong link between telework arrangements and better recruitment and retention. They observed that half of the companies they surveyed felt that boundaryless work arrangements were highly successful in both attracting workers and retaining employees It is interesting to note that the Ceridian (2000) study found that younger workers were twice as likely as older workers to see more benefits and fewer problems with boundaryless work arrangements.

But how does this affect the bottom line? AT&T (2000d) estimate that by retaining employees through the practice of telework, companies can save over $14,6000 per teleworker (average cost of recruiting an employee). NetWorld Fusion (2000) notes that greater retention means improved quality of work and lower human resource demands for retraining and replacing personal.

OTHER ORGANIZATIONAL BENEFITS OF TELEWORK

5. *Improved motivation.* Telework programs can increase motivation as employees who are permitted to work from home often interpret this as a sign that their manager/employer trusts them, is confident in their abilities, and is willing to give them more autonomy and control over their work.

6. *Increased time available to work.* Telecommuters contend that it takes productive time out of the day to "wind down" from and mentally prepare for the stresses associated with commuting to and from work. This is time that is then available and productive to them when they work at home. While studies are by no means definitive, the current wisdom is that up to half the commuting hours saved by telecommuting may be given directly back to the company as additional work hours (Nie, 1999). Additional savings of productive time are realized as a reduction in the use of company paid time to meet personal or family needs (i.e. teleworkers have less of a need to take a sick day to take children to appointments, be home for a delivery or repair etc.) (Boyd, 2000). Finally it has been estimated that around 20 percent of onsite employees' time is lost due to factors over which they have no control (i.e. office politics). This time is "available" to those who work from home (Boyd, 2000).

7. *Organizational flexibility*. There are a number of examples of organizational flexibility offered in the literature. For example, remote work can allow people to work in dispersed teams that can be assembled and reassembled as the needs of the organization change. It also allows the organization to create teams representing the best skills and experience for the project regardless of geography and time zones and with a minimal need for travel (this benefit is referred to in the literature as "spatial reach").

8. *Flexible staffing*. This feature of telework is particularly attractive to organizations who have peaks and troughs of workloads. In this case, remote work enables staff to work peak hours without having to travel. This is particularly beneficial when the time commuting to and from work is as long or longer than the amount of extra work-time required.

9. *Resilience*. Telework means that work can continue uninterrupted during and after inclement weather (e.g., the "Great Canadian Icestorm" of 1998), a natural disaster, a strike, special events (it proved invaluable during the Olympics), highway construction or during an energy or transportation emergency which may prevent normal access to the conventional office site.

10. *Enhanced customer service*. Customer services can be extended beyond the working day or the working week without the costs of overtime payments or the need for staff to travel at unsocial hours.

11. *Schedule flexibility*. Teleworkers are more productive when they can schedule their actual work time during their most effective periods (i.e. accommodate their personal clocks) and around the other demands in their lives. While telework is not a substitute for daycare, it does provide telecommuters with greater flexibility in scheduling this type of care.

12. *Tax incentives*. There are also potential tax incentives for employers who permit work from home as governments are taking a more active role in promoting the social and environmental benefits of telecommuting (NetWorld Fusion, 2000).

13. *Compliance with legislation*. Allowing people to work from home will allow companies to comply with legislation such at the USA's Clean Air Act (requires large companies to reduce the number of automobiles commuting to work on a daily basis), and the USA's Disabilities Act (requires organizations to make reasonable accommodations to enable disabled employees to perform their jobs) (Matthes, 1992).

Barriers to the implementation of telework

With all these benefits it would seem that telework should be a fairly "easy sell" to employers and managers. Unfortunately, this is not always the case. Telework can represent a dramatic shift in how many organizations conceptualize work and the workplace (Shore, 2000). As noted previously, the literature on barriers to telework is not as well developed or as extensive as that on benefits. This is not surprising as much of the research on telework has been funded by organizations or groups who have a vested interest in the growth of this work arrangement (i.e. telework associations, consultants, high-technology companies). The barriers that were reported on in the literature are divided into three main groupings in the discussion below: drawbacks to employees, drawbacks to employers, and unintended negative consequences to society.

DISADVANTAGES TO EMPLOYEES

The main disadvantages to employees who telework outlined in the literature include professional and social isolation, overwork, greater conflict between work and family, greater conflict with colleagues at work, and the costs associated with setting up a home office (Baruch, 2000; Baruch and Nicholson, 1997; Bailey and Kurkland, 2000; TBS, 2000; Dannhauser, 1999; Shore, 2000; Reingold, 2000). Details on each of these disadvantages are given below.

1. *Professional and social isolation.* Some individuals who telework may experience a sense of isolation from the office environment and reduced social interaction with colleagues. The European Telework Association (2000) for example found that some people, whose work didn't require regular contact with others, felt lonely or isolated when teleworking for long stretches of time – they needed the "camaraderie" of working at an office. Telework may also reduce employees' sense of belonging to the organization. Recent research has found that the risk of isolation and no sense of belonging are highest when employees telework full-time but minimal if employees work at home one or two days a week (AT&T, 2000a).

Probably the most well researched drawback to telework is the idea that employees who decrease their visibility in the office by working from home may damage their career objectives because of the "out of sight, out of mind" phenomenon. This concern is particularly prevalent in situations where there is no independent way for a manager to assess whether or not the teleworker is "doing a good job" when working from home (i.e., professional telework). Fortunately, the research that has been done in this area can be used to refute this concern. A recent study of 17,000 teleworkers done by Joanne Pratt for AT&T indicates that teleworkers receive a higher proportion of promotions than their stay-at-work counterparts. Contrary to the notion that telework imposes career obstacles, more than 60 percent of survey respondents reported that teleworking has affected their career positively; 33 percent reported no career effect either way.

2. *Overwork and increased work–life conflict.* Research indicates that telecommuting has introduced some new stresses including the inability to place appropriate boundaries around the workday, greater work–life conflict and overwork. Employees who telework have 24-hour access to their work and are often tempted to work longer hours. Employees who are unable or unwilling to control the amount of time they spend in work (see the discussion below on who should work from home) are more

likely to find that telework extends the amount of time they spend in work-related activities. The European Telework Association (2000) found that some people reacted to an unstructured home-based work environment by becoming workaholics because they found it difficult to switch off from working. This group concluded that individuals who need the externally imposed pressures of "office hours" to assist the transition between work time and private time are not well suited to telework.

3. *Increased tension at work.* Non-teleworking colleagues often have issues with telework arrangements that managers and teleworkers need to consider when implementing this work arrangement (AT&T, 2000c). Research has suggested that conflict with colleagues and managers may occur with telework arrangements due to the following sentiment: "when you are in the office, no one doubts whether you are working or not . . . when you work at home, people don't really believe that you are working" (Duxbury et al., 1998). Tensions increase when the criteria used to assess employee suitability for telework arrangements are not objective and transparent. For telework programs to work, non-teleworking colleagues need to be reassured that:

- teleworkers will meet their commitments,
- teleworkers will be as accessible as if they were in the office, and
- their own workloads will not increase because teleworkers are offloading tasks usually performed at the office.

4. *Costs of setting up a home office.* Many teleworkers bear the costs of setting up at home in return for the opportunity to work there (Dannhauser, 1999). Just under half (46 percent) of teleworkers who participated in the recent Telework America study paid for both their equipment and its maintenance with the employer covering all costs in only 29 percent of the cases (Telework America 2000, 2000). Employees who participated in a 1998 survey conducted by Kensington Technology Group reported that they paid about $3,500 just to set up shop at home (Dannhauser, 1999). While many work for companies willing to share the cost, some 44 percent said their employers didn't even pay for essentials like computers and phones (Shore, 2000).

DISADVANTAGES TO ORGANIZATIONS

The Treasury Board of Canada provides the following comprehensive list of the potential organizational disadvantages of teleworking (TBS, 2000):

- Teleworkers cannot be visually monitored. In order to have efficient monitoring, there must be greater emphasis put on work measurement and productivity. In many cases, however, these measures have not been identified and are not in place.
- A cultural change may be required to encompass the new work arrangements and necessitate leadership and support from both managers and colleagues.

- Some individuals may feel that employees who telework are not really working, even though this is contrary to evidence that telework usually results in greater effectiveness and efficiency.
- Companies may face increased liability exposure for home workers.
- Data security is more difficult to ensure for those who work at home.
- Unions may resent the loss of proximity to their members.
- Meetings may become harder to schedule.
- The technology infrastructure needed to support telework may be too expensive.
- Emergency actions involving the telecommuter may become harder to take.

DISADVANTAGES TO SOCIETY

Any social change as large and as pervasive as one modifying the locus of work for a quarter or more of the workforce is likely to carry with it a number of unintended consequences. Nie (1999) expressed the following concerns in this regard:

- The workplace currently represents one of the major centers for friendship, personal contact, and collegiality in contemporary society. Its importance has grown steadily in this regard as other areas have declined (e.g., small towns where everyone knew each other have been replaced by large cities and bedroom communities; extended families are now more geographically dispersed). Telework may increase employees' sense of isolation.
- Ongoing face-to-face connections foster trust and personal integrity in people's business dealing. The more isolated work is from other parts of one's social world, the more business ethics may suffer as anonymity can lead people to believe they can get away with shoddy behavior.

TBS (2000) also notes that there is a potential for telework to contribute to a loss of business for downtown merchants, for transportation companies, and for automobile-related industries and trades.

● Implementing a Successful Telework Program ●

Too often when people conclude that "telework doesn't work for us" or "telework doesn't work," the reality is that they made a mess of the implementation process. This section outlines what can be done to capture the gains promised by virtual offices and telework. It is divided into five sections. The first outlines when telework is and is not applicable while the second looks at who should telework. This is followed by a discussion of what needs to be done to ensure a successful telework program. Included in this section is discussion of things that key stakeholders such as managers and teleworkers can do to increase the probabilities of success. The fourth section presents a number of key success factors for implementing telework. The section ends with discussion of how two best practice organizations, Merrill Lynch and IBM, implemented their telework programs.

When to consider telework arrangements: when not to implement telework

Telework only yields benefits when applied in the right circumstances and in the right way. European Telework (2000) identifies the following key areas that have to be right in order for telework to yield benefits rather than problems.

- *The task and whether telework is a good way to do this task set.* It is not the job title but the job duties that determine whether work is suitable for teleworking (Shore, 2000). Not all tasks are best performed in a distributed, self-managing environment. There are many tasks (e.g., design or other creative work) that gain considerably from the very close interactions of a team working together in one room. Telework is, however, possible for almost any office-based task and for an increasing range of industrial tasks. Writers have compiled lists of necessary telework tasks and job characteristics (e.g., Baruch and Nicholson, 1997). Job traits often included in this list include individual control of work pace and little need for face-to-face interactions. Before teleworking both employers and employees should ask themselves: is it appropriate for me to do this task at home? Will it enhance the way this task set is performed?

- *The employing organization.* Telework works best in companies where there is a lot of networking, where employees are empowered to act and think for themselves, and where management is by results. Such organizations are highly networked, tend to gravitate toward arrangements such as telework, and take a fairly informal approach to telework (European Telework, 2000). Other companies have management systems and cultures that are not (yet) well adapted to the flexibility that telework can entail. For example, it is hard to introduce telework into an organization that has not yet implemented electronic networking (i.e., e-mail, online discussions) or into an organization where the management approach is bureaucratic and strongly hierarchical. It is also difficult to implement telework into an environment where managers lack the skills or confidence to manage at a distance or do not trust their employees not to underperform.

- *The domestic (home and family) setting.* Here there are both physical and emotional aspects to be considered. Physically, the main requirement is the ability to create a workspace within the home where the teleworker can (at least partially) isolate themselves from domestic activities and family role responsibilities but at the same time "close the door to work" when they are focussing on their family. Many homes are not well equipped for telework. It is difficult, for example, to telework effectively if the task requires close concentration and the home environment is a small apartment with young active children, noisy neighbors, etc. Emotionally, it is important that telework be a good fit with the rest of the family. Research would suggest that it takes the family time to adjust to a teleworker who is "physically present but mentally preoccupied" (European Telework, 2000).

- *The individual's personality, experience, and preferences.* Home-based telework is inappropriate for some people. Those who are not "self-starters," for example, may need the external discipline provided by set hours and a managed environment. Telework is also not the right arrangement for an employee who wants opportunities to socialize, make new contacts, etc. This issue is discussed in greater detail in the following section.

When does personality matter?

Even if all factors are appropriate for telework, it is still possible that an employee may have a personality that makes home work inappropriate for them personally. Experience has shown that successful teleworkers are well-disciplined and organized self-starters who can work independently. They are results-oriented, being able to set their own deadlines and goals. They have a history of reliable and responsible performance, are trustworthy, and require minimal supervision (TBS, 2000). It is important to note, however, that what some people find attractive about telework others find unattractive. Factors to consider include:

1.   *Ability to apply self-discipline and self-analysis to work.* Teleworkers have to apply self-discipline (or self-management) to ensure that an appropriate amount and quality of work is done and that satisfactory results are achieved as telework is, by definition, unsupervised. Some people have problems with this and respond better to a clearer differentiation between work and home/leisure environment than is provided by commuting to an employer-managed workplace (European Telework, 2000). Other research shows that one of the keys to a successful telework program is selecting teleworkers who can break up their tasks into two groups: those that are best done in the traditional office and those that are location-independent and therefore teleworkable (Telework America 2000, 2000).

2.   *Reactions to working alone.* Some people find it easier to focus on work without the distractions of a busy office – others need busy surroundings to motive them.

3.   *Reactions to an unstructured work setting.* Some people optimize their performance when they can work at whatever time suits them personally – others need the routine of regular hours and external prompting to start and finish work.

4.   *Need for commute time.* Some people appreciate the time they can save by not commuting – others find value in the daily routine of travel and use the time as a mechanism for transition from work role to home role.

5.   *Comfort level with office technology.* Not all telework jobs require a high degree of technical knowledge but some familiarity with technology is necessary.

Unfortunately fewer than 20 percent of teleworkers get intensive training in the use of their technology (Telework America 2000, 2000).

How to ensure a successful telework implementation

"Telework touches the whole work environment, not just the individual who does it" (AT&T, 2000a). When a telework program starts, everyone should be consulted, including bosses and colleagues. During the telework implementation phase, however, managers and teleworkers are the key stakeholders and their actions can make or break the program. What does the research suggest that managers and employees need to do to help ensure a successful telework experience?

WHAT DO MANAGERS NEED TO DO TO ENSURE SUCCESS?

What does it take to manage teleworkers? For telework arrangements to be effective, managers need to do following (NetWorld Fusion, 2000; AT&T, 2000c):

- Develop a telework plan which includes both long-term and short-term goals. Since teleworkers often need to make independent decisions, it is important that they understand:

  - the goals of the company,
  - the objectives of their work group,
  - their own role in achieving these goals.

- Produce a written telework agreement. Many employers are suspicious of telework because they are fearful of reduced worker accountability and its effects on productivity. A written agreement that spells out all aspects of the job (i.e., ownership issues, compensation for worker expenses, performance evaluation criteria, frequency of required office attendance, legal considerations, etc.) can help alleviate these fears.
- Use technology to stay in touch with teleworkers.
- Rethink and redesign the way certain jobs are performed.
- Adopt location-independent ways of measuring performance and results: managing teleworkers is done using results rather than observation.
- Transition teamwork towards more electronic-based collaboration. The work team also needs to invest some time and effort to build the team as a team (i.e., time to socialize).
- Use planning skills to effectively distribute work so that in-office personnel and teleworkers are treated equally.
- Establish regular means of communication with the teleworker as effective, regular communications help clarify work expectations, due dates, and questions and keep teleworkers "in the loop." Schedule regular progress reviews.

- If the arrangement is not working out, drop out of the program. Telework arrangements do not work for every job or every employee. They will not rectify poor performance problems.
- Take care to include teleworkers in all group activities (i.e., staff meetings, events).
- Evaluate and reward teleworkers using the same criteria as are used with those who remain in the office. Working away from the office means working to deliver results, not just to register "face time" in the office. Virtual workers need to know they will be rewarded if they develop individual skills and the results follow.
- Take training which equips them to manage virtually.

WHAT DO TELEWORKERS NEED TO DO TO ENSURE SUCCESS?

Research suggests that telework has a greater chance of succeeding when teleworkers (see Church, 2000):

- Establish a routine for use when working from home: planning and scheduling must replace relying on chance encounters in the office.
- Establish goals and assignments for days when teleworking. Set deadlines.
- Designate a separate workspace at home and make sure that it is set up so it is efficient.
- Work out the rules and roles with others at home so that family does not interfere with work.
- Maintain regular communication with their managers, their colleagues and their clients. Good (electronic) communication must replace informal contacts and "eyeball" management when people work remotely.
- Are easily accessed by managers, colleagues, and clients.

Key success factors with respect to implementation of telework

Research turned up two excellent sets of key critical success factors for the implementation of telework programs. The one was developed by consulting company Ceridian (2000) in conjunction with its research on the boundaryless office. The other was developed by the Treasury Board of Canada (TBS, 2000) for use in training initiatives undertaken as part of the Government of Canada's federal telework program. The lists are quite different and have quite different focusses, but when considered together provide a comprehensive list for those interested in either implementing or researching the implementation of telework arrangements.

CERIDIAN SUCCESS FACTORS

Ceridian (2000) research identified the following key success factors with respect to implementing boundaryless work:

- *Begin with research.* Look at company history, culture, readiness, overall budget. Identify best practices and talk to other companies who have had successful results.
- *Set goals and standards.* Include in the business plan criteria for measuring the results and productivity of telework arrangements which can be used to establish criteria for rewards and incentive programs.
- *Communicate clear, measurable expectations to the entire employee population.* i.e., roles, responsibilities, office hours, equipment, furnishings, frequency of face-to-face meetings, reporting requirements, work assignments, professional goals.
- *Invest in resources and essential tools.* Determine the technology and resources needed to support telework arrangements.
- *Identify a pilot group and test the program before wide-scale implementation.* Test employees' office equipment and procedures on a small group before rolling out to the entire organization.
- *Provide training and ongoing support.* Include sessions for managers, teleworkers and co-workers. Provide help lines and e-mail and forums for workers and managers to discuss best practices and challenges.
- *Leverage practices in recruiting and retention.* Be prepared to discuss telework arrangements in the hiring or employment process.
- *Review practices periodically.* Telework is not for everyone. Nor does it work for all types of work. The arrangements need to be reviewed periodically and adjusted when specific situations arise.

TBS SUCCESS FACTORS

The Treasury Board of Canada (TBS) started offering telework arrangements to all eligible federal public services (just over 200,000 people) in the early 1990s. An evaluation of this policy was conducted in early 1996 after telework arrangements had been in place for three years. This review confirmed that the telework policy was meeting its objectives. In December 1999 the TBS issued the permanent Telework Policy endorsing its commitment to create a workplace of choice. The following information comes from a document prepared to accompany its telework training efforts.[2]

The Treasury Board of Canada states up front that "Telework success is based on the basic principles of trust, respect and collaboration." They then identify the following keys to the success of teleworking programs (TBS, 2000):

- Dispel the myth that "visibility equates to productivity" by ensuring that managers manage by results rather than by visual presence. Performance expectations need to be quantifiable and qualitative and should be similar for teleworkers and for employees who perform similar work in the office.
- Have senior management show visible support for the program (perhaps by teleworking occasionally themselves).

- Telework must first be feasible from an operational perspective (i.e., the employee can work away from the office without negatively affecting their performance; client service is not adversely affected).
- Telework arrangements must also be cost-effective: up-front costs can be recuperated over a reasonable time. The recuperation of costs may be in terms of increased productivity, reductions in absenteeism, savings in recruitment costs, facility savings.
- Telework is a voluntary option subject to management approval. Employees must want to telework; managers should agree that this arrangement is feasible from both operational and budgetary perspectives.
- Requests to telework are assessed on a case-by-case basis.
- Telework arrangements can be terminated at any time with reasonable notice from either party.
- Advanced planning by all parties is key. Supervisors must plan workloads and meetings in advance and ensure that these are well communicated. Teleworkers must plan their work to ensure that there is sufficient work to do at home and that they have the necessary tools, references, etc. to be able to carry out the work.
- Details of the telework arrangement need to be discussed and agreed to in advance (a written document is particularly helpful here).
- All terms and conditions of employment and collective agreement provisions continue to apply.
- Colleagues must not be adversely affected by telework arrangements: workloads must be equitably distributed to ensure that employees at the office are not burdened with the teleworker's responsibilities.
- There must be ongoing monitoring of the program including feedback from the team, the client, the teleworker, and the manager.
- Security of information and files is ensured. Employees must be well briefed on aspects of the safe custody and control of sensitive information.
- While telework can provide valuable assistance with dependent care (i.e., time saved commuting can be spent with family members, less need for before- and after-school care, increased ability to attend daytime school functions, go to the doctor) teleworkers must have some form of dependent care for the days when they work at home (i.e., telework arrangements do not eliminate the need for outside dependent care services).
- Communication with colleagues at work: it is not only important for the teleworker to maintain excellent ongoing communications with his or her manager and vice versa, but also that the colleagues know the teleworker's schedule and the tasks being carried out at home.
- Good communication at home: it is also important for the teleworker to ensure that any persons living with the teleworker understand that he/she is working and to work out any home schedules to minimize any disruptions.

Case studies

Many companies have launched telework programs that failed dismally (Bresnahan, 1998) Two companies which have been identified as "Best Practice" with respect to their telework programs are Merrill Lynch and IBM (Bresnahan, 1998). These companies have completely different cultures and had radically different reasons for implementing the program (Merrill Lynch wanted to earn the loyalty of its IT employees; IBM wanted to save a few million in real estate dollars). How they implemented their programs is, however, illustrative for companies thinking of pursuing this option.[3]

IBM

Between 1991 and 1993 IBM lost $16 billion, cut some 117,000 jobs, and took more than $28 billion in restructuring charges. Telecommuting was one of the strategies IBM used to get out of this slump. In 1995 the 10,000 salespeople who survived the cuts "found themselves without a home (or rather, with only a home!) as dedicated office space was now shared at a four to one employee to office space ratio and telecommuting became mandatory." Because salespeople and consultants were used to working remotely and were grateful to still be employed, IBM did not encounter the resistance that such a drastic downsizing typically engenders.

Even though employees were willing to telework, a number of problems still arose. These included:

- *Technology barriers.* Even though IBM has a technically sophisticated staff, the skills required to use a host-based system which links directly to the network are quite different from those needed to use a laptop. People had to get used to working a different way.
- *Communication challenges.* IBM's culture had always focussed around meetings, but lengthy status meetings over phone lines were awkward. Managers did not know how to monitor productivity and employees felt out of the loop. Even worse, customers and clients complained they could not reach consultants. IBM overcame this problem by developing a sophisticated e-mail, voice mail, and corporate intranet system.
- *Determining how to enable its scattered workforce to have regular social interaction with colleagues.* Meetings became difficult because salespeople and consultants were mobile and IBM would rather they were in the field serving customers than working at a central location. IBM overcame this challenge by having an executive responsible for drawing employees together for social activities and retreats.
- *How to assimilate new employees into a virtual workforce.* This was overcome by implementing a seven- to ten-day course for all new employees which covers all the basics about working for IBM and gives them a chance to work with peers. New hires are also assigned two mentors: one for professional development and one which handles business-related questions. Part of a mentor's performance pay is dependent on their mentoring abilities.

What was the impact of the telework program at IBM? Bresnahan (1998) reports that telecommuting has saved the company significant dollars in real estate. By having 10,000 employees mobile, IBM estimates that it saves $75 million per year. Employee productivity is estimated to have increased 20 percent and an employee survey showed that 75 percent of employees said that teleworking had a positive impact on overall morale. Employees are working longer hours, getting more done an hour, and are happier overall. Moreover, customer service has never been better.

MERRILL LYNCH

Merrill Lynch was amongst the first companies that decided that they should sanction formal telework programs to attract and retain employees (Dannhauser, 1999). Merrill Lynch has 54,000 employees scattered in 40 countries. The company is heavily dependent on its IT department. Difficulties in recruiting and retaining employees in this area was the impetus for the implementation of their telework program. In 1995 the company set up a task force to address issues of concern to the 1,700 programmers in the Private Client Group. The committee's goal "was to become the most appealing IS employer in the market." After much argument the company decided to launch a telecommuting venture that would cost $500,000 up front and $3,000 each year thereafter for each teleworking employee. Company executives were convinced to implement the program by figures showing that the cost of the telework program was anticipated to be much less than the cost of continually losing and replacing IS staff. The company began its telework project by first establishing rules and processes to govern work away from the office. These rules included the following:

- An employee cannot telework until they have been with a new product for 90 days. Even then the employee is required to go to the workplace at least once per week. This stipulation was added to ensure that employees maintain strong ties to their programs and their co-workers.
- Once an employee has decided to telework, both they and their manager must attend a day-long training program.
- After the training, the manager and employee must go through a technical interview to determine technology requirements. Those who demonstrate the quality to telework get a phone line, laptop with docking station and modem from the organization. The employee is responsible for the purchase of his or her own office furniture.
- As a last step before working from home each employee must spend two weeks in a telecommuting simulation lab at Merrill Lynch. This lab was set up to simulate the home telework experience. They employee is located away from where they work, given the same equipment they will have at home, and exposed to a number of distractions (i.e., the simulation lab is by a busy street). During this two-week period, the teleworker is expected to communicate with managers as if they were already telecommuting. This experience prepares them for working outside the office.
- Home offices are inspected for safety and conduciveness to productivity

Even though Merrill Lynch felt they were incredibly well prepared to implement telework, they found in retrospect that they had underestimated the need for technical support. To remedy this they assembled a five-person IT support group dedicated to solving problems for remote workers, who are available from 7 a.m. to 7 p.m. and on call the rest of the time. They also built a corporate internet where people could post announcements and updates, reserving e-mail for more immediate communication needs.

And what has been the impact of this program? Bresnahan (1998) notes that three years after its inception employee satisfaction is up 30 percent, *Working Mother* voted Merrill Lynch one of the 100 best places to work, and *Business Week* named it one of the top family friendly firms to work for. Dannhauser (1999) notes that Merrill Lynch reports saving from $5,000 to $6,000 per office per year in overhead costs.

● Telework and Work–Life Balance ●

Work–family conflict occurs when an individual has to perform multiple roles such as worker, spouse, and parent (Duxbury et al., 1998). Each of these roles imposes demands on their incumbents requiring time, energy, and commitment to perform the role adequately. The cumulative demands of multiple roles can result in role strain of two types: overload and interference. Overload exists when the total demands on time and energy associated with the prescribed activities of multiple roles are too great to perform the roles adequately or comfortably. Interference occurs when conflicting demands make it difficult to fulfill the requirements of multiple roles (Duxbury et al., 1998).

Both the popular press and the research literature emphasize the personal, family, and social benefits gained from the flexibility afforded to teleworkers as the reason for the re-emergence of telework (Owen et al., 1995). While the Bureau of National Affairs (BNA, 1992: 4) indicates that "telecommuting as a flexible workplace option to help balance family and work responsibilities is growing" it is difficult to gauge the accuracy of this statement as "It is difficult to get an accurate assessment of the total telecommuting population, much less the workers who do so just for family reasons."

At the present time there is an intense debate in the literature regarding the relationship between telework arrangments and work–life balance. This debate is summarized below. Those interested in a more complete discussion of this topic are referred to Duxbury et al., 1998.

View 1: Telework helps parents balance work–family conflict

The view that telework will help employees balance the work and family demands is widely held. Many researchers claim that the opportunity to work at home is just what today's dual-income couples need to help them cope with heavy demands at work as well as home. Company policies on telework are frequently based on the premise that telework arrangements will make it easier for employees to balance work and family. The Treasury Board of Canada, for example, states that one major objective of their initiatives in this area is "to allow employees to work at alternative locations thereby achieving a better balance between their work and personal lives" (Treasury Board, 2000). Researchers report that many teleworkers cite need to balance work and family as the major reason for working at home (see Duxbury et al., 1998 for references).

How can telework reduce work–family conflict? Suggestions include: (1) increased work-time and work-location flexibility; (2) increased control over the pacing and scheduling of work; (3) decreased time in commuting may give employees more time for their families; (4) the idea that work at home makes it possible for employees to provide emergency care for sick children or better mesh their hours of work with their families' schedules; (5) better relationships at home; and (6) increased satisfaction with childcare.

There is some empirical support for positive spillover between telework and the ability to manage household tasks and childcare arrangements. Hartman et al. (1992) reported the following four positive outcomes that teleworkers experienced from telecommuting: (1) greater personal flexibility; (2) reduced time spent commuting; (3) increased productivity when working from home; and (4) the ability to spend more time with the family. Olson and Primps (1984) discovered that professional teleworkers felt that their relationships with their children had improved since they began to telework. Huws's (1990) study of clerical teleworkers reports that, for most teleworkers, working at home offered a number of advantages including flexibility and the opportunity to combine work with childcare. Hill et al. (1996) found that teleworkers who were parents of young children were more likely to feel that telework helped them combine work and family responsibilities. Finally Higgins, Duxbury, and Lee (1993) and Duxbury et al. (1998) report that employees with greater work-time and work-location flexibility were better able to constructively balance competing work and family responsibilities.

Work by Duxbury et al. (1998) provides one of the first rigorous empirical examinations of how telework arrangements affect work–family conflict (i.e. pre-test post-test control group design; use of multiple data-collection techniques). The findings from this empirically rigorous study offer strong support for those who contend that telework arrangements help employed parents balance competing work and family demands. Both the quantitative and qualitative findings reported in this study suggest that telework helps dual-income parents to: (1) increase their control over the work and family interface; (2) ease some of the tensions associated with combining a career with parenting; and (3) achieve a better balance between their work roles and their family roles.

View 2: Telework increases work–family conflict

While some of the literature on the consequences of telework has stressed the opportunities this work arrangement will create for performing both work and family roles more fully, much of the literature contends that working at home may increase stress by increasing the permeability of the boundary between work and family domains and making it more difficult to juggle work and family schedules (see Duxbury et al., 1998 for relevant references). This body of literature maintains that the home office is a "cyberspace sweatshop" that blurs the boundaries between work and home life resulting in increased rather than decreased levels of stress and conflict and negative spillover from work to home. Christensen (1988: 6), for example, suggests that the idea that telework will help employees balance complex work–family problems "is a cruel illusion, implying that a woman will be able to resolve these problems by simply changing the place where she works."

Why would telework increase stress and conflict between work and family? Studies in this area offer a number of possible mechanisms by which this may occur: (1) studies on employees who work at home often show that they spend a greater percentage of their time on paid work activities; (2) the flexibility gained through telework benefits work rather than the family; (3) working at home gives contrasting messages to employers (telework maximizes productivity by making it easier for employees to work) and families (telework increases the employees' availability for family activities); and (4) for many employees, the journey to and from work provides a "buffer" between work and family roles which reduces the transfer of stress from one life domain to the other. A recent study of home-based work (Heck, Walker, and Furry, 1996) noted that home workers cited the following three main disadvantages of working from home: can't get away from work, family interrupts work, and work interferes with family.

● Telework Research: Where Are We? Where Do We Need To Go? ●

Serious comprehensive studies on telework date back to the 1970s (i.e., Nilles et al., 1976). Unfortunately, despite this long history, the growth in the number of teleworkers, and the extensive publicity given to this work arrangement, sound empirical research in this area is surprisingly limited. The literature that does exist has been at a fairly superficial level and is full of contradictions (Westfall, 1998; McCloskey and Igbaria, 1998). This section presents an overview of the empirical research on telework. It seeks answers to the following questions: How much empirical research has been done in this area? What are the methodological limitations of this research? What questions remain to be answered?

How much empirical research has been done on telework?

Bailey and Kurkland (2000) in a recent review of the academic telework literature found 75 published field studies and more than 50 other articles or book chapters published since Jack Nilles coined the phrase "telecommuting" in 1973 (Nilles et al., 1976). They conducted their search as follows:

- they searched library databases like ABI/Inform and PsychoInfo using the following keywords: telework, telecommuting, remote work, and
- they used a "snowball" technique whereby citations in articles were mined for further references.

The field studies represented a wide range of disciplines including transportation, urban planning, information sciences, organizational behaviour, ethics, law, and sociology (Bailey and Kurkland, 2000) suggesting that telework research is multi-disciplinary in nature. The academic articles took the form of essays on topics such as the future of teleworking (Handy and Mokhtarian), methodological issues (Kraut, 1989; Mokhtarian et al., 1995; Mokhtarian, 1991), legal and union issues (e.g., DiMartino and Wirth, 1990), gender issues (Holcomb, 1991; Huws, 1991), and considerations of time and space (Perin, 1998).

Other indications of the depth of the empirical work in this area come from an extensive review of the academic telework literature conducted by McCloskey and

Igbaria (1998). These authors identified 32 empirical studies of teleworking which they classified into five broad types: pilot studies, usage, beliefs/perceptions, work attitudes/outcomes, and work–life issues. They enumerated the concerns associated with each of these lines of enquiry:

- *Pilot studies* are typically confined to one organization and are based on the experiences of participants who were likely self-selected. This makes the generalizability of the results from pilot studies quite limited. Pilot studies are also flawed in that they tend to focus on easily measured constructs and ignore the more complex constructs. On a positive note, pilot or case studies may give researchers the ability to study telework over time.
- *Usage.* This line of research focusses on identifying the extent of telework participation. The lack of a common definition of telework unfortunately makes it very difficult to compare research on telecommuting usage.
- *Beliefs/perceptions.* Many of the larger studies on telecommuting examine only the perceived impacts of telecommuting. Although these studies provide insight into the attitudes and beliefs about this work arrangement, the usefulness of this line of enquiry is quite limited. "Just because employees who have never telecommuted believe telecommuting will result in less career advancement does not necessarily mean that limited career advancement will be an outcome" (McCloskey and Igbaria, 1998: 341).
- *Work attitudes and outcomes.* Several studies have tried to establish the advantages and disadvantages of telecommuting. While some studies have focussed only on the employee, others have explored the attitudes of both employees and managers. Yet others have compared teleworkers to non-teleworkers on aspects of their work and on their work attitudes. The number of work outcomes addressed in this body of research have, however, been quite limited.
- *Work and family issues.* Telecommuting is also believed to have an impact on family life as working from home often results in integration of and conflict between the two domains. With few exceptions, research in this area has been superficial.

Key problems with the literature

There are a number of deficiencies in the telework literature that constrain what we can conclude from it. These problems, as enumerated by Bailey and Kurkland (2000), Westfall (1998), and McCloskey and Igbaria (1998) include the following:

- sample sizes of many studies are small and poorly constructed;
- methodological weakness (i.e. broadly construed variables, poor sampling technique) render the findings suspect;
- there is no consistent, formal definition of telework (see the introduction for a discussion of this problem);
- most studies do not control for potentially significant extraneous variables;
- much of the empirical literature on telework seeks to identify its major benefits

and disadvantages;

- many of the studies on telework are descriptive and atheoretical (i.e., either lack a theoretical grounding or are unmotivated by theory);
- few studies address the economic issues of telework to any depth. Those studies that do explicitly consider costs and benefits have generally been case studies that analyze specific situations but do not attempt to develop a comprehensive and generalized overview of the economics of telework.

Details on several of these concerns are given below.

- *Lack of control of extraneous factors.*   Often teleworkers are considered a homogenous group. The reality is that there are differences in the circumstances of telework that may make an impact on the outcomes being examined. Bailey and Kurkland suggest that, at a minimum, the following factors needed to be controlled for in future research in this area:

  - level of participation in telework (i.e. whether or not telework is done on a full-time, part-time or occasional basis);
  - job type (manager, professional, non-professional);
  - gender.

- *Telework research on productivity.*   While organizations who have implemented telework programs feel that such work arrangements have resulted in decreased costs and increased productivity, there is, as yet, very little hard data to back their claims. While stories of increased teleworker productivity are rampant in both the practitioner press and academic journals, most rely on self-report data. Because most teleworkers volunteer or request to work from home, they will possess a natural bias to claim success. Compounding the difficulties linking telework and increased productivity is the fact that many teleworkers report increased hours when working from home, suggesting that teleworkers may be confusing improved productivity with an increase in the absolute amount of work performed (Bailey and Kurkland, 2000).

Critical evaluation of the empirical data indicates that the evidence for productivity gains is not highly compelling. Westfall (1998: 258) offers a number of criticisms of this data, including the fact that:

> many of the references are anecdotal reports of programs within organizations with no indication of the methodology or qualifications of the people who evaluated the results. Some of the examples come from within the telecommunications and computer industries which have vested interests in reporting results favourable to telecommuting. Some of the increases in productivity noted in the literature are so large (e.g., 50%, 65%, 144% and 200%) that they raise questions about the data for the telecommuters or the comparisons (or perhaps the effectiveness of the management of these employees prior to telecommuting!)

In most cases reported productivity gains are based on subjective perceptions rather than actual measurement of output (Westfall, 1998). Westfall (1998) offers a number of alternative explanations for these productivity gains including a placebo (or Hawthorne) effect, inflated perceptions of productivity (people tend to think they are more productive that they really are), an artifact of the type of work being done at home (i.e., employees engage in lower productivity activities like meetings when at the office) or re-engineering of the jobs rather than telecommuting.

- *Research is atheoretical.* Bailey and Kurkland (2000: 28) concluded that research in this area had been "dominated by atheoretical studies seeking to establish the advantages and disadvantages of what is lauded as an alternative work arrangement." They also noted that the most rigorous telework research to date exists within the transportation literature in the form of predictive models (Bailey and Kurkland, 2000). Future studies need to be grounded in theory to have greater generalizability.

Directions for future research

Most available articles on this topic are found in the business press and on the internet, and either offer only cursory treatment of this topic or are purely anecdotal and speculative in nature. Conclusions drawn from the current body of empirical research on the impact of telework are frequently limited by small sample sizes, the lack of longitudinal data, and inadequate control groups. These limitations have resulted in contradictory results and the inability to form a cumulative body of telecommuting research. Clearly, more empirical research is required in this area to provide human resource professionals and managers with information to make strategic decisions about the future of telework arrangements.

Academic interest in telework is on the rise (Bailey and Kurkland, 2000). Sound, well-designed, theoretical research is needed to answer the following fundamental questions:

- Who teleworks? Why? What happens when they do?
- Why do companies offer the various types of telework programs? Why do employees use the various types of telework programs?
- Why are companies/managers reluctant to let employees telework? Are these concerns legitimate? What can be done to alleviate these concerns?
- What impact does telework have on productivity? Employee satisfaction? Work–life balance? Stress? Workloads?

To answer these questions, future research needs to be more vigilant in identifying and controlling for extraneous factors that may contribute to differences in the experiences and outcomes of telecommuting. They also need to be methodologically more rigorous (larger sample size, use well-established measures for antecedents and outcomes, grounded in theory) and cover a broader range of industries and sectors. Well-designed research on why telework is not being adopted would also prove useful. Researchers should recognize that telework is not one construct but rather many, depending on things such as technology, location of work, and time spent away from the office. Similarities and differences between the different types of telework need to be identified and their impacts determined. Furthermore, studies should be expanded to include not just the teleworker and their manager but their colleagues and clients, as this work arrangement might have a wider impact that needs to be fully understood. Finally studies comparing teleworkers to non-teleworkers should be expanded to address a broader range of outcome variables.

GLOSSARY

alternative officing. Different workplace strategies that have changed the design of the workplace and how people work (i.e. telework, hoteling).

flexible working. This is an employer-centered concept that includes a wide spectrum of new working practices including flexible working hours, flexible work location, flexible employee contracts, etc. Home-based telework is often one element of a "flexible working company" but the overall concept includes significant rethinking of the whole employment policy and its consequences.

home-based office. Well-defined area that contains all the furniture, equipment, and supplies the individual needs to work from home.

hot desks. Instead of each employee who is "based" at a particular office having a personally "owned" desk, employees who happen to be there on a particular day use any available desk on that day. Each desk has a standard "office systems" and the employee has a "personal" carousel in which his or her personal files are stored. This carousel is wheeled to the "hot desk" and kept there while the employee is around.

hoteling. "Shared workstations," consisting of a work surface, computer and telephone, to be used by employees who are working temporarily or part time in a specific place and/or on a specific project or who work in an environment where employees have flexible hours. These workstations are generally located within an existing office environment so those users have access to equipment such as copiers, printers, and fax machines. Since many desks in conventional offices are only occupied for as little as 20 percent of the working day (European Telework, 2000) the savings in office overheads obtained by sharing offices can be dramatic.

mobile workers. Employees who work from multiple locations in a single day. They are typically equipped with portable technology such as a cellular phone, notebook computer, portable printer, and cellular modem. These employees work out of a "virtual office."

nomadic teleworking (mobile work). Nomadic workers are those whose primary work activity entails considerable necessary travel and for whom their "place of work" is wherever they happen to be (e.g. salespeople, service engineers, executives). Such teleworkers rely on tools such as notebook PCs, mobile telephones, voice and FAX mailboxes, messaging services, and remote access. The needs of this group are gradually being recognized by airports, airlines, hotel chains, etc.

offshore telework. Shifting jobs away from one's own region, town or country. Telework and the technology that support it are neutral – they neither create job opportunities nor destroy them. What they do is to present opportunities. European Telework (2000) indicates that work opportunities arise where there is the right combination of costs, skills, and entrepreneurship.

remote workers.   Employees who spend some portion of their week away from the regular office. The two most common types of remote work are telework and mobile work.

telecenter.   An alternative office closer to customers or to worker's home than his/her traditional office.

telecottages.   A special class of telecenters, named because of their origins in rural villages. The telecottage movement started in Scandinavia and has now spread to many other parts of Europe. The original focus of telecottages was to bring technology and relevant skills to people in remote villages who lacked opportunities to gain these skills by working for hi-tech employers, who generally cluster in and around urban centers.

telepresence.   The concept of being "virtually present" somewhere other than your physical location (AT&T, 2000a).

televillages.   The development of a whole community that is "wired" and connected to the "global village" through broad-band communications. This village supports the work and lifestyle of employees who participate in the networked economy.

telework.   A work arrangement in which an employee regularly works at an alternative worksite such as the employee's home, a telecenter, or other worksite which saves the employee a more lengthy commute by reducing vehicle trips to a main worksite. A main worksite is where the employee normally works when not working at an alternative worksite. To be considered as telework, the arrangement must be continuously and regularly used, averaging at a minimum once per week. Taking work home to perform after hours is not considered telework.

virtual office.   With a portable computer, pager, and cellular phone as needed a "mobile" worker can work anywhere (i.e. home, while traveling, at a customer site).

NOTES

1   A flaw that we too are about to commit. Although the data cited below are the most current estimates available at the time this chapter was being written, they will be dated by the time you read this chapter.
2   Full details on the Government of Canada's Telework program are available at www.tbs-sct.gc.ca.
3   The information presented below is a summary of material presented by Bresnahan, 1998.

REFERENCES

AT&T (2000b). *The Future of Telework: Many New Kinds of Tele-feasible Work Are Coming.* URL: <wysiwyg://41/http:www.att.com/telework/artib/future_tele_2html>.
AT&T (2000b). *Telework for Managers: Can Telework Benefit your Business Situation?* URL: <www/att/com/telework/getstart/gs_bemef.html>.
AT&T (2000c). *Telework for Managers: Adjustments (You May Need to Make Some).* URL: <www/att/com/telework/getstart/gs_adjust.html>.
AT&T (2000d). *Employee Retention: Telework is a Powerful Way to Keep and Attract Workers.* URL: <www/att/com/telework/artib/empl_ret.html>.
Bailey, D., and Kurkland, N. (2000). A review and new directions for telework research: Study telework not teleworkers. Working Paper, Stanford University.

BNA (1992). *Telecommuting: Its Role and Value in Work and Family Programs.* BNA Special Report No. 50. Washington, D.C.: BNA Plus.

Baruch, Y. (2000). Teleworking: Benefits and pitfalls as perceived by managers and professionals. *New Technology, Work and Employment*, 15, 1.

Baruch, Y., and Nicholson, N. (1997). Home sweet work: Requirements for Eeffective home working. *Journal of General Management*, 23, 15–30.

Boyd, P. (2000). *Six Organizational Benefits of Telecommuting.* URL: <http://pw2.nctcom.com/-pboyd/orgbens.html>.

Bresnahan, J. (1998). Why telework? *CIO Enterprise Magazine*, January.

Ceridian (2000). *The Boundaryless Workforce.* URL: <http://ces.ceridian.com/info/article/display/1,1197,5167,00.html>.

Christensen, C. (1988). *Women and Home-based Work: The Unspoken Contract.* Boulder CO: Westview Press.

Church, J. (2000). New tules for the virtual workplace. *HR Bookmark.* URL: <http://www.hrbookmark.com/CoverStory/cover070199.shtml>.

Cyber Dialogue (2000). *Small Business/Home Office Trend Report.* Washington: US Small Business Advisory Service.

Dannhauser, C. (1999). Who's in the home office? *American Demographics*, July. URL: <http://www.demographics.com/publications/ad/00_ad-ad/9907–ad009797.html>.

DiMartino, V., and Wirth, L. (1990). Telework: A new way of working and living. *International Labour Review*, 129, 529–54.

Duxbury, L., Higgins, C., and Neufeld, D. (1998). Telework and the balance between work and family: Is telework part of the problem or part of the solution? In M. Igbaria and M. Tan (eds). *The Virtual Workplace.* Hershey, PA: Idea Group Publishing, pp. 218–55).

Egan, B. (1997). Feasibility and cost benefit analysis. Paper presented at the International Telework Association Conference, Crystal City, VA.

European Telework (2000). *Telework and Telecommuting: Common Terms and Definitions.* URL: <www.eto.org.uk/faq/faq02.html>.

Gerson, J., and Kraut, R. (1988). Clerical work at home or in the office: The difference it makes. In K. Cristensen (ed.). *The New Era of Home-Based Work.* Boulder, CO: Westview Press, pp. 49–64.

Gordon, G., and Kelly, M. (1986). *Telecommuting: How to Make it Work for You and Your Company.* Englewood Cliffs, NJ: Prentice Hall.

Haddon, L., and Lewis, A. (1994). The experience of teleworking: An annotated review. *International Journal of Human Resource Management*, 5, 193–223.

Handy, S., and Mokhtarian, P. (1995). Planning for telecommuting: Measurement and policy issues. *Journal American Planning Association*, 61, 99–111.

Harrington, S., and Ruppel, C. (1999). Telecommuting: A test of trust, competing values and relative advantage. *IEEE Transactions on Professional Communication*, 42, 223–39.

Hartman, R., Stoner, C., and Arora, R. (1992). Developing successful organizational telecommuting arrangements: Worker perceptions and managerial prescriptions. *SAM Advanced Management Journal*, 57, 35–42.

Heck, R., Walker, R., and Furry, M. (1996). The workers work at home, In R. Heck, A. Owen, and B. Rowe (eds). *Home-Based Employment and Family Life.* Washington, D.C.: National Academy Press, pp. 41–74.

Higgins, C., Duxbury, L., and Lee, C. (1993). *Balancing Work and Family: A Study of the Canadian Private Sector.* London, Ontario: National Centre for Research, Management and Development.

Hill, J., Hawkins, A., and Miller, B. (1996). Work and family in the virtual office: Perceived influences of mobile telework. *Family Relations*, 45, 293–301.

Holcomb, B. (1991). Socio-spatial implications of electronic cottages. In S. Brunn and
    T. Leinback (eds). *Collapsing Space and Time: Geographic Aspects of Communications and
    Information*. London: Harper Collins.
Huws, U. (1991). Telework: Projections. *Futures*, 23, 19–30.
Huws, U., Korte, W., and Robinson, S. (1990). *Telework: Towards the Elusive Office*. New
    York: Wiley and Sons.
Korte, W., Robinson, S., and Steinle, W. (1988). *Telework: Present Situations and Future
    Development of a New Form of Work Organization*. Amsterdam: North-Holland.
Kraut, R. (1987). Telework as a work style innovation. In R. E. Kraut (ed.). *Technology and
    the Transformation of White Collar Work*. Hillsdale, NJ: Lawrence Erlbaum, pp. 49–64.
Kraut, R. (1988). Homework: What is it and who does it. In K. Cristensen (ed.). *The New Era
    of Home-Based Work*. Boulder, CO: Westview Press, pp. 30–48.
Kraut, R. (1989). Telecommuting: The trade-offs of home work. *Journal of Communication*,
    39, 19–47.
Luukinen, A. (1996). A profile of Finnish telework: Survey results concerning the nature,
    extent, and potential of telework in Finland. In A. Luukinen (ed.). *Directions of Telework in
    Finland: Report by the Finnish Experience with Telework Project*. Helsinki: Ministry of
    Labour (Finland), Publication of the Labour Administration, pp. 1–22.
Mannering, J., and P. Mokhtarian (1995). Modeling the choice of telecommuting frequency in
    California: An exploratory analysis. *Technological Forecasting and Social Change*, 49, 49–
    73.
Matthes, K. (1992). Telecommuting: Balancing business and employee needs. *HR Focus*, 69,
    3.
McCloskey, D., and M. Igbaria (1998). A review of the empirical research on telecommuting
    and directions for future research. In M. Igbaria and M. Tan (eds). *The Virtual Workplace*.
    Hershey, PA: Idea Group Publishing, pp. 338–58.
Mokhtarian, P. (1991). Telecommuting and travel: State of the practice, state of the art. *Trans-
    portation*, 18, 319–342.
Mokhtarian, P. (1998). A synthetic approach to estimating the impacts of telecommuting on
    travel. *Urban Studies*, 35, 215–41.
Mokhtarian P., Handy, S., and Salomon, I. (1995). Methodological issues in the estimation of
    the travel, energy and air quality impacts of telecommuting, *Transportation Research Record*,
    29A, 283–301.
Mokhtarian, P., and Salomon, I. (1996a). Modeling the choice of telecommuting: 2. A case of
    the preferred impossible alternative. *Environment and Planning A.*, 28, 1859–76.
Mokhtarian, P., and Salomon, I. (1996b). Modeling the choice of telecommuting: 3: Identify-
    ing the choice set and estimating binary choice models for technology based companies.
    Environment and Planning A., 28, 1877–94.
Mokhtarian, P., and Salomon, I. (1997). Modeling the desire to telecommute: The importance
    of attitudinal factors in behavioral models. *Transportation Research Record*, 31, 35–50.
NetWorld Fusion (2000). *How to Manage Telecommuters*. URL: <http://www.cnn.com/2000/
    TECH/computing/06/19/telecommuting.idg/index.html>.
Nie, N. (1999). Tracking our techno future. *American Demographics*, July. URL: <http://
    www.demographics.com/publications/ad/00_ad-ad/9906–ad990601.html>.
Nilles, J. (1994). *Making Telework Happen: A Guide for Telemanagers and Telecommuters*.
    New York: Van Nostrand Reinhold.
Nilles, J., Carlson, F., Gray, P., and Hannerman, G. (1976). *The Telecommunications/Trans-
    portation Tradeoff: Options for Tomorrow*. New York: Wiley.
Novaco, R., Kliewer, W., and Broquet, A. (1991). Home environmental consequences of com-
    mute travel impedance. *American Journal of Community Psychology*, 19, 881–909.

Olson, M., and Primps, S. (1984). Working at home with computers: Work and nonwork issues. *Journal of Social Issues*, 40, 97–112.

Olson, M. (1985). Do you telecommute? *Datamation*, 31, 129–32.

Owen, A., Heck, R., and Rowe, B. (1995). Harmonizing family and work. In R. Heck, A. Owen, and B. Rowe (eds). *Home-Based Employment and Family Life*. Washington, D.C.: National Academy Press, pp. 1–14.

Perin, C. (1998). Work, space and time on the threshold of a new century. In P. Jackson and J. van der Wielen (eds). *Teleworking: International Perspectives: From Telecommuting to the Virtual Organization*. London: Routledge, pp. 40–55.

Reingold, J. (2000). There's no place (to work) like home. *Fast Company*, November. URL: <www.fastcompany.com/online/40/workhome.html>.

Ritter, G., and Thompson, S. (1994). The rise of telecommuting and virtual transportation. *Eno's Transportation Quarterly*, 48.

Robertson, K. (1997). How remote workers impact office space. *Telework International: Electronic Edition*, 5, 2. YRL: <http:/www.klr.com/news5201.html>.

Shamir, B. (1992). Home: The perfect workplace. In S. Zedeck (ed.). *Work, Families and Organizations*. San Francisco, CA: Jossey Bass, pp. 272–311.

Shamir, B., and Salomon, I. (1985). Work at home and the quality of working life. *Academy of Management Review*, 10, 455–63.

Shore, J. (2000). *Telework: The Future is Now*. Office of Government Wide Policy. URL: <http://www.pueblo.gsa.gov/telework.html>.

Stanek, D., and Mokhtarian, P. (1998). Development models of preference for home based and center based telecommuting: Findings and forecasts. *Technological Forecasting and Social Change*, 57, 53–74.

TBS (Treasury Board of Canada) (2000). *Telework: Balancing Work/Life Demands*. Ottawa: TBS.

Telework America 2000 (2000). *Research Results*. URL: <http://www.telecommute.org/twa2000/research-results-summary.shtml>.

Toffler, A. (1980). *The Third Wave*. New York: Morrow.

US Department of Transportation (1993). *Transportation Implications of Telecommuting*. URL: <http:/www.bts.gov/NTL/DOC/telecommute.html>.

Westfall, R. (1998). The microeconomic of remote work. In M. Igbaria and M. Tan (eds). *The Virtual Workplace*. Hershey, PA: Idea Group Publishing, pp. 256–87.

Changing Organizational Forms

9

The Virtual Organization

WAYNE F. CASCIO

For many employers the virtual workplace, in which employees operate remotely from each other and from managers, is a reality now, and all indications are that it will become even more prevalent in the future. Virtual organizations are multi-site, multi-organizational, and dynamic (Snow et al., 1999). At a macro level, a virtual organization consists of a grouping of units of different firms (e.g., other businesses, consultants, contractors) that have joined in an alliance to exploit complementary skills in pursuing common strategic objectives (Dess et al., 1995). The objectives often focus on a specific project, such as a defined objective in research and development, a multi-faceted, complex consulting project, or a legal case involving multiple issues (Igbaria and Tan, 1998).

In the entertainment industry, virtual organizations are common. For example, in making a movie, producer, director, film editors, workers who construct and deconstruct movie sets, special-effects specialists, actors, actresses, and scores of people who provide indirect services collaborate to make the movie. All of these individuals, independent contractors, companies, and consultants (some of whom have overlapping memberships) work intensely on a temporary basis to complete a specific project. When the project is over – poof! – they split up again to pursue their own interests and peddle their talents elsewhere. That is the essence of a virtual organization. It is a temporary collaboration. In fact, one observer has referred to this phenomenon as an "organizational tent," as opposed to a conventional organization, referred to as an "organizational palace" (Hedberg, 2000).

In the context of intact, work organizations we define virtual work arrangements as those in which employees operate remotely from each other and from managers. This represents a dramatic change in how we work, and it alters the very concept of an organization as a fixed location where people gather to perform work. Before discussing virtual organizations in more detail, however, let us provide perspective by painting a broad brush view of some important changes that are helping to shape new organizational forms.

● The Information Revolution ●

Sparked by new technologies, particularly the internet, the corporation is undergoing a radical transformation that is nothing less than a new Industrial Revolution. This time around, the revolution is reaching every corner of the globe and in the process, rewriting the rules laid down by Alfred P. Sloan, Jr. (the legendary chairman of General Motors), Henry Ford, and other Industrial Age giants. The twenty-first-century corporation that emerges will in many ways be the polar opposite of the organizations they helped shape.

Many factors are driving change, but none is more important than the rise of internet technologies. Like the steam engine or the assembly line, the net has already become an advance with revolutionary consequences, most of which we have only begun to feel. The net gives everyone in the organization, from the lowliest clerk to the chairman of the board, the ability to access a mind-boggling array of information – instantaneously from anywhere. Instead of seeping out over months or years, ideas can be zapped around the globe in the blink of an eye. That means that the twenty-first-century corporation must adapt itself to management via the web. It must be predicated on constant change, not stability, organized around networks, not rigid hier-archies, built on shifting partnerships and alliances, not self-sufficiency, and constructed on technological advantages, not bricks and mortar (Byrne, 2000; see also Colvin, 2000).

The organization chart of the large-scale enterprise had long been defined as a pyramid of ever-shrinking layers leading to an omnipotent CEO at its apex. The twenty-first-century corporation, in contrast, is far more likely to look like a web: a flat, intricately woven form that links partners, employees, external contractors, suppliers, and customers in various collaborations. The players will grow more and more interdependent, and managing this intricate network will be as important as managing internal operations (Byrne, 2000)

Three factors are key drivers of new forms of organization – globalization, technology, and electronic (e-) commerce. Let us consider each of these in turn.

Globalization

The global village is getting smaller every day. Satellite dishes in the world's most remote areas beam live television feeds from CNN and MTV. Internet booksellers like Amazon.com provide 24-hour-a-day supermarkets for consumers everywhere. CUC International, an electronic shopping network whose only product is a catalog, sells everything but stocks nothing. It simply takes orders from consumers over the internet, and, for a small commission, passes those orders on to the manufacturers who actually ship products directly to consumers.

At its core, the globalization of business refers to the free movement of capital, goods, services, ideas, information, and people across national boundaries. Markets in every country have become fierce battlegrounds where both domestic and foreign competitors fight for market share. Companies compete just about everywhere, especially when economic conditions give them a substantial price advantage. As an example, consider Hong Kong's airline, Cathay Pacific.

The airline's computer center has moved to Sydney, where the land costs only 1 percent of a comparable site in Hong Kong. Its revenue-accounting back office has been shifted to Guangzhou, China, and even some its aircraft maintenance is now done in Xiamen on the South China coast, where labor costs only 10 percent to 20 percent of Hong Kong levels. The labor-intensive part of its reservations, such as special meals for passengers, is handled out of Bombay (Kraar, 1997).

It is no exaggeration to say that, regardless of the shifting political winds in Tokyo, Berlin, Washington, Beijing, or Budapest, the shrunken globe is here to stay. Today Tokyo is closer than the town 100 miles away was 30 years ago (after all, routine long-distance phone use did not begin until the 1970s).

And tomorrow? Our networks of suppliers, producers, distributors, service companies, and customers will be so tightly linked that we literally will not be able to tell one locale from another. No political force can stop, or even slow down for long, the borderless economy (*Business Week*, 1994).

Technology

It is no exaggeration to say that modern technology is changing the ways we live and work. The information revolution will transform everything it touches – and it will touch everything. Information and ideas are key to the new creative economy, because every country, every company, and every individual depends increasingly on knowledge. Technology facilitates the rapid diffusion of information and knowledge. It is the engine that enables virtual organizational forms.

Without information and knowledge, workers in virtual workplaces would become emasculated and ineffective. Fortunately technology and enlightened management practices can ensure that this does not happen. Where we work, when we work and how we communicate are being revolutionized, as a "seamless" web of electronic communications media – e-mail, voice mail, cellular telephones, laptops with modems, hand-held organizers, video conferencing, and interactive pagers – makes teamwork and mobility a reality. Not only is work becoming seamless as it moves between home, office, and phone, but it also is becoming endless as it rolls through a 24-hour day (*Business Week*, 1997).

To be viable, virtual offices require four types of information:

1. online materials that can be downloaded and printed;
2. databases on products and customers that are accessible from remote locations;
3. well-indexed, automated central files that are accessible from remote locations;
4. a way to track the location of mobile workers.

As an example of the technology that enables virtual work arrangements, consider "groupware." "Groupware" refers to computer-based systems that are designed explicitly to support groups of people working together. This is what enables virtual interactions (Ishii et al., 1994). Groupware includes components from simple to sophisticated. The simplest forms are e-mail and newsgroups. In the middle are forms routing and document management. Sophisticated groupware includes interactive systems that link employees with one another and with customers. Interactive video conferencing that incorporates document cameras with zoom features using WYSIWIS technology ("what you see is what I see") is an example of this. Corporate intranets, which contain up-to-the-minute information on everything from the company's stock price to benefits options, afford some of the highest gains now available from groupware. The goal of groupware technology is simple: to promote and improve interaction among individuals (Aannestad and Hooper, 1997). This is collaborative empowerment. A third factor driving new forms of organization is electronic (e-) commerce.

E-Commerce

Consider this forecast: "The Internet will change the relationship between consumers and producers in ways more profound that you can yet imagine. The Internet is not just another marketing channel; it's not just another advertising medium; it's not just a way to speed up transactions. The Internet is the foundation for a new industrial order. The Internet will empower consumers like nothing else ever has . . . The Web will fundamentally change customers' expectations about convenience, speed, comparability, price, and service" (Hamel and Sampler, 1998).

Whether it's business-to-business (B2B) or business-to-consumer (B2C), electronic (e-) commerce is taking off. As an example, consider Enron Corporation of Houston, Texas. Once a distributor of natural gas through its extensive pipeline system, the company launched web-based Enron Online in November, 1999. By July 2000 it had revolutionized the energy-trading business, tallying more than $1 billion in average *daily* trading transactions. More than 800 products were being traded on Enron Online, including natural gas, electricity, coal, plastics, and even excess bandwith (Smith and Lucchinetti, 2000; see also *Fortune*, 2000*)*.

In the automobile industry, consider this scenario from Ford Motor Co. CEO Jac Nasser. He pictures the day when a buyer hits a button to order a custom-configured Ford Mustang online, transmitting a slew of information directly to the dealer who will deliver it, the finance and insurance units who will underwrite it, the factory that will build it, the suppliers that provide its components, and the Ford designers brainstorming future models. To buyers it will mean getting just what they ordered, delivered right to their doorstep in days (*Business Week*, 2000b). Although there are plenty of risks associated with this scenario (ibid.), e-commerce is encouraging the reinvention of manufacturing, and it would be foolish to underestimate the ultimate outcome.

Data compiled by *The Wall Street Journal* illustrate the extent of the online revolution. The percentage of households online has rocketed from about 15 percent in 1996 to an estimated 60+ percent in 2003 (Anders, 1999). At present, both B2B and B2C transactions comprise only about 1 percent of commercial and retail transactions (Blackmon, 2000). However, the internet is still in its infancy, and many experts expect that eventually it will be a major factor in pricing. The idea is that prices will be driven downward as B2B online markets allow an endless number of suppliers to bid competitively for contracts with big manufacturers.

Retail e-commerce sites, so the thinking goes, will cut consumer prices by pitting a multitude of sellers against one another, allowing web-surfing buyers to identify quickly the lowest possible price for any good. Web-based search engines will provide buyers with more information – and bargaining power – about products than ever before. Whether those predictions come to pass will depend on several factors, the most important of which is how much economic activity finally does move online (Blackmon, 2000). The value of goods ordered over the internet and shipped to homes was $20 billion in 1999, about 1 percent of traditional retail sales. That is expected to rise to $180 billion by 2004 (O'Reilly, 2000). As you read this, and as you ponder the future of e-commerce, consider one inescapable fact – all of the people who make e-commerce possible are knowledge workers. The organizations they work for, regardless of their form, still have to address the human resource challenges of attracting, retaining, and motivating them to perform well.

Clearly the factors of globalization, technology, and e-commerce are driving and enabling new forms of organizations, such as virtual ones. However, in making the business case for virtual work arrangements, there are potential advantages as well as disadvantages and they need to be recognized (Cascio, 2000).

Potential Advantages of Virtual Workplaces

- **Reduced real estate expenses.** IBM saves 40 percent to 60 percent per site annually by eliminating offices for all employees except those that truly need them (O'Connell, 1996; see also *Business Week*, 1996). Northern Telecom estimates the savings gained from not having to house an employee in a typical $8' \times 8'$ space, considering only rent and annual operating costs, at $2,000 per person per year (Cooper, 1997). Others estimate the savings at $2 for every $1 invested (McCune, 1998).
- **Increased productivity.** Internal IBM studies show gains of 15 percent to 40 percent. US West reported that the productivity of its teleworking employees increased, some by as much as 40 percent (Matthes, 1992).
- **Higher profits.** Hewlett-Packard doubled revenue per salesperson after moving its salespeople to virtual workplace arrangements (O'Connell, 1996; *Business Week*, 1996).
- **Improved customer service.** Andersen Consulting found that its consultants spent 25 percent more "face time" with customers when they did not have permanent offices (O'Connell, 1996; *Business Week*, 1996).
- **Access to global markets.** John Brown Engineers & Constructors Ltd., a member of the engineering division of Trafalgar House, the world's third largest engineering and construction organization with 21,000 employees around the globe, was able to access local pharmaceutical engineering talent at a project site in India. Using virtual work arrangements, the firm was able to traverse national boundaries, thereby enabling it to work with and present a local face to its global clients. This enhanced its global competitiveness (Grimshaw and Kwok, 1998).

- **Environmental benefits.** At Georgia Power, 13 percent of the workers at headquarters are teleworkers (150 people). This has reduced annual commuting mileage by 993,000 miles, and automobile emissions by almost 35,000 pounds (McCune, 1998). A US government study showed that if 20,000 federal workers could telecommute just one day a week, they would save over 2 million commuting miles, 102,000 gallons of gasoline, and 81,600 pounds of carbon dioxide emissions each week. The emissions savings for one week under this arrangement are equivalent to the amount of carbon dioxide produced by the average car over 9.3 years (Green Commuter, 1998).

Potential Disadvantages of Virtual Workplaces

Offsetting these advantages, however, are some potentially serious disadvantages that managers should consider carefully before institutionalizing virtual work arrangements: setup and maintenance costs, possible loss of cost efficiencies, cultural concerns, isolation, and lack of trust.

- **Setup and maintenance costs.** For individual employees, the additional cost required to equip a mobile or home office varies from roughly $3,000 to $5,000, plus about $1,000 in upgrades and supplies every year thereafter (Clark, 1997). In addition, to be viable, virtual offices require four types of information: online materials that can be downloaded and printed, databases on products and customers that are accessible from remote locations, well-indexed, automated central files that are accessible from remote locations, and a way to track the location of mobile workers.

  Technology is the remote worker's lifeline. In the absence of the administrative and technical support that one might find at the home office, the technology must work flawlessly, and technical support should be available 24 hours a day, seven days a week, or at least a "help desk" should be staffed from 8 a.m. to midnight. Decision-makers need to consider the incremental costs associated with setting up and maintaining virtual workplaces.

- **Loss of cost efficiencies.** When expensive equipment or services are concentrated in one location, multiple users can access them. When the same equipment or services are distributed across locations, cost efficiencies may be lost. For example, in the securities industry, certain real-time information sources are necessary. Most stock quotes are available on the internet on a 15-minute delay, which is adequate for most people's needs. However, for brokers and traders quoting prices to customers, it is imperative that quotes be up to the second. Companies such as Bloomberg, Bridge Financial Systems, Reuters Quotron, and ILX Systems provide this real-time service. Each is willing to install its system at the customer's place of choice. Typically it costs about $1,200 per month for the first installation of such a system, and about $200 per month to install each additional system in the same location. When a securities firm needs this information for 50 brokers, along with related services (e.g., CDA Spectrum, Multex.com's Market Guide, and First Call/Thomson Financial), it is more cost-effective to have all employees at one location, rather than working at multiple different locations (Arko et al., 1999).

- **Cultural issues.** Virtual organizations operating in the global arena often have to transfer their business policies and culture to work with dispersed business teams across collaborating organizations, geography, and cultures. This can lead to potential clashes of business and national cultures, which, in turn, can undermine the entire alliance (Serapio and Cascio, 1996; see also Cascio and Serapio, 1991). In addition, if the members of a virtual organization or a virtual team are not empowered to make decisions, then the technology that enables such collaboration will add little value, and the competitive advantage associated with rapid responses to demands in the market place will be lost.
- **Feelings of isolation.** Such feelings can undermine the effectiveness of virtual work arrangements because most people need social contact, acceptance, and face-to-face interaction (Baumeister and Leary, 1993; see also Hogan, 1998). Indeed, some level of social interaction with supervisors and co-workers is essential in almost all jobs. Without it, workers feel alienated, isolated and "out of the loop" with respect to crucial communications and "face time" with decision-makers who can make or break their careers (Hogan, 1998).
- **Lack of trust.** A key ingredient to the success of virtual work arrangements is trust that one's co-workers will fulfill their obligations and behave predictably. Lack of trust can undermine every other precaution taken to ensure successful virtual work arrangements, such as careful selection of employees to work in the virtual environment, thorough training of managers and employees, and ongoing performance management.

● The Need for Jobs, Employees, and Managers to Fit Virtual Work Arrangements ●

Virtual work arrangements are not appropriate for all jobs, all employees, or all managers. With respect to jobs, it is necessary first to understand the parameters of each job that might be considered for a virtual work environment. To do so, one must be able to answer questions such as the following (Apgar, 1998). What function does the job serve? Is the work performed over the phone? In person? Via the computer? All of the above? How much time does the employee need to spend in direct contact with other employees, customers, and business contacts? Is the location of the office critical to performance? Does it matter whether the job is 9 to 5? Is it important for others to be able to reach the employee immediately?

Jobs in sales, marketing, project engineering, and consulting seem to be suited best, because individuals in these jobs already work with their clients by phone or at the clients' premises. Such jobs are service- and knowledge-oriented, they are dynamic, and they evolve according to customer requirements (Townsend et al., 1998). Even in these jobs, however, virtual work arrangements are not recommended for new employees or those who are new to a position because newcomers require a period of socialization during which they learn to adapt to their new company, new environment, and new managers and co-workers. It takes time to learn business skills, how things are done in the new company or new position, why they are done, and the dos and taboos of the company's culture.

For employees whose jobs are appropriate for virtual work arrangements, and who demonstrate the appropriate temperament (internally motivated self-starters who know their jobs well and are technically self-sufficient), they key is to work with them well ahead of planned transitions. Firms such as Lotus, IBM, and Hewlett-Packard have written guidelines, training, and networks of peers to facilitate the transition. For example, Hewlett-Packard's guidelines for virtual workplaces address topics such as who can participate, family and household issues, remote office setup, and administrative processes.

Just as not all employees are suited to work away from their primary business locations during scheduled work hours, not all managers are suited to manage employees with virtual work arrangements. Those who are seem to have the following characteristics:

- An open, positive attitude that focusses on solutions to issues rather than on seeking excuses to discontinue virtual work arrangements.
- A results-oriented management style. Those with high needs for structure and control are unlikely to be effective managers in virtual work environments.
- Effective communicator, whether formally or informally, and whether employees are working remotely or are at the primary business location.
- Able to delegate effectively, and to follow up to ensure that work is accomplished.

One might argue that the characteristics listed above apply to progressive managers in conventional as well as virtual work environments. While that may be true, the need for these characteristics is greater in virtual environments that lack the attributes of traditional social contexts, such as physical proximity, verbal and non-verbal cues, norms of behavior, and, in the case of teams, a sense of cohort.

Assuming that virtual work arrangements are appropriate, and that employees with the "right" profile are available, how should organizational decision-makers proceed? Two types of virtual work arrangements that are becoming more popular are virtual teams and telework. In the following sections we consider each of these.

● Virtual Teams ●

In a virtual team, members are dispersed geographically or organizationally. Their primary interaction is through some combination of electronic communication systems. They may never "meet" in the traditional sense. Further, team membership is often fluid, evolving according to changing task requirements (Townsend et al., 1998). Such an arrangement provides several advantages:

- It saves time, travel expenses, and eliminates lack of access to experts.
- Teams can be organized whether or not members are in reasonable proximity to each other.
- Firms can use outside consultants without incurring expenses for travel, lodging, and downtime.

- Virtual teams allow firms to expand their potential labor markets, enabling them to hire and retain the best people regardless of their physical location, or, in the case of workers with disabilities, whether or not they are able to commute to work.
- Employees can accommodate both personal and professional lives.
- Dynamic team membership allows people to move from one project to another.
- Employees can be assigned to multiple, concurrent teams.
- Team communications and work reports are available online to facilitate swift responses to the demands of a global market. For example, Veriphone uses a "relay race" to develop software products faster than its competitors. Here is how it works. Software engineers at Dallas headquarters work a full day on a project, then, using groupware, they put their work product online on the company's intranct. As the Dallas employees are leaving work, their Veriphone counterparts in Honolulu are arriving. The Honolulu engineers begin working where their Dallas counterparts left off. They then work a full day, and hand off their work product to their Veriphone counterparts in Bombay, who are just coming to work. As the Bombay software engineers are leaving work, they transmit their work product electronically back to headquarters in Dallas, where their counterparts are just arriving for the next day's work. Electronic communications media make the relay race possible. Clients benefit from the firm's speedy response to their needs.

Disadvantages of virtual teams

Of course the major disadvantages of virtual teams are the lack of physical interaction – with its associated verbal and non-verbal cues – and the synergies that often accompany face-to-face communication. These deficiencies raise issues of trust. Trust is critical in a virtual team because traditional social control based on authority gives way to self-direction and self-control. Members of virtual teams need to be sure that everyone will fulfill his or her obligations and behave in a consistent, predictable manner. An empirical analysis of the development of trust in 29 global virtual teams that communicated strictly by e-mail over a six-week period found that teams with the highest levels of trust tended to share three traits. First, they began their interactions with a series of social messages – introducing themselves and providing some personal background – before focussing on the work at hand. Second, they set clear roles for each team member, thus enabling all team members to identify with one another. Third, all team members demonstrated positive attitudes. Team members consistently displayed eagerness, enthusiasm, and an intense action orientation in all of their messages (Coutu, 1998; see also Jarvenpaa et al., 1998).

There are two lessons from this research: first impressions are critical, and especially in virtual work environments, initial messages need to be handled well. Keep the tone of all messages upbeat and action-oriented. Just one pessimist in the group has the potential to undermine trust in the entire virtual team, and lack of trust affects overall group productivity. Not surprisingly, low-trust teams were less productive than high-trust ones.

Culture and customs may also work against virtual teams. For example, in high-context cultures, such as those in the Middle East and Asia, what is not said is often more important than what is said. Can workers in those cultures adapt to a virtual team arrangement? There is little or no research evidence to go on, but it is an engaging hypothesis that workers in low-context cultures, such as English-speaking countries where it is possible to be very precise with words, will report higher levels of satisfaction and productivity when working in virtual teams than their counterparts in high-context cultures.

Making virtual teams work

Perhaps the most common forms of virtual teams are task forces and project teams. These are temporary groups (e.g., in legal cases, consulting projects, or within-company task forces). As we noted earlier, such teams are formed for the explicit purpose of solving a particular problem or performing a specific task. When the problem has been solved or the task completed, the virtual team disappears and team members go back to their normal duties. Task forces and project teams have an unusual mix of autonomy and dependence (Gersick and Davis-Sack, 1990). On the one hand, they typically are free, within broad limits, to proceed with the work in whatever way members find appropriate. On the other hand, they do their work at the behest of some other person or group, and therefore members depend considerably on their client's preferences.

In a virtual team, patterns of authority and social interaction are very different from those of a team that interacts physically, such as an operating-room team or a basketball team. To function as a team, it is necessary to have some real inter-dependencies among team members. Otherwise all that remains is a loosely coupled group. It is important, therefore, to define roles clearly so that members can collaborate to accomplish work. It is also important to have a clear leadership structure in order to minimize ambiguity about who has the right to decide what (Hackman, 1990). Ground rules like these are even more imperative in a virtual team, because of the physical separation of members from clients and each other.

● Teleworking ●

Another form of virtual work arrangement is telework, that is, work carried out in a location that is remote from central offices or production facilities, where the worker has no personal contact with co-workers, but is able to communicate with them using electronic means (Gupta et al., 1995). Teleworking is a popular and rapidly growing alternative to the traditional, office-bound work style. As of 2000, an estimated 24 million Americans regularly or occasionally use telework arrangements. That's up from 8.5 million in 1995 (Dunham, 2000). Survey results indicate that employees want more opportunities for telework, and that their top priority is to gain the flexibility to control their own time (*Business Week*, 2000a; see also Conlin, 1999). Some companies are actively encouraging the trend. Thus in February 2000 both Ford Motor Company and Delta Air Lines announced that they were giving employees personal computers for home use (Rivenbark, 2000). To many people, telework means working at home. However, in addition to work-at-home arrangements, telework may assume at least three other forms:

- **Hoteling.** At Ernst & Young in Washington, D.C., workers call a central reservations center, provide a personal identification code, along with the date that space is needed. Available space includes workstations and meeting rooms. On arrival, the employee's name is on an office door, and requested files and supplies are inside. Phone numbers are forwarded, and a concierge is available. Ernst & Young has hoteled eight offices and is converting seven more. The company has found that the longer workers operate under this arrangement, the less they focus on the office and more on the customer (*Business Week*, 1996).
- **"Hot desking."** Each of 20,000 IBM employees, primarily those in sales and service, share offices with four other people, on average. Cisco Systems, a technology firm in San Jose, California, has several thousand people sharing a variety of spaces around the world. As we noted earlier, however, virtual work arrangements like hoteling and hot desking are not for everyone (*Wall Street Journal*, 1997). It is important to consider carefully issues such as setup and maintenance costs, possible loss of cost efficiencies, cultural concerns, isolation, and lack of trust.
- **Telework centers.** These are corporate office environments in miniature that offer more technology than an employee has at home. Located in residential neighborhoods, small groups of employees report to work near home, rather than commute. Centers, such as the Ontario Telebusiness Work Center in Southern California, offer electronically equipped suites to companies (O'Connell, 1996). The advantage: a suburban location minimizes commuting time, while maximizing productive time.

Effect of teleworking on productivity and adjustment

When teleworking is appropriate in a given situation (right job, right person, right reason, right boss) firms report that people's strategic planning skills go up dramatically because they have blocks of time to think (Warner, 1997). People themselves say they are as much as 40 percent more productive while working away from the office, because they have fewer distractions. While such self-report data are encouraging, they do not substitute for rigorous empirical research on this issue. At present there is no simple conclusion regarding the effects of teleworking on productivity. Much depends on the way that productivity is measured, and on whether effects are observed over short or long time periods (Rapp, 2000). There is a pressing need for controlled, empirical research to inform decision-makers, as the number of organizations and individuals that adopt such arrangements increases year by year in developed countries everywhere.

It is also important to note that if people are coerced into work-at-home arrangements, they may rebel or fail to develop the kinds of work habits that will enable
them to be productive. Can parents with pre-school-age children work at home in a
productive manner? Can workers who have been supervised closely on their jobs for
years adapt to the near-total autonomy that teleworking offers? Can they learn to
focus on results rather than simply efforts (e.g., "being seen" at the office working
either early or late)?

Finally, it is important to address the political implications of teleworking arrangements. "Out of sight, out of mind" is still very true in many organizations. Might
teleworkers be unwittingly sacrificing access to desirable assignments or career-en-
hancing positions because they and their work are not noticed by key gatekeepers in
an organization? How might organizational structures be modified to ensure that
teleworkers are afforded the same considerations as their office-based counterparts?
These are pressing questions for which we as a profession do not yet have answers.

Some possible remedies include the following. Teleworkers need to send a few
more voice mails and e-mails to keep the boss informed, and technology makes this
possible – laptops and computer servers that give mobile employees access to company files. "Mix and match" arrangements, in which workers spend one or two days
a week at the office, where they can interact with managers and colleagues, seem to
work best. In fact, AT&T found in an employee survey that fully one-third of
teleworkers would look for other work if they were forced back into the office fold!
More than 70 percent reported that they were more satisfied with their jobs than
before they started teleworking, and 75 percent reported feeling more satisfied with
their personal and family lives than before starting work at home, for reasons including better relations with spouses and children, improved morale, and less stress
(Jackson, 1997). The next section reports empirical research on this issue.

Telework and the balance between work and family demands

Little empirical research has examined the effect of telework on the work–family
relations of teleworkers. However, a recent study done in three Canadian organizations is an exception. Researchers collected information from four groups (teleworkers,
managers, co-workers, and a control group) two weeks before and six months after
the introduction of telework (Duxbury et al., 1998). They collected data from questionnaires as well as telephone interviews. Statistical analyses revealed that there were
no significant changes in work–family conflict, stress, and the ability to manage personal or family time for respondents in the control, co-worker, and manager groups
over the course of the study. However, teleworkers had significantly lower levels of
interference from work to family, significantly lower levels of interference from family to work, and significantly fewer problems managing their family time than they
did prior to teleworking. These data support the positive view of telework. They
suggest that working from home helps employed parents balance work and family
demands (Duxbury et al., 1998).

The dark side of telework

There are down sides to telework, especially for some companies and managers who believe that teleworking causes resentment among office-bound colleagues and weakens corporate loyalty. They also note that teleworkers miss out on last-minute office meetings and cannot interact as readily with other workers. In fact, most of 650 employers recently surveyed by CareerEngine.com, a New York-based network of career websites, said they expect to hire fewer people who work at home. However, few publicize their negative sentiments, especially in the tight labor markets in which most of them compete. Some internet start-ups are exceptions in their outspoken opposition. Said one executive of an internet services firm in San Francisco: "We need people working side by side, in the office, sharing ideas" (B. Beasley, cited in Dunham, 2000: B18). Based on our earlier comments about the need to ensure that the situation is right for telework (right job, right employee, right boss), many such concerns are probably well placed. Telework arrangements would not be appropriate under those circumstances.

As an example, consider the experience of Spherion Corporation, a human resources consulting firm. The company treats telework as an "all-or-none" phenomenon. It offers employees two options: either full-time telework arrangements over six-month periods, or no telework at all. The company permits only existing employees (not new employees) to use telework, and to do so for no more than six months at a time. Employees can use teleworking arrangements multiple times, but they must work in the office for a year before doing so again. As one employee noted, "It's hard to put a value on what you lose when you don't have eye-to-eye contact." Another emphasized, "you just miss out on the value of hallway conversations and the quickly scheduled five-minute meetings" (T. Chamberlain and R. Marcy cited in Dunham, 2000: B18).

These are precisely the reasons why "mix-and-match" programs are so appropriate. In fact, a study that sought to determine the preferences of teleworkers in Australia and Singapore found that more than 50 percent of the respondents in both countries preferred to use telework arrangements two days a week (three days in the office). Roughly 20 percent preferred one day a week, another 20 percent preferred three to four days per week, roughly 5 percent preferred full-time telework arrangements, and roughly 5 percent preferred none at all (Dick, 2000). In summary, most workers preferred part-time telework arrangements that permit some interaction with colleagues in the office. In most work situations, these are the arrangements that will work best.

The current state of research on telework

A critical analysis of 32 published empirical research studies on teleworking found them to be plagued with methodological problems, such as small sample sizes, lack of control groups, heavy reliance on self-reports, and failure to control extraneous factors, such as employment status, job type, and the level of participation (McCloskey and Igbaria, 1998). There is a strong tendency in the published research to treat both full-time and part-time employees who telework as a homogeneous group. This unwise decision makes it difficult to interpret study results. Moreover, gender and employment status are often related, as many studies have found that part-time workers are predominantly women, while full-time workers are predominantly men.

Teleworking lends itself to both professional work (low division of labor with internal control) and clerical work (high division of labor with external control) (Ford and Butts, 1995; see also Olson, 1987). It is likely that the experiences and outcomes of teleworking will differ for these jobs. However, many researchers have included both clerical and professional/managerial employees in their samples in examining attitudes and outcomes associated with teleworking.

Finally, it seems reasonable to expect differences in the attitudes and experiences of teleworkers depending on the amount of time that they work at a remote location (Kraut, 1989). Most of the literature suggests that there should be a balance between teleworking and working in the traditional office environment. Productivity studies have shown that working at home two to three days per week is optimum, with working more or less at home resulting in lower productivity (McCloskey and Igbaria, 1998). Studies that do not consider the relative level of teleworking participation may therefore miss an important explanation for any subsequent differences in attitudes or outcomes.

Implications of telework research for decision-makers

Decision-makers should be skeptical of claims about the effects of telework, especially if the claims are not grounded in rigorous empirical research. For example, several studies have suggested that the level of teleworking participation will have a negative impact on visibility, and, therefore, on career advancement (Austin, 1993; see also DuBrin and Barnard, 1993; Dutton, 1994). From the perspective of office politics, this is the "out-of-sight, out-of-mind" argument. However, empirical research has not addressed this issue. Before drawing conclusions about telework and framing organizational policy on this issue decision-makers should also consider the extent to which research findings might apply to their own industries and organizational cultures, and to employees at different stages of their careers.

Researchers can help promote better organizational decisions in several ways. They can do so by disentangling the organizational and personal effects of level of participation on teleworkers, by exploring potential differences in outcomes by gender and level of job, and by identifying salient personal characteristics of successful teleworkers. This kind of research can help guide organizational policy decisions, and also important decisions that individuals make relative to their careers and lifestyles.

Training managers and employees for telework

In a telework relationship, time is not important. This is one of the harder lessons for managers of teleworkers to learn, and many have to rethink completely how they view supervision. They need to understand that managing someone they can't see differs considerably from walking around offices to see that employees are at their desks at 8 in the morning. In fact, experts say that learning to make the transition from managing time to managing projects is critical and will determine the success of an organization's telework program (Grensing-Pophal, 1998). Here are some suggestions on how to help managers and employees make that transition.

Before a telework arrangement is finalized at Merrill Lynch, process consultants study how employees in a given area communicate, how they do business, and they identify for the manager of a work area what the barriers to teleworking will be. Doing so helps to alleviate managers' concerns and focusses attention on areas that need to be addressed. Formalized training for telework is divided into teleworker training, supervisor and manager training, and team training in which teleworkers and their managers come together to discuss issues that affect their relationship. Some organizations also set aside time to train and educate the entire staff, from the mail room to the board room (Grensing-Pophal, 1998).

In teleworking arrangements, issues beyond technology are at work. Cultural, managerial, and interpersonal implications also need to be addressed. For example, in Finland, cultural norms about the role of work in everyday life, military traditions ("you do not leave your friend"), and the shame of women as well as men associated with not having a full-time job, have retarded the growth of teleworking (Suomi, 2000).

Assuming teleworking is feasible, however, it is important to do three things well. One, begin training with workers and managers together so they hear the same message, understand the business case for implementing telework arrangements, and can discuss ways to address important issues. These include the lack of face time (which may create resentment among workers who remain in the office), potential losses in creativity due to lack of personal interaction with co-workers and managers, and potential losses in productivity due to absence from the office. Two, include presentations from employees and managers who already have experience with telework arrangements. Three, focus on developing a "deliverables" mentality. That means measuring productivity on the basis of the results of assignments and projects, rather than hours spent in the office.

Project management is especially important in instances where teleworkers or virtual members are not part of the same organization. Each person is hired to accomplish a specific task, and that person often has no vested interest in monitoring the end result. If a manager is not proactive in monitoring the progress of the overall project and the usefulness of the final product, the team's productivity will never result in improved profitability.

The time frame for completion can cause problems for some managers who are new at managing teleworkers or virtual teams. Most managers establish completion dates, which are necessary. However, completion of a project may be delayed if managers do not establish milestone activities. A milestone activity is a critical-completion point within the overall duration of a project. Through the use of milestones, a manager can see early in a project's life cycle whether or not the necessary pieces are progressing satisfactorily. This allows corrections and changes during the project that ensure timely completion, or at least forewarn of problems (Arko et al.,

1999). The principles of effective project management are not new, and they do not change in virtual work environments. They simply become more important.

A further issue is naive expectations about what working away from the office is really like. To provide a realistic preview for prospective teleworkers, Merrill Lynch uses a simulation lab, a large room that contains work stations where employees work for two weeks without physical contact with their managers. Even if their managers are in the building, workers cannot leave the lab to discuss issues face-to-face. After the two-week trial, some employees decide that telework is not for them (Grensing-Pophal, 1998). While some firms use short, self-scored surveys to help workers identify how likely they are to succeed as teleworkers, there is really no substitute for a job tryout, as a simulation lab provides.

A final component of telework training, in addition to up-front involvement of managers, is back-end involvement of managers. Specifically, consider bringing managers into the evaluation process about six months after the implementation of the telework program, using productivity measurements as the basis for a business case analysis. Examine the impact of telework on outcomes such as productivity, cost, and customer satisfaction. Such an evaluation allows for adjustments or enhancements to the program, or, alternatively, to its discontinuance.

● Conclusion ●

Globalization, technology, and electronic commerce, all of which are associated with the information revolution, are driving the development of new forms of organizations, such as virtual organizations. Virtual organizations are multi-site, multi-organizational, and dynamic. While virtual organizations form and disperse in response to specific projects or objectives, virtual work arrangements are common among intact organizations. In virtual work arrangements employees operate remotely from each other and from managers. Two of the most popular types of virtual work arrangements are virtual teams and telework.

In a virtual team, members are dispersed geographically or organizationally. Their primary interaction is through some combination of electronic communication systems. Such arrangements have advantages as well as disadvantages. To make virtual teams work, it is important to define roles clearly so that members can collaborate to accomplish work. It is also important to have a clear leadership structure in order to minimize ambiguity about who has the right to decide what.

Telework refers to work carried out in a location that is remote from central offices or production facilities, where the worker has no personal contact with coworkers, but is able to communicate with them using electronic means. It is a popular and rapidly growing alternative to the traditional, office-bound work style, but it is not appropriate in all circumstances. For example, when the job involves working with clients by phone or at the clients' premises, as is the case with jobs in sales, marketing, project engineering, and consulting, telework may be appropriate. In addition employees need to be experienced, technically self-sufficient, and internally motivated. Managers who function best under these arrangements are effective communicators and delegators, and emphasize managing by results more than managing by time. However, there is a pressing need for controlled, empirical research to inform decision-makers, as the numbers of organizations and individuals that adopt such arrangements increase year by year in developed countries everywhere.

In implementing virtual work arrangements, cultural, managerial, and interpersonal implications need to be addressed, along with communication and performance management issues. Doing so requires a systematic approach to design and implementation of the program, and there are no shortcuts. In order to realize the full potential of virtual work arrangements, the arrangements have to "fit" the structure within which an organization operates, and its ways of dealing with employees, customers, and suppliers. When they do, organizations may benefit through improved performance and productivity, while at the same time finding it easier to attract and retain employees. Employees and managers may benefit by taking advantage of flexible work schedules that permit greater personal control over where, when, and how they work. Virtual organizations and virtual work arrangements are not appropriate in all settings, but careful attention to the kinds of issues presented here can ensure that when they are implemented, they have the greatest likelihood of paying off handsomely for all involved.

REFERENCES

Aannestad, B., and Hooper, J. (1997, November). The future of groupware in the interactive workplace. *HRMagazine*, pp. 37–42.

Anders, G. (1999, July 12). The online revolution. *The Wall Street Journal*, p. R6.

Apgar, M., IV (1998, May–June). The alternative workplace: Changing where and how people work. *Harvard Business Review*, pp. 121–36.

Arko, D., et al. (1999). Virtual teams. Unpublished manuscript, University of Colorado Executive MBA Program, Denver, CO.

Austin, J. (1993). Telecommuting success depends on reengineering the work processes. *Computing Canada*, 19, 37–8.

Baumeister, R.F., and Leary, M.R. (1993). The need to belong: Desire for interpersonal attachments as a fundamental human motivation. *Psychological Bulletin*, 117, 497–529.

Blackmon, D.A. (2000, July 17). Price buster: E-commerce hasn't had an impact on the economy's overall price structure. Yet. *The Wall Street Journal*, pp. R12, R26.

Business Week (1994, May 23). Borderless management: Companies strive to become truly stateless. *Business Week*, pp. 24–6.

Business Week (1996, April 29). The new workplace. *Business Week*, pp. 105–13.

Business Week (1997, November 24). Power gizmos to power business. *Business Week*, p. 190.

Business Week (2000a, January 10). The new world of work: Flexibility is the watchword. *Business Week*, p. 36.

Business Week (2000b, February 28). At Ford, e-commerce is job 1. *Business Week*, pp. 74–8.

Byrne, J.A. (2000, August 28). Management by Web. *Business Week*, pp. 84–96.

Cascio, W.F. (2000). Managing a virtual workplace. *Academy of Management Executive*, 14, 3, 81–90.

Cascio, W.F., and Serapio, M.G., Jr. (1991, Winter). Human resource systems in an international alliance: The undoing of a done deal? *Organizational Dynamics*, pp. 63–74.

Clark, K. (1997, November 24). Home is where the work is. *Fortune*, pp. 219–21.

Colvin, G. (2000, March 6). Managing in the info era. *Fortune*, pp. F6–F9.

Conlin, M. (1999, September 20). Nine to 5 isn't working anymore. *Business Week*, pp. 94–8.

Cooper, R.C. (1997). Telecommuting: The good, the bad, and the particulars. *Supervision*, 57, 2, 10–12.

Coutu, D. (1998, May–June). Trust in virtual teams. *Harvard Business Review*, pp. 20–1.

Dess, G.G., Rasheed, A.M.A., McLaughlin, K.J., and Priem, R.L. (1995). The new corporate architecture. *Academy of Management Executive*, 9, 3, 7–18.

Dick, G.N. (2000, September). Telecommuting in Australia and Singapore. *Proceedings of the 5th Annual Telework Workshop*, Stockholm, Sweden.

DuBrin, A.J., and Barnard, J.C. (1993). What telecommuters like and dislike about their jobs. *Business Forum*, 18, 13–17.

Dunham, K.J. (2000, October 31). Telecommuters' lament. *The Wall Street Journal*, pp. B1, B18.

Dutton, G. (1994). Can California change its corporate culture? *Management Review*, 83, 49–54.

Duxbury, L., Higgins, C., and Neufeld, D. (1998). Telework and the balance between work and family: Is telework part of the problem or part of the solution? In M. Igbaria and M. Tan (eds). *The Virtual Workplace*. Hershey, PA, Idea Group Publishing, pp. 218–55.

Ford, R.C., and Butts, M. (1995). Questions and answers about telecommuting programs. *Business Horizons*, 38, 66–72.

Fortune (2000, September 4). *Fortune*'s fastest growing companies. *Fortune*, pp. 180–6.

Gersick, C.J.G., and Davis-Sacks, M.L. (1990). Summary: Task forces. In J.R. Hackman (ed.). *Groups That Work (and Those That Don't)*. San Francisco: Jossey-Bass, pp. 146–53.

Green Commuter (1998). <http://libertynet.org/cleanair/green/summer98/greentext8-98.html>.

Grensing-Pophal, L. (1993, December). Training employees to telecommute: A recipe for success. *HRMagazine*, pp. 76–82.

Grimshaw, D.J., and Kwok, F.T.S. (1998). The business benefits of the virtual organization. In M. Igbaria and M. Tan (eds). *The Virtual Workplace*. Hershey, PA, Idea Group Publishing, pp. 45–70.

Gupta, Y., Karimi, J., and Somers, T.M. (1995). Telecommuting: Problems associated with communications technologies and their capabilities. *IEEE Transactions on Engineering Management*, 42, 4, 305–18.

Hackman, J.R. (ed.) (1990). *Groups That Work (and Those That Don't)*. San Francisco: Jossey-Bass.

Hamel, G., and Sampler, J. (1998, December 7). The e-corporation. *Fortune*, pp. 80–92.

Hedberg, B. (2000, September). Organizing in the new economy, between inside and outside. *Proceedings of the 5th Annual Telework Workshop*, Stockholm, Sweden.

Hogan, R. (1998). Reinventing personality. *Journal of Social and Clinical Psychology*, 17, 1–10.

Holland, B., and Hogan, R. (1999). Remodeling the electronic cottage. *The Industrial-Organizational Psychologist*, 36, 2, 21–2.

Igbaria, M., and Tan, M. (eds) (1998). *The Virtual Workplace*. Hershey, PA: Idea Group Publishing.

Ishii, H., Kobayashi, M., and Arita, K. (1994, August). Interactive design of seamless collaboration media. *Communications of the ACM*, 37, 8, 83–97.

Jackson, M. (1997, November 21). Telecommuters love staying away, new survey shows. *The Denver Post*, p. 4C.

Jarvenpaa, S.L., Knoll, K., and Leidner, D.E. (1998). Is anybody out there? Antecedents of trust in global virtual teams. *Journal of Management Information Systems*, 14, 4, 29–64.

Kraar, L. (1997, May 26). The real threat to China's Hong Kong. *Fortune*, pp. 85–94.

Kraut, R.E. (1989). Telecommuting: The trade-offs of home work. *Journal of Communication*, 39, 19–47.

Matthes, K. (1992 December). Telecommuting: Balancing business and employee needs. *HR Focus*, 69, 3, 3.

McCloskey, D.W., and Igbaria, M. (1998). A review of the empirical research on telecommuting and directions for future research. In M. Igbaria and M. Tan (eds). *The Virtual Workplace*. Hershey, PA, Idea Group Publishing, pp. 338–58.

McCune, J. C. (1998). Telecommuting revisited. *Management Review*, 87, 10–16.

O'Connell, S.E. (1996, March). The virtual workplace moves at warp speed. *HR Magazine*, pp. 51, 77.

Olson, M.H. (1987). Telework: Practical experience and future prospects. In R.E. Kraut (ed.). *Technology and the Transformation of White Collar Work*. Hillsdale, NJ: Lawrence Erlbaum.

O'Reilly, B. (2000, February 7). They've got mail! *Fortune*, pp. 101–12.

Rapp, B. (2000, September). Teleworking: Where are we and where are we going? *Proceedings of the 5th Annual Telework Workshop*, Stockholm, Sweden.

Rivenbark, L. (2000, April). Employees want more opportunities to telecommute, report reveals. *HRNews*, pp. 14–16.

Serapio, M. G., Jr., and Cascio, W. F. (1996). End-games in international alliances. *Academy of Management Executive*, 10, 1, 62–73.

Smith, R., and Lucchinetti, A. (2000, August 28). Sink or swim. *The Wall Street Journal*, pp. A1, A10.

Snow, C.C., Lipnack, J., and Stamps, J. (1999). The virtual organization: Promises and payoffs, large and small. In C.L. Cooper and D.M. Rousseau (eds). *The Virtual Organization*. New York: Wiley, pp. 15–30.

Suomi, R. (2000, September). Telework in Finland – why and why not. *Proceedings of the 5th Annual Telework Workshop*, Stockholm, Sweden.

Townsend, A.M., DeMarie, S.M., and Hendrickson, A.R. (1998). Virtual teams: Technology and the workplace of the future. *Academy of Management Executive*, 12, 3, 17–29.

Wall Street Journal (1997, September 2). "Office hoteling" isn't as inn as futurists once thought. *The Wall Street Journal*, p. A1.

Warner, M. (1997, March 3). Working at home – the right way to be a star in your bunny slippers. *Fortune*, pp. 165, 166.

10

Designing Change-Capable Organizations

EDWARD E. LAWLER III

Organizations are increasingly operating in a business environment that is character-ized by rapid change and increasing performance demands. As a result, organizations face the challenge of accomplishing two, often conflicting, objectives: performing well and changing in order to adapt to their business environment. In most cases, the changes they make must be quick, skillfully executed, and clearly targeted at imple-menting an effective business strategy. Change that occurs every few years as part of a special change effort is no longer adequate. It too often is late and disruptive. Change needs to be constant and rapid in order to allow organizations to move at the speed of business. The importance of change in today's environment virtually guarantees that organizations which do not change will quickly become "corporate dinosaurs," headed for extinction because they no longer fit the current environment (Lawler and Galbraith, 1994).

Organizational change has been a persistent topic of discussion in the field of or-ganizational behavior and organizational effectiveness for many decades. Numerous books and articles have been written about how to manage change (see e.g. Beer and Nohria, 2000; Hamel, 2000; Nadler, Shaw, and Walton, 1995). They typically em-phasize the importance of leadership, employee involvement, and incentives in over-coming resistance to change. The classic model of change identifies three phases of change: the first involves creating dissatisfaction with the current state so that an organization will abandon its traditional ways of operating; next, the organization is expected to go through a period of change which is followed by a period of stability. This way of thinking about change is becoming obsolete. For more and more busi-nesses, periods of stability are a thing of the past. The environment is changing too rapidly for organizations to enjoy periods of stability. In order to be effective organi-zations must continuously change. Thus, in today's business environment organiza-tions have to be built to change, not changed as a result of a special change program or effort that is in response to a change in technology or the business environment.

Creating organizations that are designed to change calls for a special mindset with respect to organization design. Instead of striving to produce a fine Swiss watch with all of the movements interconnected so that it consistently produces the same behavior, organizations need to be designed in ways that stimulate change. This means creating an organization that encourages experimentation, learning about new practices and technologies, and a commitment to continuously improve performance. Accomplishing this requires designing organizations that have structures, reward systems, communication processes, and human resource management practices that are designed to change, and that encourage organizations to continuously and rapidly change. Before discussing how this can be done, we need to consider some basic points concerning organization design and effectiveness.

● Competitive Advantage ●

Many of the historical sources of competitive advantage such as geographic location, physical assets, and access to capital simply are not sustainable sources of competitive advantage in the today's economy (Mohrman, Galbraith, and Lawler, 1998). What is available as a source of competitive advantage? The answer is an organization's ability to perform effectively. That is, its ability to organize and manage its financial capital, technical knowledge, and its human capital. Doing this is a complex challenge and it needs to be driven by a business strategy, which identifies the kind of organizational capabilities and core competencies that an organization needs to develop.

Organizational capabilities

In order to be successful, organizations must have capabilities that allow them to coordinate and motivate behavior in ways that are tuned to the marketplace and produce levels of performance that differentiate them from their competitors. Every organization must understand what capabilities it needs in order to compete in its market and then develop them by creating the appropriate organizational designs and management systems (Lawler, 1996).

What are some key organizational capabilities? In many respects, the ability to change rapidly is the ultimate competitive advantage. It is the ultimate competitive advantage because it potentially enables an organization to stay ahead of its competitors and meet the increasingly higher performance standards that the environment presents.

Organizational capabilities don't exist in one place – in the heads of a few technology gurus or in a set of patents. They rest in a combination of the skills and knowledge of the workforce and the reward system, culture, processes, and overall design of an organization. They typically require the coordinated behavior of many individuals and systems.

In most cases, it is not enough for an organization to simply have one capability that is world-class. In today's highly competitive environment it is often necessary for an organization to have several capabilities that are at least world-class in the ability of the organization to execute them. Thus, it is a bit of an over-simplification to focus

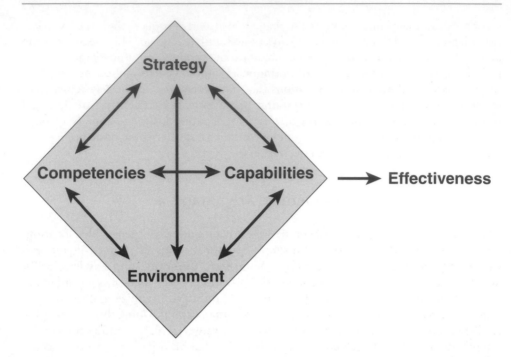

Figure 10.1 The Diamond Model

on just rapid change, but by doing it we can highlight the features of an organization which allow it to be change-orientated and adaptive. Thus, for the rest of the chapter the focus will be on the design features which an organization should have in order to create a continuous change capability.

Core competencies

Core competencies, also a possible source of competitive advantage, are technical areas of expertise such as Boeing's expertise in the aerodynamics of flight, Microsoft's expertise in computer science, Honda's competency in making gasoline engines, and Sony's ability to miniaturize products (Hamel and Prahalad, 1994). The longevity of the competitive advantage an organization gains from its core competencies depends on how easy they are to copy and develop. There is always the risk that others can duplicate or capture them because they often reside in the minds and skills of a small number of employees. The easiest way to acquire competencies in these cases is to hire key employees away from an organization that has them. Employees may also leave on their own and take core competencies with them to create new, competing organizations. In some cases organizations have been able to perform effectively for decades without having to develop new competencies, but this is becoming much less common. With the development of more and more disruptive technologies, organizations increasingly need to develop new core competencies (Christensen, 1997).

It is up to an organization's executives to manage the development of a strategy that identifies the kind of performance that is needed, to communicate the need for that performance through mission and values statements, and to develop the needed competencies and capabilities. This relationship is shown in the Diamond Model (see figure 10.1), which shows that organizational effectiveness results when there is a fit among four points: (1) strategy, (2) competencies, (3) capabilities, and (4) the environment.

• The Star Model •

The most useful way to think about the features of an organization in relationship to organizational capability and core competencies is to use the Star Model. It is a well-known model that has been used for decades to identify the key elements of an organization and focus on the issue of strategy and strategy implementation (see e.g. Galbraith, 1973). Figure 10.2 presents the Star Model. When you take into account the interconnections in the Star Model, it becomes obvious that if you wish to make a significant change in an organization's performance, all of the five elements must be examined and possibly changed, because a change in one element of the organization has implications for the rest. The challenge is to develop an approach to

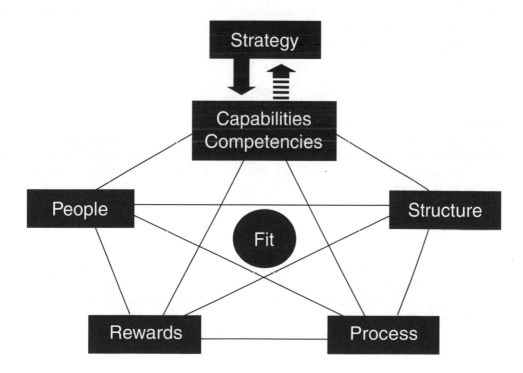

Figure 10.2   The Star Model

organizing that considers all five of the elements and how they fit together to create an organization with the strategy, competencies, and capabilities it needs to succeed. A brief review of the five points on the star follows.

Strategy

In the Star Model, business strategy is the cornerstone design element. It needs to define the kind of organizational performance that is needed, the types of organizational capabilities and competencies that are needed, and how an organization intends to respond to its business environment. An organization can do a terrific job of implementing strategy, but unless it offers the right products or services, correctly identifies potential customers, and secures adequate financing, among other factors, it will not succeed.

Structure

The second point on the Star Model is the organization's structure – that is, how people are grouped together, who reports to whom, how tasks are assigned, and the nature of the jobs within the organization. Critical decisions still need to be made about how individuals are grouped together, how major decisions are made, how many levels of management are created, and a host of other factors. In many respects, because these decisions are the fundamental building blocks of an organization, they must be closely articulated with strategy.

Rewards

The third point on the Star Model, reward systems, must fit closely with an organization's strategy so that they reward the correct behaviors. They also need to be closely articulated with the need for human resources since they are critical in attracting and retaining individuals. Further, they are crucial in making all the elements of an organization operate effectively.

Processes

Management processes, the fourth point on the Star Model, are the systems that an organization puts into place to help control, manage, inform, and direct its members' behavior, both individually and collectively, so that they focus on the correct strategic actions. Management processes include information and communication systems, budgeting and financial measurement systems, and the behavior of managers, particularly those involved in decision-making and setting direction for the organization.

As with the other points on the star, if the measurement, communication, and other key processes are out of alignment or are nonexistent, an organization cannot perform effectively. Some key communication processes – such as meetings and social events – are relatively informal, but most are formal. Budgets, quality controls, and financial information systems are formal means of measuring and communicating performance results. Strategic fit with respect to these systems often means correctly measuring the behaviors that the strategy says are important and that need to be motivated in order for the strategy to be successfully implemented.

People

The final point on the star is people, the organization's human resources. Individual performance is critical to an organization's functioning effectively. In order to ensure it, organizations must have individuals with the right skills and knowledge who are motivated to perform effectively. No organization can operate successfully if its employees cannot do the work that is assigned to them. Organizations can assure themselves that individuals have the skills, abilities, and capabilities necessary to perform well by selecting and hiring the right people and then developing and training them.

Organizational culture

The five-pointed Star Model does not identify the final determinant of organizational performance: corporate culture. It is omitted because it is not a design parameter. Instead, it develops as a result of the influence of all the major elements of an organization. Some versions of the Star Model put culture in the center of the star to emphasize its importance and indicate that it is influenced by all elements on the star but cannot be directly controlled in the same sense that the major design elements can be. An organization, for example, is seen as valuing innovation not simply because it says it does but because the reward systems, work design, and information processes all support and encourage those behaviors that lead to innovation.

It is often possible to determine whether an organization is likely to perform in a particular way by looking at its culture, because culture "says" what people in the organization should do and what will be rewarded. The challenge in changing culture is to identify what points on the star give the current culture its characteristics and then to figure out how to change them so that the organization can operate with a new and more functional culture. Culture is often difficult to change because individuals in the organization have signed up to work there and have continued to work there because they like the existing culture as well as the reward practices and organization design that created it. Thus they are likely to resist change.

A considerable amount of the writing on organizational change and change management emphasizes the importance of having an organizational culture that is change-friendly. It talks about the importance of valuing risk-taking, supporting entrepreneurial behavior, and developing a willingness on the part of individuals to accept change. There is little doubt that these are important cultural features of an organization and that the culture of an organization is critical in determining how easily and effectively it will change. The challenge is to create a culture which values change, risk-taking, and adaptation to a changing environment. Indeed measuring the culture of an organization and finding out whether it is supportive of change is a powerful way to determine whether the effort to design a change-ready organization has been successful. In that respect culture is an indicator of the success of an organization design effort rather than a design feature of the organization that can be directly altered. What can be directly altered are the points on the star. The challenge therefore is to create an organization design that produces a culture which favors change.

● Fit and the Star Model ●

An important principle of the Star Model has been that organizational effectiveness is greatest when there is a fit among the points of the star. In particular, the emphasis has been designing processes, reward systems, structures, and human capital that produce the capabilities that are required for the implementation of the strategy. Fit is important according to the Star Model because it is required in order to produce the kind of capabilities that provide for competitive advantage. It occurs when all the points on the star are aligned in a way that they support each other and, in combination, support a particular business strategy. In most cases, an alignment is sought that supports a highly focussed set of behaviors. In the case where an organization wants to develop a change capability, it may be important to create a type of misfit. As we will see when we discuss the different points on the star, it may be that a particular degree and kind of misfit is in fact desirable.

● Types of Change ●

In thinking about designing for change capability it is worth distinguishing between two types of change: evolutionary and transformational. Evolutionary change refers to the continuous adjustments, improvements, and product alterations that organizations need in order to satisfy the increasing demands of customers and to keep up with current changes in technology. It usually does not require an organization to alter its core competencies, but may involve a shift in its organizational capabilities. Transformational change refers to major changes in an organization's core competency or competencies, product mix, markets, and business models. It usually requires an organization to develop new capabilities. Examples of transformational change include Corning moving from being a consumer products company to becoming a fiber-optics company, and Nokia moving from being a wood products company to being a wireless communications technology company.

The capabilities that are needed to execute transformational and evolutionary change often require different organization designs. Because they are similar capabilities, some of the same practices that encourage transformational change can also support evolutionary change, but some practices are clearly more appropriate for transformational than for evolutionary change and vice versa. Thus, a key issue with respect to the design of an organization is the degree to which it needs to be designed for transformational or evolutionary change. As we discuss each point of the star, consideration will be given to any differences in how it should be designed in order to optimize the capability for each type of change.

● Organizational Structure ●

The first point on the star that is typically considered after strategy is organizational structure. The traditional functional organization structure fits a steady-state world in which the movement of information is expensive and needs to be carefully controlled. It clearly does not fit a world of cheap, high-speed communication and rapid organizational change (Mohrman, Galbraith, and Lawler, 1998). What kind of structure or structures fit and encourage the development of an organizational change capability that will allow an organization to respond effectively to a rapidly changing environment? No single structure is always optimal. However, it is possible to identify a number of structural options which support organizations having the capability to change.

An organization that is structured around small, relatively autonomous business units is a good example of one that has a structure that enables rapid change (Galbraith, Mohrman, and Lawler, 1998). With business units it is relatively easy to change the mix of businesses that a corporation is in while keeping the organization focussed on particular products, market segments, and customers. Thus, it enables an organization both to execute a transformational change with respect to its mix of businesses and to have units which themselves are rapidly changing and adjusting to their environment. This structure makes it easy to add new business units that are acquired through acquisitions. Clearly, acquiring new businesses and business units is a quick and effective way to change an organization. Cisco, the very successful internet company in the United States, has exactly this change strategy and has used it to become one of the most valued corporations in the world.

A business unit structure lends itself to the use of new venture startup units within a corporation. This approach is particularly useful when an organization has a new transformational technology that it needs to bring to market but has no established units that are prepared to handle it, either because they do not have the capability or because it threatens them (Christensen, 1997).

With a business unit structure, it is possible to have a variety of reward systems, processes, and individuals in the organization as a whole, but to have fit among these points of the star within each unit. Internet-related businesses are a good example of the kind of transformational businesses that may be put in a new unit. In a business unit structure, new ventures that are transformational can be started and protected from the rest of the organization by being put in a separate business unit until they have reached critical mass. At that point, they may join an existing business unit, be maintained as a competing business unit within an organization, or spun out as a separate company. A business unit structure is not particularly helpful as far as creating new organizational capabilities that are corporate-wide. It can make it easier to develop them in particular parts of the company, but transferring them to the rest of the organization can be difficult.

The network organization structure is another approach that enables rapid continuous change in an organization. In a network organization, multiple independent organizations are typically linked together and constitute different parts of the value chain (Mohrman, Galbraith, and Lawler, 1998). A classic example of a network is the structure of Nike, Benetton, and other fashion businesses. In a network, one organization, typically the organizer of the network, takes responsibility for design and marketing while other organizations work as manufacturers, sellers, advertisers, etc. Change is relatively easy because all it requires is adding new network members who bring new competencies or capabilities. Information technology is a major enabler of network organizations. Historically, they were difficult to manage because of the tremendous cost of moving information from one business to another. With modern information technology organizations can now develop the capability to coordinate a long multiple organization value chain in ways that make network organizations practical and, in many cases, very effective.

One final approach to organization structure warrants mention here. The front/back organization structure typically has relatively independent units that constitute the front of the organization and another set of relatively independent units that constitute the back (Mohrman, Galbraith, and Lawler, 1998). The front is typically organized around geography, consumers, or market segments. The front-end units are relatively independent of each other and are designed to focus specifically on selling and marketing products to their customers. The back of the organization is typically made up of units that supply the front with products and/or services. They too are relatively independent of each other, but need to relate effectively and closely to the front. Again, information technology is key in making this type of organization effective because it enables the kind of communication and coordination that is needed to coordinate the front and back pieces of the organization. Front/back organizations are relatively easy to change because new products and services can be added simply by adding independent units to the back while new markets and customers can be addressed by adding new units to the front. These changes usually represent evolutionary change rather than transformational change and highlight the point that front/back organizations are generally more effective at evolutionary change than transformational change.

● Reward Systems ●

The reward systems in most traditional organizations use pay systems that are based on job size (Lawler, 2000). Large pay increases usually can only be obtained through getting promoted to a higher-level position. Individuals often resist reorganization and organizational change precisely because they disrupt the career paths of individuals and cause a reallocation of work that may decrease the size of an individual's job.

Most traditional pay systems reward performance with merit pay increases. Particularly in low inflation periods, these increases are often just a few percent of someone's pay and are tied to a performance appraisal of how well an individual does his or her job. Research evidence shows that merit pay plans do little to motivate performance but may act as an obstacle to change (Heneman, 1992). Even the simplest change in job duties or responsibilities can call for a major revision of the performance measurement process that determines individual pay and thus changes are sometimes resisted by both the appraiser and the individual who is being appraised. Further, since all that most individuals have to do to receive a pay increase is perform well in their job, there is little incentive for the individual to look for better work processes or support reorganization efforts that are likely to improve the overall performance of the organization. In this and many other ways, reward systems tend to encourage individuals to resist change, to grow their jobs, and to focus on their personal situations.

Reward systems do not have to be sources of resistance to change. Quite the opposite can be true: they can support and encourage change if they are properly designed (Lawler, 2000). They have the potential to motivate individuals to accept change and to change their skills and abilities in ways that will make change efforts successful (Beer and Nohria, 2000). What is required? The answer is simple to state but difficult to implement. Individuals need to be rewarded for learning, developing and possessing the key skills an organization needs in order to implement its strategy and individuals need to be rewarded not on the basis of their performance but on the performance of their business unit and/or organization.

Paying individuals based on their skills, knowledge, and of course, on their market value is a relatively new idea but it is gaining wider and wider acceptance (Lawler, Mohrman, and Ledford, 1998). In essence it argues for rewarding individuals for what they can do rather than the job they are doing at the moment. It allows organizations to structure reward systems which reward individuals for continuously learning and changing their skill sets in ways that fit the changing nature of an organization's business. Thus, instead of resisting change individuals potentially welcome it because it leads to their having an opportunity to learn new skills and get paid more. It can be particularly supportive of change efforts that are targeted at creating new organizational capabilities and probably most useful in evolutionary change efforts.

The research on organizational change clearly argues that change will only occur if individuals have a reason to change. Individual-pay-for-performance systems give individuals a reason to perform their own job well but, rather than giving them a reason or reasons to change, they give a reason not to change. The best alternatives in most cases to individual-pay-for-performance are profit-sharing or stock-based plans that reward individuals for the overall success of the organization. In the case of large organizations, the plans may need to focus on business unit performance or team performance instead of total organization performance.

When organizations base pay on organizational performance it not only creates a reason to change, it provides a reason to implement and effectively operate the desired strategic and operational change. My research shows that the implementation of most change efforts that are directed at capability building – total quality management, knowledge management, and re-engineering – are more effective when pay is based on organizational performance (Lawler, Mohrman, and Ledford, 1998). Rewards for organizational performance motivate individuals to continually ask how they can do things better and of course, reward them when in fact, they do things better. Failure to change means deteriorating performance and as a result fewer financial rewards so it is not a surprise that individuals are more focussed on how to improve performance and more willing to accept change when they are paid based on the profit and stock performance of their organization.

In addition to creating pay systems that reward organizational members for organizational performance, it may be useful to reward them for critical individual behaviors. This is particularly true in organizations that are looking for transformational change instead of continuous evolutionary change. Organizations such as Enron have created specific bonus plans to reward individuals who start new ventures and break the mold of the traditional way of doing business. In essence, they reward good risk-taking and thinking that is outside the mold of standard operating procedure. It is an effective way to maturate individuals to stay with their organization instead of leaving to start a new corporation.

Rewards for new venture efforts in companies can take the form of individuals being given equity in the new ventures. This is particularly effective when the venture is high-risk and very different from the existing business of the organization. It is a way of creating "big hairy audacious rewards" for people who take major risks with their careers and thinking in order to create transformational business opportunities for their organization. It also is consistent with the idea of varying the practices of an organization in order to fit different performance needs.

● Human Capital ●

In order for change to occur individuals must support it and have the skills necessary to implement it. Having a reward system which rewards change and skill development is one piece of creating an organization in which human capital seeks change and learns the new skills and abilities that are necessary to implement it. However, it is only one step; other human capital management practices need to be in place in order for an organization to continuously change.

In many respects readiness to change starts with the basic HR systems in an organization. In traditional organizations they are based on jobs and because of this individuals are focussed on their job. Change typically requires a redefinition or elimination of jobs and, as a result, may be a threat to individuals. The alternative to traditional job-based human capital management is a human capital system that is based on skills and knowledge (Lawler, 1994). In this approach, individuals are hired based on their skills, abilities, and the degree to which they are a good fit for the future direction of the organization. They are also recruited on the basis of a value proposition that is focussed on change, growth, and development, and rewards which are dependent upon learning and performance. Some theorists in the HR field have called this approach to recruiting and employment the employability contract. It emphasizes the importance of individuals gaining and learning skills so that they will be employable and it de-emphasizes the idea of job security and lifetime employment.

It is perhaps slightly counterintuitive to argue that an employability contact will lead to less resistance to change than will traditional approaches that emphasize job security. However, my research suggests quite strongly that an employability contract which states that individuals need to perform, learn, and change in order to retain their job leads to more effective organizational change and transformation than one that tells people they are secure and have a job for life (Lawler, Mohrman, and Ledford, 1998). Although security may be satisfying for some individuals it doesn't seem to be a motivator of change. Quite the contrary, it seems to encourage individuals to continue to do what they have done in the past rather than to think about how they can improve and how their organization needs to change.

Implementing an employability contract needs to start with a selection process that includes a realistic preview of the nature of the organization and the importance of continuous change. Once an individual has joined an organization it involves a career system that gives individuals information about career options but expects them to manage their own career. It provides them with learning opportunities rather than placing them on career tracks. In a highly predictable world, carefully orchestrated laid-out careers may make sense, but in a world in which things are changing rapidly it is unrealistic to expect management to provide individuals with a dependable career map or for that matter with a secure job.

The fit aspect of the Star Model might argue for creating an organization that has a homogeneous group of individuals. That is, individuals who are similar in their tolerance of risk, willingness to innovate, and desire for certain kinds of rewards. With similar individuals it is relatively easy to design reward systems, jobs, and other organizational features that are appealing to the members of the organization. In essence a one-size-fits-all approach can be taken. However, this may be exactly the wrong approach to take in order to create an organization with a change capability. Particularly if an organization is expecting to go through transformational change, it may be very important to have a heterogeneous population of employees.

Organizations that emphasize change often talk about the importance of having some "wild geese" employees who are willing to take risks, break from the mold, and champion change efforts. Staffing an organization with a variety of individuals starts with the selection process and a concerted effort to hire a variety of individuals. However, simply hiring diverse employees is not sufficient. If the organization systems and treatment of people are homogeneous, individuals who do not fit the mold will tend to turn over and in the long term the organization will end up with a homogeneous workforce.

Essentially there are two ways to ensure that an organization maintains a somewhat diverse workforce. The first is to rely on the business unit model. As was mentioned earlier, it can be used to allow business units to treat people differently, develop different capabilities and competencies. The second is to individualize the systems within an organization so those individuals who differ significantly in their preferences and behaviors can have their needs met by the organization (Lawler and Finegold, 2000). This is not a simple feature to build into an organization but with modern information technology it is increasingly possible to give individuals the choice of how they are rewarded, what benefits they get, what kind of career tracks are available to them, and so on. Of course, having a variety of individuals in an organization has a cost, not only an administrative cost but also a coordination cost. Thus, it is probably best used when an organization is particularly concerned about the importance of being able to develop a capability for a transformational change. It is important for evolutionary change but not as much individualization is required in order to produce an organization that is capable of evolutionary change.

● Business Processes ●

The decision-making and communication processes in an organization are critical to its ability to change. Rigid, hierarchical, secretive decision and information processes tend to produce inwardly focussed business processes which produce organizations that are difficult to change and resistant to recognizing that change is needed. Change needs a reason, it needs a driver. The best driver of most change is information about the environment that indicates that the old ways of doing business are not appropriate. In order for this realization to drive change throughout an organization, individuals at all levels need information about the environment and how it is changing.

Information systems and decision processes which provide individuals throughout the organization with real-time business information and decision-making opportunities are a good way to get information about environmental change into an organization and to call attention to the need for continuous change. With modern information technology it is now possible to put the business of an organization on everyone's desk. There is no excuse for individuals not understanding the environment, the business strategy of their organization, and the financial model of the organization. With virtual closes, individuals can get immediate information about how the organization is performing and be kept highly informed about an organization's performance. This is precisely what has been done at companies like Cisco which deliver ongoing financial information to all employees on a daily basis. Each employee has a portal that provides relevant business information.

The business processes of an organization need to allow some experimentation and risk-taking. Without experimentation and risk-taking it is impossible to learn about more effective ways of operating and to develop new products that will lead to transformational changes. It is also often important to have enough resource slack so that individuals have access to the financial resources that are needed to experiment with doing things differently and to develop new products. 3M is famous for its policy of allowing individuals 15 percent free time to experiment and develop new products and processes that they think have a chance of being successful. In terms of financial resources, organizations can create pots of money that can be awarded to individuals who have ideas about new products or processes that can change the organization. This is particularly important in producing transformational change.

The leadership processes of an organization are a particularly critical determinant of an organization's ability to successfully change. Many discussions of organizational change start and end with a discussion of leadership (see e.g. Conger, Spreitzer, and Lawler, 1999; Kotter, 1996; O'Toole, 1995). Leaders clearly are important in creating a change capability in an organization and in leading change. Leaders need to do two seemingly contradictory things in order to create and support change in an organization. First, they need to provide a clear sense of strategic direction for the organization and provide a compelling mission for the organization. Typically this leadership function needs to be done by senior managers. Although it is important that they get input from others in the organization, the reality is that in a rapidly changing business environment they often have to change strategy quickly and in a somewhat top-down manner. This is particularly true in the case of transformational change.

Setting strategy however, is only one part of being a successful leader of change. Leaders also need to communicate and enroll people in the strategy and vision. This is where the second element of leadership comes into play. In order to change, organizations need not just leadership from the top that is strong and provides a compelling strategy and reason for change, they need leaders throughout the organization. Leadership itself needs to become an organizational capability so that individuals throughout the organization are capable of taking leadership roles with respect to changing the business and business processes in the areas where they work. Leadership cannot become an organizational capability unless the senior leaders in an organization support the development of leaders throughout the organization. They need to make leadership development an important organizational objective.

The view that leaders are needed not just at the top of an organization but throughout the organization is somewhat different than the tradition in many companies of focussing on developing leaders for the top-level position. It argues for broad-scale leadership development that focusses on both producing the few senior leaders that are needed to set strategic direction and provide leadership at the top and on developing individuals throughout the organization who are capable of developing key leadership behaviors. Strategic leadership at the top is particularly important to executing major transformational changes in the organization. On the other hand, leadership throughout the organization is critical to the kind of continuous change that is needed in many organizations. It leads to small but important changes in relationships with customers, the ability to satisfy customers quickly and decisively, and to change processes in ways that reflect the changing nature of the customer base and the environment.

• Key Strategic Issues •

Putting in place the right organization design features is basic to creating an organization that is capable of continuous change and improvement. In discussing the practices that are appropriate for each point in the star, we have identified the key practices that are needed to create a change capability in an organization. At this point it is important to look at some of the strategy issues that are important in managing an organization that is effectively able to change.

Type of change

Perhaps the most difficult call for any organization to make involves determining the type of change of which it needs to be capable. Transformational change requires different things than does evolutionary change. It requires somewhat different reward systems, structures, processes, and in many cases different human capital. Thus, organizations, which have a high probability of facing the need for dramatic transformational change, need to build a somewhat different kind of organization.

Perhaps the best way to think of the need for a change capability is that at a minimum most organizations need to develop the capability for evolutionary change. But when an organization senses that it may need to make a transformational change, it needs to take special steps to prepare the organization. This will usually require financial processes that offer venture funding opportunities for individuals, structures that include special new venture units which have major change experience, and reward systems that offer large rewards to those who create transformational change. Finally, it may also need to recruit some "wild geese" who are willing to champion radical change.

What to keep stable?

Keeping certain elements of the organization stable while allowing others to change can be an important facilitator of change. The key question of course, is what should be kept stable and what should be allowed to change? How much and what should be kept stable is partially determined by the kind of change the organization needs to make. Much more can be kept stable in an organization that needs continuous evolutionary change than in one that needs transformational change. In the case of the latter, stability may simply be commitment to a certain mission and a way of dealing with individuals that produces a culture that is supportive of change. Beyond that, it may also include some reward system practices such as stock options, profit-sharing, and a continued focus on customers and the external market.

In the case of a situation where evolutionary change is desired more can be kept stable. For example, more of the HR systems can be constant than can the basic organizational structure. Many of the key processes can also often be kept stable, particularly those having to do with the measurement of business success and communicating business information to all employees.

Internal competition

Change can be stimulated by both internal and external competition. It is hard to argue against maximizing the focus on external competition. Competing against an external competitor is a powerful motivator and can be supportive of change. A more difficult issue to resolve is how much internal competition an organization should encourage. With respect to building a change capability, the most important issues concern competition among different business units. Competition between units can be quite healthy, particularly if it stimulates innovation and change in order to win the competition. However, it may also lead to a failure to share ideas and as a result, to poor development of core competencies and organizational capabilities.

As a general rule, high levels of competition are probably best when transformational change is needed. Tolerance of internal competition is particularly important when new business areas need to be developed and tested, even though they are a direct challenge to existing products or services. Indeed, this brings a second issue front and center, how much should an organization cannibalize its own products? In rapidly changing technologies and businesses the right answer is usually as much as it can (Christensen, 1997). The reason is simple: if an organization doesn't come out with a better product a competitor certainly will and the long-term result will be loss of market share. Particularly in the high-tech world, internal competition, even if it means cannibalizing products and stealing customers, is an important feature that needs to be designed into most organizations because it is a powerful creator and motivator of change.

Use of outsourcing

Outsourcing a variety of services and key parts of the value chain can be a powerful way to enable an organization to change. It creates an opportunity to make significant changes simply by changing a vendor or supplier. The use of outsourcing, however, contains a number of risks and needs to be used with some caution. For example, it runs the risk of creating a competitor who takes what they have learned as an outsourcer and uses it to produce competing products. It also runs the risk that many of the services and processes are done in a way that does not provide competitive advantage. Outsourcing organizations often do the same thing for many organizations; thus what they do usually does not operate as a competitive differentiator. The key to building a successful change capability in an organization does not depend as much on how much is outsourced as it does on what is outsourced. It is particularly critical to keep things that provide a competitive advantage for an organization inside.

Outsourcing is a way to create both evolutionary change and transformational change, but it is probably most useful for evolutionary change. Exceptions to this include cases where research that advances new products or processes is outsourced and situations where an outsourcer is able to create an entirely new business model. Instances of this happening are relatively rare and thus, in most cases, outsourcing should not be counted on as a way to produce transformational change. It can, however, produce evolutionary change because outsourcers who focus on a particular business process can often improve on an organization's business processes and performance.

● Building a Change-Capable Organization ●

Organizations can be built to change, but doing this requires a conscious and continuous effort to ensure that a change capability is nurtured and supported by the key practices of the organization. The capability to change does not rest in any single system or any single individual; instead it rests in the systems, practices, and history of an organization. In many ways, the ability to change is the ultimate competitive advantage in today's information economy. An organization which is able to develop a superior change capability can respond to the rapid technological, economic, and political changes which are altering the very face of business worldwide. The future belongs to change-capable organizations. As has been stressed in this chapter, a change capability can be systematically developed in an organization. It does not need to be and should not be left to chance.

REFERENCES

Beer, M., and Nohria, N. (2000). *Breaking the Code of Change*. Boston: Harvard Business School Press.

Christensen, C.M. (1997). *The Innovator's Dilemma*. Boston: Harvard Business School Press.

Conger, J.A., Spreitzer, G.M., Lawler, E.E., and Associates (1999). *The Leader's Change Handbook*. San Francisco: Jossey-Bass.

Galbraith, J.R. (1973). *Designing Complex Organizations*. Reading: Addison Wesley Longman.

Hamel, G. (2000). *Leading the Revolution*. Boston: Harvard Business School Press.

Hamel, G., and Prahalad, C.K. (1994). *Competing for the Future*. Boston: Harvard Business School Press.

Heneman, R.L. (1992). *Merit Pay*. Reading: Addison-Wesley.

Kotter, J.P. (1996). *Leading Change*. Boston: Harvard Business School Press.

Lawler, E.E. (1994). From job-based to competency-based organizations. *Journal of Organizational Behavior*, 15, 3–15.

Lawler, E.E. (1996). *From the Ground Up: Six Principles for Creating the New Logic Corporation*. San Francisco: Jossey-Bass.

Lawler, E.E. (2000). *Rewarding Excellence: Pay Strategies for the New Economy*. San Francisco: Jossey-Bass.

Lawler, E.E., and Finegold, D. (2000). Individualizing the organization: Past, present, and future. *Organizational Dynamics*, 29, 1, 1–15.

Lawler, E.E., and Galbraith, J.R. (1994). Avoiding the corporate dinosaur syndrome. *Organizational Dynamics*, 23, 2, 5–17.

Lawler, E. E., Mohrman, S. A., and Ledford, G. E. (1998). *Strategies for High Performance Organizations: The CEO Report*. San Francisco: Jossey-Bass.

Mohrman, A.M., Galbraith, J.R., Lawler, E.E., and Associates (1998). *Tomorrow's Organization: Crafting Winning Capabilities in a Dynamic World*. San Francisco: Jossey-Bass.

Nadler, D., Shaw, R., and Walton, E. (1995). *Discontinuous Change*. San Francisco: Jossey-Bass.

O'Toole, J. (1995). *Leading Change: The Argument for Values-Based Leadership*. New York: Ballantine Books.

Company Initiatives to Improve New Working Arrangements

11

Formal Mentoring: The Promise and the Precipice

TERRI A. SCANDURA AND ETHLYN A. WILLIAMS

Mentoring is a dyadic relationship in which an older, more experienced organizational member fosters the growth and development of a junior employee into a competent professional. Research suggests that mentoring involves vocational or career development, psychological support, and role modeling (Dreher and Ash, 1990; Kram, 1985; Levinson, Darrow, Klein, Levinson, and McKee, 1978; Noe, 1988; Scandura, 1992). Protégés benefit from vocational career support as they receive sponsorship and coaching on the job. They receive psychosocial support in the forms of friendship and advice. Allen, Russell and Maetzke (1997) found that career and psychosocial functions were strongly related to protégé satisfaction with the relationship. Mentors may also serve as role models (Dreher and Ash, 1990; Kram, 1985; Scandura and Ragins, 1993). Mentoring may increase job satisfaction, career attainment, salary, and organizational commitment, and is also associated with lower intent to leave the job and reduced role stress (Baugh, Lankau, and Scandura, 1996; Fagenson, 1989). Organizations often encourage mentoring through formal programs, since mentoring may play a role in increasing performance and improving work attitudes (Murray, 1991). Mentoring provides employee training, development, and socialization. Given the potential benefits to be gained through mentoring, it is not surprising that it has become a tool for promoting the growth and development of junior members in organizations (Burke and McKeen, 1989; Hunt and Michael, 1983).

Ramsey (1999: 3) notes that "mentoring works today because it teaches lessons that aren't taught anymore or aren't available elsewhere." It is also an effective means for coping with the rapid pace of organizational change (Kram and Hall, 1995). Viator (1999) notes that formal mentoring relationships are typically different from informal mentorships. Siegel, Rigsby, Agrawal, and Lavins (1995) make this distinction in their descriptions of the relationships. They note that informal mentoring involves a powerful patron forcefully shaping the protégé's career while in the formal relationship the mentor serves as sponsor and guide (pointing out mistakes to be avoided and giving career advice).

● Formal Programs ●

This chapter examines the characteristics of formal mentoring programs, explores the features that may be important for success, and analyzes organizational reports on the purpose for which the programs are established. The majority of recommendations for formal programs as well as their descriptions come from practitioners who report on the experience of one formal program. Thus, researchers must be careful in applying these recommendations and descriptions. Based on the limited information that is available on formal programs we will present the results of three recent investigations of formal mentoring: a survey of employed MBAs, an interview study of protégés in a formal program, and a survey of Human Resource Directors regarding mentoring program characteristics.

Formal mentoring often results from programs that assign protégés to mentors based on the similarity of their interests and experience (Chao, Walz, and Gardner, 1992; Douglas, 1997; Fagenson-Eland, Marks, and Amendola, 1997; Noe, 1988). Noe (1988) describes formal mentoring programs as programs in which individuals are assigned to a mentor. Cunningham (1993) describes formal mentoring programs as those in which the organization assigns or matches mentors and protégés, they have top management support, an extensive orientation program, clearly stated responsibilities for each party, established duration and contact, and they emphasize realistic expectations concerning the relationship. Zey (1985) also emphasizes the importance of realistic expectations. Two key differences noted by Ragins and Cotton (1999) between formal and informal mentoring is that there is usually the voluntary assignment or matching of mentor–protégé pairs in formal programs while informal mentorships develop spontaneously. Also, the length of both types of mentorship varies, with informal relationships normally lasting for a longer period of time.

Bragg (1989) estimates that one-third of major companies in the US have formal mentoring programs yet Ragins and Cotton (1999) note that these programs are being developed without the guidance of empirical research. Gibb (1994) notes that evaluations of formal mentoring need to take account of learning, psychosocial and career benefits, what the costs are, and how the program contributes to the accomplishment of the organization's broader objectives. The impetus behind the establishment of formal mentoring programs is to foster the positive outcomes associated with mentoring relationships, especially for career development and employee training and socialization (London and Mone, 1987). Noe (1988) found that formal mentorship offered various benefits, stating, "protégés reported receiving beneficial psychosocial outcomes but limited career functions (e.g., sponsorship, coaching, protection) from the assigned mentor" (Noe, 1988: 473). Burke and McKeen (1989) noted that since some formal programs provide organizational support and rewards for mentoring they might allow women and other minorities greater access to mentors. The increase in formal mentoring programs during the 1990s may also have been in response to the increasing turbulence of the business environment and increased downsizing (Jossi, 1997).

Research by Dirsmith and Covaleski (1985) suggests that formal mentoring programs are often found in large public accounting firms. Viator (1999), however, notes that little is known about the structure and processes of formal mentoring programs at large public accounting firms, including what matching processes are used, who receives mentoring, who provides mentoring, how the formal structure rewards such actions, and how the program is evaluated. Mentoring programs have been found in business settings (Kram, 1986) as well as in education (Merriam, 1983), nursing (Yoder, 1990), law offices (Riley and Wrench, 1985), police departments (Fagan and Ayers, 1985), and the federal government (Klauss, 1981). Companies such as Deloitte and Touche, Ernst and Young, KPMG Peat Marwick, Price Waterhouse-Coopers, Micrografix Inc., Service Inc., Colgate Palmolive, and American Bankers Insurance Group have established formal mentoring programs.

Gibb (1999) evaluated formal mentoring programs from a social exchange theory perspective which assumes that we seek to maximize benefits and minimize costs. He concluded that formal mentoring might succeed when it allows for the realization of mutual benefits. He suggests that formal programs will fail in environments where there are too many people or where there is no effective reciprocal altruism. Gibb (1999: 10) also applied communitarian theory which maintains that "people act in a prosocial, virtuous way as they are bound by core values, established and maintained by being members of a community." Thus, people may act without any expectation of reciprocal favors. Gibb (1999) further suggests that formal mentoring might succeed where there are strong communities, regardless of the organization's size. Thus, formal programs might succeed when community members perceive that mentoring fits with achieving communitarian ends. This research suggests that formal programs may succeed where there is a balance between social exchange and communitarian ends (Gibb, 1999).

Lindenberger and Zachary (1999) suggest that formal program success and failure lie in the ability to build capacity and integrate learning continuously. They recommend having solid business reasons for establishing the program, having strong top management support, ensuring that the program supports company values, having an advisory team with diverse members, training mentoring partners, benchmarking the practices of other successful programs, and building a program that supports the informal mentoring relationships that already exist. The development of successful mentoring relationships may reinforce protégés' confidence in their ability to advance in the organization, and may increase satisfaction with their current position in the organization (Baugh et al., 1996). Developmental relationships can also build organizational commitment, as promotions may seem more attainable when one has a mentor (Scandura and Williams, 1998). Organizations may be willing to encourage mentoring through formal programs since mentoring may play a role in increasing performance and improving work attitudes. For these reasons, many organizations are interested in implementing formal mentoring programs (Clawson, 1996; Murray, 1991).

Publications on formal programs (Cunningham, 1993; Geiger-Dumond and Boyle, 1995; Gibb, 1994; Lindenberger and Zachary, 1999) make a number of recommendations including: (1) providing visible support from top management; (2) involving employees in the development of the program; (3) providing training; (4) not mandating partnerships; (5) trying to allow each party to select the other; (6) ensuring that the mentor is outside the formal chain of command of the protégé;

(7) promoting a long-term association; (8) eliciting feedback from participants; and (9) trying to tie achievement to the broader initiative. Lindenberger and Zachary (1999) made recommendations for formal mentoring programs based on the development of a mentoring program at Brown-Forman Corporation. They recommend that short-term goals be set such as increasing productivity, building relationship networks, and building career management skills. They also suggest that a mentoring program should be developed if and when there are clear business reasons such as the sharing of organizational knowledge or accelerating the development of future leaders.

● The Promise ●

Research indicates that mentoring is associated with benefits to organizations and their members (Dreher and Ash, 1990; Whitely, Dougherty, and Dreher, 1991). Noe (1988), however, suggests that organizations cannot expect formal mentoring relationships (those established through formal programs) to deliver the same types of benefits as those received in informally established relationships. Protégés in formal assignments may report less vocational and psychosocial support. Research does suggest, however, that while informal mentorships may provide greater benefits than formal ones, formal mentorships do provide benefits beyond having no mentoring relationship and do not appear to adversely affect outcomes such as job satisfaction, organizational socialization, and salary (Chao, Walz, and Gardner, 1992). Chao et al. (1992) found that protégés in informal mentorships reported more favorable outcomes (organizational socialization, satisfaction, and salary) than non-mentored individuals. However, there were no significant differences in outcomes between informal and formal protégés. Seibert (1999) found that protégés with formal mentors reported greater job satisfaction than non-mentored employees.

Recently, Fagenson-Eland, Marks, and Amendola (1997) sampled individuals from two technology organizations owned by the same parent company. One of these organizations had a formal mentoring program. In contrast to Chao et al. (1992), Fagenson-Eland et al. (1997) found no difference between formal and informal mentorships on career mentoring, but found greater psychosocial mentoring in informal mentorships. Given these discrepancies, more research is needed which examines benefits that might be derived from different types of mentoring relationships.

Ragins and Cotton (1991) noted that women might be more likely to seek formal mentoring programs as substitutes for informal mentorships since they face greater barriers than men in establishing informal relationships with mentors. Organizations may also target women for formal programs to help them overcome the "glass ceiling" (Catalyst, 1993; Herry, 1994). Scandura and Williams (2000) note that mentoring can be transformational, thus having positive effects on work attitudes (Bass, 1990). Mentoring appears to have incremental effects over and above transformational leadership (Scandura and Williams, 2000). Thus it appears that leaders who mentor can have a profound effect on employees. For this reason, training senior managers to mentor may enhance their leadership. Research by Burke (1984), for example, found that employees often report that their supervisors provide them with mentoring. It therefore appears that the organizational context is ideal for mentoring relationships and that mentors need not be outside the organization. Burke (1984) noted that organizations might not successfully mandate that all managers become mentors, but they can create mechanisms that will facilitate the process.

Ragins and Cotton (1999) found that protégés in same-gender relationships reported more challenging assignments from formal mentors and male protégés with formal mentors reported receiving more counseling than females with formal mentors, and more than male and female protégés with informal mentors. Ragins and Cotton (1999) also noted that potential short-term benefits might be realized such as on-the-job training and the early development of career and performance goals. Ragins and Cotton (in press) noted that although formal mentors are likely to be viewed as providing lower levels of mentoring functions than informal mentors, satisfying formal relationships surpassed dissatisfying or marginal (limited in scope and degree of mentoring functions provided) informal relationships.

Viator (1999) surveyed 3,000 certified public accountants in order to assess whether formal mentoring programs in large public accounting firms are effective in providing mentors to employees. While his research suggests program characteristics that might lead to protégé satisfaction, it is important to note that over 83 percent of respondents reported also having concurrent formal and informal mentoring relationships. Important considerations for the program included having both mentor and protégé input in the design and having formal mentors meet regularly with protégés to set goals and objectives for the mentorship. Klauss (1981), in his investigation of formal mentoring in the federal government, concluded that formal mentor relationships in management and executive development programs could benefit the protégé, mentor, and organization. He advises the careful identification of the potential mentors, protégé involvement in mentor selection, providing training (role assignment), having the protégé ultimately take responsibility for the relationship, and providing realistic expectations for each party.

Forret, Turban, and Dougherty (1996) suggest that the pairing process in formal mentoring programs is critical for the development of mentoring relationships. Chao, O'Leary-Kelly, Wolf, Klein, and Gardner (1994) also suggest that when the mentor initiates the relationship, the relationship may be enhanced. Thus, initiation may play an important role in the way mentoring relationships develop. The most beneficial method of pairing may be through facilitating interaction and familiarity that allows mentors and protégés to select each other (Scandura and Williams, 1998). Formal mentoring may result from programs that pair protégés with mentors based on the similarity of their interests and experience (Chao et al., 1992; Fagenson-Eland, Marks, and Amendola 1997; Noe, 1988). Jossi (1997) suggested that employees could find stability and support through mentoring relationships. Thus, formal programs may be most effective when the need for mentorship exists, and this need is recognized and accepted by all parties involved in the formal program. Ensuring that there is a willingness to devote time, effort, and a sense of commitment to the relationship may be necessary for success (Burke and McKeen, 1989).

● The Precipice ●

Formal mentoring programs have been seen as a way to develop employees and provide opportunities for minorities. Many programs, however, have encountered problems as members report discomfort and protégés appear to receive fewer benefits than protégés in informal mentoring relationships. Difficulties in formal mentorships (supervisor–subordinate pairs) may arise from the imposed structure of the relationship (Tepper, 1995). Unrealistic expectations may be held for mentors (as the evaluation of formal programs may require that the relationship be successful), while those employees not selected for a program may feel discouraged, and create negative morale within the organization (Scandura, 1998). The potential also exists for problems with matching individuals, and in identifying potential mentors. Kaye and Jacobson (1995) suggest that a better alternative might be to substitute the dyadic relationship with interactive mentoring groups. This can evolve into a learning group, as the responsibility for mentoring becomes that of the peers as well as the mentor's.

Recent research (Williams, 2000) suggests that one-on-one mentoring between a supervisor and subordinate can lead to jealousy, especially where the remaining (unmentored) subordinates feel neglected. Habler and Lowe (1985) note that this may occur where a supervisor singles out a high performer for mentorship. All subordinates should be able to benefit from the leader's developmental interactions, and regular and focussed team events may be needed to ensure that this happens (Kaye and Jacobson, 1995). The manner in which the mentoring relationship is initiated, however, may have strong implications for how much success is realized. Kram (1983) notes that protégés are usually those who are seen as having talent and a positive attitude toward work while Healy and Wechert (1990) also note that those accorded the status of protégé are normally perceived as showing exceptional promise. This suggests that how the mentor and protégé select each other is very important and it may well be the case that this type of relationship cannot be mandated or "organized" or even coordinated but may need to develop through a natural selection process.

While research on both formal and informally initiated mentorships has emphasized the associated benefits, there is increasing recognition of the potential that formal mentorships have for becoming dysfunctional relationships (Scandura, 1998). Formal mentors are often selected by protégés based on their competence and there is less likely to be the mutual respect, friendship, and mutual attraction as might be found in an informal mentoring relationship (Ragins and Cotton, 1999); in informal mentorships the mentor typically views the protégé as a high performer or having the potential for high performance (Ragins, 1997). Both types of mentorship may be viewed as high-risk, since the success or failure of the protégé in the organization may be attributed to the mentor's ability. In an informal mentorship there may be greater levels of commitment to the relationship by both parties since mutual interest exists. Since the familiarity of each party with the other plays a key role in initiation, informal relationships will be more likely to involve the vocational, psychosocial, and role-modeling elements of mentoring. However, since the purpose of many formal programs is to advance task- and career-oriented goals for protégés (Gray, 1988), the time spent together tends to be less than in informal mentorships and thus there may be less psychosocial support and role modeling.

Ragins and Cotton (1999) reported that protégés with informal mentors reported more benefits than those with formal mentors (more career and psychosocial functions). They also found that those in informal mentorships reported higher compensation and promotions while there were no differences between those with formal mentors and non-mentored individuals. Female protégés also reported receiving less coaching, role modeling, social, counseling, and friendship functions than males with formal mentors. In their discussion of "marginal" mentors Ragins and Cotton (in press) describe these relationships as limited in the amount of mentoring provided. This marginal mentoring may occur in cases where organizations establish formal programs for the purpose of providing on-the-job training or job orientation (Murray, 1991).

Protégés may receive some confirmation, acceptance, learning, and feedback in formal mentorships. However, they may also experience anxiety and confusion and place less value on a relationship that they perceive as contrived (Noe, 1988). There may also be a lack of personal commitment to relationships that are not formed on the initiative of a mentor or protégé (Kram, 1985). The career/goal orientation that is embodied in formal relationships may capitalize on the organizational promotion of good citizenship behavior. This may result in the participation of individuals who, rather than being prepared for the mentoring role, are motivated to mentor for organizational recognition. Informal mentorship on the other hand usually develops out of a mutual interest and both mentor and protégé experience personal development. Thus, mentors may be more motivated to provide career development to protégés they select.

Formal protégés may experience pessimism, especially when they are not involved in choosing the mentor (Phillips-Jones, 1982; Wilson and Elman, 1990). Tepper (1995) found that informal protégés reported using direct and extracontractual influence tactics rather than regulative and contractual tactics to maintain relational stability. He found that formal protégés used more contractual and regulative influence tactics, which suggests that the context in which formal mentoring occurs is more threatening than that for informal mentorships. Recent work on what might be referred to as the "dark side of mentoring" describes dysfunctional relationships in which protégés reported having dissimilar attitudes, values, beliefs and being in assigned mentoring relationships (Eby, McManus, Simon, and Russell, 1998). Scandura (1998) warns that the power dynamics within a supervisory mentoring relationship may give rise to dysfunction. She highlights the importance of having mechanisms in place to end or assist with mentoring relationships that encounter difficulties. Mismatches often occur in formalized mentoring and may result in relationships characterized by discontent, anger, jealousy, resentment, sabotage, deception, or harassment. Such negativity can have serious detrimental consequences and highlight the danger of possible incidents of personal damage to either party involved. Given that formal mentoring poses both promise and precipice for organizations, there is a clear need for more research. In the following sections we summarize our recent research on formal mentoring.

● Survey of Protégés in Formal Programs and Informal Relationships ●

We were interested in investigating the differences between protégés in informal and formal mentoring relationships. Our analyses go beyond previous research since we compared mentoring relationships in terms of initiation: protégé-initiated, mentor-initiated, mentor- and protégé-initiated, and formally initiated. Previous research suggests that the way that mentors and protégés are matched can allow the formal program to have more informal characteristics and thus be more successful. By examining type of initiation we can make suggestions on what matching processes might make formal mentoring programs more successful.

A questionnaire was administered to 400 respondents, most of whom were employed on a full-time basis and in a Masters of Business Administration (MBA) program at a university in the southeastern United States. Respondents were asked to rate their most current mentoring relationship. Mentors were described as influential individuals in the work environment who had advanced experience and knowledge and were committed to providing upward mobility and support to the career of the protégé (Ragins and Cotton, 1991; Ragins and Scandura, 1994; Scandura and Ragins, 1993). Thirty-five responses were dropped due to missing data. Those in formally initiated mentorships also reported having been assigned to the mentor.

Respondents were classified as non-mentored individuals (N = 91) if they responded as never having had a mentor during their career. Classification of respondents in formally initiated mentorships (85) was based on the response of "formal organizational program" to the question "Who initiated this relationship?" Individuals who responded with "self," "mentor," or "both" to this question were classified as participants in informally initiated mentorships (189). We controlled for (1) whether the protégé was in a current mentoring relationship and (2) duration of the mentorship (Chao et al., 1992). Thus, for reports on mentoring functions, the final sample was 76 in the "formally initiated" mentoring group and 174 in the "informally initiated" mentoring group.

The average age of respondents was 30.7 years with 57.8 percent male. Seventy percent of respondents were employed in the service industry. Sixty-one percent had bachelor's degrees and 32.1 percent master's degrees, with 80.3 percent at or below the level of middle management in their organizations. The respondent mix by race was 47.7 percent white, 6.8 percent black, 28.5 percent Hispanic, and 5.8 percent Asian. The average work experience was 5.3 years and the average duration of the mentoring relationship was 1.4 years (1 year for formally initiated mentorships and 1.63 years for informally initiated mentorships).

Mentoring. Respondents completed an 18–item measure of mentoring functions (Scandura, 1992). A 5-point response scale was used ranging from 1 = "strongly agree" to 5 = "strongly disagree." The items presented were designed to tap career development, psychosocial support, and role modeling. The reliability coefficient (Cronbach's alpha) for career development was .70 (7 items), for psychosocial support .75 (4 items) and for role modeling .87 (6 items) (Nunnally, 1978).

Career expectations.   A six-item measure of respondents' perceptions of their likelihood to be promoted by their organization was administered (Scandura and
Schriesheim, 1991). The reliability coefficient for this measure (Cronbach's alpha)
was .78.

Organizational commitment.   The 15-item Organizational Commitment Questionnaire (OCQ) was administered (Mowday, Steers, and Porter, 1979). The Cronbach
coefficient of reliability obtained for this sample was .80.

Job satisfaction.   The 20-item short form of the Minnesota Satisfaction Questionnaire (MSQ) was administered (Weiss, Dawis, England, and Lofquist, 1967). Individuals reported their level of job satisfaction. The Cronbach reliability coefficient
was .88.

Since the mentoring functions were moderately correlated an overall multivariate
analysis of variance (MANOVA) was run by type of mentorship (formally initiated
and informally initiated) and was significant (Wilks Lambda = .938, F = 2.60, $p <$
.05). Using analysis of covariance (ANCOVA) we tested the differences between the
various types of initiation. The duration of the mentorship and having a current
mentor were significant covariates. Protégés in relationships initiated by both mentor
and protégé reported higher means on the mentoring functions than protégés in relationships initiated by the protégé. There was a statistically significant difference for
the career development function (3.98 vs. 3.74; $p <$ .05). Protégés in relationships
initiated by the mentor reported higher means on the mentoring functions than those
in relationships initiated through formal organizational programs. There was a statistically significant difference for the career development function (4.02 vs. 3.53; $p <$
.05). Protégés in relationships initiated by both mentor and protégé reported higher
means than formally initiated relationships on career development (3.98 vs. 3.53; $p <$
.05), psychosocial support (3.52 vs. 3.12; $p <$ .05) and role modeling (3.95 vs. 3.58;
$p <$ .05).

Since the outcome measures of career expectations, organizational commitment,
and job satisfaction were moderately correlated, an overall MANOVA was run using
all three outcome variables by mentorship group (formally initiated, informally initiated, and non-mentored) and was significant (Wilks Lambda = .950, F = 3.091, $p <$
.01). For career expectations and organizational commitment, mean scores reported
by informal protégés were higher than means reported by formal protégés (3.67 vs.
3.45), which were higher than means reported by non-mentored individuals (3.19).
Results of the one-way ANOVA and *post hoc* analyses (Scheffé tests) revealed statistically significant differences between informal protégés and non-mentored individuals on career expectations.

Protégés in informal mentorships reported higher levels of career development and
role modeling than protégés in formal mentorships. Thus, our results are consistent
with those of Chao et al. (1992) for career development. Fagenson-Eland et al. (1997)
however, found only psychosocial support but not career development nor role
modeling to be significantly different between formal and informal mentorships. The
difference between our results and Fagenson-Eland et al. (1997) for career development and role modeling might be due to the different sampling strategies used.

Fagenson-Eland et al. (1997) compared two sister organizations under the same parent company, one having a formal mentoring program. This suggests that more research is needed that examines the elements of psychosocial support that vary by type of mentorship.

When the mentor initiates the relationship, and when both the mentor and protégé are committed to the mentorship (both mentor- and protégé-initiated), the career development function was higher than for protégé-initiated relationships. It appears that the mentor's initial commitment and interest in the protégé has implications for career development since *post hoc* analyses also revealed that mentor-initiated relationships (as opposed to protégé-initiated ones) provided more career development than formal ones. Also, protégés in relationships initiated by both the mentor and protégé perceived more career development, psychosocial and role-modeling functions than protégés in formal relationships. The initiation of the mentoring relationship may have important implications for how the relationship develops. Thus, one factor in the success of mentoring relationships may be whether the mentor or both mentor and protégé initiate the relationship. Informal protégés also reported higher levels of career expectations than formal protégés and non-protégés. Thus, informal protégés may feel that they have greater chances for promotions, and feel more fulfilled at work compared to formal protégés and non-protégés. Consistent with previous research (Chao et al., 1992) there were no differences between formal and informal protégés on other outcomes.

● Interviews with Protégés in a Formal Mentoring Program ●

An interview project was conducted with a large bank in the southeastern United States. Interviews were conducted with 16 protégés involved in a formal mentoring program for management trainees. The program involved 22 protégés who were matched with senior executives who had volunteered to serve as mentors in the program. Protégés were provided with a list from which they could select a mentor and were asked to list their first and second choices in the event that an individual was selected by more than one protégé. Also, if a desired mentor was not on the list a protégé could request him/her and that person would be added to the list if willing to serve in this role. A kickoff breakfast was organized for mentors and protégés to receive guidelines for the program.

Mentoring relationships in this program seemed to work best when either (a) the protégé knew the mentor prior to the program (they picked someone from the list that they already knew or nominated someone not on the list) and/or (b) after the relationship began, the mentor and protégé actually worked together on projects. The flexibility of the program with respect to the matching process seems to pay off in the eyes of the protégés. Despite strong feelings about the matching process being flexible, however, protégés said that having the program formalized had certain benefits such as "increased commitment to mentoring" and "assuring responsibility for the mentor's role."

Interactions with mentors included going to lunch/breakfast, seeing customers together, and stopping by the office to talk. Interview reports indicate that the protégés felt that the program was a success and gave descriptions of the benefits they received. Benefits reported included the receipt of advice and encouragement, role modeling, loyalty, support, help, and having someone to call on for career advice. The individuals interviewed also described the conditions that had facilitated the development of successful mentoring relationships:

1. The matching process for mentors and protégés must allow each party to select themselves into the relationship by basing decisions on prior knowledge of each other. Management can also facilitate interaction through project assignments.
2. Each party should have the freedom to discontinue the relationship at will or have access to mediation processes where conflicts threaten working conditions or task accomplishment.
3. Having the program formalized creates responsibility for mentoring.
4. The program provides access to the mentoring process for those who do not have informal mentors.

• Survey of Human Resource Directors •

Questionnaires were mailed to 500 companies in various industries that employ 3,000 employees or more. The Human Resource Directors of these companies were asked to report on the characteristics of their organizations' formal mentoring programs. These companies are located all over the United States of America and include industries ranging from manufacturing to education. A recent study by Ragins and Cotton (in press) examines the perceived effectiveness and design of formal mentoring programs and the benefits of these formal programs. Some of the measures employed in this research are drawn from Ragins and Cotton (in press).

Seventy-two Human Resource Directors responded. Fifty-eight reported that their organizations did not have a formal mentoring program. The majority of those without a formal program were in manufacturing (17) and sales and services (25). Three organizations were in the transportation sector, four were in construction and maintenance, six were in health care, two were in education and one in the category "other" (farming). The average number of employees that they reported for their organizations was approximately 15,500. Human Resource Directors from 14 organizations reported that their organizations had a formal mentoring program. Eight of these organizations were in the sales and services sector, two were in construction and maintenance, two were in education, one was in manufacturing, and one was in transportation. The average number of employees for these organizations was 4,000.

The purposes for which the programs were established included training and development, succession planning, socialization, role modeling and orientation, career development, improved retention, change management, and to provide assistance and support. These were all aligned with organizational objectives. The age of these programs ranged from one month to 14 years. The number of participating mentors ranged from six to 150 with the number of protégés ranging from six to 200. One organization in the services (technology) sector reported having six different mentoring programs. These were geared toward different sets of organizational members (new hires, minority members, office professionals, project managers, management coaching, and voluntary mentoring for those not in a program). Our reports therefore reflect responses received for 19 formal mentoring programs.

For 12 of the programs each mentor had only one protégé, while for the remaining seven programs the number of protégés ranged from one to four protégés per mentor (construction and sales and services sectors). For 13 programs all mentor–protégé pairs were assigned while for the remaining six, one program (construction company) reported that pairs were formed informally on the job site, two programs reported that relationships were protégé-initiated (sales and services sector), and three programs reported that relationships were mentor-, protégé- or mutually initiated (sales and services sector). The relationships were intended to last from four months to two years. For the majority of the programs participation was voluntary for both mentors and protégés, with most mentors being males and an equal distribution of male and female protégés. Mentors were, on average, two levels above protégés and the majority were superiors outside the chain of command (for nine programs) and peers (for five programs). There were equivalent proportions of mentors both inside and outside each other's departments. Mentor–protégé pairs met least often on a daily basis and more often on a weekly, bimonthly, and monthly basis, and the time spent together ranged from an average of half an hour per week to eight hours per week. The majority of programs recognized mentors using bonuses, write-ups in newsletters, promotions, performance appraisals (when mentoring was a part of their job description), plaques, awards, company apparel, and recognition dinners.

The majority of programs made attempts to evaluate the program using methods including the review of financial results, focus groups, surveys, interviews, feedback sessions, phone calls, and meetings with the training officer. Three Human Resource Directors reported on the results of their programs and felt they were successes. The Human Resource Directors also reported the characteristics that they felt were necessary for the success of formal mentoring programs. The characteristics reported include an appreciation of the differences between the mentor and protégé, commitment by either party, training, learning exchange among pairs, assistance from a mentoring coordinator, recognition of mentors, support and publicity from top management, making mentoring part of the corporate culture, a clear understanding of protégé needs, patience, a willingness to learn, and a willingness to teach.

● Conclusion ●

Despite the potential for dysfunctions in formal mentoring relationships, it seems that under certain key conditions, this process can work effectively for protégés, mentors, and the organization. Organizations desiring to benefit from mentoring within their organizations may need to focus on fostering relationships by creating an environment that facilitates networking among employees at various levels in the organization. Comparing different types of mentorships may reveal the critical elements for success that can be simulated in formalized mentoring relationships and they might be facilitated through training and appropriate pairing techniques. More research is needed on the implications of the matching process in mentoring programs since it appears that perceptions of who initiated the relationship may affect the development of mentoring from the protégé's point of view. If mentors select protégés, mentoring may be more effective than if protégés alone initiate. Our survey results further suggest that when both parties are involved in the matching process (i.e., both initiate the relationship), the most effective relationships develop.

Interviews with protégés in the banking context indicate that having prior knowledge of each other facilitates the mentoring process. The time spent together is also important for the developmental relationship and allowing the pairs to tackle work-related assignments together promotes understanding and learning. It also appears that protégés prefer to choose their mentor than be forced into a relationship. Where the relationship fails to develop in a positive direction, protégés appear to be in favor of discontinuing the relationship or having a third party assist. Protégés also seem to value formal programs for their ability to give them the opportunity to gain access to mentoring.

Based on the survey of Human Resource Directors of mentoring programs it appears that mentoring programs are present across many sectors. Programs are generally implemented to support organizational objectives and to help employees achieve organizational goals. While mentoring programs have been used in the past, they are gaining more popularity as organizations learn more about how the process works and research helps to guide their implementation and evaluation. Some organizations even have mentoring coordinators who recognize the need to monitor and facilitate the process. It appears that one-on-one mentoring is also being coupled with group mentoring since there may not be enough mentors to assign to each person in need of a mentor. Many mentoring programs still find it most efficient to assign mentors to protégés, but more programs are trying to create a more informal pairing process by allowing each party to select into the relationship.

Our results indicate that while organizations allowed mentors and protégés to be inside or outside each other's departments there seemed to be a recognition that peers can effectively mentor each other and, where the mentor is at a higher level in the organization, then it is important that he/she be outside the protégé's chain of command. Whereas Burke (1984) found that many protégés reported that their supervisors provided mentoring, this may be more common or even advisable where the mentorship evolves naturally. The company-wide attention that being part of a formal program entails may apply more pressure for success and thus strain supervisor–subordinate relationships. To attain success in formal programs it appears important that mentors and protégés join the program voluntarily and that making mentors accountable can increase their level of commitment to the relationship. Thus, many programs evaluate and recognize the mentor for their contribution and some even build mentoring into their job descriptions so that performance with respect to employee development can be formally appraised and rewarded.

Thus, some common elements that appear to be important in formal mentoring programs are providing training to mentors and protégés, maintaining support from top management, and ensuring the commitment of each party. Other issues that need to be considered include what makes a mentor effective. Mentorship might be, in part, dispositional, and some individuals may have "natural" tendencies to mentor others. It appears that role modeling may be a unique function that cannot be instilled through training. However, it does seem possible that skills such as coaching and providing social support may be learned. Thus, research that continues to examine the functions of mentoring appears warranted, to better isolate what aspects of mentoring can be learned and what aspects are dispositional (Scandura, 1992). Perhaps training programs that facilitate effective relationship development, listening, and feedback skills can increase the occurrence of mentoring in organizations. This is an area that is worthy of future research since many organizations are attempting to formalize the mentoring process, often without the necessary support from training programs (Clawson, 1996; Ragins and Cotton, in press).

Some recommendations for mentoring programs include creating a structure that ensures regular one-on-one meetings, formally recognizing mentors for their involvement to encourage participation, and eliciting public commitment on the part of mentors. Having short biographies/personal sketches of mentors and protégés available might also enhance the matching process. The goals of the program need to be stated clearly and a trial period implemented for each party to get to know each other and determine their compatibility (Scandura and Lankau, 1998). Mentors and protégés need to receive training that outlines their separate roles and guidance on how to develop the relationship. Managing the complexities of the relationship dynamics rests with the mentor and protégé, but management support should be forthcoming.

We agree with Ragins and Cotton (1999) that organizations should offer formal mentoring in partnership with informal mentoring. These programs should mimic the dynamics in informal mentorships so that protégés can receive the greatest benefits. It may well be that instead of helping a formal relationship along even where there seems to be an incompatible match, organizations should allow the ones that are not working to dissolve and recommend that the protégé try to establish an informal relationship whether inside or outside the organization's boundaries. Keele, Buckner, and Bushnell (1987) suggest that the organization's goal should be to create conditions conducive to network formation rather than formal mentoring programs since the protégé may defer personal responsibility for career development to the mentor. Since formal programs are less successful than informal mentorship, organizations should encourage employees to form networks with ties to higher-level managers, peers, employees, and outsiders. Keele et al. (1987) suggest that the organization can foster such networks by allowing opportunities for cross-departmental interactions, implementing reward systems to reinforce the development of peers and lower-level employees, diversifying teams in the organization, having "fast-track individuals" on teams, and providing training on how to build relationships and achieve goals. Network relationships may be a source of career and psychosocial support and places the power of development with the individual; such a network is more likely to produce an informal mentoring relationship than any organizational program.

REFERENCES

Allen, T.D., Russell, J.E., and Maetzke, S.B. (1997). Formal peer mentoring: Factors related to protégés satisfaction and willingness to mentor others. *Group and Organization Management*, 22, 488–507.

Bass, B.M. (1990). *Bass and Stodgill's Handbook of Leadership*. New York: Free Press.

Baugh, S.G., Lankau, M.J., and Scandura, T.A. (1996). An investigation of the effects of protégé gender on responses to mentoring. *Journal of Vocational Behavior*, 49, 309–23.

Bragg, A. (1989). Is a mentor program in your future? *Sales and Marketing Management*, 141, 54–9.

Burke, R.J. (1984). Mentors in organizations. *Group and Organization Studies*, 9, 353–372.

Burke, R.J., and McKeen, C.A. (1989). Developing formal mentoring programs in organizations. *Business Quarterly*, 53, 76–9.

Catalyst (1993). Mentoring: A guide to corporate programs and practices. New York: Author.

Chao, G.T., O'Leary-Kelly, A.M., Wolf, S., Klein, H.J., and Gardner, P.D. (1994). Organizational socialization: Its content and consequences. *Journal of Applied Psychology*, 79, 730–43.

Chao, G.T., Walz, P.M., and Gardner, P.D. (1992). Formal and informal mentorships: A comparison of mentoring functions and contrast with nonmentored counterparts. *Personnel Psychology*, 45, 1–16.

Clawson, J.G. (1996). Mentoring in the information age. *Leadership and Organization Development Journal*, 17, 6–15.

Cunningham, J.B. (1993). Facilitating a mentorship program. *Leadership and Organization Development*, 14, 15–20.

Dirsmith, M.W., and Covaleski, M.A. (1985). Informal communications, nonformal communications and mentoring in public accounting firms. *Accounting Organizations and Society*, 10, 149–69.

Douglas, C.A. (1997). *Formal Mentoring Programs in Organizations: An Annotated Bibliography*. Greensboro, NC: Center for Creative Leadership.

Dreher, G.F., and Ash, R.A. (1990). A comparative study of mentoring among men and women in managerial, professional and technical positions. *Journal of Applied Psychology*, 75, 539–46.

Eby, L., McManus, S., Simon, S.A., and Russell, J. (1998). *Does Every Cloud have a Silver Lining? A Study of Dysfunctional Mentoring Experiences*. Proceedings of the Southern Management Association meeting. New Orleans: LA.

Fagan, M.M., and Ayers, K. (1985, January). Police Mentors. *FBI Law Enforcement Bulletin*, 8–13.

Fagenson, E.A. (1989). The mentor advantage: Perceived career/job experiences of protégés vs. non-protégés. *Journal of Organizational Behavior*, 10, 309–20.

Fagenson-Eland, E.A., Marks, M.A., and Amendola, K.L. (1997). Perceptions of mentoring relationships. *Journal of Vocational Behavior*, 51, 29–42.

Forret, M.L., Turban, D.B., and Dougherty, T.W. (1996). Issues facing organizations when implementing formal mentoring programs. *Leadership and Organization Development Journal*, 17, 27–30.

Geiger-Dumond, A.H., and Boyle, S.K. (1995). Mentoring: A practitioner's guide. *Training and Development*, 49, 51–4.

Gibb, S. (1994). Evaluating mentoring. *Education and Training*, 36, 32–9.

Gibb, S. (1999). The usefulness of theory: A case study in evaluating formal mentoring schemes. *Human Relations*, 52, 1055–1075.

Gray, A.A. (1988). Developing a planned mentoring program to facilitate career development. *Career Planning and Adult Development Journal*, 4, 9–16.

Habler, B., and Lowe, R. (1985). The mentoring relationship in organizations. *Proceedings of the Southeastern Organizational Development Group*, 26–31.

Healy, C.C., and Wechert, A.J. (1990, December). Mentoring relations: A definition to advance research and practice. *Educational Research*, 32, 17–21.

Herry, W. (1994). Corporate mentoring can break the glass ceiling. *HR Focus*, 71, 17.

Hunt, D.M., and Michael, C. (1983). Mentorship: A career training and development tool. *Academy of Management Review*, 8, 475–85.

Jossi, F. (1997). Mentoring in changing times. *Training*, 34, 50–4.

Kaye, B., and Jacobson, B. (1995). Mentoring: A group guide. *Training and Development*, 49, 23–7.

Keele, R.L., Buckner, K., and Bushnell, S.J. (1987). Formal mentoring programs are no panacea. *Management Review*, 76, 67–8.

Klauss, R. (1981). Formalized mentor relationships for management and executive development programs in the federal government. *Public Administration Review*, 41, 489–96.

Kram, K.E. (1983). Phases of the mentoring relationship. *Academy of Management Journal*, 26, 608–25.

Kram, K.E. (1985). *Mentoring at Work*. Boston: Scott, Foresman, and Company.

Kram, K.E. (1986). Mentoring in the workplace. In D.E. Hall (ed.). *Career Development in Organizations*. San Francisco: Jossey-Bass, pp. 170–201.

Kram, K.E., and Hall, D.T. (1995). Mentoring in a context of diversity and turbulence. In S. Lobel and E. Kossek (eds). *Human Resources Strategies for Managing Diversity*. Oxford: Blackwell Publishers.

Levinson, D.J., Darrow, C., Klein, E., Levinson, M., and McKee, B. (1978). *The Seasons of a Man's Life*. New York: Alfred A. Knopf.

Lindenberger, J.G., and Zachary, L.J. (1999). Play "20 questions" to develop a successful mentoring program. *Training and Development*, 53, 12–14.

London, M., and Mone, E.M. (1987). *Career Management and Survival in the Workplace*. San Francisco: Jossey-Bass.

Merriam, S. (1983). Mentors and protégés: A critical review of the literature. *Adult Education Quarterly*, 33, 161–73.

Mowday, R.T., Steers, R.M., and Porter, L.W. (1979). The measurement of organizational commitment. *Journal of Vocational Behavior*, 14, 225–47.

Murray, M. (1991). *Beyond the Myths and Magic of Mentoring: How to Facilitate an Effective Mentoring Program*. San Francisco: Jossey-Bass.

Noe, R.A. (1988). An investigation of the determinants of successful assigned mentoring relationships. *Personnel Psychology*, 41, 457–79.

Nunnally, J.C. (1978). *Psychometric Theory*, 2nd edn. New York: McGraw-Hill.

Olian, J.D., Giannantonio, C.M., and Carroll, S.J. Jr. (1985). Managers' evaluations of the mentoring process: The protégé's perspective. Presented at the Midwest Academy of Management meetings, St. Louis, MO.

Phillips-Jones, L. (1982). *Mentors and Protégés*. New York: Arbor House.

Ragins, B.R. (1997). Diversified mentoring relationships in organizations: A power perspective. *Academy of Management Journal*, 22, 482–521.

Ragins, B.R., and Cotton, J.L. (1991). Easier said than done: Gender differences in perceived barriers to gaining a mentor. *Academy of Management Journal*, 34, 939–51.

Ragins, B.R., and Cotton, J.L. (1999). Mentor functions and outcomes: A comparison of men and women in formal and informal mentoring relationships. *Journal of Applied Psychology*, 84, 529–50.

Ragins, B.R., and Cotton, J.L. (in press). Marginal mentoring: An examination of the effects of type of mentor, gender and program design on work and career attitudes. *Academy of Management Journal*.

Ragins, B.R., and Scandura, T.A. (1994). Gender differences in expected outcomes of mentoring relationships. *Academy of Management Journal*, 37, 957–71.

Ramsey, R.D. (1999). Do you have what it takes to be a mentor? *Supervision*, 60, 3–5.

Riley, S., and Wrench, D. (1985). Mentoring among women lawyers. *Journal of Applied Social Psychology*, 15, 374–86.

Scandura, T.A. (1992). Mentorship and career mobility: An empirical investigation. *Journal of Organizational Behavior*, 13, 169–74.

Scandura, T.A. (1998). Dysfunctional mentoring relationships and outcomes. *Journal of Management*, 24, 449–67.

Scandura, T.A., and Lankau, M.J. (1998). From research to practice: A current look at mentoring programs in organizations. Presented as part of a joint symposium for the Careers, and Management Education and Development divisions. Academy of Management Meeting, San Diego, CA.

Scandura, T.A., and Ragins, B.R. (1993). The effects of sex and gender role orientation on mentorship in male-dominated occupations. *Journal of Vocational Behavior*, 43, 251–65.

Scandura, T.A., and Schriesheim, C.A. (1991). *Effects of Structural Characteristics of Mentoring Dyads on Protégé Outcomes*. Proceedings of the Southern Management Association meeting. Atlanta, GA, pp. 206–8.

Scandura, T.A., and Williams, E.A. (1998). *Initiating Mentoring: Contrasting the Reports of Protégés in Assigned and Informal Relationships*. Proceedings of the Southern Management Association meeting. New Orleans, LA.

Scandura, T.A., and Williams, E.A. (2000). *Relationships as Tutorials in New Career Contracts: Augmenting Effects of Mentoring on Transformational Leadership*. Proceedings of the Southern Management Association meeting. Orlando, FL.

Seibert, S. (1999). The effectiveness of facilitated mentoring: A longitudinal quasi-experiment. *Journal of Vocational Behavior*, 54, 483–502.

Siegel, P.H., Rigsby, J.T., Agrawal, S.P., and Lavins, J.R. (1995). Auditor professional performance and the mentor relationship within the public firm. *Accounting, Auditing and Accountability Journal*, 8, 3–22.

Tepper, B.J. (1995). Upward maintenance tactics in supervisory mentoring and nonmentoring relationships. *Academy of Management Journal*, 38, 1191–205.

Viator, R.E. (1999). An analysis of formal mentoring programs and perceived barriers to obtaining a mentor at large public accounting firms. *Accounting Horizons*, 13, 37–53.

Weiss, D.J., Dawis, R.V., England, G.W., and Lofquist, L.H. (1967). *Manual for the Minnesota Satisfaction Questionnaire*. Minneapolis, MN: Industrial Relations Center, University of Minnesota.

Whitely, W., Dougherty, T.W., and Dreher, G.F. (1991). Relationship of career mentoring and socioeconomic origin to managers' and professionals' early career progress. *Academy of Management Journal*, 34, 331–51.

Williams, E.A. (2000). *Team Mentoring: New Directions for Research on Employee Development in Organizations*. Toronto: Academy of Management Annual Meeting.

Wilson, J.A., and Elman, N.S. (1990). Organizational benefits of mentoring. *Academy of Management Executive*, 4, 88–94.

Yoder, L. (1990). Mentoring: A concept analysis. *Nursing Administration Quarterly*, 15, 9–19.

Zey, M.G. (1985). Mentor programs: Making the right moves. *Personnel Journal*, 64, 53–7.

12

Self-Assessment Models and Quality/Excellence Awards

B. G. DALE

● Introduction ●

If a process of continuous improvement is to be sustained and its pace increased it is essential that organizations monitor on a regular basis what activities are going well, which have stagnated, what needs to be improved, and what is missing. Self-assessment provides the framework for generating this type of feedback about an organization's approach to continuous improvement. It helps to satisfy the natural curiosity of management as to where their organization stands with respect to the development of Total Quality Management (TQM).[1] Self-assessment against the criteria of a quality award/excellence model is now being given a considerable amount of attention by organizations throughout the world as the means on which to base the evaluation and diagnostics. The main reason for this increasing interest is the Malcolm Baldrige National Quality Award (MBNQA), which was introduced in America during 1987, and the European Quality Award (EQA), introduced in Europe during 1991. There is little doubt that these awards and models have raised the profile of TQM throughout the world and provide the mechanism for quantifying, by means of a points score, an organization's current state of TQM development. There are many definitions of self-assessment provided by writers such as Conti (1993) and Hillman (1994), but an all-embracing definition is provided by the European Foundation for Quality Management (EFQM) (1999a):

> Self-Assessment is a comprehensive, systematic and regular review of an organization's activities and results referenced against the EFQM Excellence model.
>
> The Self-Assessment process allows the organization to discern clearly its strengths and areas in which improvements can be made and culminates in planned improvement actions that are then monitored for progress.

There are a number of internationally recognized models, the main ones being the Deming Application Prize in Japan, the MBNQA in America, and the EFQM Excellence Model in Europe. Although there are some differences the models have a number of common elements and themes. In addition, there are many national quality/excellence awards (e.g., the Hungarian National Quality Award, the Irish Business Excellence Award, and the Australian Quality Award for Business Excellence) and regional quality awards (e.g., the North West Excellence Award): see European Quality (2000). Most of the national and regional awards are more or less duplicates of the international models, with some modifications to suit issues which are of national or local interest. In America alone there are over 60 state and regional award schemes. Blodgett (1999) provides data from the National Institute of Standards and Technology (NIST) which shows that interest in state and local awards in America is experiencing considerable growth (e.g., in 1998 there were 830 applications compared to 36 for the MBNQA). Since the establishment of these awards there has been an explosion in published material describing them (e.g., Brown, 1996; Cole, 1991; Conti, 1997; Hakes, 2000; Lascelles and Peacock, 1996; Nakhai and Neves, 1994; Porter and Tanner, 1996; and Steeples, 1993).

The models on which the awards are based and the guidelines for application are helpful in defining TQM in a way in which management can easily understand in all types of organizations – small, large, public, private, manufacturing, and service. This is one of the reasons behind the distribution of thousands of booklets outlining the guidelines and award criteria. The majority of companies requesting them have no intention, in the short term, of applying for the respective awards; they are simply using the criteria of the chosen model to assist them to diagnose the state of health of their improvement process and provide indications of how to achieve business excellence. They help organizations to develop and manage their improvement activities in a number of ways. For example they:

- Provide a definition and description of TQM which gives a better understanding of the concept, improves awareness, and generates ownership for TQM amongst senior managers.
- Enable measurement of the progress with TQM to be made in a structured manner, along with its benefits and outcomes.
- Educate management and employees on the basic principles of TQM.
- Encourage annual improvement, which provides the basis for assessing the rate of improvement.
- Force management to think about the basic elements of the organization and how it operates; through this organizational change is facilitated.
- Provide, through scoring criteria, an objective-based measurement system, gain consensus within the organization on the strengths and areas for improvement of the current approach, and help to pinpoint the key improvement opportunities.
- Share best practices and facilitate organizational learning.
- Develop a more cohesive company working environment.

Ritchie and Dale (2000), based on detailed research carried out in 10 companies,

Table 12.1   Benefits of the self-assessment process

Category	Benefits
Immediate	• Facilitates benchmarking • Drives continuous improvement • Encourages employee involvement and ownership • Provides visibility in direction • Raises understanding and awareness of quality-related issues • Develops a common approach to improvement across the company • Used as a marketing strategy, raising the profile of the organization • Produces "people-friendly" business plans
Long-term	• Keeps costs down • Improves business results • Balances long- and short-term investments • Provides a disciplined approach to business planning • Develops a holistic approach to quality • Increases the ability to meet and exceed customers' expectations • Provides a link between customers and suppliers
Supporting TQM	• Helps to refocus employees' attention on quality • Provides a "health check" of processes and operations • Encourages a focus on processes and not just the end product • Encourages improvements in performance

summarize in table 12.1 the benefits of self-assessment against a Quality/Excellence Award Model. A full listing of the benefits which have been found to result from the self-assessment process is given in the EFQM (1999a).

To use any self-assessment method effectively as a business tool for continuous improvement, various elements and practices have got to be in place and management needs to have had some experience with TQM to understand the questions underpinning the concept. The decision to undertake self-assessment needs to be fully considered from all angles and management must be fully committed to its use. In my view the use of self-assessment methods based on the quality/excellence award models are best suited to those organizations that have had a formal improvement process in place for at least three years. This is supported by Sherer (1995), the Managing Director of Rank Xerox (Germany), who in explaining how the corporation won the EQA says "Do not use the Award Programme, your application for the EQA, as an entry point into your quality journey. It is something you should do after you have been on the road for a long time." He also goes on to comment: "Do not try to run for the award too early." A similar point is made in the Deming Prize Guide for overseas companies (Deming Prize Committee, 1998): "It is advisable to apply for the Prize after two to three years of company-wide TQM implementation efforts or after top management has become fully committed and has begun to assume a leadership role." Having made this point, the models underpinning the quality/excellence awards are also helpful in demonstrating to those managers in organizations inexperienced in TQM what is involved. However, they must understand the potential gap that can exist between where they currently stand in relation to TQM and the model of the award being used in order to make comparisons.

This chapter opens by investigating the replacement of quality and TQM by excellence in the award models and this is followed by describing the Deming, MBNQA, and EFQM models. It then examines the self-assessment process, and the associated success factors and difficulties.

● Quality, Total Quality Management, and Excellence ●

In recent times there has been a drive to change from quality and TQM to excellence in the criteria of quality/excellence models. In the 1999 version of the model, the members of the steering group responsible for the development of the revised model appear to be proud of how they have progressively stripped out reference to TQM and quality both in the criteria and areas to address. Nabitz et al. (1999), in describing the move from quality management to organizational excellence, point out that: "The word quality does not appear in either the sub-criteria or the areas to address"; and "In the new model, the switch from total quality management to organizational excellence is a fact." This development has, in turn, been followed by national quality bodies such as the British Quality Foundation (BQF). However, it is noted that there is a lack of consistency in the use of quality, excellence, and business excellence in the designations given by national bodies in their specific quality/excellence awards; see European Quality (2000).

The potential for confusion in terms of the language used in the description of what used to be termed TQM, but is now classed by those involved in the self-assessment process as business excellence or excellence, is considerable. For example, at the November 1999 British Excellence Award ceremony the following terms were used during the course of the ceremony: Business Excellence; Excellence; Total Quality; Continuous Improvement; Quality Improvement; Continuous Improvement Programme; Process of Continuous Improvement; and Quality of Service. The master of ceremonies punctuated and attenuated the first two terms at regular intervals during her announcements and introductions. Listening from the sidelines it was almost as though the words "quality" and "total quality management" had been struck out of her prompts and notes and replaced with "excellence" and "business excellence," with no particular rationale in term usage – if the word is mentioned a sufficient number of times and in a loud and authoritative voice, then people will start to accept and believe in the term.

This replacement language raises a number of issues, including:

1. If "quality" is replaced by "excellence" in the awards and models (e.g., UK Quality Awards to UK Business Excellence Awards, and Irish Quality Association to Excellence Ireland), for the purpose of consistency, should this not extend to *quality* in the European Foundation for Quality Management and

the British Quality Foundation? Another logical progression would be take out the word *quality* in the European Organization for Quality, American Society for Quality, International Academy for Quality, Institute for Quality Assurance, Quality Department, Quality Manager, Quality Policy, Advanced Quality Planning, Quality Plans, Quality Assurance, and Quality Control.

2. Many trees have been sacrificed in the cause of writing about quality issues in papers, conference proceedings, books, reports, etc. When the published material is studied, are the readers expected to override the word "quality" with "excellence"? This, as a logical development, would also involve some rebadging of tools, techniques, and systems which are commonly associated with quality, such as Excellence Function Deployment, the Seven Excellence Control Tools, Excellence Management Systems, Excellence Costing, Acceptable Excellence Level, Advanced Excellence Planning.

3. It also presents an interesting challenge for the writers and users of quality-related standards.

It has taken some considerable time to get across to employees within an organization and to the general public the importance of quality, its management and improvement. It can also be argued that this form of term replacement not only marginalizes quality but also reinforces the belief that TQM is a fad and quality and its management is no longer an important issue for business. A question which needs to be addressed is whether a new set of terms will undermine the undoubted progression which has been made in quality during the last two decades in the Western world. Whatever the sceptics think about TQM, continuous improvement, quality assurance, or whatever the approach is badged, there have been considerable improvements in the products and services which are used in everyday life. The following comment by Cole (1999) encapsulates this view: "It [the quality movement] left in its wake a greatly expanded infrastructure, a partial adaption of a variety of quality methodologies, and a renewed focus on how to serve customers better and how to use business processes to improve competitive performance." The words "business excellence" and latterly "excellence" in terms of the EFQM model have been in regular use for at least three years but it was only in the 1999 guidelines that a definition was put forward and the principles outlined. However, there is no rigorous definition of "excellence" and what, if any, is the difference from "business excellence." This leads to the view that it is just a play on words.

In the EFQM (1999) guidelines, "excellence" is defined as: "Outstanding practice in managing the organization and achieving results, all based on a set of 8 fundamental concepts." These fundamental concepts of excellence are: "Results orientation; customer focus; leadership and constancy of purpose; management by processes and facts; people development and involvement; continuous learning, innovation and improvement; partnership development; and public responsibility" (EFQM, 1999).

In the draft revision of the ISO 9000 series, the principles of quality management are defined in DIS ISO 9000 (2000) as: "Customer focus; leadership; involvement of people; process approach; system approach to management; continual improvement;

factual approach to decision making and mutually beneficial supplier relationship." Allowing for interpretation of these individual principles it can be seen that there is little or no difference between quality management and excellence. This lack of clear water in definitions is confirmed when comparison is made with the 10- and 14-point cluster summaries of the teachings of Crosby, Deming, Feigenbaum, and Juran and with what has been written about by writers such as Dale (1999) as the elements and practices of TQM. It should also be mentioned that there is no attempt to define excellence in DIS ISO 9000 (2000).

● Award Models ●

The Deming Application Prize

The Deming Prize was set up in honor of Dr. W.E. Deming, back in 1951, in recognition of his friendship and achievements in the cause of industrial quality. Deming, through the royalties received from the text of his "Eight Day Course on Quality Control" contributed to the initial funding of the Deming Prize. The prize was developed to ensure that good results are achieved through the implementation of company-wide control activities. It is based on the application of a set of principles and statistical techniques.

The author has led four missions of European manufacturing executives to Japan to study how they manage quality. It is clear from the evidence collected that the Deming Application Prize criteria have produced an almost standard method of managing quality; see Dale (1993). Compared to the West, there is much less company-to-company variation in the level of understanding of TQM and in the degree of attainment. This has helped to promote a deep understanding of TQM amongst all employees. Rather than argue about the merits of a particular approach, system, method or technique, the Japanese tend to discuss how to apply the TQM approach more vigorously through a common core level of understanding. The Deming Prize Committee (1998) outlines the following results which have been achieved in applying for the Deming Application Prize:

- Quality stabilization and improvement.
- Production improvement/cost reduction.
- Expanded sales.
- Increased profits.
- Thorough implementation of management plans/business results.
- Realization of top management's vision.
- Participation in and improvement of the organizational constitution.
- Heightened motivation to manage and improve as well as to promote standardization.
- Harnessing power from the bottom of the organization and enhanced morale.
- Establishment of various management systems and the total management system.

The original intention of the Deming Application Prize was to assess a company's use and application of statistical methods; later in 1964 it was broadened out to assess how TQM activities were being practiced. The award is managed by the Deming Application Prize Committee and administered by the Japanese Union of Scientists and Engineers (JUSE). It recognizes outstanding achievements in quality strategy, management, and execution. There are three separate divisions for the award. The Deming Application Prize, the Deming Prize for individuals, and the Quality Control Award for Factories. The Deming Application Prize is open to individual sites, a division of a company, small companies, and overseas companies. The Deming Prize was initially restricted to Japanese companies, but since 1984 has been open to companies outside of Japan. It is awarded each year and there is no limit on the number of winners. On the other hand, the committee reserves the right not to award the prize in any year. It is made to those "companies or divisions of companies that have achieved distinct performance improvement through the application of company-wide quality control" (Deming Prize Committee, 1998). Data collected by Dale (1993) suggest that it has become customary in Japan for organizations wishing to improve their performance to apply for the Deming Application Prize. This arises from the continuous improvements which are necessary to qualify for the award, along with the considerable prestige associated with winning the prize.

The Deming Application Prize is comprised of 10 primary categories (see table 12.2) which in turn are divided into 66 sub-categories. Each primary category has six sub-categories apart from quality assurance activities, which has 12 categories. There are no predesignated points allocated to the individual sub-categories. It is claimed that the reason for this is to maintain flexibility. However, discussions with JUSE indicate that the maximum score for each sub-category is 10 points. This checklist is prescriptive in that it identifies factors, procedures, techniques, and approaches that underpin TQM. The examiners for the Deming Application Prize are selected by JUSE from quality management experts from not-for-profit organizations. The applicants are required to submit a detailed document on each of the prize's criteria. The size of the report is dependent upon the number of employees in each of the applicant company's business units, including the head office. The Deming Prize Committee examines the application document and decides if the applicant is eligible for on-site examination. The committee chooses the two or more examiners to conduct this examination. Discussions by the author with JUSE suggest that considerable emphasis is placed on the on-site examination of the applicant organization's practices. It is also evident that the applicant organization relies a great deal on advice from the JUSE consultants. JUSE would also advise an organization when it should apply for the prize.

In 1996 the Japanese Quality Award was established. This is an annual award that recognizes the excellence of the management of quality. The concept of the award is similar to the EFQM model with emphasis placed on the measurement of quality with respect to customer, employees, and society. The eight criteria on which the award is based are similar to the MBNQA.

Table 12.2   Quality Award Criteria

(a)   *Deming Application Prize*
       Category

   Policies
   Organization
   Information
   Standardization
   Human resources development and utilization
   Quality assurance activities
   Maintenance/control activities
   Improvement
   Effects
   Future plans

(b)   *Malcolm Baldrige National Quality Award*

Category	Max.
Leadership	125
Strategic planning	85
Customer and market focus	85
Information and analysis	85
Human resource focus	85
Process management	85
Business results	450
TOTAL	1,000

(c)   *European Quality Award*

Category	Max.
Leadership	100
Policy and strategy	80
People	90
Partnerships and resources	90
Processes	140
Customer results	200
People results	90
Society results	60
Key performance results	150
TOTAL	1,000

The Malcolm Baldrige National Quality Award

The Malcolm Baldrige National Quality Improvement Act of 1987 – Public Law 100–107, signed by President Reagan on August 20, 1987 – established this annual US quality award, some 37 years after the introduction of the Deming Prize. The award is named after a former American Secretary of Commerce in the Reagan administration, Malcolm Baldrige. The Baldrige National Quality Program is the result of the cooperative efforts of government leaders and American business. The purposes of the award are to promote an understanding of the requirements for performance excellence and competitiveness improvements and to promote the sharing of information on successful performance strategies. The MBNQA guidelines contain detailed criteria that describe a world-class total quality organization. The criteria for performance excellence are available in business, education, and health care versions. The program and award are managed by the National Institute of Standards and Technology (NIST), an agency of the US Department of Commerce. The MBNQA recognizes US organizations for performance excellence.

Up to two awards can be given each year, out of the average number of 60 applicants in each of five categories: manufacturing businesses, service businesses, small business (defined as independently owned, and with not more than 500 employees), education organizations, and health care organizations. The latter two categories were introduced in 1999 and in that year half of the 52 applicants were from these two new categories. Since its inception, in a single year there have never been less than two and no more than five awards. Any for-profit domestic or foreign organization and not-for-profit education and health care organization located in the US that is incorporated or a partnership can apply. The applicant can be a whole firm or a legitimate business unit. The award is made by the President of the United States, with the recipients receiving a specially designed crystal trophy mounted with a gold-plated medallion. They may publicize and advertise their award provided they agree to share information and best practice about their successful quality management and improvement strategies with other American organizations.

Every Baldrige Award application is evaluated in seven major categories with a maximum total score of 1,000 (US Department of Commerce, 2000). These are: leadership (125 points), strategic planning (85 points), customer and market focus (85 points), information and analysis (85 points), human resource focus (85 points), process management (85 points), and business results (450) points) (see table 12.2 and figure 12.1). The seven criteria categories are sub-divided into 19 items and the items are further defined by 27 main areas to address. The seven categories embody 11 core values and concepts – customer-driven quality, leadership, continuous improvement and learning, valuing employees, response, design quality and prevention, long-range view of the future, management by fact, partnership development, public responsibility and citizenship, and results focus.

The criteria and processes are reviewed each year to ensure that they remain relevant and reflect current thinking and, based on experience during the intervening period, their wording and relative scores are updated. It should be mentioned that like the EFQM model the MBNQA criteria were developed originally by the business fraternity, management consultants, and academics.

Figure 12.1   Baldrige criteria for performance excellence framework: a systems perspective
Source: US Department of Commerce (2000).

The framework (see figure 12.1) has three basic elements: strategy and action plans, system, and information and analysis. Strategy and action plans are the set of customer- and market-focussed company-level requirements, derived from short- and long-term strategic planning, that must be done well for the company's strategy to succeed. They guide overall resource decisions and drive the alignment of measures for all work units to ensure customer satisfaction and market success. The system is comprised of the six Baldrige categories in the centre of figure 12.1 that define the organization, its operations, and its results. Information and analysis (category 4) are critical to the effective management of the company and to a fact-based system for improving company performance and competitiveness.

The evaluation by the Baldrige examiners is based on a written application (this summarizes the organization's practices and results in response to the Criteria for Performance Excellence) of up to 50 pages and looks for three major indications of success:

- *Approach*. Appropriateness of the methods, effectiveness of the use of the methods with respect to the degree to which the approach is systematic, integrated and consistently applied, embodies evaluation/improvement/learning cycles and is based on reliable information, and evidence of innovation and/or significant and effective adoption of approaches used in other types of applications or businesses.
- *Deployment*. The extent to which the approach is applied to all requirements of the item, including use of the approach in addressing business and item requirements and use of the approach by all appropriate work units.
- *Results*. The outcomes in achieving the purposes given in the item, including current performance, performance relative to appropriate comparisons and/or benchmarks, rate, breadth, and importance of performance improvements, demonstration of sustained improvement and/or sustained high-level performance and linkage of results to key performance measures.

The assessors will use these three dimensions to score an applicant. Most entrants tend to score within a fairly narrow range on "approach," and a few fall down on "deployment," but it is "results" that separate the real contenders from the rest. High scoring on "results," which are heavily weighted towards customer satisfaction, requires convincing data that demonstrates steady improvement over time, both internally and externally. Experience has shown that, even with a good internal approach and deployment strategy, it takes time for results to show.

Following a first-stage review of the application by quality management experts (i.e. leading management consultants, practitioners, and academics), a decision is made as to which organizations should receive a site visit. The site visits from a team of six to eight assessors take from two to five days. The visits are used to verify information provided in the application and clarify issues raised in the assessment of the application. The assessors have to be fair, honest, and impartial in their approach. A panel of judges reviews all the data, both from the written applications and site visits, and recommends the award recipients to the NIST. Quantitative results weight heavily in the judging process, so applicants must be able to prove that their quality efforts have resulted in sustained improvements. The thoroughness of the judging process means that applicants not selected as finalists get valuable written feedback on their strengths and areas for improvement. The detail of the report is related to the scores achieved and this is considered by many organizations to be valuable consultancy advice.

The European Quality Award

The European Quality Award was launched in October 1991 and first awarded in 1992. The award is assessed using the criteria of the EFQM excellence model. This was created by Europe's leading senior managers, academics, and consultants under the auspices of the EFQM and European Organization for Quality (EOQ) and supported by the European Commission. The EQA was broadened in 1996 to include public sector organizations and in 1997 a special category for small and medium-sized enterprises (SMEs; organizations of fewer than 150 employees) was introduced. According to the EFQM the EQA was intended to: "focus attention on business excellence, provide a stimulus to companies and individuals to develop business improvement initiatives and demonstrate results achievable in all aspects of organizational activity." Whilst only one European Quality Award is made each year for Company, Public Sector, and SME, several European Quality prizes are awarded to those companies who demonstrate excellence in the management of quality through a process of continuous improvement. The EQA is awarded to the best of the prizewinners in the categories of companies and public service organizations (i.e. health care, education, and local and central government), that is the most successful exponent of TQM in Europe. The winner of each of the three awards gets to retain the EQA trophy for a year and all prizewinners receive a framed holographic image of the trophy. The winners are expected to share their experiences at conferences and seminars organised by the EFQM.

The EFQM excellence model is intended to help the management of European organizations to better understand best practices and to support them in their leadership role. The model provides a generic framework of criteria that can be applied to any organization or its component parts. The model is based on eight fundamental concepts: results orientation; customer focus; leadership and constancy of purpose; management by processes and facts; people development and involvement; continuous learning, improvement, and innovation; partnership development; and public responsibility. The EQA is administered by the EFQM. The EFQM in developing the model and the EQA drew upon the experience in use and application of the MBNQA. The model (EFQM, 1999b) is structured on the following nine criteria which companies can use to assess and measure their own performance:

- *Leadership*. 100 points (10 percent). How leaders develop and facilitate the achievement of the mission and vision, develop values required for long-term success and implement these via appropriate actions and behaviors, and are personally involved in ensuring that the organization's management system is developed and implemented.

- *Policy and strategy*. 80 points (8 percent). How the organization implements its mission and vision via a clear stakeholder-focussed strategy, supported by relevant policies, plans, objectives, targets, and processes.

- *People*. 90 points (9 percent). How the organization manages, develops, and releases the knowledge and full potential of its people at an individual, team-based and organization-wide level, and plans these activities in order to support its policy and strategy and the effective operation of its processes.

- *Partnerships and Resources*. 90 points (9 percent). How the organization plans and manages its external partnerships and internal resources in order to support its policy and strategy and the effective operation of its processes.

- *Processes*. 140 points (14 percent). How the organization designs, manages, and improves its process in order to support its policy and strategy and fully satisfy and generate increasing value for its customers and other stakeholders.

- *Customer results*. 200 points (20 percent). What the organization is achieving in relation to its external customers.

- *People results*. 90 points (9 percent). What the organization is achieving in relation to its people.

- *Society results*. 60 points (6 percent). What the organization is achieving in relation to local, national and international society as appropriate.

- *Key Performance results*. 115 points (15 percent). What the organization is achieving in relation to its planned performance.

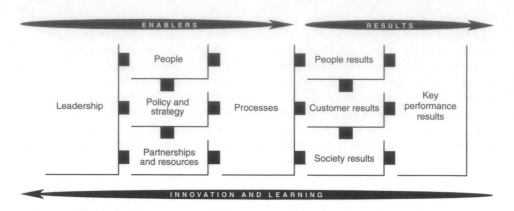

Figure 12.2
Source: EFQM (1999a).

The criteria, which are shown in table 12.2, are split into two groups, "Enablers" and "Results" (illustrated in figure 12.2). The feedback arrow indicates the importance of sharing knowledge, and encouraging learning and innovation. The scoring framework consists of 1,000 points with 500 points each being allocated to enablers and results. The nine elements of the model are further divided into 32 criteria. For example, leadership is divided into four parts and people into five parts. The model is based on the principle that processes are the means by which the organization harnesses and releases the talents of its people to produce results. In other words, the processes and the people are the enablers which provide the results. The results aspects of the model are concerned with what the organization has achieved and is continuing to achieve and the enablers with how the organization undertakes key activities and how the results are being achieved. The rationale for this is that "Excellent results with respect to Performance, Customers, People and Society are achieved through Leadership driving Policy and Strategy, People, Partnership and Resources, and Processes" (EFQM, 1999b). Each of these nine criteria can be used to assess the organization's progress to excellence.

The EFQM model is based on what is termed the RADAR logic – Results, Approach, Deployment, Assessment, and Review. The last four elements are used when assessing the enablers and the results element is obviously used to assess results. "Results" cover what an organization achieves and looks for: the existence of positive trends and sustained good performance; comparisons with previous, current, and future targets; comparison of results with competitors and best-in-class organizations; understanding the cause-and-effect relationships that prompt improvements; and that the scope of the results covers all relevant areas. The "Approach" covers what an organization plans to do along with the underlying reasons. It needs to be sound, systematic, appropriate, prevention-based, focussed on relevant needs and be integrated with normal operations and support organizational policy and strategy. "Deployment" is the extent to which the approach has been systematically deployed and implemented down and across the organization in all relevant areas.

"Assessment" and "review" relate to both approach and deployment. They will be subject to regular review cycles and measurement with appropriate learning and improvements planned and taken.

The scoring is done on a sliding scale over five levels – 0 percent range indicates no evidence, implementation or results; 25 percent represents just getting started; 50 percent indicates some progress being made; 75 percent indicates considerable progress; and 100 percent is indicative of excellence.

The EFQM model does not stipulate any particular techniques, methods or procedures which should be in place. The organizations that put themselves forward for the award are expected to have undertaken at least one self-assessment cycle. Following this a 75-page report is written for large companies and public sector organizations and 35 pages for SMEs. Once the application has been submitted to the EFQM headquarters, a team of four to eight fully trained independent assessors examines each application and decides whether or not to conduct a site visit. The assessors comprise mainly practising managers, but also include academics and quality professionals. The site visits provide the opportunity for the assessor to evaluate the application document, in particular deployment issues and check issues which are not clear from the document. Irrespective of whether or not the company is subject to a site visit, a feedback report is provided to the company that gives a general assessment of the organization, a scoring profile for the different criteria, and a comparison with the average scores of other applicants. For each part-criterion the key strengths and areas for improvement are listed. The feedback report for those organizations visited contains more detailed information. A jury, comprising seven members from business and academia, reviews the findings of the assessors to decide the European Quality prizewinners. The EQA is made to the organization judged to be the best of the prizewinners.

• The Self-Assessment Process •

Self-assessment uses one of the models underpinning an award to pinpoint improvement opportunities and identify new ways in which to encourage the organization down the road of organizational excellence. On the other hand, audits, with which self-assessment is often confused by the less advanced organizations with respect to their development of TQM, are carried out with respect to a quality system standard such as the ISO 9000 series; these, in the main, are looking for non-compliance and are assessing to see if the system and underlying procedures are being followed. In DIS ISO 9000 (2000) audit is defined as: "Systematic, independent and documented process for obtaining evidence and evaluating it objectively to determine the extent to which audit criteria are fulfilled."

The first European survey on self-assessment was completed by a research team drawn from UMIST (UK), the Ecole Supérieure de Commerce de Paris (France), the University of Valencia (Spain), Universität Kaiserslautern (Germany), the University of Limerick (Ireland), and Erasmus University Rotterdam (The Netherlands). The research which was carried out by postal questionnaire obtained data from 519 organizations and is reported by Van der Wiele et al. (1996a and 1996b). The five most important reasons for organizations starting self-assessment were to:

- Find opportunities for improvement.
- Create a focus on a TQM based on either the EFQM or MBNQA model criteria.
- Direct the improvement process.
- Provide new motivation for the improvement process.
- Manage the business.

This ranking provides a clear indication that internal issues are the most important motivation for organizations starting formal self-assessment. In some organizations a self-assessment process is introduced in response to changes in operating environment, company direction, and competitors. The need for improvement is now recognized in most cases, however well an organization may be doing. This is encapsulated by the comment: "Even if you are good now, you still have to get better."

After gaining the commitment of management to the self-assessment process and carrying out the necessary education and training, the following are the main steps which an organization should follow in setting about self-assessment:

- Assess what the organization has done well.
- Identify what aspects could be improved upon.
- Pinpoint gaps and what elements are missing.
- Develop an action plan to pick up the pace of the improvement process.

A key aspect of the process is take a good hard and honest look at the organization in order to identify its shortcomings, keeping in mind at all times a golfing analogy: "You will never become a better golfer by cheating." The process, on average, usually takes about three months.

There are several methods by which an organization may undertake self-assessment. Each method has advantages and disadvantages and an organization must choose the one(s) most suited to its circumstances, varying in complexity, rigor, and resources and effort. Some organizations prefer to go for a full award simulation approach after using a matrix chart or questionnaire for educational purposes. Other organizations choose a more incremental approach. In general, organizations develop from using a simple approach to one more complex, unless they have some external stimulus affecting the pace at which they address the process. These methods are outlined in detail in the EFQM *Assessing for Excellence: A Practical Guide for Self-Assessment* (EFQM, 1999a). The broad approaches which can be used separately or in combination are:

- *Award simulation.* This approach, which can create a significant workload for an organization, involves the writing of a full submission document (up to 75 pages) using the criteria of the chosen quality award model and employing the complete assessment methodology including the involvement of a team of trained assessors (internal) and site visits. The scoring of the application, strengths, and areas for improvement are then reported back and used by the management team for developing action plans.

  Some organizations have modified and developed the criteria of the chosen award model to: suit their own particular circumstances, provide more emphasis on areas which are critical to them, make the criteria easier to understand and use, and to reduce some of the effort in preparing the application document. In some cases a corporation or holding company has set a minimum score which each of its facilities has to achieve within a set time frame. Once an internal award has been achieved its continuation will require the successful completion of a subsequent assessment, usually within two years after the initial award has been granted.

- *Peer involvement.* This is similar to but less rigid than the award simulation approach in that there is no formal procedure for data collection. It gives freedom to the organization undertaking the self-assessment to pull together all relevant documents, reports and factual evidence in whatever format it chooses against the appropriate model being used.

- *Pro forma.* In this approach each criterion is described and the person(s) carrying out the assessment outlines the organization's strengths, areas for improvement, score, and evidence which supports the assessment in the space provided on the form. It is usual to use one or two pages per assessment criterion.

- *Workshop.* This approach is one in which managers are responsible for gathering the data and presenting the evidence to colleagues at a workshop. The workshop aims to reach a consensus score on the criterion and details of strengths and areas for improvement identified and agreed.

- *Matrix chart.* This requires the creation of an organization specific matrix or using one of those produced by one of the award bodies (e.g. Excellent North West). It involves rating a prepared series of statements, based on the appropriate Award model on a scoring scale. The statements are usually contained within a workbook which contains the appropriate instructions. The person(s) carrying out the assessment find the statement which is most suited to the organization and notes the associated score. The assessment usually takes about 30 minutes.

- *Questionnaire.* This is usually used to carry out a quick assessment of a department's or organization's standing in relation to the award model being used. It is useful for gathering a view on employee perceptions with respect to the criteria of the model being used. It involves answering a series of questions and statements, which are based on the criteria of the award model being used, using a yes/no format or a graduated response scale. It is usual to ask for the appropriate evidence underlying the answer. The workbook in which the questionnaire is contained usually encourages notes to be made on improvement actions. After the questionnaire is completed a report is prepared identifying strengths and areas for improvement based on the numerical scores and written comments.

The choice of approach is dependent upon the level of TQM maturity. Organizations with less experience should use the simpler methods, whilst those more advanced should adopt the more searching methods.

In recent times a number of self-assessment packages based on software have come on to the market which claim to simplify the self-assessment process and provide a benchmark of progress against other organizations. Typical examples are the British Quality Foundation's Assess Rapid Score (this employs a questionnaire which is completed and compiled by a team; it is useful when starting out on self-assessment and requires little previous experience) and Assess Valid Score (this is similar to Rapid Score but is more sophisticated with the ability to store strengths, opportunities for improvement, and evidence). These approaches require input from one individual, although they can be re-run by others and results compared to give a more comprehensive set of findings.

Assessment against a model, whether by internal or external assessors, has three discrete phases:

Phase 1   The gathering of data for each criterion.

Phase 2   The assessment of the data gathered.

Phase 3   Developing plans and actions arising from the assessment and monitoring the progress and effectiveness of the plan of action.

It is not the purpose of this chapter to regurgitate the details of a self-assessment process but simply to list the key issues which need to be considered by those organizations undertaking self-assessment for the first time:

- Reach agreement and be clear on the motivation for undertaking self-assessment and articulate the long-term expectations from the process.
- Senior management must be committed to the self-assessment process and be prepared to use the results to develop improvement plans.
- The people involved in the process need to be trained (i.e. training of assessors, training of employees who gather data, and the training of employees responsible for processes which are going to be assessed).
- Communicate within the business the reasons for and what is involved in self-assessment.
- Decide the self-assessment method(s) to be used.
- Plan the means of collecting the data:
  - decide the team and allocate roles and responsibilities for each criterion of the model;
  - develop a data collection methodology and identify data sources;
  - agree an activity schedule and manage as a project.
- Decide the best way of organizing the data which has been collected.
- Agree the means of coordinating the process.
- Present the data, reach agreement on strengths and areas for improvement, and agree the scores for the criteria. A decision needs to be made on whether or not

Increasing complexity
of approach

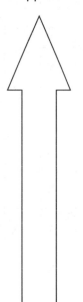

A   Award submission
B   Award simulation
c   Blue/Green cards (a measurement tool in assessing information
    presented in a report form)
D   Externally assessed award-based questionnaire, e.g., Excellence
    North West
    EFQM Report (without external assessment)
E   The Business Driver (simplified questionnaire based on the BEM)
F   Others (alternative models that have assisted in understanding the
    BEM and the development of company-based improvement models,
    e.g., British Gas Improvement Matrix)
G   A report based on the self-assessment criteria
H   Option Finder (flexible computer simulation questionnaire which
    aids the decision-making process – can be based on the BEM)
I   Assess (computer-simulated questionnaire based on the BEM)
J   Questionnaires (formulated and customized by individual
    organizations when addressing the self-assessment process)
K   Pro formas (used in conjunction with workshops)
L   Workshops
M   A3 Matrix (used as an educational tool in workshops – provides an
    overview of criteria incorporated in the BEM)

Figure 12.3   Approaches used in the self-assessment process

to publicize the scores of individual departments, if the assessment has been
done on a departmental basis.

- Feedback to facilitate organizational learning.
- Prioritize the improvements, develop an action plan, and ensure that the ownership is with appropriate people.
- Regular review of progress against the plan.
- Ensure that self-assessment is linked with the business planning process. This is
  important to ensure that the areas for improvement are turned into actions
  which are implemented. Therefore only if an organization has a business plan
  that is known to its various business units, and that business plan has specified
  within it items for improvement related to whatever model is being used, will
  self-assessment be considered a success.
- Repeat the self-assessment.

Ritchie and Dale (2000) point out that organizations approaching self-assessment
can experience difficulties in planning the process and allocating the appropriate
resources. They have developed a "model," in the form of two matrices which shows
the characteristics and level of TQM understanding that an organization should
demonstrate before employing any self-assessment approach. The prerequisite

Self-assessment approaches

Prerequisite characteristics (of company/business unit)	A	B	C	D	E	F	G	H	I	J	K	L	M
• Long-term vision	✓	✓	✓	✓									
• Ability to see the "bigger picture"	✓	✓	✓	✓									✓
• Supportive directors	✓	✓	✓	✓									
• Open-minded management	✓	✓	✓	✓			✓						
• Commitment and involvement at all levels in the process	✓	✓	✓	✓	✓	✓	✓						
• Knowledge of TQM toools and techniques	✓	✓	✓	✓	✓	✓							
• Ongoing continuous improvement strategies	✓	✓	✓	✓	✓	✓	✓						
• Ongoing performance monitoring processes	✓	✓	✓	✓	✓	✓	✓	✓	✓	✓	✓		
• Cross-functional integration	✓	✓	✓	✓	✓	✓	✓	✓	✓	✓	✓		
• Good communication networks	✓	✓	✓	✓	✓	✓	✓						
• Possess an up-to-date working knowledge of all systems and processes	✓	✓	✓	✓	✓	✓	✓	✓	✓	✓	✓	✓	
• Corporate culture that welcomes change	✓	✓	✓	✓	✓		✓						✓
• Identification of "sponsors" for analysis	✓	✓	✓	✓			✓		✓	✓	✓	✓	✓
• Trained assessors	✓	✓	✓	✓				✓	✓	✓	✓	✓	✓

Educated staff regarding the self-assessment process	✓	✓	✓	✓	✓	✓	✓	✓	✓	✓	✓	✓
Welcome objective views on performance of business and processes	✓	✓	✓	✓	✓	✓						
Advocate the development of teams and quality groups	✓	✓	✓									
Computer literacy							✓	✓				
Acknowledgment of the benefits of the self-assessment process	✓	✓	✓	✓	✓	✓	✓	✓	✓	✓	✓	✓
Ability to identify where self-assessment fits in with business strategy	✓	✓	✓	✓	✓	✓	✓	✓	✓	✓	✓	✓
Incorporation of self-assessment results into business plans	✓	✓	✓	✓	✓	✓	✓	✓	✓	✓		
Coordinating self-assessment for the purpose of continuously improving the business processes	✓	✓	✓	✓	✓	✓	✓	✓	✓	✓	✓	✓

Figure 12.4 The minimum characteristics that a company should exhibit, pre-adoption of prescribed approaches to self-assessment

characteristics change depending on the technicality of the approach involved. The ones detailed are those that an organization needs to actively pursue and practice in order to successfully adopt self-assessment. This "model" is summarized in figures 12.3 and 12.4.

● Success Factors in Self-Assessment ●

A key to the success of self-assessments is that the assessments have to be written down by the assessors. If the assessments are purely verbal then they will have far less power. Something written down has a life of its own and it can be referred to again and again. It can also be related to a business plan and to a subsequent improvement plan and can be part of a PDCA cycle. Written assessments also mean they will be taken much more seriously by both assessors and the assessed.

Ritchie and Dale (2000) have identified the following criteria which are necessary for a successful self-assessment process:

- Gaining commitment and support from all levels of staff.
- Action being taken from previous self-assessments.
- Awareness of the use of the model as a measurement tool.
- Incorporation of self-assessment into the business planning process.
- Not allowing the process to be "added on" to employees' existing workload.
- Developing a framework for performance monitoring.

Van der Wiele et al. (1996a), in summarizing the findings of their survey, point out that self-assessment has a greater chance of success if the following conditions exist:

- Senior management are committed to the process and get involved.
- The Business Unit (BU) management team develop an improvement plan from the outcomes.
- The outcomes from the self-assessment are linked to the business planning process.
- Senior management monitor targets for the improvement plan developed.
- The management team of a BU present their plan to the senior management.
- The people who undertake the self-assessment will need relevant training.

It is always be difficult to clarify the impact of self-assessment on an organization's business results. However, those organizations with considerable experience of self-assessment do have a very positive perception of the impact of the techniques on their business performance.

● Difficulties with Self-Assessment ●

There are a number of problems that hinder the self-assessment process. These are nicely summarized in table 12.3.

Table 12.3 Difficulties experienced with the self-assessment process

Difficulties

- Lack of commitment and enthusiasm
- The time-consuming nature of the process
- Not knowing where to start
- Selling the concept to the staff as something other than an "add-on" to their existing duties
- People not realizing the need for documented evidence
- Lack of resources: time, manpower, finance
- Maintaining the self-assessment skills of the assessors
- Lack of cross-functional integration between departments and units
- Getting the assessment done in time to link it into the business plans

Source: Ritchie and Dale (2000)

Research carried out by Dale and Coulambidou (1995) indicates that the problems experienced are created by a lack of senior management support, lack of ability to plan self-assessment effectively, and a low level of TQM maturity.

● Summary ●

Self-assessment on a systematic basis by an organization against one of the models described in this chapter can prove extremely useful in assisting it to improve its business performance. However, if used in an artless manner by organizations just starting out on the quality journey and without an adequate vision of TQM by the senior management team it will not provide the necessary results and may even push the organization down blind alleys. It can also lead to the risk of gathering a considerable amount of data which is then not able to be put to effective use. When used in such a naive way the emphasis tends to be on training staff as assessors, assembling data, preparing long reports, and assessment and annual points scoring, without the development of the all-important action plans and the solving of the day-to-day quality problems. The focus tends to be on meeting a minimum set number of points for an internal award and what activities should be concentrated on to increase the score, rather than what are the priorities to increase the velocity of the improvement process. As a consequence the ongoing, day-to-day quality problems which beset the organization will not be resolved. It is also observed that senior management become obsessive about gaining some form of award (regional or national) within a set time frame.

In using self-assessment it is important that management attention is focussed on the identification and implementation of planned and prioritized improvements and not on the mechanics and techniques of the assessment process or with the obsessive scoring of points. If this is not done they will run into the problems of self-deception.

The benefit of using self-assessment against one of the recognized models is not the winning of the award but its adoption as a methodology to assess progress, using appropriate diagnostics, and identify opportunities for improvement, not forgetting the need to satisfy and delight customers. This measurement of progress on a regular basis and comparison of scores from assessments is a confirmation to the management team that real improvement and achievement has taken place. The quantification of performance in terms of numbers is important for senior management. It is also important that the management team of the organization buy in to the self-assessment process and are enthusiastic about its use. This applies, in particular, to developing action plans to address the outcomes from the self-assessment. They must also be clear on their objectives for self-assessment. When used in the correct manner, the challenge, effort, and involvement help to generate an environment in which it is enjoyable to work.

It would appear that the MBNQA and EQA have generated an industry of its own in running training courses and advising how to understand the assessment process and detail requirements of the award criteria. In organizations this often creates an internal expert who, after intensive external training, applies the knowledge gained in providing advice to the local management team as to how each of the individual criteria can be interpreted and applied to their own particular area of activity. A danger inherent in this is that the "expert" keen to demonstrate their knowledge ends up in detailed discussion on the mechanics of self-assessment and consequently the purpose of self-assessment is often lost in the ensuing debate. Another worrying trend is that some organizations seem to believe that using one of the models as the standard and almost as a checklist approach will automatically lead them to TQM. In such organizations people will continually use the terms "excellence model" and "quality award" almost as a comfort factor to ensure that all will be right with their continuous improvement efforts. There is also the danger of treating self-assessment against one of the recognized models as a panacea, which is clearly not the case.

An organization has to be fairly advanced in TQM to be able to use self-assessment in an effective manner; what is not in place cannot be assessed. Registration to ISO 9001 can be a useful first step towards TQM; however, there is a large gap between these requirements and what is portrayed in the EFQM and MBNQA models. Those organizations which have recently acquired ISO 9001 registration and are not advanced in their quality management activity would benefit from studying one of these models to gain an insight into what is necessary in order to develop a TQM approach to managing the business. Having identified the gap, they need to look at methods of introducing the basics of TQM, such as a consultancy package, the teachings of the quality management gurus, or a simple improvement framework. Once the basics are in place, then the organization should return to self-assessment to assess progress, and identify the next steps.

NOTE

1   Throughout this chapter TQM is used, rather than Excellence or Business Excellence. The rationale for this is explained in the section "Quality, TQM, and Excellence" on pages 261 to 263.

REFERENCES

Blodgett, N. (1999). Service organizations increasingly adopt Baldrige model. *Quality Progress*, December, 74–6.

Brown, G. (1996). How to determine your quality quotient: Measuring your company against the Baldrige criteria. *Journal for Quality and Participation*, June, 82–8.

Cole, R.E. (1991). Comparing the Baldrige and Deming awards. *Journal for Quality and Participation*, July–August, 94–104.

Cole, R.E. (1999). *Managing Quality Fads*. New York: Oxford University Press.

Conti, T. (1993). *Building Total Quality: A Guide to Management*. London: Chapman and Hall.

Conti, T. (1997). *Organizational Self-Assessment*. London: Chapman and Hall.

Coulambidou, L., and Dale, B.G. (1995). The use of quality management self-assessment in the UK: A state of the art study. *Quality World Technical Supplement*, September, 110–18.

Dale, B.G. (1993). The key features of Japanese total quality control: Quality and reliability. *Engineering International*, 9, 3, 169–78.

Dale, B.G. (ed.) (1999). *Managing Quality*, 3rd edn. Oxford: Blackwell Publishers

Deming Prize Committee (1998). *The Deming Prize Guide for Overseas Companies*. Tokyo: Union of Japanese Scientists and Engineers.

DIS ISO 9000 (2000). *Quality Management Systems: Fundamentals and Vocabulary*. Geneva: International Organization for Standardization.

EFQM (European Foundation for Quality Management) (1999a). *Assessing for Excellence: A Practical Guide for Self-Assessment*. Brussels: EFQM.

EFQM (European Foundation for Quality Management) (1999b). *The EFQM Excellence Model*. Brussels: EFQM.

European Quality (2000). National Quality Awards: Annual Review. *European Quality*, 7, 1, 14–29.

Hakes, C. (2000). *The Business Excellence Assessment Handbook*, 5th edn. Bristol: British Quality Centre.

Hillman, P.G. (1994). Making self-assessment successful. *The TQM Magazine*, 6, 3, 29–31.

Lascelles, D.M., and Peacock, R. (1996). *Self-Assessment for Business Excellence*. Berkshire: McGraw Hill.

Nabitz, U., Quaglia, G., and Wangen, P. (1999). EFQM's New Excellence model. *Quality Progress*, October, 118–20.

Nakhai, B., and Neves, J. (1994). The Deming, Baldrige and European quality awards. *Quality Progress*, April, 33–7.

Porter, L., and Tanner, S. (1996). *Assessing Business Excellence*. London: Butterworth Heinemann.

Ritchie, L., and Dale, B.G. (2000). Self-assessment using the business excellence model: A study of practice and process. *International Journal of Production Economics* (awaiting publication).

Sherer, F. (1995). Winning the European Quality Award: A Xerox perspective. *Managing Service Quality*, 5, 2, 28–32.

Soin, S. (1992). *Total Quality Control, Essentials: Key Elements, Methodologies, and Managing for Success*. New York: McGraw Hill.

Steeples, M.M. (1993). *The Corporate Guide to the Malcolm Baldrige National Quality Award*. Milwaukee: ASQC Quality Press.

US Department of Commerce (2000). *Baldrige National Quality Program 2000: Criteria for Performance Excellence*. Gaithersburg: United States Department of Commerce, National Institute of Standards and Technology.

Van der Wiele, T., Williams, R.T., Dale, B.G., Kolb, F., Luzon, D.M., Wallace, M., and Schmidt, A. (1995). Quality Management Self-assessment: An examination in European business. *Journal of General Management*, 22, 1, 48–67.

Van der Wiele, T., Williams, R.T., Dale, B.G., Kolb, F., Luzon, D.M., Wallace, M., and Schmidt, A. (1996). Self-assessment: A study of progress in Europe's leading organizations in quality management practices. *International Journal of Quality and Reliability Management*, 13, 1, 84–104.

13

Best Practices for Advancing Women in Business Organizations

MARY C. MATTIS

● Introduction ●

Today, competitive advantage for business organizations derives less from manufacturing processes and low costs and more from increasing the quality of the people who work in and lead corporations and firms. Human capital – creativity, analytical skills, and leadership ability of employees – is the new competitive advantage. To succeed domestically or globally companies must attract and retain the most talented employees. The demographics of today's US labor market dictate that in every industry, one of the most important new organizational goals will be for companies to attract, retain, and advance women to significant leadership roles. Research shows that the ability of companies to achieve this goal is contingent on a transformation of the organizational culture and work environment of the business enterprise as we have known it. New policies, programs, and practices are required to create a more inclusive workplace. Corporate gender initiatives that go far beyond mainstream practices, with demonstrated results, to achieve these goals – "best practices," as they are commonly referred to – are the subject of this chapter.

● Why Companies Need Gender Diversity Initiatives ●

The business case

Companies and firms can no longer afford to ignore the reality that, literally and figuratively, women mean business. Companies need women to do business and to compete domestically and globally. Women have demonstrated that they "mean business" when it comes to their career commitment. Women are in the workforce for

the long run; as a consequence, they have increased expectations of their employers.
   Demographics support the contention that women mean business for companies
and firms.

- In 1999, women accounted for 46.5 percent of the total US labor force participants. (US Bureau of Labor Statistics, 1999).

- Sixty percent of women age 16 and over were labor force participants in 1999,
  up from 38 percent in 1960 (US Department of Labor, 2000).

- In 1999, women held 49 percent of managerial and professional specialty positions (US Bureau of Labor Statistics, 1999).

- Over the last two decades, there has been especially rapid growth in the number
  of women-owned businesses in the US. As of 1997, there were 8.5 million
  women-owned businesses in the US, employing over 23.7 million people and
  generating close to $3.1 trillion in sales. One in eight (13 percent) of women-
  owned businesses in the US is owned by a woman of color. These 1,067,000
  minority women-owned firms employ nearly 1.7 million people and generate
  $184.2 billion in sales. Women-owned businesses represent both a potential
  competitive threat and a key customer focus for major corporations/firms
  (National Foundation of Women Business Owners, 1999).

- Aside from their role as business owners, women make more than 85 percent
  of total household purchasing decisions, including such major items as homes,
  cars, vacations, and home improvement (Barstow, 2000). Improving customer
  focus demands that businesses hire and retain people who reflect the
  demographics of the consumer base, especially at senior levels to provide leadership.

Demographic data also supports the contention that women mean business when it
comes to their commitment to lifelong careers. Since the 1960s women have increased
their preparedness for lifelong careers, including careers in business:

- Women now earn more than half the bachelor's and master's degrees awarded
  every year and one-third of MBAs (Digest of Education Statistics, 1999).
- Half of the undergraduate degrees in business and management, accounting,
  and mathematics go to women (Digest of Education Statistics, 1999).

A glass ceiling continues to block women's advancement to senior levels

To date, US companies have been more successful at attracting women to their workforce than at advancing them to meaningful leadership roles. Catalyst's annual cen-
suses of women's representation in corporate management and governance, along

with other studies, support the contention that a glass ceiling continues to operate to the detriment of women's advancement in US companies/firms (Catalyst, 1999; Catalyst, 1997: data in this 1997 report are drawn from 1994–5 US Census Bureau data taken from the Merged Earnings Files of the 1994–5 Current Population Survey):

- In 1999, women held just 11.2 percent of corporate board seats and just 11.9 percent of corporate officer positions in Fortune 500 companies; the change in women's representation on Fortune 500 boards between 1998 and 1999 was only 0.1 percent.

- Women hold only 8.5 percent of board seats in Fortune 501–1000 companies. More than twice as many Fortune 501–1000 companies do not have any women on their boards as do Fortune 500 companies (190 vs. 81).

- Women of color hold just 159, or 1.9 percent, of 8,463 board seats among Fortune 1000 companies for which such data was available.

- Women hold 3.3 percent of top-earner spots in Fortune 1000 companies and represent just 5.1 percent of individuals holding the most powerful and prestigious titles of chairman, CEO, vice-chairman, president, COO, SEVP, and EVP.

- Even when they achieve the rank of corporate officer, few women hold line jobs – those positions with profit-and-loss or direct client responsibility: among corporate officers men hold 93.2 percent of line jobs. The fact that, for whatever reason, women's experience continues to be largely on the staff side of business organizations, limits their potential to obtain powerful and prestigious titles and commensurate salaries.

- At the managerial level generally, for every dollar earned by white men, white women earned 74 cents; African American women earned 58 cents; Hispanic women earned 48 cents; and Asian/other women earned 67 cents.[1]

The glass ceiling also operates in other countries where recent data on women's advancement has been compiled. Catalyst's research in Canada, and in the UK (in collaboration with Opportunity Now) provides the following comparative data:

- Women make up 45 percent of the Canadian labor force and 32 percent of managers. In contrast, only 14 percent of senior private sector managers are women and women hold just 6.2 percent of seats in the Financial Post 500 companies (Catalyst, 1998).

- In the UK, 72 percent of women of working age are classed as economically active but women hold just 22 percent of management jobs and only 9.6 percent of board directorships in public and private organizations and institutions of higher education (Catalyst and Opportunity Now, 2000).

Catalyst and other researchers have identified the following as the most powerful barriers to women's career advancement (Catalyst, 1998):

- Negative assumptions and stereotypes about women, their abilities, and their commitment to careers.
- Perceptions that women's style of leadership does not fit with generally accepted norms.
- Lack of career planning that leaves women with a limited breadth of exposure to their organizations, in particular, lack of general management and line experience.
- Lack of mentoring and exclusion from informal networks, where men have typically learned the unwritten rules of success.
- Failure to make managers accountable for advancing women.
- Absence of or inadequate succession planning processes.
- "Negative mentoring" and self-selection that channels women into staff roles.
- Appraisal and compensation systems that are not uniform for men and women.
- Corporate systems designed prior to women's large-scale entry into the workplace, such as benefits systems and productivity measures that don't take into account new policies such as flexible work arrangements and the increased number of dual-career couples in the workplace.
- Other forms of "cultural discouragement," like a work environment that values long hours over actual performance or that offers limited support for work–family initiatives and limited commitment to diversity programs in general.
- Discrimination and sexual harassment.

One researcher has referred to the everyday manifestations of these barriers as "micro-inequities" (Rowe, 1990). No one of the omissions or commissions in women's work experience may seem consequential at the time of its occurrence; however, the accumulation of these micro-inequities over time is corrosive to women's morale, productivity, and ultimate career advancement.

The pipeline is leaking

Business organizations' failure to address the glass ceiling is driving turnover of women, who leave their organizations for more supportive work environments and better opportunities for advancement. Turnover studies on women who voluntarily leave their employers – "regretted losses," as they are called by some companies – show that most women who have left are pursuing better career opportunities. They are not choosing family over a career, as companies often erroneously conclude.

In today's robust economy, companies have to be concerned about recruiting the best and brightest women; but they have to be more concerned about holding on to them. Even highly technical industries and engineering companies, for whom recruitment of women is much more difficult, are increasingly aware of the need to retain the relatively scarce group of technical women they have recruited at considerable expense.

The business case for stemming the turnover of women in business organizations is compelling. Studies have shown that the cost of replacing exempt employees, especially senior managers and highly marketable personnel such as high-tech professionals and engineers, is substantial. Other "invisible" costs of turnover include the impact on the morale and productivity of work units, discontinuity of customer/client service with resultant negative impact on customer/client satisfaction, and lost of intellectual capital with the associated possibility that a former employee may become a future competitor.

While corporate and firm leaders today may embrace the need to retain and advance women in their organizations, traditional methods of achieving these goals with a white male workforce do not necessarily work with women and other nontraditional employee groups. Dynamics in the corporate culture and work environment that have favored talented men often create conditions that disadvantage talented women: formal programs are undermined by male stereotypes and assumptions about women's suitability to be selected for them; and informal opportunities – often the route to the top for talented men – are largely unavailable to women due to male discomfort with coaching, mentoring, and sponsoring women for key opportunities. New approaches are needed.

American business organizations measure what they value. Like other business results, leveraging their investment in people needs to be a key concern of companies and professional firms. As a consequence, within the broader arena of human resources management, benchmarking outcomes with regard to the retention, development, and advancement of women in order to identify best practices is becoming integral to an increasing number of leading business organizations.

● What are Best Practices? ●

A best practice is a context-specific solution to a problem or barrier, in this case, a problem or barrier related to the retention and advancement of women professionals and managers. Organizational practices, programs or policies are designated as "best practices" when they are judged by experts to be above and beyond mainstream, widely implemented practices, programs, and policies. Before and after quantitative and/or qualitative measures related to the goals of the practice should be used to evaluate whether a practice is effective at accomplishing its stated objectives.

Best practices don't exist in isolation or out of context. Since policies, programs, and practices are designed to address context-specific problems or barriers, there can be more than one "best" practice for addressing, for example, disproportionate turnover of female employees, which requires different solutions in corporations than in professional firms. It follows that while one organization's practice can be useful as a guide to addressing another organization's problems or barriers, it will need to be tailored to the second organization's specific context. Best practices are shaped by several factors: industry, organization size and market reach, structural considerations, etc. What works in one company or industry may not work in another.

Best practices evolve and change. What worked several years ago may not work now. Catalyst's experience over two decades evaluating corporate/firm initiatives points to several trends in this regard:

- Today, most diversity initiatives are designed to address diversity in the broadest sense, as opposed to a singular focus on gender issues.
- Stand-alone programs are less likely to be regarded as cutting-edge, in part because organizations have a more sophisticated understanding of diversity, including the broad range of interdependent issues that are encompassed under this heading.
- Multi-faceted diversity initiatives linking a number of best practices have become the norm, rather than the exception, as they were a decade ago.
- There is increased recognition of the need to tie diversity strategies to strategic business initiatives and to develop and articulate the business case for diversity initiatives.
- As companies/firms have gained awareness and expertise around issues presented by diversity in the workplace, initiatives that were once regarded as best practices have become mainstream.

Benchmarking best practices to retain and advance women

Typically companies benchmark industry peers or other organizations that have been reported to have best practices that are effective in enhancing gender diversity. However, most companies have policies, programs, and practices within their own walls that could be identified, rewarded, and held up to other business units for replication as practices that, relative to others within the organization, are internal "best" practices for reducing turnover and promoting advancement of women.

Companies/firms that benchmark their gender diversity outcomes against other organizations and/or among business units internally, generally focus on:

- Establishing the current status of women professionals and managers relative to their male counterparts in terms of: recruitment and retention rates; functional status in the organization and breadth of experience; access to developmental opportunities; compensation; time in grade; and promotion rates.
- Creating the business case for gender diversity including: cost of replacement and other hidden costs of voluntary turnover of valued employees; opportunity costs of failure to attract and retain women; value added to customer focus, market share, and product/services development.
- Tying diversity strategies to short- and long-term business imperatives and strategic business plans/alliances.
- Identifying and recruiting the best talent.
- Eliminating barriers to success.
- Enhancing access to opportunities.
- Evaluating the effectiveness of initiatives in place, and recommendations for revised or additional approaches.

Benchmarking is not an end in itself but a means to an end: to create a more inclusive corporate culture where women, among others, have equal access to resources and opportunities to enable them to succeed.

● Corporate/Firm Initiatives for Retaining and Advancing Women ●

Creating real change for women – change that will produce demonstrable results for women and for an organization's bottom line – is difficult and cannot be achieved by implementing a few isolated "women's programs." The underlying issues are almost always deeply embedded in the organization's culture and only an initiative aiming at systematic change will enable companies to truly capitalize on the talents of women.

Most successful gender diversity initiatives move through three stages: (1) establishment of a strong foundation based on leadership and a clear business case; (2) identification of barriers and opportunities for women through both quantitative and qualitative data collection and analysis; (3) identification and implementation of solutions through internal and external benchmarking; and (4) development of systems for measuring change and evaluating the effectiveness of solutions.

Characteristics of successful change initiatives outlined in this chapter include:

- Motivation and rationale linked to business strategy and profitability.
- Support from the highest levels of the organization.
- Built-in communication plan clearly stating how the best practices are linked to business issues.
- Built-in accountability mechanisms to ensure that initiatives cannot be ignored or undermined.

The best practices outlined below were selected from a range of initiatives that have been identified and recognized by Catalyst and other organizations as exceptional approaches to retaining and advancing women. Each example focusses on an initiative that was designed to address one of the specific barriers to women's retention and advancement discussed above.

Corporate initiative: benchmarking

BANK OF MONTREAL'S ADVANCEMENT OF WOMEN INITIATIVE

Early in 1991, F. Anthony Comper, the bank's president and chief operating officer, commissioned the Employee Task Force on the Advancement of Women to identify barriers to female advancement and to devise strategies to break them down. The mandate of the task force was to "identify the constraints to the advancement of women" and to "recommend goals and measures."

The bank's investigative phase broke new ground as part of a gender diversity initiative. The task force reviewed the bank's human resource database, interviewed 270 people, conducted 11 focus groups, and surveyed 500 former managers. But the most important thing it did was a survey of 15,000 women and men employees, asking such questions as "What is the number 1 thing that's holding women back?" and "What would you like the bank to do to help you advance?" The key finding from the task force: "Women were not advancing because of stereotypical attitudes, myths of conventional wisdom."

The task force set out on a "myth-busting" venture, countering each of the stereotypes with facts gleaned from the human resources files. The most common erroneous assumptions about women's failure to advance in the bank's executive ranks, as revealed by the survey, were:

- Women at the bank were either too young or too old to compete equitably with men.
- Because of child-rearing responsibilities, women are less committed to their careers.
- Women do not have the educational credentials to compete with men.

The best practices presented below were collected by Catalyst and approved by the companies for reprinting. Many result from the Catalyst Award evaluation process, undertaken annually, and currently headed by Marcia Kropf, VP, Research and Information Services, and Paulette Gerkovich, Director, Research. Prior to their tenure, the author of this chapter headed the awards evaluation process at Catalyst for eight years. Meredith Moore, Senior Associate, Research, compiled these practices into a database for internal use at Catalyst and developed a format for presenting them in a uniform fashion. Best practices used here are excerpted from *Cracking the Glass Ceiling: Catalyst's Research on Women in Corporate Management 1995–2000.*

- Women don't have "the right stuff" to compete for senior jobs.
- Women haven't been in the pipeline long enough to advance to senior levels.
- Time will take care of the problem.

The task force learned that these myths were false and required refutation. As a result of its rigorous research, the bank was able to demonstrate that women are equally as qualified, equally as educated, and equally as committed to their careers as men. The survey also uncovered similarities in the approaches men and women felt the bank should take to help them advance. Both talked about needing flexibility in scheduling work hours, both wanted more control over their careers, more information about management vacancies, and more access to mentoring.

To build a foundation for eliminating barriers to women's advancement, the task force issued a report detailing the information about women employees at the bank that they had compiled. Based on the survey research and the analysis of demographic data on male and female employees, the report used a myths-and-realities approach and was distributed to all staff. It included this information:

- On average, women and men are the same age.
- Although women have babies and more responsibility for child-rearing, they have longer service records at the bank, except at senior levels.

- An analysis of performance appraisals revealed that a higher percentage of women than men were ranked in the top two tiers of each level.
- The percentage of women in senior positions had grown so slowly – 1 percent a year – that it was not practical to wait for time to take care of the problem.

The initiative that resulted from the bank's research and communication efforts has several components that fall under the categories of training, career planning and performance review, and flexible work arrangements.

- *Training.* The bank has incorporated "Managing Diversity" and "Men and Women as Colleagues" into its management training curriculum and added a leadership curriculum to help managers develop a leadership style that emphasizes coaching and teamwork. It has also instituted several accreditation programs to help men and women gain credentials that will help them advance. The program addresses historical inequities in employment, in which women were concentrated in personal banking, with limited authority on how much they could lend. The bank's goal is for half the trainees in each program to be female.

- *Career planning.* Among programs that were implemented are: (1) computer-assisted self-learning courses for branch staff to increase their knowledge and skill base and become eligible for more senior positions; (2) a career information network that provides listings of job vacancies for mid-to-senior management positions; (3) a job posting system for regional positions in lower-level jobs.
  Managers and supervisors, starting at the executive level, establish annual hiring, retention, and advancement targets, and they determine how flexibility will fit into that plan. They review and update business plans quarterly.

- *Performance reviews.* Annual performance reviews include each manager's progress in reaching individual goals, as well as his or her contribution to workplace equality. Employees rate their managers on their management of flexibility.

- *Flexible work arrangements.* Employees are able to work out flexible arrangements with supervisors. "Flexing Your Options," a 100-page handbook distributed to all employees and managers, offers detailed advice on how to implement a flexible work arrangement including common questions asked by managers and how to develop a proposal for a flexible schedule, and describes varying types of arrangements. The bank assesses the impact of flexible arrangements on work. For example, the impact of a work-at-home program on translators was measured, with a finding that the amount translated by those working at home was either the same or exceeded the amount translated by persons working at an office site.

Results. In six years, from late 1991 to late 1997, the representation of women in executive ranks increased from 9 percent to 24 percent. Among senior vice-presidents, women have increased from 3 percent to 27 percent, and their representation among senior management has increased from 13 percent to 26 percent.

Corporate initiatives: moving women into line positions

CONSOLIDATED EDISON: MANAGEMENT INTERN PROGRAM

Consolidated Edison – Con Ed, as it is referred to by residents of New York City and Westchester County, NY – is one of the largest publicly owned gas and electric utilities in the United States. Motivated by changing workforce demographics and a bottom-line concern to develop and diversify management talent, Con Edison created a comprehensive strategy called "Commitment to Women With Technical Talent." The strategy was designed to recruit, develop, and promote qualified women. The centerpiece of this strategy is the Management Intern Program, which was launched in 1981 to intensify efforts to recruit women and to develop future female managers of the company. The initiative has continued to evolve. In 1993, Con Edison divided the program into several organization-based programs:

- the Field Supervisory Program for Engineers
- the Assistant Engineer Program
- the Gas Operation Management Development Program
- the Information Resources Assistant Computer Analyst Program
- the Business Intern Program (organization-wide).

Another recent change is in the administration of the program. The Management Intern Program was once run solely by the College Programs Department. Now, the Recruitment and Staffing Department hires and places the interns, and Con Ed's Learning Center is responsible for the administration of the program. Mentors assist the director of the Learning Center by providing feedback to evaluate the effectiveness of the program.

The programs generally recruit between 10 and 20 students annually. Managers conduct campus interviews with potential candidates, who are assessed according to skills identified by the Competitive Skills Team. The managers in the recruiting and staffing department select candidates for the program. They are looking for technical competence, leadership potential, and communication skills. The Gas Operations Management and the Business Intern Programs both run for two years, while the Assistant Engineer and Field Supervisory Intern Programs take three years. Each program involves several short-term, rotational assignments where the interns receive on-the-job supervision and mentoring from an assigned advisor.

After the first year, engineers go into a three-year position as first-line supervisors followed by three years in central operations. For interns who are not engineers, a one-year administrative training job follows the Management Intern Program. That year is spent in a field assignment in operations. These programs provide participants with a wide range of experience and expose them to the field environment.

Each intern is assigned a mentor from mid- or upper-level management who is responsible for tracking the intern's progress. Managers meet regularly with interns to provide guidance and assistance. The assignments are evaluated by a Functional Review Committee made up of senior-level managers and chaired by general managers. The program administrator is part of every review committee.

Results. While women make up only 17 percent of engineering students nationally, they make up more than 30 percent of the participants of the Management Intern Program. There has been a great demand for program graduates from departments. And graduates are placed into departments upon completion of the program.

CORNING INCORPORATED: WOMEN IN MANUFACTURING INITIATIVE

Corning's Women in Manufacturing Initiative (WIM) is specifically designed to increase and advance the pool of women in manufacturing leadership positions at the company. It provides women employees with critical career pathing information and development opportunities.

In 1992, Norman Garrity, then EVP of Corning's Specialty Materials Division and currently president of the Corning Technologies and co-chief operating officer, recognized a lack of women in key manufacturing positions. He formed the WIM team, comprising ten men and women in manufacturing leadership. Their mission was to identify potential issues or barriers that were keeping women from progressing into key manufacturing positions, and then to implement initiatives to break these barriers and monitor progress.

The team discovered there were issues in the advancement, retention, and recruitment of women in manufacturing. They set out to shape a clearer understanding of the women's perception of the manufacturing environment. From these data, the team constructed a powerful initiative to develop and advance women into manufacturing roles.

Corning realized its work environment in manufacturing was not working for women because the environment was decreasing productivity and causing unacceptable levels of attrition (in 1992, twice as many women as men left jobs in the manufacturing sector). Corning intends that every employee have the opportunity to fully participate, to grow professionally, and to develop to his or her highest potential. The WIM initiative helps ensure Corning uses its available pool of talent by developing women to their fullest potential, thus providing the company with a competitive advantage.

The WIM initiative includes communication and data-gathering, coaching, mentoring, a process for recruiting women into manufacturing career planning, work–life balance integration, and networking. A key element of the program is strong commitment from senior leadership.

Specifically, the initiative:

- Works to recruit women into manufacturing positions.
- Encourages managers to provide women with key developmental and networking experiences.
- Analyzes career paths to senior-level positions, thereby identifying and communicating feeder positions and key developmental experiences.
- Ensures that women who are interested in manufacturing are included in succession planning.
- Develops a manufacturing ladder to encourage movement between manufacturing and engineering.
- Emphasizes zero tolerance for any form of sexual harassment.
- Places importance on achieving a balance between work and personal life.
- Encourages increased use of both formal and informal flexible work arrangements.

To support the initiative's objectives, a career path brochure, which clarifies career planning for the manufacturing sector of the company, was developed. In addition, coaching and mentoring programs ensure that women are mentored on career development issues.

Results. The positive impact of the initiative is clear, through an increase in women employees in key positions, as well as improved employee satisfaction on diversity-related issues. From 1992 to 1996, women manufacturing employees increased from 22.4 percent to 28.5 percent, while women in "A-payroll" positions (the highest layer of management in the company) increased from 15 percent to 26 percent. There were no women plant managers when the initiative was founded. Today, five of Corning's 20 plant managers are women; an additional two women plant managers have been promoted into higher-level management positions. At the same time, the attrition rate of women employees has dropped from 8 percent to 3.5 percent.

Employee surveys reveal an improved work environment within the plants that is marked by an increased comfort level on the part of women. Employees also report an improvement in their ability to balance their work and personal lives.

Corporate initiative: mentoring programs

KNIGHT-RIDDER: BENCH STRENGTH PROGRAM

Knight-Ridder, the newspaper and information company, is competing in a fast-changing, volatile industry. Understanding that it does business in a diverse world in which economic power is increasingly wielded by women as well as men, the company recognized that newspapers and other forms of media need to reflect the communities they cover; both to maintain a standard of excellence and to be prepared to recognize business and product opportunities that might arise. In light of women's growing economic influence, Knight-Ridder wanted particularly to strengthen its position with women readers.

In 1989, Knight-Ridder's diversity task force created a mandate to advance women.

Business units were required to develop numeric targets based on regional populations and to design programs to advance women in senior positions.

Knight-Ridder's "Bench Strength" program is a formal mentoring system targeted at high-level employees, who are identified by senior managers at newspapers as being within two to three years of taking on significantly broader leadership roles. More than 40 percent of the participants are women. Corporate officers take responsibility for a group of six to eight mentees. Officers serving as mentors have a number of responsibilities:

- To talk with each mentee's editor or publisher to get an assessment of his or her strengths, weaknesses, and career aspirations.
- To have a similar in-depth talk with the individual.
- To have the mentees and their editors devise a career development plan, looking forward two to three years and including a timetable, a cost projection, and a clearly understood outcome.
- To review the plan and fine-tune it with the editor and the individual.
- To support and assist in implementing the plan and make sure the timetable is met.

Officers meet annually to discuss the individuals in the program. This creates a familiarity with these individuals for the time when job openings arise.

Knight-Ridder holds vice-presidents and supervisors accountable for results for the Bench Strength program and all other diversity initiatives. At the corporate officer and local company executive levels, bonuses are tied to performance on advancing diversity, including women. Performance reviews also contain requirements relating to diversity hiring and development. From 1990 to 1995, Knight-Ridder significantly moved the needle on women and minorities in the workforce and management representation through a five-year plan. Today, each company's strategic plan specifies steps toward its clearly defined goals for advancing diversity, including women, at management and non-management levels. The elements of the plan include:

- Any specific recruiting and hiring.
- A program for accelerating the training and experience of women and minorities, identifying individuals and projecting assignments and opportunities.
- A specific program for enlarging the pool of qualified women and minorities for jobs.
- Plans for aiding organizations in the community that promote opportunities for women and minorities.
- Plans for conducting diversity training (including gender, sexual harassment, and work–life issues) in the workplace.
- Steps to be taken to assure both the reality and perception of fairness to all employees.

Results. Women represent about 40.1 percent of Knight-Ridders's workforce and they are equally reflected among its executive ranks, at 39.6 percent, up 17 percent from 1991. A survey of the paper's readers showed a significant increase in female readership from 1991 to 1994.

Firm initiative: retention

ERNST & YOUNG: USE OF TECHNOLOGY

Professional services firms are known for their long hours, intense work environments, and demanding travel regimens. For many firms in the early nineties, this translated into a struggle to retain women professionals. One such firm, Ernst & Young, annually lost 22 percent of its women professionals and spent $150,000 per job to hire and train replacements. According to an unpublished 1996 Catalyst study of the firm, 60 percent of women employees and 57 percent of men in senior management were dissatisfied with working long hours. In response to those dramatic statistics and client demands for consistency in service, in 1996 Ernst & Young created the Office of Retention to address issues of work–life balance and women's particular needs in this area.

Ernst & Young's Office of Retention has leveraged technology to generate innovative ways to "convince employees it is safe to use flexible work arrangements (FWA)." Employees now use the electronic FWA Roadmap and FWA Database to research and apply for flexible work arrangements.

- The FWA Roadmap is an interactive tool that guides individuals through the flexible work arrangement application process by providing detailed information about the available programs.

- The FWA Database provides the personal stories of more than 500 individuals who work on flexible work arrangements. For those who worry about the potential impact of a flexible work arrangement on their career, the database provides some reassuring statistics:

    - 99 percent are satisfied with their arrangement;
    - 98 percent say their colleagues are supportive of their arrangement;
    - 97 percent say their supervisor is supportive of their arrangement;
    - 25 percent of people profiled have had a least one promotion since the database was established, five of them to partner.

By sharing these internal success stories, Ernst & Young is communicating to partners and employees alike that a flexible work arrangement does not hinder career advancement or jeopardize client relationships.

Results. Now 1,700 of 23,000 staff members – 7 percent – work a flexible work schedule, up from 1,000 in 1988. Twelve percent of those who benefit from flexible work arrangements are men.

Firm initiative: culture change

CHARLES SCHWAB & CO.: BUILDING A CULTURE. NO CEILINGS, NO BARRIERS, NO LIMITS

Over 25 years ago, Charles Schwab recognized that he could gain a market advantage by building a brokerage firm dedicated to customer needs and the recruitment and development of traditionally under-represented segments of the financial services sector. His firm was founded with the notion that an open, respectful, and inclusive culture was the key to achieving this advantage. Today, founder Charles Schwab and co-CEO David Pottruck continue to implement the original vision by demonstrating support for diversity in all business decisions and employee programs.

The Vision Quest program is a key component of Schwab's approach. Vision Quest featured a nationwide event that simultaneously brought together 5,000 Schwab employees from ten geographic locations. Its purpose was to achieve coherent thinking about Schwab's culture, vision, values, business, and marketplace. The event included speeches from the co-CEOs, videos, and an interactive business-related game. Schwab continues to conduct Vision Quest events with smaller groups of new hires as an official part of the Schwab orientation and enculturation process in order to communicate and maintain a shared vision, culture, and work approach.

Schwab focusses on recruiting diverse talent through the following programs:

- *Wings* is a recruitment program for college seniors that focusses on hiring ethnically and gender-diverse candidates. Upon graduation, candidates are placed in a month-long training program, followed by interim assignments in various Schwab departments.

- *The Management Associate Program* is a seven-month training program that focusses on developing leadership skills for high-potential business school students and Schwab employees. Participants have the opportunity to work with long-standing Schwab employees, leaders, and senior management in one field with two headquarter-based rotations.

- *Schools to Careers* is an internship program for high school students interested in intellectually and technically demanding careers. The program – which includes mentoring programs, job shadowing, work site visits, part-time work, and paid summer internships – is an additional way of promoting the company's goal of developing a talented and diverse future workforce.

Schwab also features a host of work–life programs, including:

- Informal and formal flexible work arrangements.
- A hoteling program that offers 50 off-site workstations to San Francisco employees with the goal of easing their daily commute.
- The *Balancing Work–Life* training program offered by Schwab University, and led by senior women in the organization.

- *Les Concierges Service* which acts as a "personal assistant" and is available on an unlimited basis, at no charge, to all Schwab employees. Services provided include running personal errands, doing household chores, and helping busy employees plan family vacations.

The company also offers development programs:

- Schwab has a formal mentoring program, and is a founder of Mentium 100 in the San Francisco Bay Area. Mentium 100 is a cross-company mentoring program placing senior managers with mid-level executives.
- The Women's Interactive Network is an active employee resources group that sponsors training, speakers, and seminars on women's issues.

Schwab encourages employees to become active in their communities:

- Volunteerism is encouraged, and business units frequently participate in programs such as Habitat for Humanity during business hours.
- An employee Sick Bank allows employees to donate extra, unused sick days to colleagues with life-threatening illnesses.

Results. Women currently comprise 39 percent of Schwab's workforce and 36 percent of its corporate officers. Two of the company's five vice-chairs are women and two women sit on the 12-member board of directors. Due to the strong presence of women in senior management, 77 percent of Schwab's employees ultimately report to a woman.

Corporate initiative: succession planning

MOTOROLA: SUCCESSION PLANNING WITH CLOUT

Motivated by changing workforce demographics, Motorola broadened its longstanding succession-planning practice in 1989 to accelerate the advancement of women to the vice-president level. Yet, by 1995, the company realized that most of the women who reached the VP level were white women. As a result, the then Chairman and CEO Gary Tooker challenged his direct reports to closely monitor and develop women of color so that they would be more fully represented among vice-presidents. Motorola made sure that each mechanism supporting its succession-planning process is actually targeted to women of color.

Motorola established Officer Parity Goals requiring that by year-end 2000, the percent representation of women and people of color at every management level mirror the representation of these groups in specific areas of import to the company. Human resources also monitors and provides analyses of the company's progress towards its officer parity goals and the representation of women and people of color in each of the key areas and in staff versus line positions.

Motorola's succession-planning process – the Organization and Management Development Review – identifies and tracks employees who have the potential to be promoted two levels in five years. This process is unique in that it embraces the entry and middle levels of management as well as the upper levels, which are more commonly the focus of succession planning. By developing a high-potential list that reaches lower into the organization the company ensures that there is enough representation of women and people of color, and specifically, women of color, in the pool which feeds the senior management levels. In addition, for each high potential, managers must include individual career development plans. In situations where a woman or person of color has left the company, his/her manager is responsible for ascertaining the reason for the departure.

An annual succession-planning chart – the Management Resources and Replacement Chart – is completed to identify three successors who could fill each key position. On the chart, managers first provide their "immediate successor" should their positions suddenly open. Managers also designate their planned successor or a person who is being trained and developed for the job. This "planned successor" may be the same person as the immediate successor. Finally, managers must specify the most qualified woman or person of color candidate at the time, in addition to any woman or person of color already designated as the immediate or planned successor.

Senior managers must complete development planning forms for women and people of color who are identified as having the potential to become vice-presidents within a specified time period. The development plan specifies timelines for promotions and lateral moves as well as a mentor for the high potential so that both the high potential's supervisor and mentor become responsible for helping the individual carry out her or his development plan.

Motorola's current Chairman and CEO Chris Galvin drives the initiative with strategic assistance from the HR department. Chris Galvin's direct reports, who lead Motorola's six major business operations, are each responsible for developing plans to meet the parity goals for their organizations. Progress toward these goals are reviewed on a quarterly basis. Motorola believes it is essential to have top leadership commitment and an understanding that diversity of talent is necessary to the company's success. The company uses similar processes for diversity as it does for any business initiatives: establish clear goals, timetables, and milestones to be reviewed.

Key elements for women of color include:

- Strong leadership commitment to advance women of color to the vice-president level.
- Integration of diversity and business objectives.
- Representation goals for women and people of color at every management level.
- Succession planning that includes the widest talent pool and strategic planning to develop high potentials.
- Managerial accountability for success.

Results. In 1991, there was only one woman of color among nine female vice-presidents compared with today when there are 11 women of color vice-presidents out of 54 women vice-presidents.

Corporate initiative: work–life

BAXTER INTERNATIONAL INC.: WORK AND LIFE STRATEGIC INITIATIVE

Baxter Healthcare's Work and Life Strategic Initiative began with an 18-month study to investigate work–life issues. The initial goals of the initiative were to evaluate current work–life programs, understand employees' work and life needs, and uncover management attitudes toward employees' work–life conflicts. Subsequent goals included using the fact-finding process to motivate senior managers to address work–life as a critical business issue and to dispel fears and stereotypes surrounding work–life issues. During the course of the study, the scope of work–life issues was found to be broader than anticipated, and new findings significant to human resources and the work–life field were discovered. The reach of work–life expanded to encompass more categories of employees who experience conflicts, as well as more approaches to alleviate them.

The initiative provided the impetus to incorporate work–life support mechanisms into operational aspects of Baxter. The initiative has helped to identify the extensive breadth and depth of work–life conflicts and reveal the impact the results made and continued to make on the entire organization.

The Work and Life Strategic Initiative was developed under the direction of Alice Campbell, Baxter's Director of Work and Life Initiatives. Initial input for the project was received from the Work–Life Forum, a group of HR managers that represented Baxter business units. The business unit HR staff identified how many locations would participate in the study, the findings of which would represent that particular business unit. Managers at most locations were interviewed, as well as managers at the headquarters office for that division. The CEO champions the initiative, providing ongoing role modeling and communication of his commitment.

Baxter communicates its commitment to work–life issues through a variety of methods:

- Each business unit communicated specifics about its participation in the survey to the management team, following up with a detailed report.
- The Operating Management Team used voicemail to distribute standards to all employees.
- A Work–Life homepage on Baxter's intranet site supports and provides information to employees about Baxter's work–life initiatives.
- CEO Harry Kraemer writes a monthly update to all staff that includes information about his own family and efforts to achieve balance. On the "Ask Harry" intranet site, Kraemer responds to employee questions about the company and the initiative.
- Baxter shared results of the Work and Life Initiative, internally as well as with the business community, in a full report, *The Work and Life Pyramid of Needs*.

Baxter allows for review of work–life issues for individuals and managers using the variety of mechanisms available. Supervisors at the highest level monitor results for each employee and take them into account when establishing objectives for any given year. The all-employee survey monitors results on employee issues that take into account the overall corporation. Figures are monitored quarterly for activity relating to alternate work arrangements and the Inside Advantage job-posting system. A sharp increase in the number of jobs that could be considered for alternate work arrangements occurred as a direct result of these enhancements.

Results. Between 1996 and 1998 there was an 8 percent increase of women at the managerial level, a 17.7 percent increase at the director level, and a 29.6 percent increase at the vice-president level. The percentage increase of employees of color who are officials and managers was 8.8 percent – women of color increased by 20.4 percent.

NOTES

1   These statistics were prepared for Catalyst from 1994 to 1995 US Census Bureau data by the Institute for Women's Policy Research. The data are drawn from the merged Earnings Files from the Current Population Survey in 1994 and 1995, collected by the US Census Bureau and then merged by the US Bureau of Labor Statistics.

REFERENCES

Barstow, Ann (2000). Women as targets: The gender-based implications of online consumer profiling. *Online Profiling Project*. Comment, P994809/Docket No. 990811219–9219–01, November 1, Washington, D.C.

Catalyst (1997). *Women of Color in Corporate Management: A Statistical Picture*. New York.

Catalyst (1998). *Advancing Women in Business: The Catalyst Guide* San Francisco, CA: Jossey-Bass.

Catalyst (1999a). *1999 Catalyst Census of Women Board Directors of the Fortune 1000*. New York.

Catalyst (1999b). *1999 Catalyst Census of Women Corporate Officers and Top Earners*. New York.

Catalyst (2000). *Cracking the Glass Ceiling: Catalyst's Research on Women in Corporate Management, 1995–2000*. New York.

Catalyst and Opportunity Now (2000). *Women in Senior Management in the United Kingdom*. London.

Digest of Education Statistics (1999). Chapter 3: Postsecondary education, table 258. Bachelor's, master's, and doctor's degrees conferred by institutions of higher education, by sex of student and field of study: 1996–1997.

National Foundation of Women Business Owners (1999). *Key Facts*. Silver Spring, MD.

Rowe, Mary P. (1990). Barriers to equality: The power of subtle discrimination to maintain unequal opportunity. *Employee Responsibilities and Rights Journal*, 3, 2.

US Bureau of Labor Statistics (1999). *Household Data Annual Averages*. Washington, D.C.

US Department of Labor Women's Bureau (2000). *Facts on Working Women*. March, 2000, Statistical Abstract of the United States, 1998, US Census Bureau.

14

Towards a Culture for Work–Life Integration?

SUZAN LEWIS AND JACKIE DYER

● **Overview** ●

This chapter begins by introducing the background to current discussion about work–family or work–life policies and practices. It then discusses the role of workplace culture in supporting or undermining the integration of work and personal life. The long hours culture is discussed as an example of the ways in which culture can undermine work–family policies and serve to obscure the benefits of non-standard and often innovative ways of working. It is argued that this can be particularly problematic to knowledge workers, although it can affect most sectors of the labor market. This points to the importance of looking beyond the implementation of work–life policies towards fundamental changes in workplace cultures. Culture change is described as part of an evolutionary process whereby organizations adapt to and innovate within the new world of work. The chapter includes a number of case studies which illustrate aspects of this process.

● **Introduction and Background** ●

At a time when human resources are more than ever driving the new economy, the issue of work–life integration becomes crucial for sustaining a healthy and flexible workforce. Organizations have long been urged since the 1970s to change their ways of working to acknowledge employees' family and other commitments, although the focus on culture change and on broader work–life concerns is much more recent. Initial interest in work–family issues stemmed from the growing number of women entering and remaining in all areas of the workforce and the growth of dual-earner families. These trends challenged the traditional or "male model" of work (Pleck, 1977; Cook, 1992), which assumed that the ideal employee worked continuously from the end of education until retirement, and did not allow family to interfere with work at any stage. With the concomitant implication that this would be with a single employer this is clearly an outdated notion in the contemporary labor market, although it continues to influence traditional management thinking, for example, in questioning the commitment of those who take periods out of full-time work for family reasons.

Although there has always been some recognition of the business benefits of broadening equality of opportunities, work–family issues were initially regarded as a women's issue and as primarily a social rather than a business concern. In the 1980s these issues were taken up by Human Resource professionals, and in the context of skills shortages, came to be regarded as recruitment and retention matters. This was the beginning of the business argument for the development of what became known as family-friendly employment policies. Mounting research on work–family conflict and stress, among women and men, reinforced the call for workplaces to change to take account of employees' non-work demands and to address quality of life issues which, in turn, had implications for organizational outcomes (Lewis and Cooper, 1987, 1988; Frone et al., 1997; Parasuraman et al., 1996).

During the last two decades of the twentieth century family-friendly policies grew in range and sophistication in some organizations. These policies include support for dependent care, such as workplace nurseries and financial and informational support for childcare and elder care. Periods of leave for family reasons, such as career breaks and parental leave were developed, often mandated by governments, although firms could supplement statutory provisions in order to gain a competitive edge. Other initiatives aimed to enable those with family commitments to work more flexibly, for example, by part-time work or reduced hours, job sharing, term-time-only working, compressed work weeks, and various forms of flexitime. Working from home for all or part of the working week has been increasingly feasible with the development of information technology, and this too is often conceived as a "family-friendly" measure.

However, formal family-friendly workplace policies have developed unevenly; they are more prevalent in the public sector and large private sector organizations than in smaller enterprises, and more likely to be available to skilled than non-skilled workers (Evans, 2000; Wood, 1999) (but see our case study of an agricultural firm below, for an example of an exception). Furthermore, even in those workplaces where work–family arrangements have been implemented, they have tended to be developed at the margins of organizations, focussing mainly on women, while mainstream employment practices remained largely unchanged (Lewis, 1997). Often policies are not widely communicated so that employees do not know about the provisions offered (Lewis, Kagan, and Heaton, 2000). There is also often a gap between formal policy and informal practice. There may, for example, be provision for parental leave or for short leaves of absence for family emergencies, but most employees, especially men, do not feel entitled to take up the provision, or know that to do so would be career limiting (Lewis and Taylor, 1996). Provisions are too often regarded as favors rather than entitlements (Lewis, 1997; Lewis and Smithson, forthcoming). Meanwhile, the proliferation of contracting out, temporary contracts, and other new forms of work has created a growing peripheral or contingent workforce to whom family-oriented policies often do not apply. Even statutory maternity leave becomes threatened with fixed-term contracts (Smithson and Lewis, 2000). In this context then, family-friendly policies are often developed for a core workforce; those whom the organization currently wishes to retain and motivate, but who are aware that no guarantees exist about the security of their jobs. Even core workers are often reluctant to take up work–family arrangements because of perceived job insecurity (Smithson and Lewis, 2000).

Research evaluating the outcomes of family-friendly or flexible working practices indicates that there can be considerable benefits in terms of productivity and other organizational variables (see Kossek and Ozeki, 1999 for a review) but that their effectiveness depends on how they are implemented. In particular it has been argued that their effectiveness depends on the extent to which they provide workers with the autonomy and control to work out their own work and non-work schedules and boundaries (Thomas and Ganster, 1995) (although, as discussed later in this chapter, autonomy is not always associated with work–life balance). Informal culture, particularly as represented by line managers, who may block flexibility because they are skeptical about the benefits and reluctant to depart from traditional ways of working, often prevents family-friendly policies from providing such autonomy. Increasingly then it is recognized that workplace culture is crucial to the development of real organizational change to support integration of work and personal life.

● Workplace Culture as a Barrier to the Effectiveness of Family-Friendly Policies ●

Workplace culture

Workplace culture refers to a deep level of shared beliefs and assumptions, many of which may operate unconsciously. These assumptions are usually functional initially but may persist inappropriately. For example, the "male model" of continuous work may have appeared functional at a time when male breadwinners were the norm, although it would also have contributed to the perpetuation of traditional structures, no longer appropriate for employees or businesses. A supportive work–life culture, on the other hand, has been defined as the shared assumptions, beliefs, and values regarding the extent to which organizations value and support the integration of work and family lives, for women and men (Thompson et al., 1999). Schein (1985) identified three operational levels of culture: artifacts, values, and assumptions. Formal family-friendly or work–family policies may be regarded as artifacts, that is, surface-level indicators of organizational intentions. Formal policies may indicate an organizational intention to enable workers to achieve integration of various aspects of their lives, but this is often blocked by counterproductive values and assumptions.

On the other hand, informal practice is often the way that work–life conflict is addressed, in a very positive way, particularly in smaller organizations (see e.g. Dex and Schriebl, forthcoming). The managing director of a manufacturing plant explained:

> I was aware that one of my shop floor workers, usually reliable and hardworking, started coming in late, had the odd day off sick and was continually clockwatching. Turned out that his wife had left him, but he'd managed to keep custody of his daughter. He had

support from the grandmother after school, but he had to do the school run before work and it just didn't fit with the start of work. When I realised this, I agreed that he could start later, if he'd take responsibility for site security at the end of the day. The relief on his face was reward enough, and his work mates helped him out whenever they could. Eventually, he lost custody of the girl for other reasons, which broke his heart. I believe that the court acknowledged our efforts as a supportive workplace but that wasn't the point really. It was just one father helping out another. (Dex and Schreibl, forthcoming)

The long hours culture

The impact of workplace culture in undermining formal family-friendly policies is particularly evident in relation to working time and the increasingly pervasive long hours culture, especially in white-collar, professional, and managerial jobs. In organizations where the long hours culture is the norm, long hours spent visibly at the workplace (i.e. face time) are valued because it is assumed that they represent commitment and productivity (Bailyn, 1993; Lewis and Taylor, 1996). Often employees are expected to demonstrate commitment by being willing to put work before their personal lives, at all times (Bailyn et al., 1996). Within the long hours culture time is defined as a commodity to be managed and "given" to paid work and/or family (Lewis, 1997), and those who "give" more time to work through full-time employment and long working hours are valued more than part-time or reduced-hours workers, who are assumed to be less committed and productive.

The assumption that only those who are working long hours are committed or productive obscures the value of alternative, and often more efficient, ways of working which workers often develop in order to meet the demands of work and non-work responsibilities (Lewis, 1997; Perlow, 1998). For example, Perlow (1998), in a study of engineers in the USA in a context where innovation is usually encouraged, describes how innovative ways of working were undervalued if they were thought to be introduced to make more time for family. In a study of an accountancy firm which had introduced a range of family-friendly policies, women who were working reduced hours because of childcare demands often reported that they were accomplishing as much as they had when working full-time, but that this was obscured by a long hours culture (Lewis and Taylor, 1996; Lewis, 1997). Most of their managers felt that those who worked reduced hours, however efficient, would not be promoted because they were not sufficiently committed. When pushed to explain this, one manager replied, "they do not put the hours in, or do not give enough time to their work" (Lewis and Taylor, 1996).

In many cases productivity is sustained among those working less than full time by an intensification of work, as illustrated by a senior manager, working seven hours less than the standard week in a British public sector organization:

There's things like not talking, not going off and making several cups of coffee. I can go through a whole day without having a cup of coffee if I don't have the time to think about getting up. I tend to steam through meetings, I organize meetings carefully. There's an agenda, we go through it and I also tend to wind it up a bit faster so I think that's where the 7 hours has gone in the organization aspect of it. (Lewis, 2000)

Intensification of work can itself cause stress and exhaustion (Burchell et al., 1999), but may be an effective way of achieving work–life integration if it is freely chosen. Professional and managerial staff working less than full-time hours often accept that their cut in salary is the price they must pay to legitimize more realistic hours. The long hours culture reduces the sense of entitlement for equal rewards for work accomplished in shorter hours; as one Human Resources Director explained: "Many people who are doing 'just less than full-time' patterns will say to me, or say to each other in private, what you are really buying in that element of salary is the right to go home on time with nothing on their conscience" (Lewis, 2000).

This raises issues of equity. If those working reduced hours receive reduced pay but have no fall in productivity this suggests that full-time workers are being paid more to work less efficiently. It is, however, difficult for managers to know how much to expect from employees working part-time or reduced hours because the long hours culture in many organizations makes full-time work elastic and difficult to define. The real challenge to persistent assumptions about the value of time in the workplace may be to pay people according to what they achieve rather than how long it takes them to accomplish it.

Meanwhile working hours are growing in most sectors. In a recent national survey in Britain, 42 percent of employees reported that they always or often left the workplace in a state of exhaustion, and a further 48 percent said they sometimes do so (*Social Trends*, 1999). Evidence is beginning to emerge associating long working hours with stress-related illness (Sparks, Cooper, Fried, and Shirom, 1997). Long hours can also have a negative impact on organizations. For example, more than 50 percent of a national survey of managers in the UK reported that the number of hours they work is having an adverse effect on their productivity (Worrall and Cooper, 1999). Long hours also inevitably interfere with family life. For those managers reporting working over 60 hours per week, 35 percent said that their work hours adversely affected their relationship with their partner and 33 percent their relationship with their children to a great extent (Worrall and Cooper, 1999).

As the nature of work changes, however, long hours issues are becoming particularly salient for knowledge workers, that is the highly skilled and talented workers that organizations need to support to enable them to be successful in highly competitive global markets.

Work–life integration and the "new" workforce

In the context of long working hours cultures and the pressure this places on employees and their families, the terms work–life balance or integration have emerged and replaced discussions of work–family. The work–family or family-friendly policy agenda never quite managed to throw off the implication that this was solely a woman's issue. Work–life debates aim to be more inclusive, embracing the needs of men as well as women, of those with family responsibilities other than children, and, importantly, the needs of those without current family responsibilities who just want to "have a life" beyond the workplace. This shifting discourse reflects the changes that have been taking place in the transition to a knowledge economy, which have challenged the very notions of work–family or work–life boundaries. Knowledge workers have increasingly more permeable temporal and spatial boundaries between their work and personal life, as technology enables them to work around the clock, in the workplace, at home or wherever else they take their mobile offices. Discussions about family-friendly or flexible working practices have become less relevant in this contemporary context. Knowledge workers are most likely to have access to formal or to informal flexibility and support. They have control over their own working hours, and can be flexible to fit in family or other demands, which is the goal of family-friendly policies. Yet paradoxically they are the most likely to be under pressure, to work long hours. They have autonomy to decide how they work, but this is associated with greater feelings of responsibility for getting work completed (Holt and Thaulow, 1996; Hochschild, 1997). In fact, among knowledge workers greater flexibility and autonomy are often associated with more conscientiousness and longer working hours. These longer working hours are then constructed as a choice, and pressure is intensified.

Why do increased flexibility and autonomy often fail to empower many knowledge workers to manage the boundaries between work and personal life? "Family-friendly" or flexibility policies help those, such as factory workers, who have rigid hours when they have to be present at a central workplace. But control of hours at the workplace by the clock rather than the nature or amount of work to be done is a characteristic of industrial workers and not of knowledge workers. The temporal boundaries between work and non-work are controlled instead by organizational culture for this growing segment of the workforce. Expectations of high commitment and involvement are internalized. It is these more subtle pressures that lead to workers putting in long hours or taking work home to get it finished.

One partner in a professional practice explained:

(PARTNER)   Family is taken into account. We tell people to go home. As partners, we prioritize, we say "enough is enough".

(INTERVIEWER)   So you must still be in the office to see others doing long hours, and to send them home?

(PARTNER)   True.

As the nature of the work performed is more open-ended, creative and individually styled, more complex and analytic for these workers, the boundaries between work and non-working time become increasingly blurred. Flexibility enables knowledge workers to leave work to attend children's school functions and other activities during the traditional working day. It can also enable them to work evenings and weekends and holidays.

There have been many attempts to explain the perverse findings that highly skilled workers, who often have complete flexibility and autonomy over the ways in which they work, are the most likely to work long and intensive hours. It may be because in the modern workplace there are fewer people and more work to be accomplished, so that high workloads are inevitable. It could be that the nature of the work performed by knowledge workers is more absorbing and satisfying than other forms of work.

Indeed, Arlie Hochschild (1997) has argued that for many people work has become more satisfying than home. The more time is spent at the workplace, the more difficult relationships become at home, which reinforces their desire to spend time at work. Work becomes a refuge from home, rather than home a refuge from work as was assumed to be the case in industrial times.

Another view is that managers of knowledge workers impose control of the boundaries between work and personal lives by the various ways in which they "cajole, encourage, coerce or otherwise influence the amount of time employees spend visibly at the workplace" (Perlow, 1998: 329). They do this by overtly valuing and rewarding long hours at the workplace. When commitment and productivity are difficult to quantify, as they are in most knowledge work, then they are measured by workers' willingness to work late to meet a series of deadlines, or simply to get the work done. Perlow (1998) argues that managers exercise control over these types of workers using a variety of mechanisms including, for example: creating a crisis mentality by imposing deadlines; setting meetings and reviews; monitoring employees by standing over or checking; and by modeling the type of behavior that is required – including excessive working hours (Perlow, 1998). Not all knowledge workers accept these structures, of course. While some seem to thrive on excessive work involvement, which it has been suggested might be due to personality characteristics, particularly a dependence on mastery and visibly high investment of time in the workplace for self-esteem (Kofodimos, 1993), others are assertive about sustaining a work–life balance. In some cases control is also exercised in the home. That is, a spouse or partner may insist that workers do not spend too much time at work and are available at home. However, those who reject the culture of excessive work are often less likely to be valued and promoted at work (Perlow, 1998; Lewis, 1997).

● Culture Change ●

Culture change as an evolutionary stage

Supporting work–life integration requires recognition of the role of workplace culture in creating pressures and a commitment to achieving culture change. Leading-edge employers are now recognizing the need to move beyond implementing work–family policies at the margins of organizations to achieve more fundamental culture change, with work–life balance as a strategic business issue. The Families and Work Institute in New York has described four stages in the development of US corporate responses to work–life issues in the USA, with culture change as one stage in an evolutionary process (Friedman and Johnson, 1997). These are:

- "Grass Roots" stage which focusses on childcare and women's issues.
- "Human Resources" stage in which the issues addressed and the initiatives developed are broadened, usually led by human resource departments but with support from top management. The focus is on recruitment and retention.
- Cultural change.
- Work redesign.

Cultural change involves attempts to change practice rather than policy, and the deeper assumptions, beliefs, and values which underpin these practices. It involves strategic initiatives to examine all organizational systems and not just HR systems. At this stage it is recognized that innovative work–life policies will only be effective in a supportive workplace culture. The focus shifts to work–life concerns of all the workforce, rather than specific groups of employees, with a goal of enhancing creativity, commitment, and individual contributions. If successful the systemic change that emerges brings about the fourth stage of work redesign. Awareness of how workplace culture and communication are related to work–life goals leads to a focus on work itself. Ways of working which create a synergy between organizational objectives and employees' work–life goals, i.e. win solutions, are sought.

The Ford Foundation studies

The culture change and work redesign approaches are exemplified by the Ford Foundation Studies, a program of action research undertaken by Lotte Bailyn, Rhona Rapoport, and their colleagues at a number of organizations, including the Xerox Corporation in the USA (Bailyn et al., 1996; Fletcher and Rapoport, 1996). The approach taken in these studies involved looking at total work situations through what they termed a "work–family lens." They began by surfacing the work–family concerns of the workers in specific departments and then reframed these as organizational or systemic rather than individual problems. For example, if long working hours prevented workers from having sufficient time and energy for family, or if rigid hours made it difficult for some workers to manage their family demands, this was reframed as an organizational issue. The workers with family or other commitments were not regarded as the problem, but the organizational systems which created the problems were focussed upon. The research team then engaged the work teams in examining the ways in which the work could be changed to better meet the demands of both the business and the workers. Often this involved having to surface and deal with resistance among managers or colleagues. However, all the solutions that emerged from this process had demonstrable bottom-line benefits.

The solutions that emerged were specific to each workplace or department studied, depending on the nature of the workers, the work, and the culture. So, the process is generalizable to different contexts but the solution is not. Below are some examples of the solution reached.

SOME OUTCOMES OF THE FORD FOUNDATION STUDIES

On one site where long hours were the norm, this was found to be largely the consequence of a crisis mentality, which created stress and was actually detrimental to production. Innovations to reduce the crisis mentality and culture of long hours, including setting more realistic deadlines and periods of quiet times without

---

interruptions, resulted in outcomes such as reduced time to market and the achievement of quality awards as well as work–family integration.

At another site the research team found that the frequent requests for part-time work were not due to extreme family commitments but to routine work practices leading to very long full-time hours. Innovative ways of reducing these practices also benefited the business.

At another site neither flexibility nor a drive for empowered teams was progressing well. Although there were a range of formal work–family arrangements these were subject to management discretion. There was a culture of control. Management were reluctant to allow what were seen as "benefits" because of fear of losing control. Therefore people had to manage their work–family commitments without support. Consequently there were high levels of absenteeism and turnover, as well as backlash against those who were allowed flexibility as a "favor." The innovation introduced here was to make flexible working available to everyone. Self-managed teams then found ways of accommodating this. This led to a fall in absenteeism, turnover, and backlash, plus the emergence of more genuinely empowered, self-managing teams. Another outcome was an increase in responsiveness to customers.

Thus some really innovative solutions emerged out of the process of bringing personal issues from the individual to the collective level and engaging people's energy to make innovative changes in existing work practices – which can have a positive impact on the bottom line.

The change process

Action research does not provide answers about which specific interventions will lead to culture change, as this is likely to be workplace-specific. However, it does provide important pointers about the process of change. The main themes and processes to emerge from this body of research are the importance of:

- Framing work–life as a strategic business issue.
- Communicating the business case throughout the organization.
- Confronting resistance (e.g. in managers or colleagues) and challenging assumptions.
- Involving and consulting with all employees.
- Supporting managers.
- Addressing all systems, not just HR policies.
- Development of a full range of measurable outcomes.
- Continual cycle of implementation, measurement and evaluation, feedback, identifying barriers, seeking new solutions and sustaining momentum.

FRAMING WORK–LIFE AS A STRATEGIC BUSINESS ISSUE

Often work–life balance can be integrated within a company's philosophy and mission statement. For example, Bennesse, an educational publishing company in Japan, has been developing policies to support work–life and working towards culture change, although they are aware that this is a long process within the context of Japanese society, which is slow to change. The company philosophy is to provide support for people at all life stages through their products. They attempt to provide the same support and offer the same level of choice that is offered to clients to their employees, aiming for total consistency in all they do. In the process of development they have learnt that initiatives that are linked to strategic business issues rather than more marginal work–family issues are more effective. For example, childcare leave of one year (the statutory minimum is three months) and nursing care leave to care for elderly parents or parents-in-law have been successful in their goal of retaining women; growing numbers now return to the company after this leave, although the HR managers admit it has taken ten years to change the culture sufficiently for this to happen. However, this has not had any impact on work–life balance for men. More recently a super-flex system, with no core hours, has been introduced. This was introduced as a productivity measure, not directed at women nor at work–family balance. Because it is seen as a strategic business initiative, flexitime is taken up by men and women, for a range of reasons, and is beneficial to the company.

Through the super-flex system the company claims to "encourage our employees to spend more time on hobbies and outside interests. We believe that outside stimulation will benefit the company. We think this will stimulate creativity."

ADDRESSING ALL SYSTEMS AND ENGAGING WITH RESISTANCE

Lloyds Policy Signing Office (LPSO), part of the Lloyds Corporation, introduced flexible working including a pilot teleworking scheme, a hot suite for coping with peaks of demand by using staff from other areas, with additional pay out of normal hours as well as multi-skilling, and an incentive scheme, in order to be able to better meet troughs and peaks of work. This was introduced within a broad programme of fundamental change, which included changes to charging structures, consolidation of IT systems, cost reductions and downsizing, increased accountability, the development of measurement and service standards, and bonus systems for staff based on key performance indicators. Flexible working was not conceived as a work–life balance measure, although it was recognized that employees seeking work–life or work–family balance, especially some of the women workers, would be most likely to wish to take up opportunities for flexibility. The flexible working program was regarded as crucial to the success of all the other initiatives in the change program. The introduction of flexible working, including teleworking, met with some resistance from some of the line management. However, they were persuaded to go along with a pilot scheme. The most resistant manager commented afterwards that he was completely sold on the benefits of flexible working which he could see met the needs of the business to cope with peaks and troughs as well as employees' needs.

Most action research to bring about workplace change to support the integration of work and personal life has been with professional workers. The case study below demonstrates that the process can also work well with other workers.

WORK–LIFE BALANCE IN THE AGRICULTURAL SECTOR

Long working hours are not solely the province of knowledge workers. In a recent case study, a consultancy firm worked with an agricultural plant, where the product was grown and harvested on a system very similar to "just-in time." This family business had a turnover of £3.5 million and was a major employer within the local rural community: the farmer had a number of contracts with large supermarkets, and had to respond to changing market needs very quickly. Opportunities existed for larger contracts with existing customers, but the farm was not able to expand and develop as it was held back by staffing problems. The workforce was working six days per week, up to 60 hours per week, in conditions that few office workers would imagine, far less consider working in. Staff were tired and becoming less productive as a result of their long working hours. The overtime costs were phenomenal. In spite of the opportunity for a relatively high level of pay within the sector, the firm reported a turnover rate of 72 percent and a very high short-term absence rate in the six-month period preceding the time when the Managing Director asked for specialist advice from an external consultancy. Clearly, recruitment and retention were a major issue: the high and unpredictable turnover of staff meant that the dependable and committed workers had to work excessive overtime to ensure that the crop was harvested. The long working hours were a source of complaint and, in some cases, stress and ill-health.

One of the key outcomes of the project was to discard the traditional working patterns whereby staff were required to "clock on" before 8 a.m., losing up to half an hour's pay if they were over five minutes late. More flexible start times were introduced which had a significant effect on short-term absence, and which allowed staff with family responsibilities more scope to balance their commitments. Various working arrangements, such as job-share and part-time work, were also offered. Childcare vouchers, assistance with transport to and from work and advice on pensions – with company contributions to longer serving members – were other benefits that were introduced. These initiatives helped both recruitment and retention.

Important elements of this organizational work–life balance problem and the process by which it was addressed are described below using the structure outlined above.

FRAMING WORK–LIFE AS A STRATEGIC BUSINESS ISSUE

Significant to this project was the Managing Director/owner's appreciation of work–life balance and his attitude towards his workers, to whom he felt obligated to improve the quality of their working life. He could have viewed the problem simply as a business issue – the need to get production up and to get the product on the supermarket shelves. Yet his mindset was that his staff were valuable to him – he knew that he had to address the needs of his staff with respect to their work–life balance in order to maintain a constant, high-quality staff group. This mindset is not to be underestimated.

INVOLVING AND CONSULTING WITH ALL EMPLOYEES

The implementation of changes followed a consultation exercise with the staff, comprising a series of focus groups and a questionnaire, sent to all employees. This was an unusual process for this group of staff, who historically had not been consulted on any issues. There was quite a lot of cynicism and initial resistance to participating, but eventually people opened up and gave their views quite freely. The external consultant presented a series of options to the Managing Director, who then set up an internal working party comprising staff members, to facilitate the introduction and implementation of the changes.

COMMUNICATING THE BUSINESS CASE THROUGHOUT THE ORGANIZATION

The culture of this organization had previously been one of scant employee involvement. The diagnostic process had quantified the dissent among the workforce: for example, it became clear that for staff the implication of staff shortages was that they often did not know when they would be able to leave work in the evening. Care was taken to ensure that staff recognized the link between the initiatives aimed at making the organization a more attractive employer to people with family responsibilities, and the improvements in benefits to all staff with the outcome of having a more stable workforce. The more high-quality staff the company was able to attract, the more the firm could commit to larger contracts. This increased the profitability of the firm and the job security of all staff.

CONFRONTING RESISTANCE (E.G., IN MANAGERS OR COLLEAGUES) AND CHALLENGING ASSUMPTIONS

This workforce initially reported a very high level of support from managers and colleagues if staff members had problems out of work. Yet some preferred to report sickness rather than admit to care responsibilities out of work. Attention was paid to developing a higher level of acceptance about work–life conflict as the more flexible approach to work hours enabled staff to make time up, rather than lose pay for absence. Managers and supervisors were given training in interpersonal skills which gave them confidence to confront opinion, for example on perceived levels of fairness. This was helped by the behavior of the Managing Director, an influential role model in this way.

SUPPORTING MANAGERS AND ADDRESSING ALL SYSTEMS, NOT JUST HR POLICIES

Work was organized on a team basis, each with a team leader. Each team comprised both full- and part-time workers, whose work hours were self-organized. The team leader roles introduced an element of career development where previously there had been none. The team leaders formed their own team, to help them in their new role and to organize the weekly workload. New members of staff were each allocated to a team and a mentoring system set up. Helping new staff members in the organizational socialization process in this way significantly reduced the numbers of new staff who left after a very short space of time.

The management also set up external partnerships with local childcare providers and also with local community development initiatives, often government-funded projects aimed at getting people in areas of high unemployment back to work.

DEVELOPMENT OF A FULL RANGE OF MEASURABLE OUTCOMES AND THE EVALUATION CYCLE

At the outset of this project, measurable indicators were set, including staff turnover, numbers of staff leaving within a three-month period, numbers of staff taking up more flexible work practices, reduction in short-term sickness, overtime costs, and production costs. New employees were surveyed about the perception of the organization as an employer of choice. These evaluation criteria are measured on a six-monthly basis and this information fed back to management and the working party.

● Summary ●

- Formal family-friendly policies may help some workers to integrate work and personal life and can have a positive impact on organizations, but this depends on how they are implemented.

- Informal workplace culture can support employees' work–life balance, especially in small businesses or at a departmental level. However, workplace culture is often a barrier to the effectiveness of formal work–life policies.

- In many organizations there is a long hours culture which stems from the assumption that hours of work indicate levels of commitment and productivity.

- This long hours culture can often obscure the benefits of alternative ways of working.

- Organizational culture is often used by management to perpetuate long working hours, particularly among knowledge workers, and can be counter-productive for the organization.

- Culture change towards supporting work–life balance can be viewed as one stage in an evolutionary process.

- Culture change for work–life balance is an ongoing process involving strategic planning, communication, consultation, and broad and systemic change. Companies need to be continually anticipating new issues as they arise and there is little room for complacency.

- Culture change to support work–life integration can enhance productivity and effectiveness. Case studies illustrate bottom-line benefits in a range of different types of workplace.

REFERENCES

Bailyn, L. (1993). *Breaking the Mold: Women, Men and Time in the New Corporate World.* New York: Free Press.

Bailyn, L., Rapoport, R., Kolb, D., and Fletcher, J. (1996). *Relinking Work and Family: A Catalyst for Organizational Change.* New York: Ford Foundation.

Burchell, B., Day, D., Hudson, M., Lapido, D., Mankelow, R., Nolan, J., Reed, H., Wichert, I., and Wilkinson, F. (1999). *Job Insecurity and Work Intensification: Flexibility and the Changing Boundaries of Work.* York: York Publishing.

Cook, A. (1992). Can work requirements change to accommodate the needs of dual earner families? In S. Lewis, D.N. Izraeli, and H. Hootsmans (eds). *Dual Earner Families. International Perspectives.* London: Sage.

Dex, S., and Schreibl, F. (forthcoming). Flexible and family friendly working arrangements in SMEs: Business case. *British Journal of Human Relations.*

Evans, J.E. (2000). Firms' contribution to the reconciliation between work and family life. Paper presented at the Conference on Families, Labour Markets, and the Well-Being of Children, University of British Columbia, Vancouver, Canada.

Fletcher, J., and Rapoport, R. (1996). Work–family issues as a catalyst for organizational change. In S. Lewis and J. Lewis (eds). *The Work-Family Challenge.* London: Sage, pp. 142–58.

Friedman, D., and Johnson, A. (1997). Moving from programs to culture change: The next stage in the corporate work–family agenda. In S. Parasuraman and J. Greenhaus (eds). *Integrating Work and Family: Challenges and Choices for a Changing World.* Westport, CT: Quorum.

Frone, M., Yardley, J., and Markel, K. (1997). Developing and testing an integrative model of the work–family interface. *Journal of Vocational Behavior,* 50, 145–67.

Hochschild, A. (1997). *The Time Bind: When Work Becomes Home and Home Becomes Work.* New York: Henry Holt.

Holt, H., and Thaulow, I. (1996). Formal and informal flexibility in the workplace. In S. Lewis and J. Lewis (eds). *The Work–Family Challenge.* London: Sage.

Kofodimos, J. (1993). *Balancing Act: How Managers can Integrate Successful Career and Fulfilling Personal Lives.* San Francisco: Jossey-Bass.

Kossek, E.E., and Ozeki, C. (1999). Bridging the work–family policy and productivity gap: A literature review. *Community, Work and Family*, 2, 1, 7–32.

Lewis, S. (1997). Family friendly organizational policies: a route to organizational change or playing about at the margins. *Gender, Work and Organization*, 4, 13–23.

Lewis, S. (2000). Organizational change and gender equity: Case studies from the UK. In L. Haas, P. Hwang, and G. Russell (eds). *Organizational Change and Gender Equity*. London: Sage.

Lewis, S., and Cooper, C.L. (1987). Stress in two earner couples and stages in the life cycle. *Journal of Occupational Psychology*, 60, 289–303.

Lewis, S., and Cooper, C.L. (1988). The transition to parenthood in two earner couples. *Psychological Medicine*, 18, 477–86.

Lewis, S., Kagan, C., and Heaton, P. (2000). Managing work–family diversity for parents of disabled children: Beyond policy to practice. *Personnel Review*, 29, 3, 417–30.

Lewis, S., and Smithson, J. (forthcoming). Sense of entitlement to support for the reconciliation of employment and family life. *Human Relations*.

Lewis, S., and Taylor, K. (1996). Evaluating the impact of employer family friendly policies: A case study. In S. Lewis and J. Lewis (eds). *The Work Family Challenge*. London: Sage.

Parasuraman, S., Purohit, Y., Godshalk, V., and Beutell, N. (1996). Work and family variables, entrepreneurial career success and psychological well being. *Journal of Vocational Behavior*, 48, 275–300.

Pleck, J. (1977). The work–family role system. *Social Problems*, 24, 417–27.

Perlow, L.A. (1998). Boundary control: The social ordering of work and family time in a high tech organization. *Administrative Science Quarterly*, 43, 328–57.

Schein, E. (1985). *Organizational Culture and Leadership*. San Francisco: Jossey-Bass.

Social Trends (1999). London: Office for National Statistics.

Sparks, K., Cooper, C.L., Fried, Y., and Shirom, A. (1997). The effects of hours of work on health: A meta-analytic review. *Journal of Occupational and Organizational Psychology*, 70, 391–408.

Smithson, J., and Lewis, S. (1999). Is job insecurity changing the psychological contract? Young people's expectations of work. *Personnel Review*, 29, 6, 680–702.

Thomas, L., and Ganster, D. (1995). Impact of family supportive work variables on work family conflict and strain. *Journal of Applied Psychology*, 80, 6–15.

Thompson, C., Beauvais, L., and Lyness, K. (1999). When work–family benefits are not enough: The influence of work–family culture on benefit utilization, organizational attachment and work–family conflict. *Journal of Vocational Behaviour*, 54, 392–415.

Wood, S. (1999). Family friendly management: Testing the various perspectives. National Institute Economic Review, 168, 99–116.

Worrall, L., and Cooper, C.L. (1999). *The Quality of Working Life: 1999 Survey of Managers' Changing Experiences*. London: Institute of Management.

Index